the faithful tribe

the
faithful tribe

An Intimate Portrait of the Loyal Institutions

RUTH DUDLEY EDWARDS

HarperCollins*Publishers*

HarperCollins*Publishers*
77–85 Fulham Palace Road,
Hammersmith, London W6 8JB

Published by HarperCollins*Publishers* 1999
3 5 7 9 8 6 4

A catalogue record for this book
is available from the British Library

ISBN 0 00 255863 7

Set in PostScript Times New Roman by
Rowland Phototypesetting Ltd, Bury St Edmunds, Suffolk

Printed and bound in Great Britain by
Clays Ltd, St Ives plc

To all my friends in the loyal institutions and especially to Henry

(who dragged me into this in the first place), Lorraine, Erin and

Thomas, my Northern Ireland family, who made researching

this book such a joy.

contents

list of illustrations

1. Royal Black Preceptory No 800, Clogher, County Tyrone, circa 1930.
2. Tom Reid (as baby) at his first Twelfth, Fivemiletown, County Tyrone, 1934.
3. Banter at 'The Field', Ballymoney, County Antrim, August 1989. (JFA Studio)
4. The annual re-enactment of the Battle of the Boyne at Scarva, County Down. (Bobbie Hanvey)
5. Making lambeg drums in Belfast. (JFA Studio)
6. Three generations of the Brownlees family, Ballymena, County Antrim. (Bobbie Hanvey)
7. 'If Northern Ireland Was Really "British"...' (Martyn Turner/*Irish Times*)
8. Henry, Erin and Thomas Reid outside the Orange Hall in Glenageeragh, County Tyrone, 1995.
9. Gerard Rice of the Lower Ormeau Concerned Community. (MSI)
10. Donncha MacNiallis of the Bogside Residents' Group. (*Belfast Telegraph*)
11. Martin McGuinness and Brendán MacCionnaith walk the Garvaghy Road. (Dan Chung/Reuters)
12. Robert Saulters, Grand Master. (MSI)
13. Press Conference at Craigavon, County Armagh, 27 June 1997. (*Belfast Telegraph*)
14. Garvaghy Road, County Armagh, 6 July 1997. (John Giles/PA News)
15. Apprentice Boys Pageant, Londonderry, August 1997. (Mark Stakem)
16. RUC versus loyalists in Derry, aftermath of Apprentice Boys Parade, 1997. (Mark Stakem)
17. Gerry Adams and Martin McGuinness at rally following Belfast anti-internment march, August 1997. (Mark Stakem)
18. Chinook picking up soldiers from field above Drumcree church, 10 July, 1998. (Max Nash/Associated Press)
19. Joel Patton and his supporters occupying the House of Orange in protest against the leadership, December 1997. (MSI)
20. Protest march in Sandy Row, 6 July 1998. (*Belfast Telegraph*)
21. Funeral of Jason, Mark and Richard Quinn, July 1998. (Pacemaker)
22. Harold Gracey in his caravan at Drumcree, January 1999. (Martin McCullough)

IT WAS A FEW DAYS AFTER THE BATTLE OF THE BOYNE when King William decided to pop into the local pub for a contemplative pint. He was sitting happily and peacefully with his feet up when he saw a familiar figure hunched in a corner across the room. Being of a kindly disposition, he thought he'd better cheer up the poor fellow, so he walked over, clapped him on the back and said, 'Hello there, father-in-law. How's it goin'?'

King James looked up miserably. 'Dreadful,' he said. 'After that awful hammering you gave me at the Boyne, I'm finished. I'm so, so depressed.'

King William shook his head reprovingly. 'Oh, come on, father-in-law,' he responded bracingly. 'You're getting this completely out of perspective. Everyone will have forgotten all about the Boyne within a couple of weeks.'

JOKE POPULAR IN ORANGE CIRCLES IN THE SUMMER OF 1998

introduction

'When I go to Northern Ireland, I'm looking back to my youth in the 1950s. I remember in Sheffield on Whit Monday nine Protestant Sunday schools used to parade to a service and Boys' Brigade, sea scouts, boy scouts, cubs, brownies, girl guides – scores of children walking past behind a banner carried by some adult. And we all used to go along and the preachers used to preach and everybody used to walk around talking to people you'd not seen for a year. I remember that from my boyhood and see a resonance of it in Northern Ireland. They are to some extent recreating the old virtues of family, sobriety, self-reliance, hard work and thrift.

It's the Blue Remembered Hills: you can't go back. We can all see that community and experience a sense of loss – because we know where we've come from. But it makes me feel angry that an entire community should be demonized for no greater crime than being out of fashion.'

English Orangeman

AT AN ANGLO-IRISH CONFERENCE in 1996, I was standing in the bar with two Northern Irish Orangemen when a third came up and said: 'I spent an hour last night explaining to X and Y [two intelligent and sophisticated members of the Dáil, the Irish parliament] why I'm an Orangeman. One of them has just bounced over to me and said: "We've been talking about you, and we've all decided that you can't be an Orangeman. You're too nice." To which the second Orangeman replied: 'I was in Dublin a while ago when someone in the group I was with who knew me quite well said: "Why don't you tell those awful Orangemen to stop those parades?" When I explained that I *was* an Orangeman, they all said, "You're not." I said, "I am," and they said, "You're not." "But I am." "You're not. You're not. You're not." So I said, "OK. Have it your way. Obviously when I think I parade through Belfast in a collarette on the Twelfth of July I'm suffering from delusions."' And the third Orangeman, who had always believed the southern Irish mind was so closed it was a waste of time trying to explain anything, said, 'There you are! What did I tell you?'

I spring from a southern Roman Catholic, nationalist tradition myself, but over the decades, I have become aware of my tribe's effrontery and laziness of mind where Northern Protestants, particularly Orangemen, are concerned. 'Why doesn't the British government stop those dreadful bigots from strutting through nationalist areas?' is the cry from people who've never met an ordinary Orangeman. And with the next breath they say that unionists have no culture worth talking about.

During the past few years, as I researched this book, I have met hundreds of members of the loyal institutions: the Apprentice Boys, the Orange Order and the Royal Black Institution. I have never known a community as misrepresented and traduced. In their pride and inflexibility, though, they have certainly given plenty of ammunition to their enemies. But then the qualities that enable people to endure a life under siege are not those that make for intellectual nimble-footedness and a talent for public relations.

Most members of the loyal institutions are ordinary, decent people, many of whom have endured extraordinary fear and suffering without becoming bitter. Many are among the finest people I have ever met and live lives that are an inspiring witness to their faith. And others, of course, are very bigoted and nasty.

Along the way I've asked Orangemen here and there what they hoped might emerge from my book. I enjoyed most the suggestion from the English Orangeman (who gave me the run of his library and his unpublished work on English Orangeism), Mike Phelan, that it should prove conclusively that compared to Orangemen the Knights of the Round Table were cornerboys. I've failed to do that, I'm afraid, but I hope I may have made some headway in satisfying some of my other advisers, like Henry Reid, who told me my job was to give an idea of the spirit of the ordinary Orangeman. Graham Montgomery elaborated: 'I'd like it to show that Orangemen are just men and Orangewomen just women – just people. And that they can be terribly cultured people who go to the opera or holiday abroad or can be terribly pedestrian and watch the football and eat chips and watch *Coronation Street* and go to Newcastle for a short break. That they can be ministers or businessmen or lawyers or teachers or farmers or factory-workers – or, like Dr Barnardo, be philanthropists. That they cover the whole gamut of life in any society. That there's something about the Orange that everybody, even outsiders, can identify with in some way. And that the Orange Order is something we're involved in in our leisure time – something important enough for us to actually create leisure time for it.'

The Reverend Brian Kennaway added that he'd want the book to show that the Orange Order 'is about more than parades; the perception in England and abroad is Orange Order equals parade. We are a people with our own identity and our own moral values, and we express those values within our institution. But we are also a people with a tradition and with rights and we are in the forefront of civil rights. Every Orange banner is a civil rights banner.'

Along the way, in trying to understand why members of the loyal institutions think as they do, I've had to acquire an understanding of the differences within Protestantism, get a grip on several centuries of European religious wars, look at Irish history from the perspective of besieged settlers rather than of the angry dispossessed and at British history from the perspective of the Puritan rather than the Cavalier. I've come to appreciate the virtues of a way of life that would never suit me. To anyone who believes that I am looking at Orangeism from too positive a perspective, I can say only that that is what I do in all my books: my biography of James Connolly, for instance, is sympathetic too, and I am neither republican nor socialist.

I have been much enriched by the whole experience. But I now know without a shadow of doubt that what we have on the island of Ireland are two tribes who might be from two different planets and that no amount of rhetoric will change that reality, however unpalatable it may be to wishful thinkers. It is not until men of violence give them the chance to learn mutual trust that the tribal mentality can be overcome and people can let go of the hatreds of the past.

For the most part, the tribes can be defined as being Protestant/unionist or Catholic/nationalist, though there are significant numbers of Catholics who are happy to remain part of the British state and a handful of Protestants who have become Irish nationalists.

I've interviewed many of the leaders of the loyal institutions, but I've been just as interested in hearing the views of innumerable foot-soldiers and their spouses. I can't mention all those who helped me and there are, sadly, others, particularly in the border areas, who do not wish to be acknowledged in case they or their families are in consequence put at greater risk from thugs and terrorists from either side. But since they are readily identifiable anyway, I will mention the Reverend William

Bingham and Janet, Edwin and Gail Boyd, Harrison and Beryl Boyd, Eric Brown, Bertie Campbell, the Charlton family, George Chittick, Johnny Cowan, Tony Crowe, Richard Dallas, Gerry Douglas, Tommy Doyle, Sammy Foster, Jackie Hewitt, Jack Hunter, Roy Kells, the Reverend Brian Kennaway and Liz, Alfred and Charlie Kenwell, Cecil Kilpatrick, Warren Loan, Gordon Lucy, Jim McBride, John McCrea, Lexie McFeeter, Chris and Joyce McGimpsey, Derek Miller, Lord Molyneaux, Gordon, Graham and Heather Montgomery, the late Jack Moore, Billy Moore, Noel Mulligan, Dave Packer, George Patten, Mike and Sue Phelan, the Reverend Warren Porter, Tom and Louie Reid, Bobby Saulters, Alistair Simpson, the Reverend Martin Smyth, David and Daphne Trimble, Denis Watson, Richard Whitten, Ian Wiggins and James Wilson. I am grateful also to Ian Black, Charles Fenton, David Griffin, the Reverend Gordon McMullan, the Reverend Ian Wilson, Frederick and Betty Stewart, Cephas Tay, Hilton Wickham and all the other delegates to the Imperial Council who gave so much help. To all those other Orangemen and Apprentice Boys who gave me their time and trust, I give my thanks. It has been a privilege to be welcomed into a community as you have welcomed me and to know that you expect of me only that I tell the truth as I see it.

Among the non-Orange people to whom I owe thanks are Brian Walker, who took me to my first bonfire, and to various parade companions, especially Karen Davies, Rhondda Donnaghy, Bridget and Emily Houri-can, Hugh Jordan, Shelly Kang, Gary Kent, Stephen King, Gus Legge, John Lloyd, Paul Le Druillenec, Jenny McCarthey, Gerry McLoughlin, Úna O'Donoghue, Paddy O'Gorman, Priscilla Ridgway, Mark and Margot Stakem and James Tansley. I'm grateful too to the many friends who put up with me despite thinking I must be mad to have embarked on a project that took me away so often to squelch through mud in the company of religiously-minded men in bowler hats who keep making a fuss about walking down roads. 'Oh, God, you're not going Orangeing again, are you? Be careful,' was the usual line. I'm particularly grateful, though, to the friends who listened, even if not always sympathetically, to what I reported back or those who told me I was doing something useful. Special mention must be made of two beloved and encouraging friends, Niall Crowley and Jill Neville, who died while I was working on the book, and of Paul Bew, Chaz Brenchley, Stephen Cang, Maírín Carter, Nina Clarke, Betsy Crabtree, Robert Cranborne, Colm de Barra, Barbara Sweetman Fitzgerald, Dean Godson, Graham Gudgeon, Blair Hall, Rory Hanrahan, Eoghan Harris, Kate Hoey, Eamonn Hughes, Sylvia

Kalisch, Mary Keen, Liam Kennedy, Kathryn Kennison, Kuku Khanna, Janet Laurence, Gordon Lee, John Lippitt, Robin Little, Jim and Lindy McDowell, James McGuire, Janet McIver, John and Elizabeth Midgley, Sean O'Callaghan, Eoin O'Neachtain, Henry Robinson, Des Smith, Oliver Snoddy, Veronica Sutherland, Bert Ward, Julia Wisdom and my niece Neasa MacErlean. And Martin Mansergh kindly gave me the benefit of his researches into the Orange Order.

I am very grateful to David Armstrong, editor of the *Portadown Times*, Graham Montgomery, Sean O'Callaghan, Mike Phelan and Henry Reid for reading and commenting on the typescript. Along with Brian Kennaway, Graham, Mike and Henry have been the Orangemen on whom I have most relied throughout the last few years for help, hospitality, wit and honest answers to innumerable difficult questions. James McGuire, an historian of the seventeenth-century and one of the few southern Catholics I know who has close friendships with Ulster Protestants, has been the non-Orange equivalent. My brother Owen, who is notoriously generous with his time and his scholarship, took tremendous trouble, picked up several errors, filled in several gaps and engaged for about eight hours on the telephone in healthy disagreement with me about certain passages – most of which I amended. Not only is he exceptionally well informed about the subject, but his Catholic perspective was a very useful corrective: I greatly appreciate his support and encouragement.

It was Alan Ruddock, who as Irish editor of the *Sunday Times* first gave me space to write about the Orange Order, and Aengus Fanning and Willie Kealy of the *Sunday Independent* who have since he left been my main indulgers. I quote or use here from articles of mine in both papers as well in the *Belfast Newsletter*, *Daily Express*, *Daily Mail*, *Daily Mirror*, *Daily Telegraph*, *Irish Times*, *Portadown Times* and *Spectator*.

Michael Fishwick of HarperCollins took me to lunch to discuss a completely different project, listened to my babbling about Drumcree, and said: 'That's what you're really interested in. Why not write a book about the Orangemen?' Not only was he invariably sympathetic and helpful, but he did not even raise an eyebrow when he was given a typescript which was twice the length agreed. He was lucky that time did not permit me to do a proper job on Orangewomen or juniors, not to speak of the Orange Order abroad. My agent, Felicity Bryan, wanted me to do something far more sensible, but she gritted her teeth and as always, backed me up. The HarperCollins team including Janet Law, Phyllis Richardson, Prue Jeffreys and Moira Reilly, did me proud and my editor, Kate Johnson, who came late and over-worked to the project, was a pleasure to deal with and always laughed rather than cried.

But the name of my assistant, Carol Scott, should lead all the rest. Not only did she, as usual, look after me with patience and humour, but she listened to my stories, sympathised with the sufferings of my troubled Orange friends and readily accepted that Orangemen are people too. I hope others will show a similarly open mind.

Eight Parades, a Cancellation and Some Anthropological Notes from the War-zone

I CAME TO THE LOYAL institutions bringing with me all the unconscious prejudices I had imbibed during a Dublin Roman Catholic*
childhood and a secular adulthood in London. The best way of explaining
how my views have changed is to give my own parading history; so here
is a cross-section of the dozens of parades, big and small, that I have
attended. I have tried to show how my assumptions and attitudes changed
along the way, so where I wrote at the time about a parade, I quote
relevant extracts here.

1. Belfast, 13 July 1987

At the time I was chairman of the British Association for Irish Studies
(BAIS) which, *inter alia*, sought to give public expression to all aspects
of Irish history, politics and culture. Protestant and unionist perspectives
received a decent airing at our conferences and public lectures, but we
had never heard a positive view of Orangeism – a closed, unreadable
and rather distasteful book to most academics. ('For all I know about
Orangemen after twenty years of living and working in Belfast,' said an
English academic friend to me recently, 'they could live in burrows in
the Glens of Antrim.') So I thought I had better go and look at a Twelfth
of July parade and see if I could understand what was going on.

Orangeism to me then represented thuggish, stupid, sectarian bigotry.
I had a vague feeling that Orangemen were mainly working-class, and

---

∗ This is as good a place as any to clear up a problem of language that is a running sore today in Northern
Ireland. Catholics are those who believe their Church has evolved from the ancient Christian Church; Anglicans,
many other Protestant sects and Orthodox Eastern Churches come into this category, along with those who
acknowledge the Pope as head of the Church, and who have historically therefore been termed 'Roman
Catholics'. 'We stand,' says the Orange Order, 'for the true Catholic Faith and we deny any church the right to
make exclusive claims thereto. The title "Catholic" belongs to all who own the Lord Jesus Christ as Saviour
and honour Him as Lord. They are all by His grace members of His Catholic or Universal Church. That saving
grace is confined to no single sect.'

Yet since Rome has always insisted it had exclusive use of the term 'Catholic' and since the belief that it is
the one, true Catholic Church has been a principle of Roman Catholic teaching in Ireland, it is in the psyche
of the Irish Roman Catholic that he is a Catholic, and that anyone calling him a Roman Catholic is in some
obscure way being offensive. A Southern Irish friend of mine recalled hearing the term first in the 1960s in
television coverage of an Ian Paisley speech; he and his other teenage friends gazed at each other indignantly.
'What does he mean Roman Catholic?' said one of them. 'We're not Italians.'

Orangemen are asked not to take offence but, in the interest of saving trees, throughout this book I use
'Catholic' to mean 'Roman Catholic'.

that aspiring unionist politicians cynically donned the Orange sash to help them get elected. People on the Anglo-Irish scene occasionally passed on the information that all unionist MPs, with the exception of Ken Maginness, were in the Orange Order. Since Maginness was and is a well-known liberal and one of the few unionist leaders to have friends in the Republic of Ireland, this was added evidence that Orangeism was for bigots only. It was ten years before I learned that Maginness was in fact a member of a loyal institution with an even rougher reputation: the Apprentice Boys.

Northern nationalist friends spoke of the fear that gripped them on the Twelfth of July; middle-class Protestants and Catholics alike talked of how they always got out of town for the Twelfth and a Catholic friend from Portadown did a highly amusing imitation of an Orangeman swaggering along singing 'On the Green Grassy Slopes of the Boyne', with a chorus of 'Fuck the Pope', in which we all merrily joined.

It was sobering that no one wanted to go with me. Family and friends in London thought it another of my aberrations to want to look at a lot of dreary and possibly dangerous men stomping along in bowler hats and probably rioting. And my Northern Irish friends refused out of hand, except for one Protestant with an interest in political culture who agreed to take me to a bonfire on the night before the parade. Fortunately, my Dublin friend Úna is indulgent and adventurous, so she agreed to go north.

On an impulse, when I arrived in Belfast on Friday, I looked up the Orange Order in the phone book and presented myself at the House of Orange in Dublin Road. I was making a point for the sake of it: I expected to be greeted with distrust if not hostility. Instead I was given a friendly welcome by George Patten, the executive secretary.

I explained about the BAIS and asked some basic questions about how much work had been done on Orange history. What were the chances of an outsider ever being allowed access to Orange archives? I asked idly. George Patten shook his head. He was all for objective history, he said, but he couldn't imagine the Order trusting an outsider.

Emboldened by his friendliness, I explained that Úna and I wanted to see the parade on Monday and that, being Dublin Catholics, we didn't know where to go or what to do. Had he any advice on where we should sit? And how would we find out what was going on? Explaining that he himself would not be in Belfast, for he would be on parade in the country, Patten summoned a colleague who told me where we would have the best view: he would come and brief us for a while in the morning preparatory to joining his lodge.

I loved the tour of enormous bonfires on Sunday night. Perhaps I should have been offended that effigies of the Irish and British prime ministers were being burned as a protest against the Anglo-Irish Agreement, but I wasn't. I had been rather uneasy that the two governments had made a deal without consulting unionists and that a mass demonstration of a quarter-of-a-million Protestants had been virtually ignored. Considering the massive sense of betrayal throughout the unionist community, burning effigies seemed a harmless way of letting off steam.

The following morning Úna and I seated ourselves on the pavement opposite Sandy Row – which I knew by repute as a street down which any Catholic went at his peril – and were soon surrounded by families and picnic baskets. There then arrived a contingent of five or six nasty-looking young men with tattoos, militaristic haircuts and rasping Glaswegian accents. They were carrying cartons of beer. It was a hot day and looked like being a long one so I nerved myself to ask where they had procured their supplies. 'Sandy Row,' they explained. It is a testimony to the insane levels of media exaggeration and extreme nationalist propaganda that I really thought that in the middle of the morning I was running a serious risk in exposing my Southern Irish accent in a Sandy Row off-licence, but I did, and only pride got me to my feet. The alcohol-buyers were a pretty rough-looking bunch, but everyone was perfectly civil.

When our guide arrived in his regalia, he explained a few basic essentials: that LOL on a banner or a sash meant Loyal Orange Lodge, that the numbers were originally related to the lodge's seniority, and that temperance lodges were not necessarily composed of teetotallers but of people who disapproved of getting drunk. He told us that, contrary to what he understood was Catholic mythology, Lambeg drums were not made from the skin of Catholics but of goats. He stayed for about twenty minutes and then suddenly said goodbye and vanished into the middle of a group of men who looked indistinguishable from all the rest.

Úna and I had a good time. We sipped our beer and listened to the music and marvelled at the noise and colour and spectacle and tried to understand the banners. We took pleasure in the good time that people all around us were having. I found the whole thing absolutely unthreatening except for some fife-and-drum bands composed of dangerous-looking young men, several of which, it was explained to me afterwards, came from Scotland. I felt uneasy, though, at the sight of small children wearing collarettes or band uniforms which, at the time, I took to indicate that they were being brainwashed in sectarian practices.

My martial blood was stirred by now and I was on for walking the five miles to Finaghy Field where the parade was heading, but Úna decreed lunch so we cheated and went later to the field by taxi. Even so, we were in time to walk up the lane for ten minutes with the last of the parade behind the Portadown True Blues, a tough-looking crew in military-style uniforms who nevertheless played with a verve that put a spring in one's step. And when we reached the field we saw the arresting sight of hundreds of bandsmen and some Orangemen facing the hedge-rows in a virtual semi-circle relieving themselves. Young fife-and-drum bandsmen, it was explained to me later, drink a lot of beer before and after parades.

We steered well clear of the platform and the speeches, skirted the picnicking Orangemen and their families and headed for the stalls. Having acquired red-and-white flags and hats saying 'Keep Ulster British' and 'Ulster says No', respectively waving and wearing them, we had our photograph taken at a stall and converted into keyrings. And when we had run out of amusements we headed back down the lane to find the taxi we had prudently booked to take us back to the city centre.

The ironic postscript came that evening in a restaurant. At the table next to us were half-a-dozen women having a very merry dinner with much wine and laughter. When we fell into conversation we found they were celebrating having made a vast amount of money running food stalls at Finaghy Field. They did this every year. And they were all Catholics.

2. Belfast, 12 July 1994

It was seven years before I went back, this time as a journalist with guinea-pigs in tow: Priscilla, an American Protestant, and, from Dublin, Bridget and Emily Hourican, Catholic university students. In Belfast, on the eve of the Twelfth, we were briefed by academic and political friends over dinner. The mood was sombre to begin with. In the hope of provok-ing retaliation, the IRA had murdered a prominent loyalist and riddled with bullets the house of the Democratic Unionist Party (DUP) MP, the Reverend Willie McCrae. Later we cheered up. I was a great deal less ignorant about Northern Ireland now, yet I was amazed to hear from the McGimpseys, Orangeman Chris and Orangewoman Joyce, that they saw the Order as predominantly a social organization; Joyce waxed eloquent about the socials and dances.

We repaired late to a couple of massive bonfires, built communally in Protestant areas over several days with anything from cardboard to obsolete refrigerators; large numbers of people stood around drinking and making amiable chat. My contingent were in merry form by then and disappointed that there was insufficient carousing. They learned the words of 'No Pope of Rome', which was being played in the background and is an old favourite of mine. It is elegiac, a kind of Orange *aisling*,* a vision of what life might be in a Utopian Northern Ireland, though, like most modern hard-line sectarian songs, it was composed in Scotland. Sung to the tune of 'Home on the Range', the chorus runs:

No, no Pope of Rome,
No chapels† to sadden my eye,
No nuns and no priests,
No rosary beads,
Every day's like the Twelfth of July.

I wrote afterwards:

When I last saw the parade, it was in blazing sunshine. This time it poured with rain. We collected our beer from the Sandy Row off-licence and settled on a stone wall nearby, now augmented by Gus Legge, a University College Dublin engineering student and Hourican friend who had been fired by their example to come up from Dublin independently. The first differences emerged over the paraphernalia. Priscilla, Emily and I were happy as a gesture of courtesy to wear King Billy or Ulster Flag hats and wave Union Jacks; Bridget balked at the flag but wore a hat and carried a baton decorated in red, white and blue. Gus eschewed all insignia; he felt they had political overtones and would not have waved their republican equivalents. However, he did graciously accept from me the present of a keyring which on one side said 'Keep Ulster Tidy' and on the other 'Throw your litter in the Irish Republic'.**

---

* Irish for 'vision poem'. The Irish Catholic Utopia was a country from which all the Protestants would have been evicted.

† Protestants call Catholic churches chapels.

** An Orangeman asked me to point out that such merchandise has nothing to do with the Orange Order.

I love the parade. I love the music; if you've never heard the Eton Boating Song played by fife and drum, you haven't lived. I love the daftness of some of the decorations. Ferociously muscly chaps bash drums adorned with politically-chosen flowers – orange tiger lilies or sweet william. I love trying to work out why in several groups just a few will have red or white carnations in their bowler hats. Are they office-holders in the lodge? Are some of the bowlers rounder than some of the others for significant reasons, or has a hatter gone out of business? Why was one bowler sporting a fern and another a sprig of heather? And why were not more of them sprouting the tiny plastic Union Jacks?

I love the banners – the pictures, the variety, the often baffling biblical, Irish and Scottish historical references. I love the eclecticism of a parade that includes lodges called Ark of Freedom, Rev. W. Maguire Memorial Total Abstinence, Prince Albert Temperance, Prince of Orange, Mountbatten, Martyrs of the Grassmarket – Edinburgh, True Blues of the Boyne, Martyrs Memorial (the name of Ian Paisley's church, though he is in fact in the Independent Orange Order*), the Queen Elizabeth Accordion Band, the Rising Sons of India, the Defenders, the Protestant Boys and the Loyal Sons of County Donegal. Contemporary politics was occasionally in evidence, with a clip-on 'NO DUBLIN INTERFERENCE' attached to a handful of banners. 'I didn't know there were that many Prods in Ireland,' observed Priscilla.

I love the taxis. They arrived at infrequent intervals, decorated according to the enthusiasm of the proprietor with anything from a single Union Jack to full regalia – King Billy banners, large flags, bunting and a multiplicity of political flowers. Their purpose was threefold: to transport Orangemen too old or frail to march with their lodges, drums too heavy for anyone to carry for five miles and also to pick up those who faltered along the route. I loved the moment when a dogged aged marcher dropped out, still smiling bravely, hailed an oncoming taxi uncertainly and was eventually assisted by a functionary who stopped the cab and the entire procession and helped him in. The fact that such a disciplined parade would stop unexpectedly to accommodate a falterer was typical of the humanity of the whole event. There was even a wheelchair.

I love the daft mix of clothes. From the ultra-disciplined – flute bands in vulgar brightly-coloured uniforms which depending on your perception

---

∗ I was wrong. Paisley did not join the Independents when he fell out with the Orange Order. He is, however, an Apprentice Boy.

were quasi-military, ocean-liner steward or cinema usher, complete with little caps with tassels, epaulettes and the lot – through kilts, trews, tam o'shanters, Californian drum majorettes' uniforms, complete with short skirts, white socks and white shoes, older women in sensible skirts and stout shoes, chaps with ponytails, chaps in shirt-sleeves, one man in a dinner-jacket, to the most familiar image – the men in suits and bowlers with the sashes. There were people carrying pikes, staves, batons, drums, pipes, flutes, tin whistles and umbrellas. Then there were the kids who ranged from five-year-olds of both sexes in full uniform at the head of a lodge to various tracksuited individuals or toddlers in dresses and waterproof jackets holding on to banner-cords. A few people had their faces painted red, white and blue; several others opted for coloured hair, which in a surprising number of instances ended up green.

I love the lack of ageism. The fact that, apparently unselfconsciously, lodges could accommodate marchers from toddlers to totterers.

I love the fact that they are terrifically disciplined for the first mile or so, while the TV cameras are on them; in fact, when they catch sight of them, there is extra special twirling of batons, straighter shoulders and even more histrionics on the drums.

I love the signs of fraying of tempers when they got to the third mile and were soaked through. In one accordion band the girls got stroppy with their male leaders and a full-scale rebellion about what was to be played next had to be resolved. In mixed bands like this you could especially see the social importance of the Orange Order. Joining the Sandy Row Prince of Orange Accordion Band must be the local equivalent of joining the Young Conservatives in Surrey.

I love the fact that there was much chatting with the crowd once the heat was off, that people like us were intent on locating those we knew and shouting and waving at them – it was an important form of recognition. We swelled with pride when we spotted a McGimpsey and received a wave.

I love their dogged varieties of stoicism in the face of the cruel weather. Some sported umbrellas; accordion-players perforce had to wear plastic cloaks to protect their instruments; other defiantly wore shirt-sleeves in downpours that had my contingent whingeing and fighting over our golf umbrella. Not only did they finish the march, but most of them stayed in Finaghy Field, with little to amuse but hamburger and fish-and-chip stalls, and a platform of dignitaries. When we left, the officiating clergyman had attracted an audience of only about thirty-five. Everyone else was hanging around hoping that the rain would stop, the mud would dry up and they could do what they normally did – sit on the grass, play music, drink beer and sing, until it was time to regroup and march back the five miles to Belfast city centre.

I love marching along with the parade, which we did after an hour or so in order to get warm. My choice was the Unthank Road Flute Band. And when you get into the rhythm, you understand the importance of military music.

Priscilla and Emily enjoyed themselves in the same way as I did, but Bridget and Gus did not. Bridget hates parades anyway and, like Gus, thought this one militaristic. Neither likes fife-and-drum music. There was some wistful longing for Spanish fiestas or West Indian carnivals. Priscilla caused a rethink by pointing out that this event was greatly similar to the Ancient Order of Hibernians' St Patrick's Day parade in New York, with the pipe bands, the IRA veterans and the marching Irish police in Sam Browne belts. It was agreed that because the South was unused to military trappings, it was possible to see militarism where it was not intended. What received general agreement in the end was that the parade was an expression of pride in the community and that is no bad thing.

Tiny signs of tribalism were accentuated by walking down the Falls and the Shankill. The very secular Priscilla suddenly went seriously Protestant in the Shankill Road. Here, she said, were the besieged, not the besiegers; it was a clenched-teeth community. It was a reversion to family type. 'If there have been Catholics in the family, it has never been mentioned,' she explained.

Bridget and Emily went slightly the other way, mainly because of their shock at the World Cup-related graffiti. Having been actively involved in World Cup mania in Dublin and having adored the carnival atmosphere, it passed their understanding that anyone in Northern Ireland would not have been on the side of the Ireland team. The comments on the Ireland–Holland match were bad enough: '1690 ORANGEMEN 1–0; 1994 ORANGEMEN 2–0'; 'PACKIE BUTTERFINGERS LET IT IN THE NET'. 'But we'd have supported Northern Ireland if they'd got through,' said the Houricans. 'Not the point,' said the newly politicized Priscilla. 'Being besieged leads to aggression.' And that was before we saw the comment on the Ireland–Italy match and the Loghlinisland public-house massacre: 'HOUGHTON HIT THE NET 1 – 0; UVF HIT THE BAR 6–0'.

Gus felt no tribal signals. He felt more at ease in the Falls simply because there a southern accent would be an advantage, but he was depressed by both roads and the multiplicity of 'For Sale' signs, suggesting hopeless attempts to get out.

Everyone loved the people they met from both communities and their great friendliness and were delighted when a Protestant taxi-driver said with pleasure, 'I wouldn't have expected youse people from Dublin to come up and wave on the parade.' Bridget was particularly pleased at the elderly Orangemen who said to her in the field, 'Wish you were the leader of my lodge.'

A detour on the way home via Crossmaglen yielded an impressive tribute to the British passion for freedom of speech, for signs which I had seen a year ago were still in place: 'BRITISH TERRORISTS GO HOME' and, surrounding a sketch of a chap in a balaclava, '2ND BATTALION – VICTORY TO THE PROVOS'.

Priscilla has returned to America determined to recommend the event to her Irish acquaintances, and the Dublin contingent is evangelical. A coachload can be expected next year.

3. Aughnacloy, 23 August 1995

As a result of that and other articles about Northern Ireland, I received an invitation out of the blue from a County Tyrone farmer the following year to come to the Clogher Valley, stay at his house and attend 'the Last Saturday in August demonstration with RBP No. 800'. I didn't know what he was talking about, but I was so stunned at being invited to anything by an unknown Ulster Protestant that I cut short a highly convivial holiday in Clare. 'I'm going to some kind of Orange march in the country,' I said to a Southern Irish friend who worked for peace and reconcilation in Northern Ireland. 'You must be mad,' she said. 'I'd rather cut my throat than go to an Orange march.'

Henry, my host, had decided that it was time – post-Drumcree One – for at least one journalist to attend an ordinary rural parade as a guest of what turned out to be a preceptory of the Royal Black Institution. Determined I should see it for myself and make up my own mind about it, he gave me little briefing the night before. At around nine the following morning, after his mother had provided us with a vast Ulster fry,* we

---

* Known locally as a heart-attack on a plate, this is normal rural fare and can include bacon, eggs, sausages, tomatoes, mushrooms, fried bread and potato bread, and is usually accompanied by home-made soda bread, one of the most delicious foodstuffs in the world.

drove to the little village of Clogher, six miles from the border. It was cold and intermittently showery: Ulster's is a cruel climate for a culture whose big festival days occur in the open air.

I was led first into the Orange Hall which was shared by what I now knew to be the Royal Black Preceptory and Henry showed me around. A two-storey house, it was dingy, plain and furnished in a decidedly spartan fashion with hard seats and rough trestle-tables. There was a picture of the Queen downstairs and another upstairs, a ceremonial sword and a plush seat for the Worshipful Master. The lavatory and kitchen were tiny and cheerless and there was no hot water. Men rushed in and out exchanging greetings, removing coats and putting on what I thought were black sashes but which are called collarettes, bowler hats and white gloves. The Blackmen,* as they are generally known, pride themselves on being well turned out: indeed, the only daft thing that Henry has ever said to me he said later that day. When he observed on parade a contingent from south of the border who were wanting in the white-glove department, he shook his head and said, 'Look at them poor craturs there. If we'd been in a United Ireland we'd all be in that state.'

After introducing me to some of his brethren, Henry dispatched me with instructions to wait across the road from the hall, watch them parade round the village and then proceed to the coach to travel to the main parade. Then they assembled, their band struck up and they processed up the village and round and down, watched by no more than perhaps a dozen or so people along the way.

In the coach I was seated next to the Worshipful Master who said he hoped I would come to tea in the hall afterwards and suggested that if I enjoyed a nip of whiskey, I might like to accompany him to the pub afterwards. My enthusiasm for this notion sealed our friendship, and for the rest of the journey we talked about his family. (Ulster people are so cautious of causing affront by seeming nosy that they rarely ask personal questions; during interviews on countless occasions someone would say in response to a question about his religion, 'I don't know what your faith is and I wouldn't ask but I hope I'm not giving offence,' before

---

* Ireland has few black residents and Ulster hardly any, so locals are unaware of any ambiguity when they refer to the Blackmen. One July I was standing at a reception desk in a Belfast hotel when an American woman asked if there would be any more marches that summer. 'Oh yes,' said the receptionist, 'the Blackmen parade on the last Saturday in August.' She continued finalizing the guest's account and thus missed her astounded and bewildered expression. I thought of setting the tourist right, but decided it was more fun not to.

going on to say something completely innocuous about his particular religious beliefs.)

Summing up the day in a newspaper article, I wrote:

The Clogher Valley people – who were extraordinarily welcoming – have since been described to me as among the most decent people in Northern Ireland. Dungannon, the local council, is working well on a system of power-sharing between the Ulster Unionists and the SDLP. As one council member explained: 'For most purposes it's us and the SDLP [John Hume's party] against the fascists – the DUP [Ian Paisley's party] and Sinn Féin.'* And there were many Catholics among the more than 20,000 people who picnicked in cars along the parade route.†

You can't become an RBP member without having spent two years in the Orange Order. The RBP has a reputation for being the least confrontational of loyal institutions, so I realise that what I saw in Aughnacloy was the most benign face of Orangeism. Of perhaps 90 lodges and bands, only three or four were even faintly intimidating. The exceptions were what are known as the 'kick-the-pope'** bands of young men from places like Portadown with earrings, shaven heads, vulgar and militaristic uniforms and a triumphalist swagger; in Scotland they would be on the terraces of Glasgow Rangers football club.

I've often vaguely wondered exactly what Orangemen do. 'Sinn Féin think we talk politics and plot,' said one RBP member. 'In fact what we do is to have a monthly meeting in our hall to discuss trivial points about increasing the annual dues or repairing the roof; a few times a year we have a dinner. The main reason for going is just to meet your neighbours. And the parades are days out to look forward to.'

It was with a shock of recognition that I realized that, at bottom, the Orange Order is simply a Northern Irish Protestant means of male bonding. In England chaps have their clubs in which they obey arcane rules

---

* I am told that some local Orangemen who are members of the DUP were annoyed at this remark. I am sorry to have hurt their feelings, but I record what I hear.

† I was corrected about this later. It would have been true six or seven years ago: indeed, in 1991 the wife of a Sinn Féin worker brought her children, her sunglasses and a chair with her and watched the parade. In the last few years, however, because of the increase in sectarian tension, Catholics stay away. There would, however, be many stalls and shops manned by Catholics servicing the paraders and onlookers.

** Orangemen describe them as 'blood-and-thunder' bands, Catholics (because they dislike them) and loyalist youths (because they love them) call them 'kick-the-pope'.

and organize social occasions. Some are Freemasons – cousins of Orangemen – and wear funny clothes and appear to be sinister because they conduct their proceedings in secret, but are in fact by and large a pretty harmless lot of men who just want an excuse to get out of the house. Irish Catholic men bond in pubs.*

Clogher Valley Protestants are hard-working, God-fearing, sober, frugal but warm people with a fierce pride in the land which many generations of their forefathers made so prosperous. Their RBP headquarters has so far escaped the fate of the almost 100 Orange halls attacked and seriously damaged in the past six years. It is a simple village hall with no creature comforts. The post-parade tea, at which I was made welcome both formally and informally, was – as one of them put it – 'a country dinner' of lots of meat and potatoes, and it was dry. But the Worshipful Master took me to the pub afterwards for Irish whiskey and chat with locals.

RBP 800 prided themselves on being well turned-out for the parade, in best suits, bowler hats, sash, mason's apron and white gloves; the Murley Silver Band with whom they have marched for many years has a smart uniform. Like most of the bands, the Murley men and women are devoted to music-making rather than politics and like many of the other bands has extended its repertoire far beyond 'The Sash' and military music; many bands now play the music of that Catholic Derryman, Phil Coulter.†

What is missed in television coverage of these marches is the happy aspect. Old men walk along hand-in-hand with a toddler grandchild; cars follow individual lodges bearing proud but infirm elders; and every time I moved from my marching position beside the band and caught the eye of one of the men from my host lodge, I was awarded a wink or a large beam. Afterwards I said to one of them, 'Why do you look so serious as you parade?' He was puzzled. 'It's part of the discipline.'

There is a general belief that without the twenty-five years of assault from the IRA, the Orange Order would have almost withered away. The recognition that nationalist spokesmen are wiping the floor with unionists politically and on the media makes the parades a vital means of showing

---

* I should have added, 'or in the Gaelic Athletic Association, which provides a social and sometimes political focus to their lives'.

† I remember particularly the Murley renditions of 'It's A Long Way to Tipperary', 'Pack Up Your Troubles' and 'All the Nice Girls Love a Sailor'.

that the Protestants won't go away. 'What else have we got?' asked one. Yet there is a new recognition of the necessity of taking on the nationalists at their own game. 'We've been too stiff-necked and proud to explain ourselves,' said one. 'We've got to change.' There is nothing they would like so much in the Clogher Valley as to watch on television the new leader of the Ulster Unionist Party wipe that smile off Gerry Adams's face.

There were aspects of the day I had no room to put in that article. Such as that my host – who wanted me to know how bad it could be – insisted that we sit on the wet grass and listen to an evangelist who seemed to me to be completely deranged. Or that I was totally baffled that chaps speaking from the platform referred to each other as 'Sir Knight'. I was baffled too that there was almost no reference to politics: I had a vague impression that all marches ended with a unionist politician going on about the Anglo-Irish Agreement. It was only afterwards that I discovered that the Black was concerned more with the spiritual than the political.

I didn't mention that I discovered that it was rather fun singing hymns – this was the first of my many attempts at 'O God, Our Help in Ages Past' – nor did I refer to the 'resolutions' that were proposed at what I had just learned was called a 'demonstration'. Here are the three listed in the leaflet I was given, which included this instruction about a forthcoming anniversary service: 'Sir Knights to assemble on the Augher Road beside the Filling Station at 2.45 p.m.'

FIRST RESOLUTION

In pursuit of lasting peace in our land, we stress the need to contend earnestly for the Faith: We urge all Sir Knights to continue to live in harmony with their neighbours and to do all in their power to witness to the saving truths of the everlasting Gospel. We call upon everyone to embrace the Faith once delivered to the Saints and to engage whole-heartedly in the battle against the evil forces so rampant in today's society.

SECOND RESOLUTION

We, the Members of the Imperial Grand Black Chapter of the British Commonwealth, send our loyal greetings to Her Majesty The Queen. The commemorations of the end of the Second World War enabled the British people to manifest their deep respect for Her Majesty, who has maintained the commitment and duty to Her people as displayed throughout the war by Her Father and Mother, and confirmed their conviction that the Monarchy remains the keystone of our Parliamentary Democracy.

The third one was more foxing. But then I had not yet learned how immediate for many religiously-minded Protestants is the Old Testament.

THIRD RESOLUTION

We applaud the good citizens of Northern Ireland who remained unnerved by the shocks and uncertainties since the cessation of military operations by terrorists.

We regret that little was done to prepare the population for the inevitable confusion similar to that experienced by ancient Israel when released from captivity in Egypt. *Unlike* them *we* must remain resolute and ready to take full advantage of favourable developments before the end of the year.

I didn't mention either, as I didn't want to hurt Henry's feelings, that while I understood the attraction of parades, this seemed to me a pretty weird way of enjoying yourself, interesting though I'd found the experience. Nor that living in London where I virtually never hear the national anthem, I was moved by the fervour with which those attending the service sang it at the end. Nor that I greatly enjoyed the warmth of the welcome given in the Orange Hall to a female Southern Irish Catholic (albeit an atheist – which, of course, to them is worse) and was touched that the Worshipful Master thanked me formally for bothering to come. I appreciated everyone's friendliness, liked the atmosphere in the pub and the warmth and the chat of the drinking bandsmen and women and lodge-members. And I was thrilled that RBP No. 800 was now informally my lodge.*

4. Scarva, 13 July 1996

We'd had a very jolly Twelfth the previous day in Kesh. Despite the rise in sectarian bitterness after the events at Drumcree, there had been little to see except the parade and people enjoying themselves in the manner

---

* A clarifier here. My occasional references to 'my' lodge merely denote a friendly relationship and are not intended to suggest that a male-only all-Protestant lodge has taken leave of its senses and admitted as a member a female atheist who was baptized Catholic. I have standing invitations to certain functions there, I've eaten there three times and I feel a special gratitude to the brethren for being so kind and welcoming to a nervous outsider.

of rural Protestants: a sunny day, ice-cream, picnics, soft drinks, lots of stirring music and chatting to neighbours constituted for them a veritable heaven. My English companions, Gary and Paul, who'd come to a parade for the first time, had had a surprisingly good time; we'd been entertained for lunch at the Orange Hall where, as always, I was the only woman guest, and had a chat with Lord Brookeborough, grandson of a Northern Ireland prime minister and one of the few remaining members of the Ulster gentry still in the Orange Order. He had introduced us to an Orangeman in a wheelchair, an ex-member of the Royal Ulster Constabulary, whose legs had been blown off as he helped a Catholic, who was too drunk to walk properly, to get away from a place that was being evacuated. He was a cheerful man who said he had merely done his job, had no bitterness and was grateful to God for having spared him.

Now a friend was taking Gary and Paul and me to a day that a lot of parade-connoisseurs regard as the best spectacle in Northern Ireland: the annual parade of the Armagh Royal Black Preceptories and the Sham Fight.

A Black event is prized by all of those who want to see the loyal institutions at their most disciplined, dignified and responsible. And because of the nature of the Black, a far smaller portion of the bands are 'blood-and-thunder'. So it's a splendid outing for accordion, pipe and silver bands. (One of the pleasures of a parade is to see someone I have met socially appear completely transformed. I remember gentle, slightly diffident Eric suddenly appearing in front of me resplendent in his kilt and bagpipes, exuding joy and pride in his band and his community.)

The problem with Scarva is that it has become too popular and the lane down which the parade goes is narrow. If you want to walk along with a band, you have to do so behind the families sitting in their folding chairs or on their blankets, swigging soft drinks and munching sandwiches and cake. Scarva is a bit too respectable and tame to attract yobs although there is sometimes a bit of trouble from the small lager-drinking brigade.

Our day was complicated by my needing to have a word with James Molyneaux, the Imperial Sovereign Grand Master, who was leading the parade. 'We'll go through the fields,' announced our country friend, and took off at speed to lead us over barbed-wire fences and thorn-hedges and across boggy land and through muddy puddles to find Molyneaux before he disappeared into Scarvagh House to dine with the dignitaries. When we finally made it via the back route into the field, it was already full of stalls and Blackmen and bands and families. There was no sign of Molyneaux and the platform was deserted. So I had to climb over yet another fence and go to Scarvagh House.

By this time the Sham Fight between King James II, the loyal institutions' hate figure, and their hero, King William III, was in train. It is a bizarre and rather touching event, given an emotional context because there is an oak tree in the grounds under which William is supposed to have camped on his way to the Boyne. The following year, when I actually walked the route more or less backwards about twenty yards in front of the parade, I was highly diverted that the leading marshals were a King James and a King William in vaguely period uniform, in green and red respectively, adorned with tricorne hats with appropriate cockades. It rather takes away from the mystique when the two great enemies are engaged in moving bystanders out of harm's way, but then, except for a little ritual in Orange lodges, mystique is not much prized in that part of the world.

What happens at the Sham Fight is that, when everybody has arrived in the field, King William and his main henchman General Schomberg on the one hand, and King James and General Patrick Sarsfield on the other, appear on horseback to thunderous applause followed by motley footsoldiers more or less dressed for the part. After riding round and round for a while, the kings and generals, still on horseback, fight each other with swords while their followers use swords, pistols with blanks or just generally tussle. The fight – which is supposed to represent the four Williamite Irish battles: Derry, Enniskillen, Aughrim and the Boyne – rages enthusiastically all round the field with much gunshot, shouting, laughter and cheering. By the end of the fight, James's standard has been destroyed, William's is held high and James runs away.

That year I couldn't see a thing. The following year I got the hang of it when I was allowed on the platform. But what I did have was access to the Scarva joke, for I was marooned for quite some time outside the house where Molyneaux was eating, with a Black marshal who was very fond of it. It runs: 'Who won?' (or, as he pronounced it, 'Hee wan?'), a question he addressed to me and about half-a-dozen different people over the next twenty minutes amid his chortles of delighted laughter. I learned that the accepted response is something along the lines of, 'I don't know. I'll have to ask.'

As a spectacle, the Sham Fight is a bit amateurish. 'They really should call in the Sealed Knot,' observed a journalist the following year, alluding to a collection of military history buffs who refight the battles of the

English Civil War with great attention to accuracy and expertise. But that kind of professionalism would spoil the fun. The Sham Fight is put on by local people for their neighbours and, like them, it is without pretension. It is a homely and reassuringly familiar occasion.

The marshal had been rattled by my request to see Molyneaux, not so much because he was Imperial Sovereign Grand Master and retired Ulster Unionist Party leader, but because he was having his dinner. He was so shocked at the notion that a man might be distracted from feeding even by being passed a message saying, 'Can I see you when you're free?', that though he was a friendly and obliging man, it took half an hour before he could nerve himself to do the deed.

I eventually talked and laughed a bit with Molyneaux, whose public image is dour, but who is a gentle wit, in the hallway of the Victorian house, the light filtering through the stained-glass window representing King William on a white horse; then he and his colleagues decamped to the platform to say prayers, sing hymns, make sensible speeches and move moderate resolutions. The marshal was deeply impressed that Molyneaux had come out to meet me.

The men were dozing on the grass when I got back. We stayed long enough to listen to Molyneaux's part of the proceedings and then went off and had some foul hamburgers. Paul looked around the field and pronounced that, apart from the regalia, it was exactly like an English agricultural show. We left early, because if you don't get back to your car ahead of the parade, it is possible to be stuck behind cars and coaches for an hour. And after all that fresh air and blameless activity, we badly needed beer.

5. The Apprentice Boys, 10 August 1996

I had gone to Derry* the day before with Paul, who had become a parade aficionado, to sightsee and look at the route that was causing such massive arguments. For the preceding weeks and months, horse-trading had been going on to try to gain the agreement of the Bogside Residents' Group (BRG) to a walk along the city walls by the Apprentice Boys as part of their annual commemoration of the siege of 1689. The institution reveres the thirteen apprentice boys who defied their elders and closed the gates to keep out King James's army.

---

* Technically, in 1984, the city became 'Derry' while the county remained 'Londonderry'. In practice, Catholics tend to call both Derry and Protestants both Londonderry. Those trying to avoid giving offence call the city Derry/Londonderry and humorists call it Stroke City.

Derry is not just the Mecca of the Apprentice Boys, it is their *raison d'être*. It is a cruel irony for them that it is now almost wholly in national-ist hands: of the 60,000 inhabitants of the city, only 1,500 are Protestant, and they feel vulnerable to what they believe is a policy of ethnic cleansing.

Times were tense. A month before, the volte-face on Drumcree had led to full-scale riots, complete with petrol bombs and plastic bullets, leading to the death of one protester. Alistair Simpson, the Apprentice Boys' governor, had worked tirelessly to reach agreement with the resi-dents' group. Unlike the leaders of the Orange Order, who refused to negotiate parade routes with convicted terrorists, he had agreed to meet the leader of the BRG, Donncha MacNiallais.

Simpson and his colleagues had offered various concessions about numbers, about not playing any music as they walked on the part of the walls that overlooked the Bogside, and, in desperation, had suggested that screens be erected so that no Bogside resident would have to see the Apprentice Boys and barbed wire be put in place to ensure no Appren-tice Boy could approach the Bogside even if he wanted to. Even so, agreement had proved impossible. As a reporter in the Sinn Féin organ *An Phoblacht/Republican News* put it: 'They [the BRG] sought an overall accommodation with the Apprentice Boys involving the acceptance of the principle of consent for all contentious parades, wherever and by whomever they were organized. This the Apprentice Boys were unable to deliver, and talks broke down over the issue.' From Simpson's point of view, MacNiallais had moved the goalposts beyond reach.

To pre-empt trouble, on Wednesday the Secretary of State had banned the parade from the contentious part of the walls and had moved troops in to seal them off. In a particularly surreal contribution, a Bogside resident was quoted the following day in *An Phoblacht/Republican News*. 'Why are they creating a screened walkway? . . . The suspicion is that they are to be used to allow the march to go ahead outside the view of residents.'

When I met the gentle and courteous Alistair Simpson on the Friday, he was still depressed by the last meeting he had had with MacNiallais and the insults he had had to endure and he was apprehensive about the build-up of frustration among the Apprentice Boys, but he was confident he would find a way to avert violence.

Friday afternoon was enlivened by seeing in action in front of the Guildhall the legendary Mary Nelis, Sinn Féin councillor and mother of MacNiallais, dubbed by a unionist colleague 'the republican movement's

answer to Winnie Mandela'.* Less diplomatic than her son, she had
recently observed in a speech that the Apprentice Boys should know that
those whom she represented had 'never conceded your right to exist'.
Mrs Nelis enjoys drama (she is notorious among journalists for the fre-
quency with which, in front of television cameras during nationalist protests, she appears to faint under the feet of RUC men). She was holding
forth to a small audience and a couple of television cameras about the
evils of internment (which had ended in 1975) as a warm-up for the big
anti-internment march due in Belfast on the Sunday. Behind her was a
backing group of a dozen or so youths in black hoods facing the wall
with their hands pressed up against the building, adding impact to her
rhetoric about the wicked manner in which internees had been interrogated
twenty-five years previously.

I waited until Nelis finished telling us of past injustices, tried and failed
to catch the words of some doleful song about the wrongs of internment
which was wailing over the tannoy and went into the Guildhall to meet
the unionist mayor, Apprentice Boy and Orangeman, Richard Dallas.
Since for participating in an Orange demonstration over Drumcree, Dallas
had been stripped by nationalist councillors of everything that could be
stripped from him, he could not use the mayor's room, so we sat in the
council chamber until it was needed for a function and then in the tiny
robing-room which we shared with a large vacuum cleaner.

After the meeting Paul and I walked what we could of the Derry walls
and then went down into the Bogside. It was dominated by a vast new
mural of a circle containing a faceless figure in bowler hat, black suit
and Orange collarette with a diagonal red line across. Around the circle
were written DERRY, GARVAGHY and LOWER ORMEAU. At the top was
NO CONSENT. At the bottom, NO PARADE. (A few months later *An
Phoblacht/Republican News* reported that at a discussion organized during
the West Belfast Festival, a visitor from a Christian ecumenical group said
'nationalists shouldn't demonize Orangemen', citing the 'NO SECTARIAN
MARCHES' poster with the image of a faceless Orangeman. However,
John Gormley of LOCC [Lower Ormeau Concerned Citizens], who first
produced the poster, said, 'We use that image because we don't know
what an Orangeman looks like given their refusal to meet with us and
discuss the issue.')

From the estate itself, we looked at the wall. It became clear that only

---

* Republicans irritate unionists by comparing themselves with the ANC.

a very few residents could see the walls from their houses and they would be able to see only the tops of tall people's heads. So what the BRG had been complaining about was that at nine o'clock on a Saturday morning it would be theoretically possible for some residents to see a procession of bowler hats passing silently 100 yards away.

An engagement in Tyrone meant that we could not hang around to see the march in Derry city centre organized by the BRG to demand, according to the subsequent *An Phoblacht / Republican News* account, 'equality for all the nationalists of Northern Ireland. At the rally, both Donncha MacNiallais and Martin McGuinness stressed the importance of continuing solidarity with nationalists in small villages throughout the Six Counties who each year had Orange marches forced upon them.' A protest rally was planned for the following afternoon.

On Saturday morning we arrived in blazing sunshine, left our car near where dozens of coaches were off-loading Apprentice Boys and bands and walked across the bridge and into the city. Derry is a lovely city, much improved in recent years through investment by the British government, the European Union and the foreign-owned businesses courted by John Hume and others. Although in many respects it has blossomed under nationalist rule – it is, for instance, much more cosmopolitan than it used to be – many of those who love it with irrational passion are now wholly out of power. Derry Protestants love every stone in those walls; Derry republicans seem to hate it. Certainly they are still happy to vandalize it whenever there is an excuse. It is almost as if centuries of feeling excluded have made them loathe the very buildings. Tony Crowe, Apprentice Boy and historian, observed to me:

> Derry was like a kept woman, a young prostitute, in an ironic way. When she was a young maiden she was loved and feted by the unionists and she was seen as the untaken bride and known as the Maiden City. And then when they inherited her eventually in the late 1960s, the nationalists couldn't thole her because she still carried some of the vestiges of her early whoredom. Republicans systematically bombed and buggered the city and peaceful nationalists didn't mind too much because they couldn't relate to it. Now there's no refurbishment of fine buildings like you have in the Republic in cities like Limerick: the old St Augustine's rectory was knocked down and turned into a car park. It was within the walls, so nationalists felt it didn't belong to them.

On our way to meet friends, Paul and I stopped to take a photograph of some graffiti in a loyalist area and were instantly challenged by a couple of thuggish-looking locals. Who were we? 'Journalists,' I said. 'We don't like journalists. You never write anything good about us. You're all biased.' 'We're not. We're sympathetic,' I said, having no desire to start the day with trouble. The yobs clearly thought this highly unlikely, but their aggression none the less lessened somewhat. 'Just tell the truth,' one of them said grumpily and off they went. You can always rely on loyalists to do their best to alienate, just as you can rely on their republican counterparts to woo the press politely and articulately.

We went on to the gloomy Victorian premises of the Northern Counties Club, where many Apprentice Boys were gathering for their dinner. It was 11.30 and their service at St Columb's Cathedral was now over. The news was that in the middle of the previous night the RUC had agreed to allow thirteen Apprentice Boys to touch each of the gates in Derry's walls as a symbolic re-enactment of their closing in 1690. At Butcher Gate, the RUC had asked one of the BRG stewards who was on duty all night if they could speak to MacNiallais. 'When I found that no regalia at all was involved,' MacNiallais explained to *An Phoblacht / Republican News*, 'no bands or singing or shouting sectarian remarks, I told them we had no problem with this. Myself and a group of stewards escorted them to Butcher Gate, to Magazine Gate and towards Shipquay Gate. It was all very respectful on every side.' For the Apprentice Boys, being patronized like that was very hard to bear.

We supped beer with Chris McGimpsey and several other of his brethren and left him to his big feed while we went to the Apprentice Boys' Memorial Hall, paint-spattered and pock-marked from the paint bombs and ball-bearings that are launched at it regularly from the Bogside. In a tiny garden beside it is a statue of one of the Apprentice Boys' heroes, Governor Walker. In the 1970s the tall pillar on which he stood was destroyed by a bomb; more recently another blew his hand off and damaged his face. Alistair Simpson spoke to the media and the crowd to announce that though they greatly regretted being prevented from walking the walls, they would not challenge the ban, but would walk the walls another day of their own choosing. Face was saved. The majority of the Apprentice Boys were relieved; the more militant were disappointed. Like most of the media they had been hoping for a fight.

After chatting with a few Apprentice Boys, we were led off by our friend Harry to the best watching-place, just by the walls at the top of the hill leading to the Fountain Estate, the loyalist ghetto, festooned with a mass of red, white and blue bunting and flags and the remnants of the mighty bonfire of the previous night. He wanted us to experience the sheer emotion that grips the Apprentice Boys as the walls come into view. The drawback was that instead of the usual wide variety of music, most of the bands inevitably broke into 'Derry's Walls' as they approached their Mecca. Among the crowds a woman held up a poster saying 'ULSTER PROTESTANTS DEMAND PARITY OF ESTEEM', which showed that some PR lessons *were* being learned from the enemy.

It was a wonderful parade, full of vigour and brilliance of colour and sound, heightened in its impact when compared to its Belfast Orange counterpart because of the narrowness of some of the streets through which it passed. It's a strange mixture of spectacle and intimacy and if you are on a narrow street it is easy to spot your friends as they stride past. Pointing at Mike or Graham or Chris or Jim, catching their eye and exchanging waves and smiles is one of the pleasures of parade-watching.

It was with some regret therefore that, in the early afternoon, duty called me to the Bogside to attend the three o'clock protest meeting. There was no IRA ceasefire at the time and there were fears of an organized assault on the RUC and the Apprentice Boys. Violence didn't seem likely this time, since there wasn't an awful lot for them to protest about, but one could never be sure.

My unionist friends just laughed when I suggested they might like to come with me, but Paul came along. We had to go by a longish indirect route because I had forgotten my press pass and so could not go through police lines. We got to the 'Free Derry' wall that is the Bogside equivalent of Speakers' Corner just in time to hear MacNiallais uttering the word 'Finally', thanking the two or three hundred people present for their restraint and announcing the cancellation of the rally. The pretext was a generous gesture to the Apprentice Boys; the reality was that the turnout was so poor the protest would have presented badly. And then I caught the eye of Mitchel McLaughlin, the chairman of Sinn Féin.

A plausible and likeable fellow, McLaughlin is despised by the hard men because, unlike most other Sinn Féin leaders, he never served in the IRA; his nickname in Derry is 'the draft-dodger'. He was wearing a smart grey suit and chatting to a young admirer, who told him, her eyes glowing with hero-worship, that he would have her vote. He is John Hume's main challenger for his Westminster seat.

We had not met for a year, during which time I had frequently savaged IRA/Sinn Féin in print and had defended the Orangemen's right to walk from Drumcree Church down Garvaghy Road, but McLaughlin, a complete professional, betrayed not a flicker of hostility. We shook hands: 'Ruth, you are very welcome to Derry.' Paul was similarly warmly greeted. Rather churlishly, the thought flickered through my mind that McLaughlin sounded as if he owned the bloody place. He then spent the next fifteen minutes or so explaining most courteously how I was completely wrong to have thought that Sinn Féin was behind the anti-parade agitation and expressing genuine amazement that I could have spoken up for the now 'finished' David Trimble, whom republicans were convinced had been politically destroyed by the fall-out from Drumcree.

He was called away to sort out some trouble, we nodded goodbye civilly, and Paul and I ambled up to Butcher Gate, where a small disappointed mob were looking for trouble. We returned to the parade just in time to see an alarmingly nasty-looking Ulster Freedom Fighters colour party, who should not have been part of the parade but who were ecstatically greeted by the inhabitants of the Fountain. There were other occasional jarring notes provided by militaristic bands.

The Apprentice Boys, being a mainly urban and working-class organization, attract some people who think the Orange is for wimps and the Black for old men. There have been problems with one or two clubs which are nothing more than fronts for paramilitaries and whose members turn up at parades in dark glasses and strut menacingly. (This was to be more evident the following year when two or three bands carried banners saying: 'RE-ROUTE REPUBLICANS OUT OF NORTHERN IRELAND'.) Yet these represent a tiny fraction of the participants in a parade which is largely well-disciplined and brilliantly stewarded.

We headed for the Apprentice Boys' HQ to look at some memorabilia, to find ourselves briefly caught, like the RUC, between drunken bottle-throwing loyalists and stone-throwing Bogsiders. A few minutes later, returning to the centre, we found tremendous RUC and media activity in a side-street. Cautiously peering around the armoured cars I saw the RUC extracting a dozen or so violent drunks from a pub while surrounded by perhaps twenty photographers and cameramen. At one stage a policeman almost fell over a TV camera. The yobs, of course, played up enthusiastically to their audience and obligingly created a small mini-riot with stones, glasses, bottles and anything else they could get their hands on. There was not an Apprentice Boy among them, for they had all marched over the bridge and were on their way to their coaches, but of course the violence was the scene that was shown on most news bulletins.

In 1997, the Apprentice Boys showed they were learning something about PR and began to speak of the parade as a pageant. There were lengthy discussions with politicians and residents and the nationalist SDLP mayor gave the Apprentice Boys his support. Reluctantly, MacNiallais agreed to allow the pageant's participants on to the wall, so children dressed as King William and Queen Mary and assembled attendants walked along it in the morning. There was a difficulty about the flag outside the Apprentice Boys' HQ: the union flag would be offensive. So the Apprentice Boys' historian produced a green flag with a harp in the middle, which symbolized the unity of England and Ireland in 1689. The BRG did not identify it in time to object. They have since deemed it unacceptable.

Still, an accommodation had been worked out and there was no need to put a police line between the Bogsiders and the marchers. McNiallais and some colleagues came up to look at the parade and then some of their number began taunting the most militaristic-looking bands. A few bandsmen broke ranks and there was a scuffle.

I was at the same vantage point as the year before; exaggerated rumours were spreading about the level of trouble. That was a sufficient excuse for a couple of hundred drunks from the Fountain to start throwing stones and bottles and glasses at police: none of them was an Apprentice Boy. Television cameras were there again. Loyalists, as usual, were handing propaganda gifts to the enemy.

Having had the experience craved by all journalists of being hit by a stone that didn't hurt but nevertheless gave one street-cred, I left that riot as it died down and with my English friend Mark proceeded to the Bogside. There was a crowd of children, mostly between six and sixteen, throwing stones at the police who were sealing off Butcher Gate and guarding the Apprentice Boys' building. Standing in the middle of the kids, I could see how de-humanized are policemen in riot gear: they looked more like a row of Darth Vaders than human beings. But then you can't withstand stones and petrol bombs in a woolly cardigan.

Out from the Bogside with MacNiallais came Gearóid Ó hEara, chairman of Northern Sinn Féin. He walked up to the middle of the crowd of children, put his arms around two of the littler ones and said: 'Away now down to the Bog. You don't want the international TV cameras to be seeing you behaving like Orangies.'* There was a diminution in the

---

* Another insulting term for Protestants is 'Jaffas'. Abusive terms for Catholics include 'Fenians' and 'Taigs'.

stone-throwing and some children drifted back through the gate. Then the television cameras went away. So did Ó hEara and MacNiallais. It was a dull, grey afternoon as well whiled away by stone-throwing as by anything else, so the children went back to work vigorously. A dog, who was clearly a seasoned rioter, rushed up and down between the children and the police barking, until he got hit by a stone and hobbled off whimpering. The children went on throwing stones: no grown-up came out of the Bogside to try to stop them.

MacNiallais was busy elsewhere, explaining to the media that nationalists had been assaulted during the parade and there would therefore now be no tolerance for the December Apprentice Boys' parade; it would not now be allowed to go around the Diamond in the commercial centre of Derry.

Simpson had offered to halve the normal numbers in December but the BRG were not prepared to compromise. The day before the parade, which the police refused to ban, republicans went around shops and restaurants in Derry telling them to close: this form of intimidation is carried out by republican and loyalist thugs on special occasions and few businessmen are strong enough to withstand it.* So MacNiallais was able to complain that the parade had closed down the commercial life of Derry on a Saturday before Christmas to the inconvenience of everyone.

A well-orchestrated Bogsiders' riot began behind the police lines that separated them from the Apprentice Boys. The complaint was that because Butcher Gate was closed off, they were being hemmed in; the alternative, longer, route to the city centre was unacceptable. The television showed Martin McGuinness and Mitchel McLaughlin being denied permission by the RUC to go through their lines. The riot followed shortly afterwards. There was a rare slip-up when a Sky camera took a

---

* The playwright Hugh Leonard elucidated this approach in a comment on the funeral in January 1998 of Billy Wright, the notorious loyalist terrorist: 'The town of Portadown was closed down yesterday for the obsequies of Billy Wright. Shopkeepers were "asked" to suspend business. "Your co-operation is *noted* (my italics) and appreciated," is how the request was worded. Take away the olde-worlde politeness, and the translation goes: "*Shut up shop or we'll blow your effin' heads off.*" The morality is, of course, that the more people you murder, the bigger your funeral.'

Even when operating ceasefires, loyalist and republican paramilitaries have traditionally kept control of their ghettos by kneecapping or beating half to death with iron bars or baseball bats studded with nails the disobedient or those classified as 'anti-social'; shopkeepers are brought to heel by vandalizing or setting fire to their property.

shot of McGuinness smiling broadly at the stone-throwing Bogsiders. Later in the evening, a phalanx of youngsters arrived at the city centre from the Bogside wheeling shopping trolleys full of petrol bombs, of which about 1,000 were fired at police.

The allegation that this had been a spontaneous riot resulting from the disruption of the commercial life of the city at Christmas time did not convince on this occasion. The general conclusion was that the republican leadership had thought it useful to let some of their hotheads let off steam: the bill for the city was five million; the damage to the reputation of Derry abroad incalculable.

6. Glenageeragh, 15 June 1997

'Like migratory birds, we return to the same scene every year,' said Henry, as we headed towards his Orange Lodge's annual service. 'Whole families come together from elsewhere in the province or overseas. Like Christmas, it's a time for family bonding. We tread well-trodden roads that our own blood have walked for many generations, be it to a country lane, to a rural church or through a little village or down a main thorough-fare into a town.'

Of all my Northern Irish friends, Catholic or Protestant, Henry has the greatest sense of place. A farmer who believes in working with rather than against nature, he has a view of the land that takes account of beauty as well as utility. Because he spends so much of his life in physical labour, his mind and his imagination have plenty of time to roam free and much of his intellectual energy is devoted to devising ways of making his people comprehensible to the modern world. A typical phone call from Henry will begin: 'As I was graiping the silage this morning, I was thinking that another thing that makes my lot [i.e. his people] so cussed is . . .' Or he might be in fatalistic mood: 'Well, don't worry about it: whatever we do, the rivers of destiny will find their own way into the sea of history.'

Henry had decided it was time I engaged with a past not focused on King Billy or the siege of Derry. 'We're going to where my family come from, where my blood flows, and to the burial ground of my people, Presbyterians all,' he said, as we drove along the Clogher Valley. 'Look at it. Picturesque, quiet, typical south Tyrone countryside, with its rolling hills and green grass.'

Of Scots planter stock on both sides, Henry's lines can be traced back in Ulster to the late 1700s. He stopped to point upwards. 'At the top of that hill, that's where my great-grandmother McMaster was reared, looking on to the Clogher Valley. This water here goes into the Blackwater system which runs into Lough Neagh: the Blackwater is very fertile, warm ground. The bottom end of the Foyle is good ground too, which is why in Derry there are so many Presbyterian churches along its banks. As the seagull follows the plough, the Presbyterian follows the good land. Not that my people were gifted with the best of fertile land, but slowly we kept labouring on, always trying to improve ourselves.'

A few miles down the road he had shown me, with unconcealed emotion, the remains of a small building in a tiny overgrown patch of green, which once had been a thatched house. It was there that Henry's paternal grandfather and at least seven siblings were born between 1880 and 1890. Two boys became farmers, one boy joined the Royal Irish Constabulary, and the girl married. And like so many Ulster Protestants before and after them, three of the boys emigrated, one to Canada and two to the United States.

In 1932, Henry's grandfather had taken a huge risk. He had sold this 17-acre small farm to a Catholic neighbour and bought a 120-acre farm near Omagh, twenty miles north, which had been in the hands of a bank for five years. In 1923, it had been sold for £3,500, but farm values had been plummeting and the bank ended up repossessing it. 'Grandfather gave £1,050 for it – huge money for him – and since an earlier owner had bought it from a landlord under a government purchase act, there was an annuity of £50 a year due on it too. The house was in rotten condition, with rushes six feet high, but grandfather was strong, gutsy and determined.'

Henry's maternal grandfather took an equal risk. Descended from a family of small farmers who came from Ayrshire in the 1600s, he moved from Keady in County Armagh, intended by his father to buy a particular sensible property, 'but he took a shine to a place no one else would take. His father was annoyed and wouldn't give him any financial help. But he bought the place anyway, stayed there alone for years before he married, farming, making his own bread, washing his own clothes and hanging food off the rafters at night so the rats couldn't get it.'

The Second World War put farmers on their feet, so both grandfathers prospered. The maternal grandfather wasn't as physically strong as the paternal, but he had a gift for figures, so he branched out. 'He always did his sums first before he attempted anything.' On retirement at seventy he had a lot more land as well as other businesses. We saw the farms of

Henry's aunt and Henry's cousin and the house his maternal grandfather was supposed in the first place to buy but had 'taken umbrage against'. Henry knew every twist in the road. 'This is home. Even if you had no blood connections to Clogher Valley, you'd feel attached to it: it's homely. It's always good to come back to it, irregardless of how far you go in the world. And the fact that it's green, deep land and that most of your blood comes from it, I suppose is something that endears it to you as well.'

Then in front of us was Glenhoy church. 'When Presbyterians were eventually given permission to build meeting houses, there wasn't much good land left. When we got round to getting our own piece of land around here we drew the short straw. It's damnable to dig graves here because it's pure rock a foot down: they have to bring in compressors to bust it.

'My paternal ancestors lie here. And they were all in my Orange Lodge, LOL 908. And there's the new hall we built last year.' He stopped at the top of a hill and pointed down. 'If you stepped back to 1848 (the year the church was built) you would find my great-great-grandfather walking in procession on the same country lane I now walk in one of the glens of the Clogher Valley to our little kirk on the hill. It's in the blood and calls from deep within us, our little ritual to let the outside world know we're still here.'

We were late, too late for Henry to join the assembly a mile down the road and parade like his great-great-grandfather up to the church. But as we waited he talked more about the Clogher Valley and how even though his paternal grandfather had moved away from that area he would always come back to this lodge. One of Henry's two brothers would be here today. His father would have been along too but he had to attend another Orange service elsewhere.

Henry's forebears achieved high office in the Orange Order: his father, grandfathers and great-grandfather were variously Worshipful Masters of lodges and districts and even the county. Henry confined himself to being lodge treasurer for a few years, an office which he said was undemanding: he took the extreme modernizing step of opening a bank account, he collected the dues and kept the very simple books. Although he has an intense emotional attachment to his lodge, which he had joined as a junior, he has no interest in holding office again. This is a sign of the times that in some ways worries him: 'A hundred years ago, high offices would have tended to be held by Church of Ireland clergy right up to bishops, as well as by the old gentry. Some of those lads had a lot of backbone as well as standing – and some of them were cranky and mad as hell.'

Henry told me the story of a County Grand Master of Tyrone. The improbably named Anketell Moutray was kidnapped by the IRA in 1922 with forty others and taken across the border to be used as bargaining counters for eleven IRA men from County Monaghan, who had been arrested in Northern Ireland. Moutray, who was eighty, drove his captors crazy by continuing throughout his incarceration to sing metrical psalms and 'God Save the King' without ceasing.

Henry talked of how the gentry began to disappear: compulsory purchase legislation in the late nineteenth and early twentieth centuries had required many to sell their farms and two world wars had killed off many more. The leadership of the Orange became dominated by the business and professional classes, people like his grandparents. But in Henry's generation, people like that are busier than in the past and less able to give their time and their effort to what are often the mundane details of lodge work. 'It's not that I work physically harder than my ancestors, but life has become more demanding. For instance, they didn't have to spent their evenings bogged down in paperwork.' And at higher levels within the loyal institutions, where there are endless meetings, these days people with small businesses are in danger of going to the wall.

There were very few people in the hamlet, just a few cars, a handful of wives and maybe ten or twelve children. It was a nice day and there was a silver band and it was pleasant to hear the strains of hymn music wafting up the hill and seeing in the distance the advancing procession of Orangemen, many of whom, when they finally arrived, had faces so weather-beaten that not even a townee like me could doubt their occupation.

There were only about fifty people present. The lodge has only forty brethren, of whom just over half were there and then there were guest Orangemen and other visitors. There was a pause for a chat with families, friends and acquaintances and then it was time to reassemble to walk in formation into the church. With the other non-processors, I followed them in and sat at the back of the little church in a right-hand pew along with women and children: across the aisle was the band.

The young Presbyterian minister wasn't an Orangeman. Only about 12 per cent of them are, Henry told me afterwards, because, particularly in the rural parts, it was so much a family thing; this minister had no such connections. The service was the usual mixture of hymns and prayers but I was pretty rocked by the sermon, particularly since I knew the guest preacher to be a member of the Church of Ireland. One of the twentieth-century assumptions I have learned to jettison since I started consorting with evangelical Protestants is that Presbyterians are necessarily more extreme than Anglicans. Certainly the Church of England is notoriously woolly and the Church of Ireland in the Republic is self-consciously liberal, but the circumstances of life in Northern Ireland are such that Protestants of all denominations are tougher, more evangelical, less ecumenical and inevitably more political than their counterparts elsewhere. What was on the mind of the Reverend William Hoey (who was later identified to me as the minister who had called Cardinal Daly 'a red-hatted weasel')* was Drumcree, which, being only three weeks away, was on the minds of most people in Northern Ireland.

Reverend Hoey was certainly a lively and opinionated speaker, lukewarm only in his condemnation of loyalist paramilitaries who at the time were uttering various threats. In the Foreign-Officespeak that has been adopted and popularized by Sinn Féin and their counterparts in the Progressive Unionist Party, he said they weren't 'helpful'. He then reverted to Old-Testamentspeak and got stuck into the story of Nebuchadnezzar, who set up a golden image which all had to worship on pain of being cast into a fiery furnace; this appeared to be a metaphor for Drumcree. What bothered me slightly was that while Shadrach, Meshach and Abednego emerged from the furnace unscathed, as an unbeliever I wasn't convinced that following the Reverend Hoey's recommendation to trust in the Lord was going to be enough to extract the Orange Order unscathed from Drumcree. However, the preacher wasn't worrying his congregation that much: at least four or five of the bandsmen had fallen asleep. Sunday afternoon following a large lunch is normally a time for hard-working countrymen to have a rest.

We sang our hymns and said our prayers and emerged into the sunshine. After some more chatting with ministers and friends, the men reassembled. A familiar face to which I couldn't put a name smiled at me: I learned later he was a member of my Black Lodge. The silver band struck up a hymn and along with a few children I followed the Orangemen down the hill. We passed perhaps four houses on the way; the inhabitants

---

* In 1996, after Drumcree Two, the subtle, learned and sophisticated Cardinal Daly – like most of the population of Ireland – went nakedly tribal. In an emotional and often bitter television interview he declared himself betrayed and shocked by the decision to let the Orangemen down the Garvaghy Road and thereby reinforced the prejudices of all those loyalists who doggedly believe that Catholic clergy are, at best, closet republicans and, at worst, tribal witchdoctors.

were sitting in their gardens looking mildly interested. The only residents we upset were a collection of sheep who ran in panic to the opposite end of their field. After a mile or so the procession stopped, the Orangemen turned to face across the fields, the band struck up and we all sang the national anthem. Men resumed chatting for a while and then took off in their cars for home.

Henry and I walked back up the hill to where he had parked. 'Forty years ago,' he said, 'this is what Drumcree was like. That's what they don't understand. We don't need anybody to see us parading.' 'A woman rang up the David Dunseith phone-in programme on the BBC the other day,' he added, 'and said "The trouble over parade routes only comes when these so-called nationalists move into these areas"'. It was unfortunately a very logical statement which would strike a chord with every Protestant in Portadown.

'What have you got here? Four houses in a little over half a mile and only a few black cows and a few horny sheep to contend with. There are hundreds of parades like this. At Drumcree, the point of view of the Portadown man is: "My father and my grandfather walked through that way. Why should I change?"' For inarticulate and threatened people, walking the territory is their way of expressing their link with the past.

When we got home, he showed me 'Title Deeds',* a poem that to Henry best describes the passion of the Scots-Irish dissenters for the land they have tilled for centuries, which is understood by so few outside their community, especially those who still see them as foreigners and usurpers. Its inspiration was Genesis 23:20: 'And the field and the cave that is therein were made sure unto Abraham for a possession.'

> Grey, twisted stones, half hid in careless grass,
> Scribed with faint names of those who sleep below,
> Who once saw winter into summer pass,
> Felt dawn in Ulster, watched her sunset glow
>
> O'er every hill they furrowed with the plough,
> On the white walls of homestead and of byre
> Loved beyond death, even as men love them now,
> With a devotion burning like a fire.

---

* My brother pointed out that the poem was based on Longfellow's 'The Jewish Cemetery at Newport', which laments the fate of the Jews at Christian hands.

Graves of the men of Ulster, who came forth
To seek a better country than their own,
As Abraham from Ur once quested north
Obedient to the faith which led him on.

Obedient down the wandering of the years
Through many a hope deferred, a plan delayed,
Claiming the land for ever by his tears
Shed at the grave where his dear dust was laid.

So by these graves we claim the country still,
This land made rich by sacrifice and tears,
Held with such passionate love, such stubborn will,
Torn from the people oft down bitter years,

Spoiled by the hirelings of a servile court,
Harried by prelates of a faith denied.
The rebels' plunder and the landlords' sport,
Yet loved of those who tilled her fields, and died,

And dying passed into her kindly mould
To sanctify for us each kirkyard green,
Each sheltered vale and every hillside cold,
And little highways where their feet have been.

Thus do we claim our country from the lord
As Abraham claimed his at Machpelah's cave,
From age to age still runs the changeless word,
'The land is his who claims it by a grave.'

It came as no surprise that such an anti-Episcopalian poem had been written by a Presbyterian minister. What was more surprising was that he was a distant kinsman of Henry's, for I had thought all of his blood were farmers or businessmen apart from the odd engineer. And Henry was able to tell me the story that had inspired such ardent love of Ulster and such bitter denunciation of his ancestors' persecutors.

The paternal family of the poet, John Worthington Johnston, had farmed south of the border in County Monaghan from King William's time until, in the 1860s, as a result of some skulduggery by the landlord and his steward, who wanted the prosperous farm for himself, they had to move. In the Clogher Valley, Johnston's grandfather started afresh and turned unproductive land into a fertile farm; he had seven children, including one who became Henry's great-grandmother. When Johnston died at fifty-one, his eldest son took over, ran the farm and then became a Presbyterian minister. He had a church in County Antrim and then for a long time served in Dublin. His son John, who was born south of Dublin, was only twelve when his father's church, the Abbey, was burned down during the 1916 Easter Rising.

John Johnston graduated from Trinity College Dublin with first-class honours in Classics and from Cambridge University with a first in Theology and then, like his father before him, became a minister in County Antrim. In October 1942 he joined the 1st Battalion of the Royal Ulster Rifles, in the 6th Airborne Division, and served as one of the small number of 'parachute padres' until invalided out in 1945 after a parachute jump that went wrong. Of his three daughters, one became a distinguished historian and the other two senior civil servants, one of whom later became, like her father and grandfather, a Presbyterian minister.

The story of the Johnstons is an illustration of how, until very recently, almost the only acceptable way for any rural Presbyterian to follow an intellectual route was through the ministry. And equally graphically, his poem shows how even one of the loftier intellects among Presbyterian ministers kept true to his roots. Being elected by the members of their congregation, and running their kirk hand-in-hand with their elders, keep ministers humble and in touch with reality.

In his book on Presbyterians, the Reverend John Dunlop described the Bible as 'the book of a pilgrim people', which goes a long way towards explaining why they identify so much with the Israelites of the Old Testament, an aspect of their collective psyche represented throughout the rituals of the Orange and Black institutions. There was not a man walking in an Orange collarette down that hill from Glenageeragh, thinking about Drumcree, in whom Johnston's poem would not have struck a deep chord.

7. Rossnowlagh, 5 July 1997

The annual Orange parade in Rossnowlagh, County Donegal, in the Republic of Ireland, challenges two beliefs: the first that Orange marches are inherently territorial and triumphalist; the other that a United Ireland would stamp out the Protestant identity.

The truth is more complicated. Northern Irish Orangemen love the Rossnowlagh parade because there is no trouble and nothing to prove:

citizens of the Republic of Ireland – in so far as they are aware of the parade's existence – are happy about it because they think it shows how tolerant they are. Yet the Orangemen of the Republic of Ireland are very aware that since the foundation of the Irish Free State, for a variety of reasons – including persecution by the IRA at a local level – Orangemen are down to just one parade a year at the seaside and away from any towns. And all Protestants, North and South, are aware that since partition, while the Catholic population of Northern Ireland has increased steadily, the Protestant population in the Republic has decreased from 10 to 3 per cent. Many believe that they were persecuted; some that they were ethnically cleansed.

Still, Rossnowlagh is every romantic Orangeman's idea of a happy family day out. You have the countryside, you have the seaside and there are no protesting nationalists. The parade is policed by two or three amiable gardaí. Or, as one Orangeman put it to me: 'You walk into Rossnowlagh and there'll be one guard saying: "How're ye doin', boy?"'

It is an outing, it is an adventure, for it involves foreign travel and it is a way of linking up again with those of your comrades, your brothers, who found themselves after partition on the wrong side of the border. Of all the parades I attended, it was the one most redolent of a school outing in an innocent world: no khaki, no guns, no nasty graffiti, not a hint of violence and therefore, of course, no television cameras. Yet, since Rossnowlagh happens the day before the Drumcree church parade, a lot of people present were fearful about what might happen the following morning. So was I, but being a stranger there, my more immediate concern was how to find the right place on time and where to park my car.

There had been consternation among some of the Northern Irish brethren when they discovered that I was going to Rossnowlagh on my own. Gordon was distressed because a business engagement meant he couldn't drive me there. Roy was on my mobile worrying that because of a funeral he couldn't take me, but he gave me details of how to find people there who would look after me and invited me to tea in his Orange Hall in Fermanagh on my way home. Brian was frustrated too at not being able to come; he contemplated but proved unable to bring forward the service he was taking at a different funeral.

How long to get there, I asked Graham, whose favourite parade it is but who this year was doing duty elsewhere looking after the young at a Bible study camp. 'Well, of course it's fine while you're in Northern

Ireland,' he explained, 'because the roads are very good, but once you get over the border the roads are absolutely dreadful, so you'll have to allow about two hours.' 'You lot are always going on about the Republic's bad roads like a kind of defence mechanism,' I said. 'It's not confined to that,' he said. 'Every time I spend a few days in the Republic of Ireland I know more than ever I don't want to be part of a United Ireland.' He paused. 'But then maybe when you're abroad, you always see the worst of it the longer you're there.' 'Why doesn't that apply to home?' I asked, and he replied, 'Oh, that's different. That's like saying that your house needs a bit of renovation.'

I left my Orange friends in Portadown, noting as I looked back that there was an Ulster flag flying from a flagpole above my bedroom window. As I drove along the excellent roads fretting about Drumcree I got depressed once again about how deceptively tranquil is the country-side and how awful the sufferings of many of its inhabitants. You come out of Armagh into the Clogher Valley and thence to Fermanagh of the lakes and everywhere is lovely and well-tended and apparently peaceful; the fields are neat and the cattle sleek and the adolescent lambs are gambolling, yet road signs throw up reminders of atrocity after atrocity and latterly, reflecting my new preoccupations, of lower-level inter-communal cruelties and sectarian strife and the burning of Orange halls and the vandalizing of Catholic churches and the boycotting of decent shopkeepers from both tribes.

Then I knew I was in Donegal, for the roads had, in truth, suddenly become very bad. Seeing from a sign that my destination was, however, only 8 kilometres away, I thought Graham had been making rather a fuss, but then I got caught behind a bus with a shamrock on the back which crawled all the way to Rossnowlagh; it turned out to be a shuttle-bus for transporting fragile Orangepeople around the place.

Rossnowlagh farmers are happy annually to make a few bob out of this incursion from the North so there was no shortage of paying car parks. It was a sunny day, I wandered back to the assembly point and watched out for the people I was supposed to be linking up with, but inevitably I'd forgotten half the relevant details, like the number of their lodge, and was confined to wandering about the place asking people if they knew a big man with a moustache who came from Cavan. But then another coach drew up at the assembly point and out of it emerged the friendly face of the Grand Master, Bobby Saulters.

Bobby Saulters is sunny-natured, humorous and fatalistic, which in his difficult position is just as well. He is also without self-importance. As he stood there clutching his bowler hat and beaming at people, he was ribbed about something he had said on television that had annoyed the Orange hard-line pressure group known as the Spirit of Drumcree. 'Ach,' said Bobby, laughing, 'you should have heard what was on my answering machine when I got home.'

Like all Orangemen of my acquaintance, Saulters cannot see you without worrying that you might be hungry. Having established that, unlike the brethren in the coaches, I had not stopped for refreshment along the way, he said we must go to the meeting hall for tea. We wandered up and joined a queue of Orangemen and their families: there was no VIP line, no notion in anyone's mind, let alone his, that the Grand Master deserved any special attention other than a warm welcome for having come all the way from Belfast.

By now a veteran of church and Orange and village halls and refreshment tents in fields, I marvelled with Saulters that we were given proper crockery. Here catering was not left just to the ladies: a clergyman was in charge of selling sandwiches and a layman in charge of the teapots. The whole event was very much a community effort by local Protestants. I had a sandwich and refused cake, but Saulters was so worried that I might faint from hunger on the parade that eventually he persuaded me to parcel up a cake in a napkin and put it in my bag for later. I ate it in the afternoon sitting on the grass during the service.

There seemed to be far more women than usual in the Rossnowlagh parade. I studied their clothes for a while. There was a wide variation in the dress code probably reflecting differences between rural and urban and middle-class and working-class backgrounds. One lodge had everyone dressed identically, regardless of what suited their colouring or size, in another everyone wore a suit and hat of the same colour but in different styles, another permitted skirts of any colour but all jackets were black and there was one in which they wore their best outfits, which were all different.

I ambled along with the parade in company with Gerry, an Irish journalist (I think we were the only media representatives there). We enjoyed the sunshine and the walk and the music and talking politics and people. When we reached the little seaside town, it proved to be unpretentious and unspoiled. There were the usual stalls selling fast food, books and souvenirs. Most people settled down by the sea or in the field and ate their own picnics.

The hotel was full up, crammed with feeding dignitaries or Orangepeople who had pre-booked – the usual number swollen by the presence of some members of the Imperial Grand Council – but my companion and I got into the bar because we were journalists. The manager depressed us by telling us that for the first time ever, they had no guests staying this year because of the parade. They had never had any problems at Rossnowlagh; there never had been any tension and it had always been seen as a day for both communities. But Drumcree Two had changed the climate and people were frightened.

Having looked at the more interesting stalls we settled down in the field waiting for the usual problems of whistling microphones and missing speakers to be resolved by the hosts. I recorded some of the speeches. Most memorable was the thoughtful address by Dr Warren Porter, Presbyterian clergyman and an Assistant Grand Master of the Orange. It was no accident that he chose as the text on which to preach these verses from 1 Peter 2:

> Dearly beloved, I beseech you as strangers and pilgrims, abstain from fleshly lusts, which war against the soul.
>
> Having your conversation honest amongst the Gentiles: that, whereas they speak against you as evildoers, they may by your good works, which they shall behold, glorify God in the day of visitation.
>
> Submit yourselves to every ordinance of man for the Lord's sake: whether it be to the king, as supreme;
>
> Or unto governors, as unto them that are sent by him for the punishment of evildoers, and for the praise of them that do well.
>
> For so is the will of God, that with well doing ye may put to silence the ignorance of foolish men:
>
> As free, and not using your liberty for a cloak of maliciousness, but as the servants of God.
>
> Honour all men. Love the brotherhood. Fear God. Honour the king.
>
> Servants, be subject to your masters with all fear; not only to the good and gentle, but also to the froward.
>
> For this is thankworthy, if a man for conscience toward God endure grief, suffering wrongfully.
>
> For what glory is it, if, when ye be buffeted for your faults, ye shall take it patiently? but if, when ye do well, and suffer for it, ye take it patiently, this is acceptable with God.

The message could not have been plainer, and it was echoed by other platform speakers who implicitly or explicitly urged restraint. Here are a few extracts from speeches which – apart from coded messages about Drumcree – are typical of how Orangemen greet each other from platforms.

Right Worshipful County Grand Master, Most Worshipful Imperial Grand Master, Most Worshipful Brother Saulters, County and District Officers, brethren, sisters, ladies and gentlemen, it's my pleasure and privilege to have the distinct honour indeed to be here today at such an excellent gathering. As I look out across this wonderful crowd, the colourful display, the respect, the dignity and the discipline that we've just shown, it typifies what many Orange gatherings are about and that they do no harm to anybody whatsoever . . . I would like bring to the members of Donegal County Grand Orange Lodge fraternal greetings from the County Fermanagh Grand Orange Lodge. It is a pleasure indeed and a privilege to represent County Fermanagh here this afternoon and I look forward to welcoming those of you who can come next Saturday to County Fermanagh to our demonstration there.

Orangemen know what they're about. They show that responsibility, that dignity, that restraint and that discipline. That's what we are about. That's what we project to the world. That's what I trust, ladies and gentlemen, we always will be about.

It's been my pleasure to be here and I thank Donegal for the warmth of welcome, for their hospitality and for the real dignity that they have shown this afternoon. Thank you very much.

He was answered by an aged Orangeman.

Thanks, Brother Foster, for your kind words. In regard of the County of Donegal I could be possibly one of the oldest Orangemen here today. I have been connected with the County Donegal Grand Lodge for over sixty years, and I have been attending the Twelfth of July parades for somewhere around seventy-five years. And I want people to see the way the Orangemen here and our brothers of Northern Ireland are and we never had no friction whatsoever. We came and went home peacefully and quietly and there was no act of discredit to our collarettes.

Then Antrim:

> Most Worshipful Grand Master, Imperial Grand Master, Worshipful County Grand
> Master, brethren, sisters and friends.* Being the last speaker I feel that I want to
> on this first occasion associate myself sincerely with all that the previous speakers
> have said. I came down with the North Antrim District Lodge and we had a
> wonderful trip down. This has been my first time down into the demonstration here
> and I would like to take this opportunity today on behalf of County Antrim Grand
> Orange Lodge to bring the good wishes of our County to the brethren of County
> Donegal here and all the brethren in the Republic of Ireland. We do appreciate what
> you have done for the good of our institution and we do wish and pray them God's
> help as they work for the extension of God's Kingdom here. Thank you very much
> indeed.

Finally there were the 'few words of thanks' on behalf of the County
Grand Master, officers and members of County Donegal Grand Orange
Lodge to all the brethren of the Grand Lodge of Ireland, county Officers,
district officers, sisters, today 'for this grand and glorious day that we're
having here in Rossnowlagh'. There were thanks too to the 'Reverend
Brother' who had conducted the service, to the giver of the 'inspiring
address', to all the visiting lodges and bands who had attended, to County
Grand Lodge for leading the parade, to the brethren of the district and
the lodges for all their support and 'heartfelt thanks to the Grand Master
for visiting us, thanks to the ladies of Rossnowlagh, thanks to the owner
of the land . . . we hope with God's help that we'll all be here next year
. . . and may God bless you all and have a safe journey home and may
we have a pleasant weekend'.†

Gerry and I walked back to the car park ahead of the parade. He had
to file a report and I was rushing back to Northern Ireland to get the
low-down on the latest negotiations over Drumcree.

∗ Orangemen report frequent confusion on the titles front. My favourite example was the Australian who got
so muddled about whether to call a visiting dignitary 'Most', 'Right' or 'Very' Worshipful, that he lost his grasp
completely and addressed him as 'Most Adorable Brother'.

† I mentioned to a Orangeman on one occasion that I had left in the middle of a set of speeches because
they were awful and I couldn't bear any more. He laughed. 'My favourite moment at these events,' he said, 'is
when after a particularly excruciating performance, the seconder gets up and says: "I would like to second
the motion so ably proposed by Brother X."'

8. Lurgan, 26 October 1997

It was Reformation Sunday. I had been held up in Belfast and had to drive at illegal speeds to get to Lurgan before the parade set off. I am vague about distances, but I realized I was getting close when soldiers, police and Land Rovers began to appear.

As I reached Lurgan and parked the car at the end of the main street, I could see a ceremony was in full swing. Denis Watson, the County Armagh Grand Master, and officials of the Lurgan male and female lodges were laying wreaths at the war memorial. Watching respectfully were twenty or thirty men in suits, a couple of dozen women in big Sunday hats and maybe twenty girls. All were wearing Orange collarettes.

Standing slightly to the side were the preacher for the day, the Reverend Brian Kennaway, and Graham Montgomery, who was holding, upside-down, a pile of six bowler hats, for those performing the remembrance ceremony needed to be bareheaded. Typically, despite the solemnity, I got an immediate smile and nod from Brian and Graham and the other three or four Orangemen I knew.

Only a couple of dozen locals watched this small parade walking to the annual Reformation Sunday service at Brownlow House, the headquarters of the Royal Black Institution, who make the Victorian Gothic building available for Orange use also. It was being rebuilt, having been damaged the previous year by petrol bombs on the day before the Apprentice Boys' march in Derry. Many of the treasures of the Royal Black Institution were destroyed or damaged; it is costing about £8 million of public money (from the fund for compensation for terrorist damage) to repair and refurbish the house. The band, the Craigavon True Blues, seemed incongruous: they were a typical 'blood-and-thunder' band, containing young men one would rather avoid in a dark alley who wore bright blue uniforms and played the hymns like a call to battle. It is hard to avoid mixed feelings about these bands: on the one hand the macho, aggressive aura is off-putting; on the other, they're wonderful to walk along with. That is why the republican bands that have emerged in the past decade or so are mirror-images of them.

So I walked along the pavement keeping pace with the band for the mile or so to Brownlow House. Here and there, a few residents came out of their houses and watched with the air of people pleased to have some diversion on a dull Sunday afternoon. We walked up the drive, someone opened the door and the members of the Orange Order went upstairs. The drummers wiped the perspiration from their faces and, along with the rest of the band, turned and went home.

Slightly ill-at-ease, although I had been invited, I followed the worshippers up the stairs and went to the back of the room. I knew many knew I'm from a Catholic background, and some of them even knew I'm an atheist, and I was nervous that my presence might therefore be offensive to some of them. But I was overlooking the determined hospitality of the rural Orangeman.* Denis Watson summoned me to the front bench, where I sat between Graham and a man I had met before, who gave me a big grin and said with heavy irony: 'That was a very offensive parade, wasn't it?' It wasn't the moment to tell him that you wouldn't have to be neurotic or republican to find the Craigavon True Blues a bit much. The Worshipful Master of the lodge then removed my anxieties by making a kind reference to me in his opening remarks. I realized then that Orangemen are as unselfconscious about welcoming you to their worship as to their houses.

Brian Kennaway is a Presbyterian minister whose religious belief he describes as being 'expressed in the simplicity of the Gospel recovered at the Reformation of the sixteenth century. That simple biblical religious belief affirms that salvation can only be achieved *by grace* alone *through faith* alone *in Christ* alone, revealed to us in the *scriptures* alone.' For someone from the Roman Catholic tradition, the Calvinist dismissal of good works as an aid to salvation is always disconcerting, but Kennaway makes it clear that if you have faith, 'good works will follow as evidence'. He quotes William Fenner: 'Good works are a good sign *of* faith but a rotten basis *for* faith.'

---

* I once went to a Portadown Black 'Last Saturday' where my companion and I were taken to eat in the Orange Hall and therefore became honoured guests, even though James was from the British Foreign Office – an institution which as a consequence of the Anglo-Irish Agreement is believed by most unionists to be intent on selling them out. After the meal, we stood with some friends in the field waiting for the speakers on the platform to get going. We were spotted by an officer who felt we had to be given some mark of respect. Two chairs were brought down from the platform, placed in front of the crowd and we were summoned. 'No, no, please, I'm fine,' said James, who is of a retiring disposition. More experienced in the ways of Orangemen, I sat down without protest and eventually he too was persuaded to sit. Within a minute he had spotted an elderly woman and had given her his seat. Down from the platform came the officer, carrying another chair; this time James accepted his fate. For the whole of the service, except when on our feet for hymns and the national anthem, the three of us sat there, apart from those on the platform the only people among the thousands present not standing or lying on the grass.

I'd sung more hymns in the last couple of years than I had in the rest of my life and I'd become pretty expert at 'O God, Our Help in Ages Past' and 'Stand Up, Stand Up for Jesus', but I didn't know three of the robust hymns that Kennaway had chosen. However, a large Orangeman was valiantly playing the tunes on a tiny electronic keyboard and I sang along as best I could.

Kennaway took as his biblical text 2 Chronicles 34, where King Josiah deals with false gods by having their altars broken down and their carved and molten images broken in pieces. As he read to us of the burning of the bones of the idolatrous priests upon their altars, Graham grinned at me broadly. (At the end of the service I went up to Kennaway and asked genially: 'Brian, when you go off to lynch the priests, can I come too?' He looked at me in horror and said, 'Surely you didn't think I meant . . .' and then laughed when he realized I was pulling his leg.)

It was a very instructive service for me, for Kennaway is evangelical and radical as well as very intelligent. Of all the services I've been to, it was from this that I learned most about what religious Orangemen truly believe and why the Reformation is so immediate to them. It was an exemplary service, too, in its clarity and homely informality.

Kennaway was determined to show his audience of old and young, and many shades of Protestantism, why they owed gratitude to God for giving men like Calvin, Knox, Luther, Wyclif and Zwingli and their successors 'all the gifts of understanding so that they translated your word into the common language of the people of the day . . . We thank you that your work is not static or stagnant: it is a living word.'

He gave thanks that 'the word lives by your spirit in the hearts and lives of men and women and boys and girls,' and wished that it would 'really live in the hearts and lives of our people throughout this island.'

His sermon was about the relevance of his Old Testament text to the sixteenth-century Reformation.

We are here today to give thanks to God for the Protestant Reformation. And we make no apology for doing precisely that. Because we have everything to give thanks to God for in the Protestant Reformation of the sixteenth century. We do so today, because this is the nearest Sunday to the last day of the month, because it was on the 31st of October 1517 that Martin Luther nailed his 95 theses to the church door at Wurtemberg . . . There was nothing particularly dramatic in this nailing theses or statements or propositions to the church door. There were no newspapers. Indeed if you go to any university today you'll see noticeboards and all sorts of announcements and notices nailed to those noticeboards. That was a simple way that Martin Luther had of drawing attention to issues which concerned him.

Not all the theses were worth reading, he pointed out, and read out some that were, several of which were about the 'the over-enthusiastic sale of indulgences or letters of pardon from the pope'. There was some more about what was owed to Luther's successors and then he came to the heart of his homily:

It seems to me that we're very good at drawing parallels in our local situation in Ulster to other situations in the world, but we're not so good when it comes to drawing parallels to our spiritual situation in Ulster with spiritual situations in the scriptures. And for that reason I wanted to draw the parallel today because the problem of Ancient Judea is exactly the same as the problem of Ulster. It's spiritual. Brethren and sisters, you had better believe it.

The answer therefore to the problems of Ulster is not a new political initiative. The answer to the problems of Ulster is a spiritual initiative, because the problems are fundamentally and basically spiritual problems. May I quote words spoken a few weeks ago by the County Grand Chaplain, William Bingham, when he addressed a fringe meeting at the Labour Party Conference:

'As I look around Britain today, I look at the situation not only as an Orangeman, and an Ulsterman, but as a Christian – indeed a Christian minister. I am committed to Orangeism, but I am supremely committed to Christ. I recognize that my approach to religion – indeed many people's approach to religion in Northern Ireland – is out of tune with the times in England but I do feel passionately that Christ and the gospel has provided the answer to the deepest needs of society and that peace and reconciliation begin at the Cross.'

The parallel with ancient Israel, Kennaway went on, was that

every time she went wrong spiritually, she went wrong politically. Every time she went after other gods, she lost her political battles . . . We are in danger of becoming a race merely of political Protestants . . . if we get away from the centrality of the word of God . . .

I believe in the principles of the loyal Orange institution, but I wonder do we all believe in these principles? . . . We have to make sure that our principles and our practice run parallel . . . I cannot help but fear that will ultimately be our downfall. We will become political Protestants and we will abandon our biblical principles. You see as I often say to groups of Orangemen and I make no apology for saying it again and saying it here: 'If you are involved in something or you're doing something which you know in your heart of hearts is out of keeping with the principles of scripture, then do, I beg you, not only for your soul's sake – and that's far more important than anything else – but for the sake of the institution which you profess to love, *change your ways or resign.*

    Oh, we have great principles, we have noble principles, but our condemnation will be when the world points the finger at us and asks where is our practice? Our principles and our practice ought to be the same. Do we want to see change? Do we really want God to bless us? Do we really want God to intervene in a situation in Ulster where if we are honest with ourselves we know it is only God's intervention that can save us . . . People like to draw parallels to our present crises to the turn of the century – the Home Rule crisis – but some things are different, you know. And you'd better believe it. You see God played a more significant part in our nation at the beginning of the century. People were fundamentally more religious. And when they sang the words of that hymn we sang – 'O God, our help in ages past, our hope for years to come', they actually meant it. Do we? What's the answer?

    The answer is reformation and revival under the anointing of the spirit of God.

After we had sung the final hymn – a setting of the 46th psalm about God our trusty shield who makes wars cease – and, of course, the national anthem, and most people had left, Kennaway anxiously questioned those of us remaining about whether he had got his message through. Had he been direct enough? Always, my biggest culture shock when I go to the Ulster Protestant heartlands from London or Dublin, is once again to realize to what extent they say what they mean and mean what they say. It is no wonder they have such difficulty with the English desire to fudge and the southern Irish desire to please everyone.

A few of us stayed on for a chat and they showed me some more of the damaged Brownlow House. I asked about the band and was told that it was regarded as a major breach of Orange etiquette that its members had not come to the service. They shouldn't, said one of them, be hired if they weren't prepared to participate in the religious part of the proceedings. There was criticism, too, of the martial way in which they had banged out the hymn tunes. But one of the Orangemen shrugged. 'What can you do? There are only two local bands and they're both blood-and-thunder, because that's what the young men like, and there'll be bad feeling if we don't hire locals.' 'If necessary,' said Brian Kennaway, who is notorious for not suffering gladly either fools or yobs, 'we could dispense with a band and parade down the road whistling.'

So once again, another own goal by decent Protestants and another example of the how perception and reality are at odds where the Orange Order is concerned. Here was a service attended by believing Christians, who listened intently to the message that they should live their lives as witnesses to God. Most of these people are the salt of the earth. But because they hire the local band, an outsider observing their parade could well have gone away with an image of drum-beating bigots.

A Cancellation, 9 August 1997

I was over from London for the Apprentice Boys' parade which was to take place the next day, when just before midnight came the news that the Newtownbutler Residents' Association was determined to block a small Black parade through the town early the following morning. So Mark and I decided to go there before we went to Derry.

The situation in Newtownbutler was particularly sad. Despite tragedies like Enniskillen and all the border murders, Fermanagh Protestants are notoriously less bigoted than those of any other Northern Ireland county. Newtownbutler had a cross-community historical society and a Thursday Club for the elderly and prided itself on its harmoniousness. As one resident put it in the summer of 1996: 'When there was a death both communities attended the wake house and the funeral.' And a local SDLP politician told a journalist that cooperation was the norm: 'It's the so-called sick-cow syndrome. It doesn't matter if it is a Protestant or a Catholic cow. I remember once there was a cow in distress and the owner was away. A neighbour called to borrow something on the farm and saw the cow and called in others and by the time the calf was born, the DUP, the UUP, Sinn Féin and the SDLP had been there to help. That cooperation is there yet, but it is most definitely under threat.'

It was Drumcree Two and the subsequent boycotting of Protestant businesses that had made the difference. Within two months of Drumcree, Catholics and Protestants were boycotting alike and sectarian tensions had provided fertile ground for the establishment of a Newtownbutler Area Residents' Association to try to block parades.

By August 1997 Newtownbutler was radicalized and no Catholic residents were prepared or able to challenge the Residents' Association, which was able to swell its ranks when necessary by bringing in reinforcements from outside. What caused particular offence to Protestants were the protesters from the nearby town of Clones, in County Monaghan in the Irish Republic.

Mark and I arrived around 7 a.m. in Newtownbutler to find a group of disconsolate young men. Some of them had just arrived, a few were still arriving and others had been up all night fearful that the police would seal off the main street. Some of them seemed drunk. Not long before they had been told that the Blackmen had cancelled their parade. A smashed window was testimony to their frustration.

We walked up to the top of the village and then back to the bottom because I was shivering and Mark had a sweater in the car. A few RUC men arrived and took up their position at the top of the main street, well away from the protesters. They were in good humour because, as they confirmed, the parade had been cancelled. They would not have to face insults, stones, petrol bombs and maybe worse.

We wandered back to the protesters and found that some of them were still deeply reluctant to believe this had happened. It might be a cunning ploy. It might be that if the protesters left, the Blackmen would arrive and stage their parade after all. I couldn't help. These were cross young men. It was not a gathering where one could explain that the Royal Black Institution didn't approve of telling lies.

Protesters stood around grumbling for a while and then matters were enlivened by the arrival of a red-headed American woman in army boots who engaged the residents' leader in conversation for the next fifteen minutes or so. Mark and I stood by fascinated, for here in the flesh was the living embodiment of the Noraid* stereotype – the American who was more republican than the republicans, whose crassness and bigotry made even Sinn Féin twitch.

She lived in Derry it emerged, and had done so for two years. She had come to Newtownbutler with a carload of protest banners and was staying in a local guest-house. Amid great laughter at her own intrepidness, she explained how on the phone she had had to ask the guest-house owner if it was a nationalist household to be sure she'd be with 'our people'. She talked a lot about 'our people'. She spoke of Derry and of how Gerry O'Hara (Gearóid Ó hEárá) was 'an angel', who had

---

✴ NORAID (the Irish Northern Aid Committee) has since 1969 raised money in the United States ostensibly for the families of republican prisoners. In effect, it has freed up IRA money which could then be used to buy weapons. Its members are happy to encourage people 3,000 miles away to kill and be killed. Its organ, The Irish People, is a hymn to hate.

obligingly arranged for her to be registered for voting purposes at his brother's house.

She spoke with shining eyes of the protest movement. 'Soon they won't be able to march anywhere,' she said triumphantly. 'They should all be sent off to Scotland in a boat.' (In this at least she showed herself slightly more moderate than one of the inhabitants of Derry who recently wrote on a wall across the road from the Apprentice Boys' headquarters: 'NO MORE LONDON/DERRY/START SWIMMING.'

Gerry McHugh, the local residents' leader, was uneasy with her. He was well enough trained to know that you watch your words except in private; republicans never admit in public that they want to get rid of Protestants, and indeed many of them would never be anything like that extreme. As she ran out of steam, Mark asked her disingenuously if she'd now be going back to Derry for the Apprentice Boys' parade. 'Certainly not,' she snapped. 'I'm off to Donegal to speak Irish with my friends. Most of my friends speak Irish.'

Mark and I withdrew, leaving her to carry on encouraging Irish Catholics to hate and persecute Irish Protestants.

Some Anthropological Notes from the War-zone, 8 August 1998

The following night was to be the first time drumbeats continued to reverberate in my head long after I arrived back in London. But then I had had a double and severe dose of the war-drums. Not only had I stood on Saturday for more than two hours at the flashpoint in Derry where bands demonstrated what they thought of their old enemies from the Bogside, but I had walked along the Falls Road the next day beside republican bands vigorously putting up an aural two fingers at their Protestant neighbours in the nearby Shankill Road. The banners, the uniforms and most of the tunes were different; the motives and the methods identical.

Chris Patten, chairman of a commission on policing, watched the Apprentice Boys' parade from the safety of a window high above the Diamond, the commercial centre of Derry, thus missing the frisson shared by those of us down below who were dodging the missiles occasionally being exchanged between loyalist and republican oiks over the heads of the police who protected them from each other.

That morning, a few Bogside residents had violated the deal struck with the parade organizers and had jeered and spat when wreaths were being laid at the war memorial in the Diamond. The Apprentice Boys'

leaders, who had been making heroic efforts to make their parade acceptable to nationalists, had urged calm and good behaviour, but as each club
and accompanying band arrived at the Cenotaph, you could feel a palpable
sense of grievance about the earlier insults to their dead. Bands had been
instructed to stop the music as they passed the memorial, but they were
provoked by republican cat-calls from behind the police Land Rovers
and more seriously by accusatory bellows from a couple of dozen loyalist
drunks about 'big girls' and 'Lundys' if they stopped playing. (Lundy is
burned in effigy by the Apprentice Boys annually for having proposed
surrender during the Siege of Derry.)

The temperature increased when, in response to a waving of the Irish
flag, a yob climbed a lamppost and waved a Union Flag at his enemies.
Sporadically, the stones came flying over from the republicans and were
picked up and returned by their loyalist counterparts. 'I'm very impressed
at their range,' observed an American visitor to me as we ran. 'If they
were in the United States they'd be champion baseball players.'

The majority of bands virtuously obeyed orders, though many of them
relieved their feelings by breaking into loud martial music as soon as
they had passed the memorial. The unvirtuous lost their tempers at the
memorial itself and played to their hooligan gallery with deafening renditions of songs guaranteed to provoke the most reasonable of nationalists.
It was the drummers who provided the most fascinating tribal spectacle,
for some of them conducted war-dances on the spot, jumping around in
circles and bumping and grinding as they banged their drums and went
red and sweaty with effort and rage. The ecstatic response from some
female bystanders indicated this was the loyalist equivalent of the
Chippendales.

Both lots of would-be rioters shared a deep frustration because cross-
community agreement over the parade had removed the excuse for serious
trouble. Like hooligans everywhere, they were dying for a rumble. And
assiduously they pressed the buttons they knew would wind up the other
side. 'Fenian bastards' and 'Provo scum' calls were balanced by 'Fuckin'
Orangies' and subtleties like 'Billy Wright, bang bang' – an allusion to
the killing in the Maze prison of hard-line loyalists' favourite murderer.
Leaping up behind the police lines, they made throat-cutting gestures at
each other, whistled their preferred national anthem and waved their
colours. Yet balking them at every turn was their mutual enemy, the
ever-present and highly efficient RUC. So as they were blocked by riot
police from climbing over the barriers into each other's territory, both

sides screamed 'SS RUC', a chant first developed by republicans.

Driving away from Derry with my friend Henry, he said: 'Tomorrow I'll show you the bull-pens.' Obediently, I waited until Sunday morning to be enlightened. At the local cattlemart I surveyed the rows of heavy steel pens. 'You get two bulls together and they don't know anything except that they have to fight,' said Henry. 'And they'll break through cement walls to get at each other. All you can do is stop them seeing each other. That's what should have happened yesterday.'

'That's all very well, Henry,' I said, 'but there would have been an outcry from the Bogsiders about the police hemming them in and there would have been violence with the loyalists. And all this with Chris Patten looking down at the police from above.'

'What drives me mad about politicians – and I've no reason to think Patten's an exception,' said Henry, as we squelched back from the pens, 'is that they won't face reality. Now what you had yesterday were two lots of young fellas with hundreds of years of breeding telling them to fight each other. It'll take another hundred years to breed out that tribalism. We have to face what we're dealing with. And what we're dealing with are bad bastards who are egged on by worse bastards who nurture what nature's already given us. If people behave like animals, they have to be treated like animals.'

I thought of Henry throughout the afternoon in Belfast as I watched young children marching along with the Republican parade commemorating the twenty-seventh anniversary of internment alongside fife-and-drum bands – some wearing camouflage gear – which were blaring out the tunes of famous songs about brutal Brits and heroic Irish and martyred dead. Four or five kids sat on the edge of the platform in the lorry outside Belfast City Hall and cheered and clapped a collection of speeches from angry revolutionaries, who included an implacable ETA spokeswoman. When they had finished applauding Gerry Adams's vitriolic attacks on the RUC and the British occupying forces and the unionists, they cheered again when he sent them away with instructions to agitate until the republican wish-list had been fully granted. All the kids grasped that Sunday afternoon was that their tribe was good, the other one was bad. And every time they saw policemen or Land Rovers – there to keep them safe from loyalists – they shouted 'SS RUC'. Whatever the politicians say, while we need the bull-pens, we're a long way from peace.

2

What Members of the Irish Loyal Institutions Do

The Orangeman is a man of truth,
Who scorns all fraud and art;
And rear'd in truth, from his early youth,
He has shrin'd it in his heart;
For it proves to him a mighty shield
Against every foeman's dart;
And his life he'd yield, on the blood-stain'd field,
Ere with that bright gem he'd part.

The Orangeman is a man of might,
But trusts not in fleshly arm;
He dares to fight for freedom and right,
And he knows no vain alarm.
But strong in truth, in virtue bold,
He fears no earthly harm;
For his heart's stronghold, like his sires of old,
Is in virtue's potent charm.

The Orangeman is a man of thought,
He dwells upon glories past;
Upon battles fought and great deeds wrought,
Where blew war's deadliest blast;
And remembers mercies heaven bestowed,
When affection's waves roll'd fast;
When man's wrath o'erflowed, on life's rough road
Were thorns and brambles cast.

The Orangeman is a man of faith,
He believes what is written – all,
And reveres till death what the Scripture saith,
No matter what does befall.
He hears, as it were, from heaven's high throne,
His uprisen Master call;
And he takes his cross, and enduring loss,
Bursts through the world's dead thrall.

The Orangeman is a man of prayer,
To heaven looks for aid;
Against want and care and every snare,
For his soul's dread ruin laid.

And a prayerful man is never known
In perils to be afraid;
For God's power is shown when he alone
Can save from the foeman's blade.

The Orangeman is a man of peace,
But purity peace precedes;
And when ills increase, he cannot cease
To be warlike in his deeds.
Thus does he become a man of strife,
Of strife in a holy cause;
And when danger is rife, he would risk his life
For the King, and Church, and laws.

The Orangeman is a man of love,
He prays for his enemies,
And he'd seek to move the great King above,
On his humble bended-knees.
He loves his Bible, he loves his King,
And all good men he sees;
He loves the Orange, nor hates the Green,
And he bows to the law's decrees.

E. Harper, 'The Orangeman'

Why they join

SAM: It's part of us. My father and my grandfather were in the local
lodge. As a little boy, the Twelfth of July was a big day. I had bands
singing in my ears. It was something that was just part of your culture.
It was almost like Christmas when you were a kid. You thought it
would never come back again. So it was part of you. There was a
band attached to my lodge so I joined the band and was a member of
that band for forty-two years. There were two sets of fathers and sons
in that band.

BRIAN: I resisted it for a long time after I became a Christian in 1954.
I saw conflict between principle and practice. But having thought about
it and realized I believed in what the instititution stood for, I saw a
parallel between the church and the Orange Order. The church is
imperfect; the institution is imperfect. So I realized I should be inside.
Even in the days when I was critical of the Orange Order from outside

it, when I saw an Orange parade, I saw a particular man I knew well, and I knew that I could not apply any of my criticism of the Order to him. I chose his lodge. So you see, the ways people live their lives speak louder than anything else. This is why I feel strongly that as an institution we don't need a professional PR person; we simply need Orangemen on the ground, faithful people with integrity, for that speaks volumes.

CHRIS: There's an element of father to son, but there would be a lot of people in our lodge whose parents would never have been involved; people who just feel a need to identify themselves. As a kid I always wanted to be an Orangeman, because of what was happening with the bands. I loved the bands. My father was first in the family to be a member of the Orange Order. He joined much to the chagrin of the entire family, who thought it was a lot of crap. There was a sort of a left-wing fundamentalist Protestant element in my family. Grandfather was a Cooneyite; they didn't even believe in churches. They're almost like Quakers.

WILLIAM: I joined because some of the folk who were a little older than me that I respected a lot were in the Orange and they were folk who were Christians to begin with. They were folk who were working within the community, part of community life, and I thought, well, they're older, they're mature and they believe it's important and has something to give.

I did it undoubtedly primarily for the sake of history and identity with the Protestant people throughout the generations. My forefathers were in it, my grandfather was in it, certainly I was going to keep the lifeline so to speak. And I stayed with it through thick and thin because I believe that when you look through its qualifications and its principles, if men can live by it, it gives them a good foundation of life and it holds on to principles that society is losing at this stage, like the importance of family life and respect for elders.

If you sit in a lodge meeting and the eighty-nine-year-old speaks, everybody's quiet and gives him respect and listens. And that isn't happening generally in society. They tend to separate the young, the middle-aged and the old – even the churches tend to separate them. I think that's very important.

JOYCE: I was away for a long time and when I came home, because I was now living in a middle-class area, I took this way of reconnecting with the working-class district where I was brought up. An Orange

Lodge gave me the chance to show my loyalty to my country and my religion and to be involved socially with my own people.

MICHAEL: I was a bit of a thug when I joined. It was just after the murder of the Scottish soldiers, and I walked round Sheffield with a Rangers scarf tied round me head, a leather jacket and lots of Red Hand badges on the front ready to attack anyone who sounded like a Fenian.

All I'd got culturally was that I was a Prod and we were under attack and we were all supporting each other. So I joined the Orange Order without much of an intellectual agenda. But because I came under the influence of the prayers and the Bible at lodge meetings it reminded me of what I had had as a younger boy. It gave a context for our actions. So I abandoned the physical force idea and started to think more constructively. And the Order did that for me. It did that for a lot of people. It was a restraint on people. This is the Bible. This is your faith. It reminds you that you can't act in a manner that is inconsistent with the basic principles. You actually think about that.

ALF: I just had an interest in the Orange Order. I thought it was a good institution. There was a lot of brotherly friendship. And you met people in different places and if you were an Orangeman, you were welcome. And I just had a liking to join the Orange Order, because there's no doubt about it, lived up to, it's a good institution. There's no getting away from that.

To Alf, who was ninety when I met him and who had been a member of his lodge for seventy-two years, his involvement with the Orange Order was a matter of the greatest pride. Early in our conversation he pulled out a copy of its Laws and Ordinances and read to me, his voice trembling with emotion:

Basis of the instititution: The institution is composed of Protestants, united and resolved to the utmost of their power to support and defend the rightful Sovereign, the Protestant religion, the Laws of the Realm, and the Succession to the Throne in the House of Windsor, BEING PROTESTANT and united further for the defence of their own Persons and Properties, and the maintenance of the Public Peace. It is exclusively an Association of those who are attached to the religion of the Reformation, and will not admit into its brotherhood persons whom an intolerant spirit leads to persecute, injure or upbraid any man on account of his religious

opinions. They associate also in honour of KING WILLIAM III, Prince of
Orange, whose name they bear, as supporters of his glorious memory.

Alf is one of many Orangemen who cannot see how anyone could find
such a statement objectionable; the principle of religious tolerance is for
them an imperative. Over and over again people like him spoke to me
of the importance of respect for those of different religious persuasions.
They talk a lot of 'decent' Roman Catholics, by which they mean those
who want to live at peace and will not be taking potshots at Protestants
from behind hedges, throwing stones at their parades or voting for those
who want to drive them off what they would describe as 'the Queen's
highway', or force them into a United Ireland.

How they join

The etiquette is that you are asked, though obviously you can intimate
to an Orangeman that you would like to join his lodge. Your name will
be proposed and seconded and there will be a vote: maybe about 10 per
cent of people are excluded at that stage. Then, in theory at least, you
are vetted: 'There's supposed to be a committee in each lodge which
should actually check the qualifications and the type of character of a
candidate,' said Martin Smyth, ex-Grand Master. 'I was reading the
minutes of my lodge about three years ago and I discovered that when
I was proposed, a member of the lodge said: "There's no need to have
a censoring committee on this candidate." And another brother got up
and said this candidate should be treated like everyone else and proposed
a censoring committee. That brother was my father. It reflects the type
of man he was and perhaps reflects me too. Because I believe that things
should be done decently and in order and show no favouritism. And
whoever it is be treated equally.'

The 1997 recruitment leaflet puts it succinctly: 'If you are a practising
Protestant in the truly religious sense; regularly at your place of worship,
morally upright in your life, and if you display a tolerant spirit towards
those with whom you may disagree, then you will be welcome within
the Orange institittion.' Tolerance goes only so far, though. So frightened
is the Irish Orange Order still of the wiles of the Church of Rome that
it is afraid of converts. There is an unspoken fear that they might be
Romish (or, worse, Fenian) Trojan horses. It is therefore difficult, though
not impossible, for them to join.

Anyone wishing to join the Orange Order will be told of 'The Qualifications of an Orangeman', to which he is expected to live up. 'The qualifications show what the commission is – what's expected of people,' said another Orangeman. 'And people fall short of what's expected. They fall short of what's expected from their respective churches too, but it doesn't mean to say the whole church is entirely wrong because of that. And the same applies to the Orange institution.' He was another veteran, and he was as proud as Alf of the principles and language of 'The Qualifications' which are crucial to an understanding of the fundamental principles of Orangeism. Recently they were published with an illuminating commentary from the Chaplains' Committee of the Grand Orange Lodge for study in lodges. I have included here in italics and in brackets a section from the commentary on each part of 'The Qualifications'. Although rather long and indigestible for those unused to reading scripture, it is worth making the effort to read the whole passage.

An Orangeman should have a sincere love and veneration for his Heavenly Father (*To fear God is to treat Him with reverence and respect. . . The Orangeman 'should never take the Name of God in vain'* because to do so is to despise His Most Holy Majesty. . . God is Sovereign and God is Saviour. . . We recognize God's Royal Rule and we rest on God's redeeming work*): an humble and steadfast faith in Jesus Christ (*As Orangemen we stand by the Gospel. 'Believe on the Lord Jesus Christ and you shall be saved'. . . Payments and Penances are not required. Christ has paid all His people's debt. . . But doctrine implies duty. Brethren, let it be our care to exercise the faith we proclaim and to prove our profession by the deeds of a godly life*); the Saviour of mankind, believing in Him as the only Mediator between God and man' (*The one all-perfect Mediator excludes all others. No one else, not even his own blessed mother, can fulfil the work which He reserves to Himself.*) He should cultivate truth and justice, brotherly kindness and charity, devotion and piety, concord and unity, and obedience to the laws; his deportment should be gentle and compassionate, kind and courteous (*Loving God, we are to love our neighbour also. . . The virtues of truth, justice, kindness and charity are only visible when we put them into practice.*); he should seek the society of the virtuous, and avoid that of the evil (*We are of course but sinners saved, and we will seek the welfare of every fellow-sinner. But to share their vice would shame us and harden them. From*

---

* This is a serious cultural contrast with Irish Catholics, who blaspheme eloquently, imaginatively, profusely, unselfconsciously and with no intention whatever of giving offence. My language improves out of all recognition when I associate with most Orangemen. However, my brother points out that Protestants and Catholics are as bad as each other when it comes to claiming blasphemously that God is on their side.

such we turn away.); he should honour and diligently study the Holy Scriptures, and make them the rule of his faith and practice (*The Bible is our only infallible rule of faith and practice. To them we bow and place no mere tradition of men beside them. They are our guidelines for godly living. Their daily study is the secret of our strength.*); he should love, uphold, and defend the Protestant religion, and sincerely desire and endeavour to propagate its doctrines and precepts (*A 'Protestant' is one who 'protests for' the Evangelical Doctrine. Such was the meaning given to the word by the first Reformers. The common faith they taught is the religion we are pledged to uphold and defend. An Orangeman stands for the great truths re-discovered at the Glorious Reformation. That* **'Christ alone'** *is our only sacrifice, that it is through* **'Grace alone'** *that we can experience salvation, that justification can be received through* **'Faith alone'**, *and that the* **'Bible'** *alone, is our only rule*); he should strenuously oppose the fatal errors and doctrines of the Church of Rome, and scrupulously avoid countenancing (by his presence or otherwise) any act or ceremony of Popish Worship; he should, by all lawful means, resist the ascendancy of that Church, its encroachments and the extension of its power, ever abstaining from all uncharitable words, actions, or sentiment towards Roman Catholics (*Our Order and the Word of God prescribe a double duty to us. We are to speak the truth, and we are to speak it in love. . . Truth demands that we expose and refute the peculiar errors of the Church of Rome. Love requires that we do this in a manner which honours our Saviour. Above all we proclaim that Redemption is complete. No priestly ritual can add to the work of Christ. . . We refuse all communion with the errors of Rome nor can we share in her forms of worship. And we do all this for love of truth, and love of souls*); he should remember to keep holy the Sabbath day, and attend the public worship of God, and diligently train up his offspring, and all under his control, in the fear of God, and in the Protestant faith (*While every day is His by right He has appointed one day in seven for His special service. . . The Sabbath should be our delight. Not gloom but gladness should mark its tone. . . our children should know that it is a glad thing to go to the house of God*); he should never take the name of God in vain, but abstain from all cursing and profane language, and use every opportunity of discouraging those, and all other sinful practices, in others; his conduct should be guided by wisdom and prudence, and marked by honesty, temperance, and sobriety; the glory of God and the welfare of man [should be the motives of his actions] (*An Orangeman is to bear witness to the truth among his neighbours day by day. We claim to reverence God. How can we blaspheme His name? . . . As those who will answer to Him from whom nothing is hidden we must show by our speech and convince by our characters that we are sincere servants of the Most High.*), the honour of his Sovereign, and the good of his country, should be the motives of his actions (*Every Orangeman is*

called to be a loyal citizen of the country which gives him shelter. As a good
citizen he will be obedient to the laws of the land, his higher obligations to God
never being forgotten. All evil conspiracy and rebellion are forbidden by our faith. If
tyranny indeed may be resisted, as our history attests, no private individual has any
right to break the law for his own advantage. . . Law-abiding loyalty to Queen and
Contitution will be the hall-mark of all our public work as citizens and in good times
and bad the Orangeman will be steady. This is our duty to our country. It is also our
duty to God.).*

Orangemen admit that some lodges are neglectful on the vetting front
and that unsavoury people get in. But the democratic nature of the organization is such that nothing can be done about this. There is no way as
things stand to stop a lodge with a weak or pliable Worshipful Master
being taken over by undesirables, who in turn recruit more undesirables.
Jim Guiney, murdered in January 1998, was a paramilitary commander
as well as the Worshipful Master of his lodge.

In normal circumstances, there are checks and balances. First, the
vetting – which at the very least is supposed to ensure that anyone joining
is 'good, decent, law-abiding, of good character and attends church'.
Then there is the election procedure, which allows for black-balling. Then
sponsors are appointed to prepare the candidate for his initiation, which
involves learning by rote some simple responses to questions and is
intended to impress upon candidates the seriousness of what they are
about to become involved in.

'I was very surprised at how religiously-based it was,' observed one
newcomer. That is a common response, for where the Orange Order is
concerned, fiction is almost always stranger than fact. 'And it's much
more pedestrian than candidates expect,' said an old hand. 'That's part
of its charm.'

---

* It is insufficiently appreciated in the Republic of Ireland that while the vast majority of Catholics refused to
give their loyalty to the Northern Ireland state, most of those Protestants, including Orangemen, who found
themselves on the wrong side of the border after Partition were never disloyal to the new state. I've seen on
Orange parades in Northern Ireland those brave little contingents from Cavan or Monaghan or Donegal, still
stoutly demonstrating their pride in their religion and their affection for the crown, before going home to the
state which they have served loyally. Unlike most nationalists in Northern Ireland, southern Orangemen were
good losers.

How they are initiated

On the 12th of July in the year '89,
I first took the notion this Order to join;
Then up to the Lodge Room and there I did go,
And what I got there you will very soon know.

CHORUS: *On the goat, on the goat,*
To get in the Order you ride on the goat.

And when I arrived there I knocked on the door;
There's one they call Master who stood on the floor;
Come in and sit down you are welcome sez he,
But a goat in the corner kept lookin' at me.

CHORUS

Then the goat was brought forward, that I might get on,
After I mounted they bid him begone;
Through the Lodge window the goat he did go,
Through bogs and wild mountains and where I don't know.

CHORUS

Then after a long and wearisome chase,
The goat he arrived in the very same place,
Approaching the Lodge Room I heard them all sing
Success to the member that made the house ring.

'The Ride on the Goat'

As Orangemen frequently and plaintively point out, the organization is not a secret society but a society with secrets, and very few of them at that. How can an organization be secret, they ask, when its members parade openly in groups with banners declaring where they are from and what they stand for. 'The only secrets the Orange has are related to its ritual,' said an Orangeman. 'There has to be something mysterious to make you want to join and find out. That's what creates the male bonding. The fact that we know what the ladder stands for on our sash may not be earth-shattering, but it matters to us.' His father is in the same lodge; his mother refers to what they do in the lodge as 'playing silly buggers'. They don't take offence. 'Sure, it's childish. That's why we don't want to do these things in public. It's not because they're bad, but because they're stupid.'

I know from private and public sources the details of Orange ceremonies and rituals.* At their worst they are no more stupid than most ceremonials or rituals of guilds or fraternal societies seem to outsiders; they are certainly not sinister. Ritual accounts for less than 1 per cent of what goes on at an Orange Lodge – infinitesimal compared to what goes on among Freemasons. The most exciting event is an initiation, and mischievous brethren enjoy winding-up potential candidates by making mysterious references to 'riding the goat' (which is, in fact, a backwards acronym for 'the ark of God'†) and hinting darkly at stringent tests of courage. There are physical aspects to the initiation (the travel) which involve a blindfolded candidate having to face certain tests and travails inspired by a biblical story; in tough urban areas, especially in England and Scotland, these might be occasionally on the exuberant side, but in general the experience is rather tame. 'The initiation is a bit amusing,' one young man remarked, 'but when you come home you think it's a bit silly.' A less blasé brother describes the ceremony as 'a heady mixture of folk memory, rural Ulster Protestant tradition and ancient ritual', which is for many 'a moving experience, a rite of passage from boy to manhood, the admission to an historic brotherhood bonded by centuries of blood, fire and persecution and a spiritual experience couched in terms of the language of the deliverance and pilgrimage of the children of Israel'.**

The written-down part of the initiation involves the sponsors leading the candidate into the Lodge Room, where the Worshipful Master reads out in full the qualifications of an Orangeman and establishes that the candidate assents to these and is seeking admission to the Orange institution of his own free will. The lodge members agree to his initiation, the chaplain says a prayer and the Worshipful Master then asks the candidate at considerable length if, *inter alia*, he promises allegiance to the sovereign, her successors and the constitution; assistance to the civil authorities when called upon; fidelity to brother Orangemen 'in all just actions'; and a vow of silence about lodge proceedings to any but a

---

* Those Orangemen who worried that I might expose their cherished secrets to the world hadn't realized that most of this information was published as early as 1835, in appendices to the Report of the Commons Select Committee on Orange Lodges. Tony Gray in his book on the Orange Order also went into considerable detail. The ritual is necessarily rather dull and repetitive; what I am providing here is just a cross-section of what is most important. I am breaking no confidences, and keeping no secrets of any significance.

† Goat-rides, however, are a part of ancient rural pagan rituals.

** James Wilson in 'The Making of the Orange Order', a video which includes footage of preliminaries to an initiation ritual.

brother Orangeman. There are the promises about religion and secret societies.

'I don't think there's anything in there that would be offensive towards your Roman Catholic friends,' said a senior Orangeman who was telling me about the ceremony. He then went on to read out one request of the Worshipful Master:

> Do you promise, before this Lodge, to give no countenance, by your presence or otherwise, to the unscriptural, superstitious, and idolatrous worship of the Church of Rome? And do you also promise never to marry a Roman Catholic, never to stand sponsor for a child when receiving baptism from a priest of Rome, or allow a Roman Catholic to stand sponsor for your child at baptism? And do you further promise to resist, by all lawful means, the ascendancy, extension, and encroachments of that Church; at the same time being careful always to abstain from all unkind words and actions towards its members, yea, even prayerfully and diligently, as opportunity occurs, to use your best efforts to deliver them from error and false doctrine, and lead them to the truth of the Holy Word, which is able to make them wise unto salvation?

All that Orangemen can see or hear when they read such words are the injunctions to behave properly towards Roman Catholics. They are genuinely baffled that outsiders find such rules and language bigoted.* Perhaps the reason I have never taken offence is that I was brought up in the Republic of Ireland under the authoritarian and intolerant Irish Catholic Church and understand something of their traditional fears. Also, by the time I began to read the rules and regulations I had developed a great admiration and affection for many Orangemen.

'As far as the Orange Order's concerned,' said an aged Worshipful Master to me, 'it's not a bigoted order. It's a religious order, there to protect the religious beliefs of the Protestant people. In the very opening prayer you pray for your Roman Catholic brethren. I don't dictate to the Roman Catholic man where he should go to church; I'm as happy with him going to his own as he is to mine. I'll not condemn any man's religion – except Paisley, for he's divided everybody.

---

* They can, however, laugh at their own bigotry. There's the famous joke about the dying Orangeman who asked for a priest. 'What do you mean, a priest?' asked his one of his brethren. 'You've been an Orangeman for sixty years. Why do you want to see a priest?' 'I want to become a Roman Catholic.' 'A Roman Catholic? Have you gone mad?' 'I have not. It's just that I'd rather one of theirs died than one of ours.'

'To me the Orange is a family and if a man would live to the qualifications of the Orangeman and to what he's taught inside the four walls of
an Orange hall, he would be fit to live a good life.'

Where lodge meetings are held

All over Ulster in villages and in the middle of nowhere there are little
Orange Halls built of wood or brick, often with galvanized tin roofs. In
Dromore, for instance, Orangemen used to meet in an old army hut that
was a rapidly decaying tin shack on wooden stilts. Ulster Protestants are
frugal people and the prospect of raising enough money to buy a site
and erect a hall was daunting. Alf, the Worshipful Master, decided on
drastic action. 'I said this night, at a lodge meeting: "We must have a
hall of our own. I'll supply the material and I'll pay the contractor and
I'll get paid some time. The secretary came in the next morning and he
said to me – the only time he ever give me any praise – he says: "Churchill
the Second."'

It took some time to find and buy the right site, and then they built a
hall with a stage, which seated about three hundred so it could be used
for socials and dances as well as band-practice. It was opened in 1953
in September; in December the north wall of the church collapsed and
the church service was held in the hall for three years. Socials ended
about twenty years ago; nowadays the hall is a venue for the Duke of
Edinburgh's Award scheme. In the fullness of time, the brethren repaid
Alf; building that hall is an achievement which even forty years later he
felt was a highlight of his life.

Most halls have been built mostly through jumble sales and sales of
work and other unremitting labour by the ladies. Most would be smaller
than Alf's, though large enough to host the dances and *conversazioni*
and teas that made Orange Halls important community centres until the
advent of television and other major distractions. The furnishings are of
the plainest: mostly wooden benches and trestle tables and the most
spartan of spartan fixtures and fittings. There will always be a picture of
the Queen and usually some representation of King Billy, and the lodge
banner will be displayed on festive occasions.

In towns, the buildings are larger, since they often have to accommodate district or county functions, but austerity remains the norm.
Brownlow House, the headquarters of the Royal Black Institution (Orange
and Black men often share accommodation), was a fine house until it
was torched, though it too was plainly furnished. The two-storey hall at

Scarva is as luxurious as it gets, with the stained-glass window featuring King Billy, a spacious assembly-room and portraits and prints of Orange significance.

A 1960s building, the tall, narrow Orange HQ at 65 Dublin Road, Belfast sets the tone for the whole organization. There are a few adornments, including a portrait of the Reverend Martin Smyth, MP, Grand Master for a quarter of a century, and some William-related pictures. A small room contains an interesting hotch-potch of archives, books and memorabilia, but for the most part the building consists of spartan offices.

What happens at lodge meetings

Although the ritual and ceremonies in every Irish lodge are the same, the ambience and emphasis and what happens afterwards depend on where and who you are. I once sat in on a conversation between two Orangemen, one from Belfast and one from rural Tyrone, each of whom was amazed by the other's revelations about his lodge. The Belfast Orangeman reckoned that although all his brethren were believing Protestants, 90 per cent of his lodge hadn't been to church in years except for Orange services; he would expect churchgoers to join one of the lodges for committed, evangelical born-again Christians. His lodge was almost entirely social – more a drinking-club than anything else – although it kept to the strict rule that alcohol should not be consumed until after the formal meeting is over. Brethren paid about £60 a year in basic dues to cover rates and so on and a levy for Orange widows; any shortfall was made up by a night at the races or a big booze-up.

The brethren of the rural Orangeman's lodge were Calvinist or Free Presbyterians and 90 per cent would go to church every Sunday. Like most Orange Lodges, his was strictly teetotal. The dues were £12 a year and the difference had to be made up by jumble sales; even raffle tickets were not allowed.

For geographical reasons, rural lodges are more likely than urban to be socially mixed. These days very few of the gentry or the better-off would attend lodge meetings, though one of the exceptions is Eldon Lodge in Belfast: 'It's the toffs' lodge,' said my urban friend, 'for the great and the good; the one Stormont Cabinet ministers traditionally would have been members of. Today it has people like Josias Cunningham [Ulster Unionist Party president] or John Taylor [UUP deputy leader], who never goes but needs to have a sash available if required.

'While we shelter under the trees in the rain on the Twelfth with ham sandwiches and warm Guinness, they bring a caravan and drink champagne and eat canapés. One year they had shrubs outside. They only walk to the field. Never walk back. And they all wear bowler hats with an orange lily on the side of it. I don't know how they'd survive in an ordinary lodge.'

There are several business and professional lodges like that in Belfast. One was nicknamed the 'Cripple Lodge', because they couldn't walk – being important chaps, most of them were speaking around the country on the Twelfth. Over the years there have been lodges for special interest groups from bakers to shipworkers to soldiers, but deindustrialization has reduced their numbers dramatically. In Belfast, many lodges would have a broadly working-class catchment area. But in most rural areas, lodges have almost always been cross-class, which is one of the reasons for keeping the dues low. James Molyneaux, ex-leader of the Ulster Unionist Party, joined his local lodge in Crumlin, County Antrim, in the late 1930s.

'It was a watershed year for our little lodge when Colonel Pakenham, who was landed gentry and a member of the Senate, transferred from the toffs' lodge in Belfast to ours and became Deputy Master. My father was the WM and we were bottom of the social tier as farmers. And I used to think it very odd that this great man who had been through all these battles and all that – and had been in command in Palestine – sat there deferring to the WM and ensuring that everyone else did the same. And as DM he would have gently reproved anyone who spoke out of turn without addressing the chair.

'They decided to build a new hall and Pakenham offered to go on the organizing fundraising committee: he would bring aristocracy to events – people like Craigavon and the Marchioness of Charlemont on a couple of occasions. We were rubbing shoulders with all that. So you had the top drawer and the bottom drawer.

'There were ten or twelve workers on the Pakenham estate. And if one was first committee man or something, the colonel would have turned around and said, 'Brother Dalton, could I ask through the chair what's your view on this particular matter?' He wasn't talking down: he was giving him his place.'

There are far fewer toffs these days, but in many little lodges throughout Northern Ireland there are still farmworkers sitting with prosperous farmers along with shop assistants, bakers, road-sweepers, clergymen and the local solicitor, doctor and teacher. I have also come across several accountants and financial advisers. This may be because in that line of work they particularly need a bit of mystery in their lives, or it may be because, as educated men, like the clergymen, they take a disproportionate number of the senior officerships.

For the routine part of the meeting, the Orange Order has rules and regulations to which officers and foot-soldiers must conform. But first, a run-down of the elected officers' roles, as spelled out at their installing ceremonies. Private lodges are at the bottom of the Orange hierarchy; next come district lodges; then county grand lodges and at the top is the Grand Lodge.

The WORSHIPFUL MASTER is enjoined 'to exert your authority to maintain sobriety and good conduct, to use your best endeavours to promote harmony, good fellowship, and social virtues among [the lodge's] members, to observe strictly the laws and customs of the Institution, and to obey the orders of Superior Lodge authorities'. He is given a mallet 'as the outward and visible sign of authority to rule this Lodge; this Holy Bible which contains the precepts whereby all men, particularly Orangemen, should govern and regulate their conduct and actions through life; this book of the Laws and Ordinances, whereby you are to govern and guide this Lodge; and lastly, this warrant, which is your authority from the Grand Lodge of Ireland, under which your meetings must be held'.

The DEPUTY MASTER is required to assist the Worshipful Master and to stand in for him when required. Both he and the Worshipful Master have to confirm that they have not been given their positions 'for any private emoluments or advantage to yourself'.

The SECRETARY is required 'to attend to the correspondence and other business of the Lodge, keep a faithful record of its proceedings, and make the necessary returns to the next Superior Lodge'. He must 'keep regular, and preserve, the papers, books, seals, and other property of the Lodge entrusted to your care, having them at all times ready to produce or hand over to the proper or legal authorities, and that you will prepare and make all returns required by the Laws of the Institution or other proper authority'.

The TREASURER is required 'to collect diligently all payments to be made, and accurately account for all monies which shall come into your hands on account of, or for the use of, the Lodge, and to submit an annual financial statement duly audited by those apointed by the Lodge'.

The CHAPLAIN (preferably a clergyman) promises 'to discharge the duties of this office with due solemnity and decorum'. He is given 'this most precious Holy Bible – the very Word of the great I AM – on which the principles of the Order are surely founded, and for the purity of which many saints died at the stake. Also this Ritual, which contains the prayers and a list of those portions of Holy Writ to be read at our meetings for edification and guidance of all.' His attention is drawn to specific portions of scripture and prayers to read at the initiation, 'so that candidates entering our ancient and illustrious Order may know that they are being received into a Brotherhood whose profession of Faith, Hope and Love is well and surely founded'.

The LECTURERS instruct 'candidates for initiation into our Loyal Institution and confer upon them the two Orders [Degrees] laid down by the Grand Orange Lodge of Ireland'.

The CHAIRMAN OF COMMITTEE, 'a brother of experience and sound judgment', whose brethren 'repose great confidence in him', is the convenor. 'Always act in your Lodge, or Committee, so as to merit the confidence reposed in you by the members', which includes when required performing the duties of master and 'in all cases which shall come before you in Committee to act with fidelity and impartiality, without favour, affection, or personal ill-will to any person.'

The OTHER MEMBERS OF THE COMMITTEE are required to show 'sound judgment and strict impartiality between brother and brother . . . to discharge the duties of Master' when required, and in cases coming before the committee 'to act with fidelity and impartiality, without fear, affection, or personal dislike to any man'.

The TYLER guards the inside door 'while the Lodge is sitting; to receive and announce members and visiting brethren; to see that none enter or pass without permission from the chair; and that all wear the colours to which they are entitled'. The 'honour of the Institution should be your aim, and the safety of the portal of the Lodge room your ever constant care'. It is to the tyler that the password* has to be given. 'We have a pompous idiot of a tyler in my lodge,' observed one Orangeman. 'He's known me for twenty years, but when I turned up having forgotten the password, he wouldn't let me in. I had to wait for someone else to

---

* Like signs and grips, the original purpose of passwords was very serious: in the revolutionary period during which the Orange Order was founded, it was necessary to be able to tell friend from foe. Passwords do not change much with time. Typical would be one of those disclosed to a House of Lords Inquiry in 1825: 'Thus shalt thou say unto the Children of Israel' is answered with, 'I Am, hath sent me unto you'.

arrive who told me what it was so I could solemnly tell it to the tyler.'

The first four officers are given a badge (a special collarette) and a sign of office (e.g: gavel, pen) and ushered to a special chair; the chaplain has a special chair too and is given a collar of office; the lecturers are given regalia; the chairman of committee is given a badge and the members of the committee a badge and sign of office; the tyler gets a badge and sign and is conducted to his post.

You start out as a member of a private lodge, and can then progress up through district and county to Grand Lodge. If you are one of those people who immerse themselves in the institution, you could hold four offices simultaneously, say as Worshipful Master of your private lodge, district secretary, county grand treasurer and deputy Grand Master.

There are very few Orangemen who don't think the Order is top-heavy with chiefs, but that is part of the fun. It means that almost anyone can acquire a title which makes him a man of some consequence.

The official Order of Business at a lodge meeting is as follows:

1. The chair to be taken by the superior or senior officer present.
2. The deputy chair by the next in order.

Here is a typical ritualized exchange:

WORSHIPFUL MASTER: Bro. Deputy Master, what is the first duty of Bro. Orangemen when opening a Lodge?
DEPUTY MASTER: To see that the Lodge is Tyled, and that all present are in good standing and entitled to remain.
WORSHIPFUL MASTER: See the duty performed.
DEPUTY MASTER: Bro. Inside Tyler, see that the Lodge is Tyled.

3. A Tyler, or Tylers, to be appointed to keep the door.
4. A Steward, or Stewards, to preserve order.
5. The opening prayer to be read by the [clerical] Chaplain (if present), the brethren standing.

Gracious and Almighty God, Who in all ages hast shown Thy Almighty power in protecting righteous Sovereigns and States, we yield Thee hearty thanks for the merciful preservation of Thy true religion, hitherto, against the designs of its enemies.

We praise Thee for raising up for our deliverance from tyranny and arbitrary power, Thy servant, King William III, Prince of Orange; and we beseech Thee, for Thy honour and Thy Name's sake, for ever to frustrate all the designs of wicked men against Thy holy religion, and not to suffer its enemies to triumph; defeat their counsels, abate their pride, assuage their malice, and confound their devices.

Deliver, we pray Thee, the members of the Church of Rome from error and false doctrine, and lead them to the truth of that Holy Word which is able to make them wise unto salvation. Grant, O Lord, that Thy Holy Spirit may guide and direct our deliberations, so that in all our words and works we may glorify Thy Holy Name.

We beseech Thee to bless every member of the Orange Institution with all Christian virtues. Bless us with brotherly love and loyalty. Take away everything that may hinder our godly union and concord, so that we may henceforth be of one heart and of one soul united in holy bonds of truth and peace, of faith and charity, and may, with one mind and one mouth, glorify Thee, through Jesus Christ our Lord. Amen.

This is followed by the Lord's Prayer.

6. A portion of Scripture to be read, the brethren standing.
7. Proceedings of last meeting to be read and confirmed.
8. General qualifications to be read.
9. Admission of candidates of last meeting.
10. Preliminary communications to be read or made.
11. Dues and payments to be collected.
12. Appeals relating to election to be heard and decided.   AT MEETINGS FOR ELECTIONS
13. Election of officers.
14. Letters and other communications (if any) to be read.
15. Business arising out of either of the latter.
16. Election of candidates according to 2nd and 3rd Law.
17. Appeals (not against elections) to be heard and disposed of.
18. Reports from inferior Lodges to be heard and decided.
19. General business to be transacted.
20. Names of candidates for next meeting to be read.
21. The closing prayer to be read in the same manner as the opening one. (See Note 5.)

NOTE: Articles 8, 9, 16 and 20 to be observed in Private Lodges only; Articles 12, 17 and 18 to be observed in all except Private Lodges. The others to be observed in all Lodges.

Here is the brief closing ceremony:

WORSHIPFUL MASTER: Deputy Master and brethren, stand to order and assist me to close this lodge.

CHAPLAIN: Almighty God, Who art a strong tower of defence unto Thy servants against the face of their enemies, we humbly beseech Thee of Thy mercy to deliver us from those great and imminent dangers by which we are now encompassed. O Lord, give us not up as a prey to our enemies, but continue to protect Thy true religion against the designs of those who seek to overthrow it, so that all the world may know that Thou art our Saviour and mighty Deliverer: through Jesus Christ our Lord. Amen.

WORSHIPFUL MASTER: Deputy Master and brethren, I declare this Lodge closed until our next regular meeting, except in case of emergency, of which members shall receive, under Seal, due and timely notice.

GOD SAVE THE QUEEN

CHAPLAIN: The grace of our Lord Jesus Christ, and the love of God, and the communion of the Holy Ghost, be with us all. Amen.

The rituals and ceremonies are comforting for many Orangemen; the business part of the meeting drives many of them mad. 'Two hours of nonsense,' reported one to me, 'on when the spring-cleaning would be done, because of the complication of there being a children's crèche in the lodge in the mornings. Everyone had a point of view. It was eventually decided to wait till Christmas when there wouldn't be a crèche. But then there was a problem with the normal date of the annual service. There was much carry-on about which day and what time. It was eventually decided to leave the date as it was. Are these,' he added, 'the people that are supposed to hold the line when the whole place is going up in flames? If the Provies only knew.'

'There's no doubt about it that the meetings are boring for young people,' said another. 'What young fella of eighteen or nineteen years of age wants to go there on a Friday night? Some of the chairmen, they're mebbe sixty or seventy and they've nowhere else to go and they'd like it to go on to half ten or eleven at night. I remember one particular night there wasn't any business as such and the chairman got out the last three electricity bills to have a discussion. We could have read the minutes of the last one, had a ten-minute chat and gone home. I laughed that night.'

Most lodges try to achieve consensual agreement before anything is voted on, so everyone has a chance to get a word in. The more people who do, the more the issues become muddied.

'Get the business over quickly,' said a competent master. 'Then tea-bags, sugar, boil the kettle, have a drop of tea. Bring a couple of packets of biscuits, a few buns, and sit around for an hour or so and have a yarn. That's what makes a lodge, you know. A drop of tea and a bit of fellowship. It makes the night, you know.'

It wouldn't do in the Shankill Road, where the alcohol would be brought out after the closing ceremony, but the principle is the same.

So, too, is the way the brethren look after each other. All the loyal institutions contribute to an organization helping orphans of Orangemen or women; when a brother or sister dies, their lodge will help out financially and practically and there will be help during bad times. There is also a strong sense of loyalty to the disabled. Family values being what they are in Northern Ireland, the mentally and physically handicapped are far more a part of their family and the community than in more modern and secular societies and there are Orangemen with mental and physical disabilities. Sandy Row, No. 5 District, for instance, is passionately proud of 'Oor Wee Wullie', William Bloomer, who joined a junior lodge in 1982, 'when he began to play a full part in all the activities of his junior lodge, including football. Wor. Bro. Eddie Wright was worried that the other boys in the lodge would not be sufficiently considerate of Billy, but in the event, their willingness to carry Billy, with his wheelchair, upstairs to the lodge room and down again amazed him. When the lodge went on parade, the members took turns to push Billy along in his wheelchair without any prompting from the senior members.'

Billy Bloomer's ambition was to be a lecturer, and although his training was interrupted by a serious operation, he gained his lecturer's certificate in 1990. To mark the event, members of the class presented him with an inscribed 'Spirit of '88' Bible which Billy carries proudly to church,' continued the anonymous article in a Sandy Row Orange publication:

The real test for any lecturer occurs when he gives the lecture and address in his own private lodge for the first time.

Billy's style and delivery so impressed the members of [LOL] 1064 they gave him a standing ovation. Not surprisingly, the lodge elected him to the office of First Lecturer, and Billy's greatest pleasure is to take the floor and give instruction to new members of the Order.

The difficulties that William has overcome in his short life have been many, but the smiling face with which he greets his brethren helps to put one's own problems into perspective . . .

'Wee Wullie' is looking forward to parading to the 'field' on the Twelfth for, as he says, 'while others complain of sore feet, it's just a pushover for me'.

To the eye of the 1990s, that might sound patronizing, but to William Bloomer and his brethren, it is simply an acknowledgement of the fellowship and the respect the Ulster Protestant feels for those who know how to endure suffering without bitterness.

The Royal Arch Purple and the Royal Black Preceptories

When you have been initiated as an Orangeman, you have taken the Orange degree. You then go through a similar test, usually within six months to a year, to acquire the Purple. The history and nature of degrees are a matter of absorbing interest to many Orangemen and of very little interest to anyone else. They take their meaning of the word from the question of Isaiah in 2 Kings 20.9: 'Shall the shadow go forth ten degrees or go back ten degrees?' Degrees are therefore a measure of spiritual movement and are intended to deepen biblical knowledge.

Traditionally, there has been a difference between those who want to keep ritual to a minimum and those who thoroughly enjoy it. Some Orange leaders banned rituals and degrees borrowed from Freemasonry but those had been greatly enjoyed by simple people who wanted some mystery in their lives. The Royal Arch Purple Order, which these days is tolerated by Grand Lodge, was founded to preserve an outlawed degree. It prides itself 'on having a legitimate and historical claim to be the inheritors of the [Orange Order's] original initiation rituals and ceremonies'. The Grand Black Chapter of the Royal Black Institution traces its origins back to the Knights Hospitallers and the Knights of Malta; it came into existence shortly after the Orange Order. Many people join because they feel it offers a spiritual dimension.

'The Black would have to be more scriptural and more Bible-based, with Bible-teaching and that,' said a Mourne Blackman. 'Basically our Black meeting was like a gospel meeting. The leaders of the preceptory were all Christian fellows. The degrees would have been taught in that way. Degrees are really the drama of asking the questions behind the story. So that would occupy most of the time. My main reason for being in the institution was religious.'

'I joined the Black because I liked the parade in Scarva,' said one member. 'It was very well disciplined and well controlled, with good bands, good music. And because I was told all along that the Black institution was actually the main institution that taught the biblical principles of the Protestant faith in the various degrees that you went through. And there was more scope for teaching within it and getting our own people to have a greater knowledge of what our faith is about. The Orange wouldn't have that capacity.'

'The Black is a very graceful, decorous, sedate organization,' another Blackman explained. 'The Grand Master is in his flowing robes and the Grand Black Chapter has a procession into the chapter room with the mace being borne in front of him.'

A mutual Orange friend who has never been attracted by the Black was listening keenly. 'It's a bit popish, isn't it?' he commented, not very seriously, but with some truth. 'No, it's ceremonial.' 'Popery. Sheer undiluted popery.' 'Listen to Oliver Cromwell,' laughed the Blackman. And we fell into an absorbing discussion as to whether it was permissible to have a cross in a church and whether they thought Cromwell had been right to try to destroy all religious statuary.

Chapters of the Royal Arch Purple meet primarily to initiate Orangemen into the Royal Arch Purple degree in a ritual more elaborate than the Orange and the Purple and involving a lot of 'travel'. Black preceptories offer ten elaborate degrees: Royal Black, Royal Scarlet, Royal Mark, Apron and Blue, Royal White, Royal Green, Royal Gold, Star and Garter, Crimson Arrow, Link and Chain, and Red Cross. Where Orangemen and members of the Royal Arch Purple call each other Brother (and write to each other as Bro.), Blackmen call each other Sir Knight. However outsiders may view all this, there is no doubting its importance to many of their members. 'I gained great spiritual depth from going through the degrees,' said one of my friends. 'The ritual, the tests, the questions and answers, the drama, brought the Bible stories they were based on home to me. And the morals drawn were right.'

'It depends on how you're able to receive it,' said a Black lecturer. 'You only go a wee bit at a time. There's a lesson in every degree and the greatest lesson that I can find from any of them is where the children of Israel on the other side of Jordan built the altar and then the bigger part of their brethren saw it and thought they were worshipping false gods. And they condemned their brethren.

'And then they found out the truth – that they had built it to God and that their brethren were true Israelites, but that they had condemned them without one particle of evidence being produced. The lesson I learned I teach candidates is if you made up your mind, saying you've had a mouthful of this boy and you were just going to give him a hiding the night, just stop and think and don't make a hasty judgment on him. Wait. And tomorrow when you waken you'll have a different picture. I explain that to them.'

'The acting out of Bible stories and the signs and emblems and all that are rather like mystery plays,' points out an historically-minded Blackman. 'They helped illiterate people like many of our early members to remember scriptural truths. When properly performed by a good lecturer, these stories and truths can leave an imprint. And the tradition remains a good one. Many of our people are not book-minded, but they like and can relate to imagery.'

The role of the lecturer is crucial. They are part of an oral tradition: they explain the stories, teach degree candidates their responses and play a crucial part in the ceremonies. It is because they believe that the degree system helps people lead a better life, that so many of them give up an enormous amount of their time to pass on the oral tradition to their brethren.

Read with imagination (and with the information on Arch Purple and Black emblems given in the next chapter), 'The Black Man's Dream', a song written around 1795, gives a good indication of what is involved in the 'travel'.

> One night I thought a vision brought
>   Me to a spacious plain,
> Whereon its centre stood a mount,
>   Whose top I wished to gain;
> Orange, blue, and purple, too,
>   Were given me to wear,
> And for to see the mystery
>   They did me thus prepare.
>
> My guide a pack placed on my back –
>   With pillars of an arch –

A staff and scrip placed in my hand,
   And thus I on did march;
Through desert lands I travelled o'er,
   And the narrow road I trod,
Till something did obstruct my path
   In the form of a toad.

So then I saw what did me awe,
   Though wandering in a dream –
A flaming bush, though unconsumed,
   Before me did remain;
And as I stood out of the wood
   I heard a heavenly sound,
Which made me cast my shoes away,
   For it was holy ground.

Two men I saw, with weapons keen,
   Which did me sore annoy –
Unto a pyramid I ran
   That standing was hard by;
And as I climbed the narrow way,
   A hand I there did see,
Which layed the lofty mountains
In the scale of equity.

Blue, gold, and black about my neck,
   This apparition placed –
Into a chariot I was put,
   Where we drove off in haste:
Twelve dazzling lights of beauty bright
   Were brought to guide my way,
And as we drove thro' cypress shades
   One of them did decay.

Near to a mount I saw a fount
   Of living water flow;
I being dry, they did reply,
   To drink you there may go;
The mystic cup I then took up,
   And drank a health to all

That were born free and kept their knee
 From bowing unto Baal.

'I think we have to deal with the image of secrecy,' says William Bingham. 'Too many people see the Black as being almost masonic, which it isn't. As a group of people who have hidden agendas and secret meetings and people fishing for jobs for the boys. So I think the institution has to become more open. It has to be prepared to come forward and say, you know, this is what our degrees are about without going into great detail. We should explain to people the meanings of the degrees.

'We've tried to do this in Markethill District where about four years ago we started public meetings once a month during the months of November through to March where the scriptures related to each of the degrees were read and explained. And when we'd gone through the degrees we brought in the banners – one banner a night from each preceptory – and looked at the picture – usually a picture relating to one of the degrees – and explained to people the significance of the emblems and the signs. Things which if they are good and proper and shed light on life from scripture, are not to be kept in the dark but to be brought in the open.'

The Apprentice Boys

The Apprentice Boys, though Protestant, are essentially secular and their club meetings therefore are primarily social. 'I'm not a member of the Orange,' said one. 'But we get called "Orange bastards" anyway.

'I joined for traditional reasons. My father was in it and my son's in it. It is a city-based organization with the headquarters here in Londonderry. People join to keep up tradition. Most Protestants in Londonderry are now Apprentice Boys, though the business and professional people have mostly opted out over the last thirty or forty years. It's now mainly working class. People with a shop wouldn't want to be seen as one tradition only and perhaps lose custom from the majority of the citizens who are about 70 per cent nationalists.

'The ABs believe that the siege was one of the most historic events in the British Isles and all citizens should be proud of it. We see ourselves as keepers of the true tradition of that siege, because no one else has bothered down through the years. And in that remembrance, what basically we're doing is remembering the triumph of spirit and the supreme sacrifice made by up to 10,000 of those defenders. The tercentenary of that event in 1989 was really basically only celebrated here although it should have been celebrated all over the British Isles.'

There are no masonic overtones among the Apprentice Boys, no secret signs or grips. Essentially, it is historically rather than religiously driven, with its activities centred on its two main parades in August and December. With about an eighth of the number of members of the Orange Order, it means that the vast majority of Apprentice Boys would be Orangemen, but many Orangemen would not be Apprentice Boys. 'We think we're more unique than the Orange,' observed a senior Apprentice Boy. 'Wherever you live, you can only be initiated as a full member in Derry. And we believe that we have more companionship and are that wee bit more special than the Orange.'

What members of the Northern Irish loyal institutions go home to after meetings of their lodges, chapters, preceptories and clubs.

'Their houses are like little palaces,' used to be said of the Belfast Protestant working class. Protestants said it with pride; Catholics with a kind of patronizing contempt. Certainly, if you had no other clues, you could tell a Protestant from a Catholic street by the state of most of the gardens and what is visible of the front room, as you can tell which church they are going to from the neatness and formality of their Sunday-morning clothing.

A passion for cleanliness as an adjunct of godliness is as strange to my culture as our cheery indifference is to theirs. To the most bigoted Protestants, Catholics are dirty and untidy; to bigoted Catholics, Protestants are obsessively house-proud and fail to understand that life is for living and that it is more important to have fun with your friends than to polish the furniture. And if both the stereotypes are uncharitable in their application, there is nevertheless a lot of truth in them. Since I began to stay in Ulster Protestant, mostly Presbyterian, homes, I look about my house with a new and rather depressed eye.

The sheer fact of cultural separation means that differences in living conditions are so great as to provide a culture shock. 'George is going over to London,' observed my friend Henry to me a few months ago, assuming, I realized, that I would offer a bed if one were free. I decided to confront the matter head on. 'Henry,' I said, 'I'll get him a bed but, as things stand, I can have no Presbyterians in my house. He'd die of shock.' 'But he's a lax Presbyterian,' said Henry. 'Not when it comes to houses, he isn't,' I said. 'I've been to his, and it's as clean as everyone else's.' So as I do with all bedless Presbyterians, I found George quarters with an English friend whose house would not frighten him and I continue to invite to my disorganized and dusty house only Irish Catholics and assorted bohemians.

There is a certain uniformity about the Presbyterian home. I've never been in one without being reminded of the centrality of family life, of ordered relationships, of industry and of thriftiness – which is, however, tempered by tremendous generosity and hospitality. The people of Northern Ireland, Protestant and Catholic, nationalist and unionist, republican and loyalist, have many characteristics in common, of which the most agreeable is tremendous warmth and kindness to any stranger who is not thought to be the enemy.

There is a difference of degree about the generosity. My mother, who grew up in the south of Ireland as a game-keeper's daughter on an Anglo-Irish estate, was an inveterate observer of cultural differences between southern Protestants and Catholics. 'You go into hospital,' I remember her explaining, 'and a Catholic friend will arrive laden with grapes and chocolates and flowers and spend an hour with you and never come back because she has run out of money and is ashamed to return empty-handed. The Protestant, on the other hand, will come in bearing a modest gift, will stay for twenty minutes or so and will then come back regularly.'

Presbyterian houses tend to be neat and spotless but cosy, the kind of home where people have slippers and candlewick dressing-gowns; if you go out infrequently and work hard you want to be comfortable at home. In addition to a three-piece-suite, the most striking object in the living-room will be the enlarged, framed photographs on the windowsills, the table and the wall – the wedding photograph of the owners of the house, photographs of their parents, their siblings and their children, of big family groups and of their own children and grandchildren at various stages of development and at key moments like graduation and marriage. No child growing up in a house like that can think other than that he is the centre of his parents' lives. It is that same family-orientation that makes so many Orange parades a happy family event.

Books, other than the Bible, are uncommon except in the houses of ministers and of teachers, but even there they will tend to be tucked away in a separate study. There is no clutter of papers or newspapers and few, sometimes no, objects. There might in some houses be a glass bookcase for treasures, with a heavy emphasis on Tyrone crystal wedding gifts too special to be used. (In the other community you're more likely to have most of your fragile wedding gifts broken within a year or so of marriage courtesy of the exuberant clumsiness of yourself or your guests.) There will be a plethora of little tables so placed to ensure every person sitting in that living-room can eat and drink comfortably, for from the moment you come through the door, the lady of the house is preparing a tray full of food and drink: tea or coffee, two or three kinds of biscuits and home-made cake.

If you are there at a meal time you'll be offered meat and potatoes and two kinds of sweet. If it's not a meal time and they discover that you've missed your dinner (one o'clock) or your tea (six o'clock), your hostess will race to the kitchen to make piles of sandwiches, and fetch the home-made apple pie or whatever else is necessary to save you from starvation. Ulster Protestants are terrified lest their guests die of hunger; Ulster Catholics lest they die of thirst. Mind you, while drink is rarely on offer in a Protestant home as a part of normal hospitality, the occasional host might offer whiskey. And if you ever find yourself in a pub with a drinking Protestant, they are as lavish as any of their Catholic counterparts.

By any standards, the kindness is stunning. Arrive at a stranger's house for a night with no luggage, as I have done, and slippers and a cosy dressing-gown and spare toothbrushes and toiletries are pressed upon you with enthusiasm and efficiency. And people will put themselves out for you to an extraordinary degree. They think nothing of going thirty miles out of their way to pick you up or drive you somewhere. It's as if the sheer order and routine of their lives makes it possible for you to be accommodated however demanding are your needs.

The perception of Ulster Protestants as dour and taciturn does not long survive spending time in their houses, for they absolutely love talking and stay up late with any visitor. I've sat up till two in the morning and later having thoroughly enjoyable conversations with the most upright, temperate and even teetotal of citizens.

Orange, Black or Apprentice Boy meetings can be fitted into an orderly existence. The wives know when the husbands are going out, where they're going and who they will be with. Reactions to these activities go across the spectrum from an old-fashioned reverence for the man's important business to a genial acceptance that they're making a mystery out of a simple get-together. And in the rural areas at least, sanity and tolerance dominate the women's reaction to their men's activity; it is understood that men want to be together and that this provides an excuse. 'How have you stood it?' I asked one woman whose husband was so heavily involved in the Freemasons, the Orange and the Black that he was frequently out four to five evenings a week. 'I know he'll never come back drunk,' she said.

3

Onlookers, Participants and
Opponents: the Twelfth

Different viewpoints*

T HE BIG, BIG COLOURFUL, noisy day that was the Twelfth had a special magic in the grey, sober Belfast of earlier times. Rowel Friers, the cartoonist, remembered sticking his head out of the bedroom window full of excitement:

> I peered out to the right and there they were – the flying banners, the glinting instruments of the bands, and the bowler-hatted, white-gloved, navy-serge-suited and brown-booted Orange-sashed gentlemen of the Order, no brother's tailoring outdoing another, highly respectable, dignified and erect, they march to the rhythm of their bands. Occasionally, one of them might deign to give a regal nod of the head to an onlooker known to him, and no doubt already approved of by his brethren as an acceptable outsider.
>
> The swordbearers and deacon pole-carriers stepped out with all the demeanour of generals, now and then taking a peep at their pride and joy – the banner. Most of these, I was to learn later, were painted by a Mr Bridgett, a craftsman specializing in that particular art form. This knowledge I gleaned from the son of the said gentleman, who I met at art college some years later. Many and varied they were: gold, silver, orange, purple, blue, all the colours and more than could have adorned Joseph's coat. From portraits of William in battle, to Queen Victoria and her Bible ('the secret of England's greatness'), churches, angels, the Rock of Ages, memorial portraits to worshipful brothers who had passed on to that higher and grander lodge in the sky, it was a travelling art exhibition, before anyone dreamed of the Committee for the Encouragement of Music and the Arts or the Arts Council.

William Bingham, now a Presbyterian minister, reminisces about a much more recent period in County Armagh: 'I first paraded with the institution in 1969 in Markethill, where I was brought up. I was about six years of age when my uncle took me and my brother and my cousin with him to hold the strings of the banner: my grandmother made little Orange collarettes for us.†

✳ With the exception of William Bingham, George Chittick and Worshipful Master Charlton, whom I interviewed, and Neil Jarman, Elaine McClure and John Molden, who appeared on a radio programme, the quotes from everyone else named in this chapter come from their contributions to The Twelfth: What It Means to Me (ed. Gordon Lucy and Elaine McClure).

† Giving children pretend collarettes or lending them proper ones is common. Although Orangemen take their regalia seriously, they do not give it mystical status. I was watching a parade one day when I was

'When you were growing up, you played at being Orangemen. Weeks before the Twelfth, all the youngsters in the town got together and had a ceremony in the yard and formed their own Orange Lodge – you're talking about six-, seven-, eight-year-olds. And we used to get tin boxes and make banners out of cloth and sticks and we paraded by people's houses or up and down the yard and we had a really good time together. We were very democratic in electing a worshipful master. We voted on it and usually everyone got their turn at it.

'We really looked forward to the Twelfth: you used to think that when that was over, your summer was over. The highlight of it was gone. For us it was a day where you met all your friends from school that you hadn't seen for the weeks of the summer holidays: maybe some of their fathers were on parade or some of them were in the bands playing the cymbal or the triangles or a wee accordion or something. You all met in the field and you had tea and sandwiches and then you played around for a while and then you came home again. It was just a unique occasion. There was nothing like it the rest of the year.

'I suppose the things that you were mesmerized by were the colour – the paintings on the banners, the crowds of people – and the music – the bands. I really loved the silver bands. My father played the tenor horn and went on parade. My mother would have been making sandwiches: she did the picnic. And my sister, she didn't get parading, only the boys. She was left out of it a wee bit.

'For my aunts and great-aunts – many of whom were married to farmers – it was literally was the only day out they got in the year. The Twelfth of July came and they worked hard to get the harvest cleared up and the best suits cleaned and looked after their husbands. Rarely if ever would they have been out anywhere else except church. Certainly they'd have had no holidays. I had uncles that wouldn't miss the Twelfth of July, but they wouldn't go to their own sons' or nephews' weddings.'

Elaine McClure, Worshipful Mistress of a women's lodge, does not feel part of the community in nationalist Newry.

---

summoned into it by Chris McGimpsey, who removed his bowler, placed it on my head and said: 'That's a thank you for taking the trouble to find out about us.' I wore it slightly uneasily, afraid of giving offence, but when I consulted the Worshipful Master of my unofficial lodge he explained that no one would mind. Further, he told me that if I wanted a collarette as a souvenir, he would provide me with one. He duly sent one to me along with a miniature of Bushmills to toast it with.

I do feel very close to my friends in that town, my neighbours, but I feel that's completely different from, if you like, as a person coming from the community I come from, trying to identify with the symbols of local government in that town.

As T. S. Eliot says: 'I can connect nothing with nothing' . . . But certainly within the company of people who share the same culture as I do, I can connect. I can connect with their outlook, with the music, with the symbols on the banner, with the ethos and the reason behind a social gathering.

I walk on the Twelfth – I don't march . . . My blood family . . . introduced me to the Twelfth and now my Orange family take me along with them on the Twelfth of July. I walk in the road with the men of Sheepbridge.

I know those men. I know their ladies. I know their families, I know who they are and they're good, they're decent people. And I walk with them and in the front is the band and my cousin's in the band and I'm walking in the road and I'm thinking how like my uncle Joe our William is because Uncle Joe was the one who took me first to the Twelfth of July. And I walk in the road with them hoping they're not going too quick and I've got the right shoes on my feet and then we wait at the hall and then when all the lodges come we all walk off again and the drum beat's given and the banners are hoisted and we start on our way.

And I remember thinking last Twelfth of July how lucky I am to be part of this – and that's not to deride anyone else who comes from a different culture – but how lucky I am to be walking with such good, kind people and to have the colour and the music that I can listen to. To meet up with people that perhaps I haven't seen for the last twelve months. All you have to do is just say: 'Hello, how are you?' and the connection is made and the friendship is there. And to go back to the hall at the end of the night and have a meal and to sit again in the company of the sisters and the brethren of Sheepbridge – it's a wonderful warm feeling just of a family coming together. The Twelfth of July is our family occasion.

However, David Cook, Alliance politician and ex-chairman of the police authority, puts forward a view very common among middle-class Protestants whose liberalism doesn't extend to trying to understand the ordinary Orangeman.

The first thought about the Twelfth each year is how can we get away. I have spent most Twelfths in Donegal (often infuriated by RTE's [Radio Telefís Eireann] naive view of the Twelfth as no more than a folksy cultural festival). I have been lucky enough to be in Northern Ireland on only a handful of Twelfths in my life. One was a memorably hot day in the middle Seventies when I pushed our baby daughter in a pram from the Ormeau Road along the embankment all the way to Shaw's Bridge where I saw the drunken crowds in full swing.

I have never actually set out to watch a Twelfth parade. I have never taken my children to watch one. I have never believed that Protestantism needs to be, or indeed, can be defended by the usual public manifestations of Orangeism. And I have never been taken in by the claims that there is no other purpose in them than the display of a much loved cultural tradition. I have always known that one of the historical purposes of those public manifestations, and this remains true today for some Orangemen some of the time, is to annoy and antagonize Catholics.

The claim that the Twelfth is the greatest cultural festival in Europe, with its bands, banners and music, may, I think, be true. But I do not believe the assertion that the Twelfth is no more than a good-natured cultural event and a large family picnic. That is the purest hypocrisy and the biggest lie. The problem which the Orange Order has to face is that very few people outside their community believe the lie.

Marietta Farrell, lecturer and SDLP activist, had never heard of the Twelfth until she went to Northern Ireland from the Republic as a student in the 1970s.

I found the whole thing quite colourful and quaint if somewhat threatening. I was bemused at the sight of so many men, in what was to me, City of London business dress, looking so intent and serious. I admired the skill and the colour of the bands but I found their swagger and the wording of their songs intimidating and offensive. I was also surprised at the lack of women in the 'celebration'. From what I could see, women stood on the sidelines and cheered the men. I wondered why loyalist women were not more central in their important annual celebration. [Until Drumcree 1996] I neither thought nor learnt much more about the Twelfth. It seemed to have nothing to do with me.

To the best of my knowledge, I was never in the company of an Orangeman.

Decorations and associated festivities

Glen Barr, famous for his leadership of the Ulster Workers' Strike in 1974 and now a community worker, grew up in Londonderry.

Through all the seasons of marbles, hoops, bows and arrows, cowboys and indians, Easter eggs, Christmas stockings and bin lids to sleigh with, we always knew when the big day was near.

The Craigavon Pipe Band which practised at the top of King Street at the back of

Harry McLaughlin's carpenter shop and which we all joined at ten or eleven years of age, was at it three nights a week instead of the customary Wednesday nights. The men and women of the street were making bows from the wood shavings from Harry McLaughlin's and dyeing them red, white and blue in tin baths at the back of the band shed. The other emblems on the Arch were cleaned up and painted and all the light bulbs checked and renewed where necessary. Buntings were being rescued from old sacks and tied across the street from downpipe to downpipe.

Weeks before we headed off with hatchets and ropes to hack down branches and small trees in St Columb's Park, making sure the 'look-outs' were well positioned to follow every move of the park warden, and run the gauntlet in the Limavady Road pulling the biggest load imaginable for our 'Eleventh' night bonfire. Doing your watch in the back lane to make sure the boys from Alfred Street, Florence Street, York Street and Bond Street didn't raid the trees and rubber tyres for their fires.

The 'Eleventh' night in King Street was like a fairy tale with singing, dancing and spud roasting in the ashes. There was the usual crate of stout for the men and the navy men from the Sea Eagle Barracks next to King Street, could always be relied upon to bring out the rum and show off women from the area known as 'Navy Dolls' hanging onto their arms . . .

This was my 'Twelfth'. Collecting for the bonfire, roasting the spuds, the dancing, the singing on the 'Eleventh' night in The Fountain. Getting up on the 'Twelfth' morning and putting on the kilt, shawl, those damned spats, and the rest of the Craigavon Pipe Band uniform knowing the girls from school would be following the band all day.

The flowers must not be forgotten. Orange lilies and sweet william for the adorning of banners and drums and hats and buttonholes are easily procured in the country, but harder in parts of the city short on gardens. George Chittick recalls: 'For many many years our district always put Orange lilies on the top of the bannerette. Billy, the secretary of the district, says to me: ''George, there's a man coming down – he's called Nolan – and he'll give you a bunch of Orange lilies on the Eleventh night.'' So this wee man come down and he said to me: ''Is your name Chittick?'' I said, ''That's right.'' He says, ''My name's Nolan. Here's a bunch of Orange lilies. Now, when you're up the Lisburn Road tomorrow morning, you look out for me and I'll wave at you.'' So I went up the road with the lilies on the bannerette and there's this wee man standing. He smiled at me and I nodded and he said, ''Dead on.'' So that was all right.

'Billy says to me. ''George, you know that wee man Nolan come down to see you." I says, "Aye." "He's an RC." "Is that right?" "I work with him and him and me were friends and he always said to me he had a huge set of Orange lilies in his back garden and he'd give some for the bannerette." "Dead on." So it went on for a number of years. Up to 1994, Mr Nolan come down every Eleventh night with these flowers and I took them off him and thanked him very much and put them on the bannerette. 1995: I was down that night and no Orange lilies arrived. I thought it was because of Drumcree. I said, "Maybe that's it. Maybe he doesn't want to." But then about two months later on the Lisburn Road this lady comes to me and says, "Is your name Chittick? Are you from Sandy Orange Hall?" I said, "That's correct." She says, "Well, I'm Mr Nolan's daughter and I'm sorry to tell you me father passed away last May." "Oh, I says, I'm very sorry about that." She says, "I made an awful blunder. Before he died he said to me: 'Don't you forget on the Eleventh night to take the Orange lilies down to Sandy Row', and," she says, "I forgot." And I say, "It's just one of those things. You can't do nothing about it. Don't worry about it." "No," she says, "but you'll never get any more Orange lilies." I says, "Why?" And she says, "It's a big house and I had to sell it." So I says, "I understand that, ma'am. I understand that." But she says, "I have a wee present for you." And she brought me out four bulbs. She says, "I rescued them."

'So they're planted in my garden now and they will for ever and ever I hope be the lilies that will be carried on the bannerette.'

The clothes

'What should I wear to go to an Orange parade?' I asked my friend Janet, who knows about such things because she was brought up Presbyterian in Cookstown and had an Orange father.

'Frock,' she said firmly. 'No rocks.'

For Orangemen, sartorial decisions are a matter for each lodge. Standards vary dramatically. At the most respectable end, particularly in rural areas, clothes are very important. There are Orangemen who would never have bought a suit if it weren't for the Twelfth and whose brethren would be horrified if they arrived with a speck of dirt on the white gloves or a dent in their bowlers. And there will be strong views about whether flowers should decorate hats and jackets.

Why bowlers? Because they were a mark of respectability for Orangemen's fathers and their fathers' fathers, and in a deeply conservative culture there has to be a very good reason to make any break with tradition. That is tough on those who hate and loathe their bowler hats. There is the occasional middle-aged man who is enhanced by a bowler, but on the whole it is an unflattering article and on some people looks downright ridiculous.

At the other end of the spectrum – most likely to be the Belfast semi-paramilitary world – there are lodges where no one cares what you wear. To my eye, trained as I am in the ways of County Tyrone, T-shirts, tattooed arms and earrings don't go well with collarettes, but then I would be wary of arguing the point with the kind of people who think they do.

Orangewomen have greater problems. For a start, they can parade only if invited formally by the relevant hosts and if the Women's Grand Lodge agrees. Northern Irish society, especially in the rural areas, has both the virtues and defects of 1950s Britain. My experience of Orangemen is that in many respects they seem to be admirable husbands, but they mostly expect their wives to be admirable housekeepers at home preparing the sandwiches rather than going on parade.

Olive Whitten, councillor and deputy Grand Mistress of the Association of Loyal Orangewomen of Ireland, has no complaints:

'I have no regrets at our members not being invited to take part in the parade. I enjoy standing on the sideline, watching the parade from beginning to end although my one desire always was to have been a playing member of a band.'

There are some parading ladies' lodges, however, who face trickier decisions about clothes than do their brethren. Some turn all the sisters out identically dressed in, for example, purple suits and white hats and shoes, but there are few outfits that suit all women, and the results are usually bad news for some. An alternative approach is to have an agreed colour but allow different styles. One lodge produced a enormous collection of different white Sunday hats. Others adopt a more *laissez-faire* approach, but still require suits and hats and gloves. And the most bohemian let their members wear what they like, secure in the knowledge that they will be properly turned-out in their best Sunday attire.

The regalia

When it comes to regalia, there are clear rules. Ordinary members of private lodges of Orange Degree only are entitled to wear an Orange sash or usually a collar (nowadays called a collarette, though many Orangemen still call it a sash) about four inches wide, with the lodge number displayed in front; a few lodges wear blue for historical reasons everyone seems to have forgotten. Having the Purple Degree requires the wearing of a sash or collarette about four and a half inches wide with a purple stripe. Members of the Royal Arch Purple have the colours reversed: purple with orange edging. Blackmen wear their Orange regalia when they parade on the Twelfth. On Royal Black Preceptory parades they wear black collarettes which may have several coloured stripes representing various of their ten degrees and presenting the symbolic connotations of a rainbow; they also wear masonic-style blue, fringed aprons and embroidered cuffs. The Apprentice Boys wear crimson sashes or collarettes to represent the blood spilt by the defenders during the Siege of Derry and the defiant flag flown from the cathedral tower.

The regalia that mean most to members of the loyal institutions, of course, are those handed down from father to son. 'When I was eighteen, I joined my grandfather's lodge,' said one. 'And my grandmother passed on his collarette, which had been his father's collarette. I don't wear his collarette now – it's getting too old to wear. But it's in a safe place and if my son wants to join I'll pass it on to him.'

'We treat our collarettes well, because they represent something important,' said another, who has five from three different organizations. 'It's important to treat them with respect.' (I saw a particularly graphic example of this at a parade where a group of Apprentice Boys could no longer contain themselves in the face of republican provocation. Before returning abuse and missiles, they took off their collarettes and put them in their pockets lest they dishonour them.)

District officers get to wear wider collars; county grand officers have silver fringes and Grand Lodge officers have gold fringes. Indications of office appear as, for instance, 'WM', 'DM', 'S', or 'T' (or even PWM for Past Worshipful Master) in front of the collarettes.

An Orangeman might wear no adornments on his collarette other than his lodge number and the insignia of his office, but many sport emblems and badges. (Apprentice Boys, being essentially secular, wear no emblems.) Emblems can be acquired rather on the charm-bracelet principle. The two most popular emblems are the self-explanatory CROWN and open BIBLE, which anyone can wear, as they can a representation of King William on his horse. Members of the Royal Arch Purple may also wear several others, including: an ANCHOR, symbolic of a safe arrival in the afterlife; the ARK OF THE COVENANT, 'the visible evidence of God's promise to be with and guide his people of Israel safely through life'; a COFFIN, as a reminder of mortality; an EYE, signifying God's omniscience; a FIVE-POINTED STAR, a reminder of the five wounds of Christ; a LADDER, whose three steps represent Faith, Hope and Charity; NOAH'S ARK, the means by which God chose to save and regenerate life on earth, thus symbolizing 'a better and purer life'; and a THREE-BRANCHED CANDLESTICK, symbolic of the light which is revealed by the Trinity of Father, Son and Holy Spirit.

The Royal Black Institution has many more again which relate to the institution and its degrees, and are biblical and have strong overtones of John Bunyan's *Pilgrim's Progress*. Among them are a BURNING BUSH; a LAMB, as in the Lamb of God; a little MAN WITH A BACKPACK, who represents a pilgrim, Joseph in Egypt; a RED HAND, a reference to the cloud no bigger than a man's hand; a ROD WITH AN ENTWINED SNAKE, which harks back to Moses, whose rod became a snake and then changed back again; a SKULL AND CROSSBONES, which is the institution's crest, representing mourning for Joseph when he was sold into slavery in Egypt and was given up for dead. The key emblem, however, is the RED CROSS which, since it represents the final degree, shows that you have taken all the others. It is red because Christ shed his blood, it is surrounded by a crown, because he was a king, but as with all Protestant crosses, it is empty, because Christ was resurrected.

Then there are badges or medals, which often relate to notable parades attended by the wearer, such as the Orange tercentenary celebration in Belfast, a Scottish Twelfth, a New Zealand jamboree or Drumcree 1995. 'Some people stick a lot of rubbish on their collarettes,' observed a senior Orangeman. 'I hate that.' Yet though like most of them he hates show, being by nature a squirrel, he has the largest private collection of badges, emblems and other memorabilia of any Orangeman I know. Most prized of all are service medals, sometimes those of a father or grandfather.

The banners

District, county and Grand Lodge officers are called upon to preside at many services and ceremonies, including the opening-up and closing-down of Orange Halls and the unfurling of new banners.

Banners are a great cause of both pride and worry to lodges. To the ordinary Orangeman, a banner sums up the spirit of his lodge. Although there is a fair amount of duplication of subjects, each banner is unique. Much deliberation will have gone into not just the choice of subject and artist, but the manner in which the lodge's name and number will be presented and what colour and style and motifs should be used for the borders. The lodge member will know who painted it, where and when.

The downside is that banners are very vulnerable: after maybe a few dozen outings, batterings from wind and rain take a heavy toll. (They take a heavy toll on the standard-bearers too: in bad weather there is a constant battle just to keep the buffeted banner aloft, especially when its silk is weighed down by rain.) A lodge might have to requisition the painting of a new banner every ten years at a cost of maybe a thousand pounds. This will not only impose a financial burden which is serious for poor lodges, but may bring about disagreement between those of the brethren who want a new version of their old banner and those who want radical change.

As that student of parades Neil Jarman points out, while banners go back to the beginning of the Orange tradition, they developed extensively towards the end of the nineteenth century as unionism felt its identity under threat from Irish nationalism. 'The banners became more standardized, more professional. The painting became of a better quality and the range of images expanded, so you moved away from the old images of a King Billy and the crown and the Bible to include a much greater range of heroes of Ulster unionism like Colonel Saunderson, later Carson, Craig. The elaboration of events from the Williamite wars and the massacre at the Bann in 1641 all appeared at those times along with biblical images which drew an analogy from the position of the Ulster Protestants to the Israelites in the biblical times.'

There is an enormous range of these large, colourful banners and they show pictorially the cultural reference points of the Protestant people. A major grievance in recent years was the BBC's decision early in the 1980s to scrap television coverage of the Belfast Twelfth because, Orangemen think, of nationalist sensibilities. Even though in recent years there has been truncated coverage, what has been lost is the informed commentary on banners and bands that put the parade and the Orange Order in its historical and cultural context. These days, the media are interested in parades only if they provoke violence.

An Ulster Society survey identified thirteen categories of Orange banner. Many Orange and virtually all Black banners are BIBLICAL, the majority being Old Testament. The BUILDINGS represented are usually of local significance; most often they are churches. A typical example of the secular is Derrymore House, Bessbrook, carried by the local lodge because the Act of Union was signed there in 1800. The HOME RULE category depicts Ulster Protestantism in its most 'no-surrender' mode, with paintings of, for instance, the formation of the Ulster Volunteers. The HISTORICAL category covers events relating to the foundation of the Orange Order and the INDUSTRIAL particularly to the proud Belfast industrial past. Both WORLD WARS are there, the most moving image being that of the 36th Ulster Division, so many of whom were slaughtered at the Somme.

You have to be dead to be on a banner: popular PERSONALITIES are Winston Churchill, Oliver Cromwell and Sir James Craig, the long-serving prime minister of Northern Ireland: brethren murdered by the IRA during the TROUBLES sometimes become the subject of their lodge's banner. Martin Luther is the reformer most often seen on REFORMATION banners and probably Queen Victoria among the ROYALTY; a very evocative banner in the latter category is that of the Great Northern True Blues, a Sandy Row railway employees' lodge, showing a train festooned with union flags carrying King Edward VII to Belfast.

The largest category, of course, relate to the WILLIAMITE period; (for example, the Mountjoy charging the boom at Derry, William crossing the Boyne, or the battle of Aughrim. All Apprentice Boys' banners are to do with the Siege of Derry. Remaining banners are scooped up under the categories of OLD FLAGS OR BANNERS and MISCELLANEOUS, which include a British bulldog and Britannia.

Banners are as carefully cherished as collarettes. David Jones, who until his teens lived in Carleton Street Orange Hall – home to many Orange lodges, including Portadown district lodge, Royal Black preceptories and Apprentice Boys clubs – where his father was caretaker, recalled one of the procedures before the Twelfth:

One of his other tasks was to extract the lodge banners from their storage places where they had been carefully laid aside from the previous year. Following the last Twelfth each banner would have been rolled up and placed inside its own long wooden box. These boxes would be taken out of their storage places, by now covered with a liberal sprinkling of a year's undisturbed dust. When opened the banner would be unrolled, hooked on to the banner poles and carefully rested against the wall in one of the largest rooms in the building. The brass or chromium fittings that sat atop the banner poles would be polished until they gleamed. The early hanging of the banners also allowed time for any creases that had formed during storage in the material to fall out. With mention of the banner poles, quite often one of the problems faced was finding them, depending on who had put them away or where they had been left.

One of my lasting impressions of that era is the banners. I can well remember as a small child looking up at them – somewhat in awe – all assembled in the one place, and each with its own unique large oil-painted scene. This was my art gallery. Before me were displayed likenesses of King William III on horseback, or arriving at Carrickfergus. A painting of Queen Victoria being presented with a Bible by one of her colonial subjects, the banner bearing the legend 'The Secret of England's Greatness'. Numerous biblical scenes were evident, amongst them Noah portrayed on the Ark with a bird returning with a twig in its beak. Then there were the banners depicting the 'Bible and Crown' and past remembered Orangemen of the area with stern emotionless faces. Still and silent they towered above me. In a few days I knew this quiet moment would change as the banners would take on a life of their own when they would leave the hall on parade. Once outside the banners, held high, would float in the breeze and seen from a distance the tops of the banner poles would bob up and down as they were carried in the procession.

The music

John Molden, a lifelong student of traditional songs, points out that Orange culture can only be understood in the context of a wide range of music, stretching back through the centuries and across much of Britain, Ireland and Europe, belonging to a genre of songs dealing with everyday matters and events. Even the most strongly expressed Protestant sentiments in local Orange songs have at one time or another been voiced in parts of English traditional music.

Orange songs are of different kinds. Some of them are openly objectionable. Some of them refer to elements of Catholic doctrine in an opprobrious way. Some of them refer to party fights and give very very one-sided and objectionable accounts. On the other hand, the accounts of those same fights given by the other side are equally offensive.

Certainly many of the songs have been based – almost parodied – upon nationalist songs. There are some songs that are, for instance, similar in form to 'The Wearing of the Green'. 'The Sash' – although not based on a sectarian Irish song – is based on an Irish song of possibly music-hall origin called 'The Hat My Father Wore' . . . They often see themselves as David, up against the world – the English establishment, the rest of Ireland . . .

There are large numbers of songs which look at incidents in Irish history . . .

where Protestants were injured, assaulted or killed. And there are large numbers of songs which say, 'Watch out. If you are not on your guard, these things are going to happen again.'

One old Orangeman whom I had the honour to talk to in his last years about songs and Orange songs in general was a pillar of his local Orange lodge and in fact a pillar of the district. He was a lecturer on Orange traditions and history and when I went and asked him, he refused to sing Orange songs to me on the grounds that he as an Orangeman had taken an oath to give offence to no man.

Molden picked out 'The Ould Orange Flute' – a 'rather amusing, fun-poking look at the distinctiveness between two groups of people' – as being one of those songs that Catholics enjoy.

In the County Tyrone, near the town of Dungannon,
Where many a ruction myself had a hand in,
Bob Williamson lived – a weaver by trade,
And all of us thought him a stout Orange blade.
On the twelfth of July as it yearly did come,
Bob played on the flute to the sound of the drum,
You may talk of your harp, your piano, your lute,
But nothing could sound like the ould Orange flute.

But this treacherous scoundrel took us all in,
For he married a Papish called Bridgit McGinn,
And turned Papish himself, and forsook the ould cause,
That gave us our freedom, religion and laws.
Now the boys in the townland made some noise upon it,
And Bob had to fly to the province of Connaught;
He fled with his wife and his fixings to boot,
Along with the others the ould Orange flute.

At the chapel on Sundays to atone for past deeds,
He said Paters and Aves and counted his beads,
Till after some time at the Priest's own desire,
He went with his ould flute to play in the choir;
He went with his ould flute to play in the Mass,
But the instrument shivered and sighed, 'Oh, alas!'
And for all he could blow, though it made a great noise,
The ould flute would play only, 'The Protestant Boys'.

Bob jumped and he started and got into a splutter,
And threw his ould flute in the blessed holy water;
For he thought that this charm would bring some other sound,
But when he blew it again it played 'Croppies Lie Down'.
And for all he could whistle, and finger, and blow,
To play Papish music he found it no go,
'Kick the Pope', 'The Boyne Water', and such like it would sound,
But one Papish squeak in it just couldn't be found.

At a council of priests that was held the next day,
The decided to banish the ould flute away,
For they couldn't knock heresy out of its head,
So they bought Bob another to play in its stead.
So the ould flute was doomed and its fate was pathetic,
it was branded and burned at the stake as heretic;
While the flames roared around it they heard a strange noise,
'Twas the ould flute still whistling, 'The Protestant Boys'.

'When I worked in Wexford [in the Irish Republic] years ago,' remembered George Chittick, 'that was my star turn. They couldn't get enough of "The Ould Orange Flute": I used to go into the bar in the hotel where I was staying. And it was great and there was good old crack and a good old laugh. I don't drink, but I used to go down to sit with them and they used to sing away there and then they'd be shouting, "Come on, come on, you have to sing the 'The Ould Orange Flute'." They used to cheer. And then, "Give us 'The Sash', give us 'The Sash'." This was before the Troubles, may I say.'

Bands decide what to play. Lodges choose the bands. 'In my young days, the bands were all flute bands,' recalled Worshipful Master Charlton from Mourne. 'There were no uniforms. And I remember our band had old police caps. I remember going and getting a bag full of discarded police caps and the women making white tops and putting a bit of elastic in them to go over the top of the caps. And getting blue ribbon and the women putting blue ribbons on them. And I remember going to Belfast and getting badges. The blue ribbons were because our lodges are blue.

'Now we've an Irish pipe band here. In Mourne there are accordion bands, pipe bands and harp bands. I was just talking to a wee girl there, her harp and flute band, they won the Ulster championship in the Ulster Hall on Saturday. And they've practised in our hall. There's better music now, but by and large the Orange hasn't changed much. Only just the standard of living.'

There are devotees of all kinds of bands, but the instruments most associated with Ulster are the flute (or fife, the small, shriller version) and the drum. Alvin Mullan wrote in 1997:

My background is rooted in [the flute band] tradition and can be traced to the late nineteeth century, when on the Twelfth 1890 my great-grandfather Alvin Mullan began playing the fife along with the drums for an Orange lodge from Tullyhogue in Co. Tyrone, as part of the demonstration. Continuing this tradition, my grandfather William Mullan, a gifted drummer, led the drum corps in Killymoon Flute Band, the local part-music flute band from Cookstown, Co. Tyrone. Due to ill health my grandfather's mantle was inherited by my father William Alvin Mullan, who led the drum corps of the band until it folded up in the 1970s (this band has recently been reformed under the same name and maintains the part-music flute band tradition in that area).

This background caused me, from an early age, to view the Twelfth as an occasion to listen to bands, view the impressive display of musical culture and long for the day when I could participate. This finally materialized on the Twelfth 1981 when I played the flute with Tullyhogue Flute Band in Cookstown on the return parade from the main demonstration. Thus my band career was launched and still continues with Corcrain Flute Band from Portadown (which I joined in 1985).

As a bandsman I regard the Twelfth as the most important parade of the year; all other parades prior to this are preparatory and any following are extra. The occasion demands much preparation. One's flute must be in top working order, the uniform clean with trousers well pressed, the shirt snow-white and ironed in case the weather demands the removal of the tunic, shoes must be gleaming, and the music holder well polished. When the band moves off on the morning of the Twelfth it is really a most enjoyable and thrilling experience. All the preparation and months of practice result in a fine display of musical talent as the band plays through its march repertoire: Galanthia, The Bulgars' Entry, Le Tambour Major, Our Director, The Pacer, Peace and Plenty, The Gladiator's Farewell, Corcrain, Coeur de Lion and others.

In addition to the musical aspect of playing in a flute band on the Twelfth, there is also the opportunity to meet other bandsmen and listen to their music. There exists amongst bandsmen a great sense of comradeship and unity of purpose. The Twelfth provides opportunity to develop this by renewing friendships, discussing problems, swapping ideas, and reflecting on past Twelfths. As a bandsman the

Twelfth means everything; it is the heart of the flute band tradition, its soul and life. Remove the Twelfth and the tradition will die.

In the early nineteenth century, Ulster flute bands came into existence, modelled on those that formed part of military bands. Initially, they played military music and paraded in martial style. Their repertoire broadened as their range of instruments increased; from 1907 these sophisticated part flute bands, complemented by a drum corps, have engaged in music contests.

The part flute bands are for connoisseurs; the 'blood and thunder' or 'kick-the-pope' bands are populist. Dominic Bryan, an academic who with Neil Jarman has done much to explain what parades are all about, exactly expresses my own mixed feelings about them.

Blood-and-thunder bands can be threatening to an outsider like myself and it is easy to appreciate why so many in the Catholic community treat them with a mixture of fear and loathing. On the other hand they are also the most entertaining part of the Twelfth in Belfast. They help create a sense of carnival which is in some contrast to the officials at the front of the parade and the religious service given at the field.

He remarks about the uniforms: 'On the one hand you have plenty of sombre dark respectable suits whilst some of the bands are in bright orange, blue and purple uniforms. And there is invariably a group of young girls dressed in the latest fashion (or the latest Rangers shirt) walking alongside their band: the Twelfth is also about teenage sexuality.'

While most bands include women of all ages, teenage sexuality is most evident among the fife-and-drum groupies or the mini-skirted standard-bearers who march in front of the most villainous-looking bands. These bands have vastly increased in number over the last thirty years as a reaction to the Troubles. Many Orangemen who hate the militarism of these bands argue that they are a vital safety-valve for young people who might otherwise become involved in paramilitary violence and that their contact with the Orange Order is crucial. 'I was not long a member of a flute band when one of our drummers was murdered by the IRA,' one now senior Orangeman told me. 'Some of us kids were full of rage. It was only the influence of older Orangemen in our lodge that stopped us getting guns; some of us would have gone out to get revenge.'

The flute bands also have the merit of being cheap. It is extremely expensive to support, for instance, a silver or a pipe band: £2,000 is nothing for a trombone. And for those lodges which hire bands, the choice can be between paying £500 for a silver band or £100 for the fife-and-drum equivalent.

The famous Lambeg drums never appear in Belfast now, but drumming matches are still popular in rural areas. The Lambeg's origins are disputed, but it is agreed that it is the ultimate tribal symbol in Ulster. It is no accident that Lambeg drumming is strongest in Armagh, where republicanism is at its most entrenched and dangerous. The staccato beat can be heard for miles, even in bandit country.

Food

There are, in my experience, two expressions so miserable as to strike pity into the hardest heart. One is that of an Indian shopkeeper who fails to make a sale; the other, of an Ulster Protestant who has discovered his dinner will be late.

Rural Protestants in particular are people with few vices; fidelity and temperance are the norm. But they do love food. I kept track one day of the eating activities of a group of Orangemen. I had arrived in Belfast at eight o'clock and was taken to a friend's house. The woman of the house, her daughter and daughter-in-law were preparing for the arrival at ten o'clock of three or four guests, who were being lavishly catered for despite the fact that there was no doubt that they would have had an Ulster fry two hours previously.

By the time the dignitary – the local county Grand Master – and the others arrived, the table was covered with five different kinds of sandwiches, sausages and home-made sausage rolls, home-made cakes and pies. There was orange squash, there was tea and there was coffee. And throughout the meal, as throughout so many of the meals I've had in Ulster, people looked at me in a worried fashion because to them my appetite seemed so small as to run the risk of my expiring at their very table from malnutrition.

Having eaten solidly, the men drove off to join their lodges and parade from their halls to the gathering point at which the main parade would begin. Those who had not had a spread like ours had the opportunity to have sandwiches or burgers before they started walking.

When the parade was over, at around two o'clock, most participants fell on the food tents in the demonstration field where ladies were raising money for various churches by selling sandwiches, cakes and tea. This kept the Orangemen going until at around six they went to their own lodge for a tea of meat and vegetables and piles of potatoes washed down with orange squash, followed by something very sweet and then by coffee and biscuits.

At lunchtime the VIPs – officers and distinguished guests – would have had a dinner in the nearest Orange hall consisting of ham and chicken and lettuce and potato salad and coleslaw and tomatoes and hard-boiled eggs and salad cream and lots of bread and plenty of something sweet to follow. My abiding memory of such dinners and teas is of ladies rushing around anxiously with food or enormous kettles, terrified lest any of their charges might be suffering from hunger or thirst for even a moment.

After all that, the non-teetotal lodges might have a nip or two of whiskey or some beer, while the drinkers in teetotal lodges might head off for a few drinks in the local pub. The serious drinkers would stay there to get plastered and the majority would go home to tea and sandwiches or biscuits before bedtime.

The Orange tooth is so sweet as to conjure up memories of one's own childhood. I sat with a radical, intellectually aggressive, zealously evangelical minister and watched him struggle with his conscience over the issue of a second piece of apple pie, for his wife had put him on a diet. Sitting with an Orangeman who has more gravitas than almost anyone I've ever met, I loved seeing his hand sneaking out almost guiltily to take a chocolate biscuit.

I have a very happy memory of a visit to London by a group of Orangemen over to talk to politicians and the press about parades. Brian Kennaway, Bobby Saulters and I went for a stroll by the Thames and the Grand Master spotted an ice-cream van. As I sat beside them on a bench in the sunshine, licking an ice-cream cornet and watching the delight my companions took in that small indulgence, I remembered what one of the few defenders of Northern Ireland Orangemen had said to me over and over again: 'They want so little. So very, very little.'

Souvenirs

In the field where a big march congregates there will be some souvenir stalls with loyal flags and red-white-and-blue hats and batons and so on, as well as tapes and T-shirts and other paraphernalia. My collection includes tea-towels – William crossing the Boyne, 'Ulster Says No' and a representation of the Union Jack – an apron with a crown over a Red Hand, and Drumcree-related keyrings.

At a big gathering there will be a stall or two selling various accoutrements supporting loyalist paramilitaries. In 1997 the nastiest was a T-shirt inscribed: 'YABBA DABBA DOO ANY FENIAN WILL DO', inspired by the LVF, whose victims had included a Catholic taxi driver who had just graduated in English Literature from Queens and an eighteen-year-old girl shot in the head as she lay in bed beside her Protestant boyfriend.

For republican kitsch, the place to go is the Sinn Féin shop on the Falls Road, where I have bought keyrings featuring Patrick Pearse, and one with the IRA slogan 'Tiochaidh ár lá' ('Our day will come') on one side and a balaclavaed chap with an Armalite on the other, as well as a tea-towel featuring the Irish flag and another with pictures of the signatories of the 1916 proclamation of the Irish Republic. I drew the line at a statue of Gerry Adams.

My favourite is the mad bigots' stall at Scarva, manned by courteous evangelists who with the help of wares like *The Awful Disclosures of Maria Monk*, *The Convent Horror*, *Escape from a Catholic Convent*, *Horrible Lives of the Popes* and *The Scarlet Woman of the Apocalypse* take one on a journey back in time.

Going home

Perhaps the best moment for me, [wrote Alan Minnis, a teacher who comes home from Scotland every year for the Twelfth] is to stand watching the parade reassemble. The colour is overwhelming, the sights and sounds heady enough to sustain me until next year (or at least until Scarva). Of course, somebody who likes the sound of his own voice and has the public speaking appeal of Douglas Hogg is on the platform delaying the proceedings, but that only gives me all the more time to remember exactly who and what I am. And then the evening. To have the fellowship of our meal, to listen to the story-tellers, the singers. And later, to sit with a cool beer with my friends and family and to talk about 'days of yore' or 'What will become of us?'

Drink does for some participants before they ever make it home.

One supreme recollection [wrote Rowel Friers] is of a country lodge returning from another townland where the celebrations had been hosted. When they started out they were led by His Majesty King William on a dapple-grey. William, pointing his sword defiantly heavenward, led his men to battle with an assurance worthy of d'Artagnan. Though hardly historically accurate in every detail, his uniform was acceptable to all but purists. Perhaps one could admit to a certain amount of antipathy towards his work-a-day wellies – without doubt a jarring note. Nevertheless, despite any flaw in his royal raiment, his mind was fixed in the period. Proudly he led his men to glory, and if ever a leader was born, this was he.

The return journey was one of obvious triumph. Flushed from a successful day at the Field, with fresh air, good fellowship and brews, they marched homeward with chins, where possible, held high. Some had their jackets hung nonchalantly over one shoulder. Here and there a tie hung crookedly from an open shirt collar, and an odd sash had changed position – no longer *de rigueur*. The battle had yet again been won and William's conquering heroes were returning. A kaleidoscope of colour – the brilliant uniforms of the bands and the glory of silken banners dancing in zigzag rhythm to the rousing music – added firmness of purpose to the multitude of boots marching muddied from the damp field. In the midst of his warriors, William sat astride his trusty, but now bored, steed. He had dropped back from the lead he held on the outward journey and was showing obvious symptoms of bottle fatigue. His hat sat at a rakish angle on a wig, now worn peek-a-boo style, and with sword pointing earthwards Billy drooped forward, nose almost buried in the horse's mane. A loyal brother on either side of the mount kept steadying hands on His Majesty, thus ensuring that he remained, if not upright, at least mounted. The Prince of Orange had revelled in the bottle, but now neither the papist James nor anything else troubled his happy mind. His Majesty's immortal memory had deserted him, and 1690 to him could just as well have been a phone number.

The historian David Hume is attached to a more sober lodge: 'And then, after the Field and the return parade, they will march back along that country road, wearier this time around, and the band will play a hymn and the National Anthem after they have all lined up outside the hall. And someone will look around at someone else and as sure as anything, say, ''Well, that's the Twelfth over for another year.'' '

'How did you get over the Twelfth?' is what his sister asks a Belfast friend of mine every year. As Catholic children in largely loyalist East Belfast, in the 1950s and '60s they spent every Twelfth in a house with the blinds down, listening to aggressive drumming sounds and fearful of violence when loyalists got drunk. 'I've no difficulty believing that most Orangemen are OK,' observed the apolitical and non-sectarian Eamonn. 'But when you're being beaten up, it's hard to care whether it's by Orangemen, bandsmen or just thuggish hangers-on. It hurts just as much.'

It was around that time that the public servant Maurice Hayes, though Catholic a fan of the Twelfth, began to sense from Catholics in other areas that they saw the marching as a threat, a means of putting them in their place, of letting them know who was boss and that they were in a minority in a society ruled by Protestants and they had better know it and behave themselves. There was annoyance too at the sheer number of marches which kept people in houses, blocked roads, business interfered with, and the further aggravation of party tunes and some 'kick-the-pope' bands which insisted on playing more loudly when passing churches or chapels and the menacing beat of the Lambeg drums.

I wondered to myself why people wanted to march at all, and why others who were annoyed could not just pull down the blinds and refuse to be annoyed?

Hayes's hope for the future is that of all sane people in Northern Ireland: that Orangemen will make more effort to explain themselves to their neighbours and that Catholics will try to understand that Orangeism is a celebration of civil and religious liberty. 'We should be able to hold on to and to encourage the exercise of a tradition which is not only important to many people, and therefore to the rest of us, but which could add to the colour and meaning of life for all.'

It will be necessary, too, for both sides to deal with the thugs that do awful things in their name.

4

The Family Abroad

A loyal band of Orangemen from Ulster's lovely land,
They could not march upon the Twelfth – processions were all banned,
So they flew off to the Middle East this dreadful law to dodge
And they founded in Jerusalem the Arab Orange Lodge.

Big Ali Bey who charmed the snakes he was the first recruit
John James McKeag from Portglenone taught him to play the flute
And as the oul' Pied Piper was once followed by the rats
There followed Ali from the lodge ten snakes in bowler hats.

They made a martial picture as they marched along the shore
It stirred the blood when Ali played 'The Fez my Father Wore'.
And Yussef Ben Mohammad hit the 'Lambeg' such a bash
He scared the living daylights from a camel in a sash.

Now the movement spread both far and wide – there were lodges by the score
The 'Jerusalem Purple Heroes' was the first of many more
The 'Loyal Sons of Djeddah' and 'The Mecca Shining Star'
And the 'Rising Sons of Jericho' who came by motor car.

The banners too were wonderful and some would make you smile
King Billy on his camel as he splashed across the Nile
But the Tyre and Sidon Temperance had the best one of them all
For they had a lovely picture of Damascus Orange Hall.

The Apprentice boys of Amman marched beneath the blazing sun
The Royal Black Preceptory were Negroes every one
And lodges came from Egypt, from the Abu Simbel Falls
And they shouted 'No Surrender' and 'We'll guard old Cairo's walls'.

But when the ban was lifted and the lodges marched at last
The Arabs all decided to march right through Belfast
And they caused a lot of trouble before they got afloat
For they could not get their camels on the bloody Heysham boat.

Now camels choked up Liverpool and camels blocked Stranraer
And the Sheikh of Abu Dhabi came in a bloody great big car
But the 'Easter Magic' LOL they worked a crafty move
They used their magic carpets and flew in to Aldergrove.

When they came to Castle Junction where once stood the wee Kiosk
They dug up Royal Avenue to build a giant mosque

And Devlin says to Gerry Fitt,* 'I think we'd better go,
There's half a million camels coming down from Sandy Row.'

The speeches at the 'field' that day were really something new
For some were made in Arabic and some were in Hebrew
But just as Colonel Gaddafi got up to sing 'The Queen'
I woke up in my bed at home and found it was a dream.
'The Arab Orange Lodge' (Sung to the air: 'The Wearing of the Green')

'THERE'S A BOND THAT ties us together – something that folk have never fully understood,' said Martin Smyth, who in his time as Imperial Grand Master and Imperial Grand President has travelled to all parts of Orangedom. 'One could go to any part of the world and find a relationship immediately. Oh, yes, like any other family, they'll be cantankerous; there'll be folk you might love, but you couldn't like. But it's a family of nations and it's fascinating.'

In 1997, the Irish Grand Lodge invited me to the social functions of the Triennial Imperial Council of the World† which, luckily for me, was that year meeting in Northern Ireland. Established in 1867, the Council has met thirty-nine times at various locations in the strongest Orange countries: Ireland, Scotland, England, Canada, the USA, Australia and New Zealand. In 1997 it was attended by representatives from those countries as well as from Ghana. There was sadness that because of the illness of Emenyo Mawule K. Aboki Essien, the dominating figure in Togo Orangeism as well as Imperial Grand President, there would be no delegates from his country, for it is there the custom that you do not leave someone who might die in your absence. Essien was well-known to many delegates, having visited almost every Orange jurisdiction in his time.

'He is a remarkable character,' observed Martin Smyth to me later, 'with a remarkable fluency in French, which would have been the language of his area, as well as his native language and English. He and

---

* The song dates from early in the Troubles when parades were banned for a time. Paddy Devlin and Gerry Fitt were leaders at the time of the largely Catholic SDLP.

† 'The name certainly has echoes of empire,' said a delegate. 'It's a bit odd that it's called imperial these days, when we've got people here from the United States and from Ghana, which aren't even part of the Commonwealth. They hang on to it for traditional reasons. There was a suggestion some years ago that the name might be modernized and, "No, no, no, you can't touch the name." It was sacrosanct.'

his people have an outward approach that I would like to see more of among our Orange people in Northern Ireland.

'Where we tend to be fatalistic, the Togo Orangemen [who have only a thousand or so members] say: ''There are many hundreds of thousands out there who qualify for membership. We've got to reach them.'' So they're going out to actually work among the people and they've built up a fairly strong social concern as well, which is why the Grand Lodge of Ireland provided them with a minibus, which allows them not just to transport people to meetings but also to go out into different areas of the country with some social work and evangelistic work with the churches.'

It was not the best timing for a Northern Ireland meeting of the Council. Some delegates had arrived early for holidays or to take part in the Rossnowlagh parade and therefore had been in Northern Ireland through the Drumcree build-up as well as the ensuing riots, and had been fending off phone-calls from home. 'Drumcree was reported in the American press,' said the wife of an American delegate, 'and of course they only saw the violence. So my daughter called up and she was very worried and she thought the whole world was going up in smoke over here and the whole country was at war. We're fine. We know things have happened, but we haven't been around it. And of course the people here wouldn't have us going to places that were at all dangerous.'

'The media show only the bad side,' said an Australian delegate. 'My wife was panic-stricken. ''Tell me you're not there,'' she said, meaning Drumcree. ''No,'' I said, ''the only thing we disturbed this morning when we paraded to church was about half-a-dozen cows and a few crows that flew out of a tree as we went past.'' '

However, spirits were generally high. For many of the foreign delegates, to parade in Northern Ireland on the Twelfth and Thirteenth was the achievement of a life-long ambition. 'It was a thrill for me,' said the Australian Grand Secretary. 'Something I always wanted to do. People cheering and waving reminded me of the days when I was a very young member in Sydney and people used to line the streets and wave the Union Jack as well as the Aussie flag and cheer. I felt a little emotional a couple of times.'

He was especially emotional because he had been the one to stop the processing in New South Wales. 'I felt old men were marching when they shouldn't have been and shared the feelings with a few others that we didn't want it on our conscience that someone would collapse in the middle of the parade because they felt they had to march. When I stood up and announced it at the lodge I was visiting, the deputy master cried "Shame, shame". It was a sad and tough decision: there was a long period of silence before someone had to get up and move the inevitable. It was like someone moving to close a lodge. No one wants to have their name down that they moved the motion to close the lodge.' Although there were a few areas showing signs of revival, numbers were down to around one thousand and Victoria was now the only Australian state left with a young enough and large enough Orange population to make a parade viable.

Parades were over in New Zealand, too, I learned. 'It's been a gradual process downward. Auckland must have been one of the last and that would be several years ago. It ended because in July it's winter – that's the main thing. The other time of the year would be November [William's birthday], but it's not the same for members to go out in November as in July. They parade in all weathers here, but in New Zealand, once the rains came tumbling down, that would be it. Many a time July the Twelfth has been a cold, bitterly biting southerly blowing: everybody just goes home.' As in all the Australian states, throughout New Zealand there are church services, dinners and other functions on the Twelfth.

The West African Grand Lodges would have reason to find the New Zealanders wimpish. 'I've paraded and preached in Togo in great heat,' said Martin Smyth. 'I preached in Lomé both in the Presbyterian and Methodist churches and was it a delight! I've never been in a congregation where folk happily danced up to the altar with smiles on their faces.'

'We are very keen on parading,' said one of the delegates from Ghana, and recommended I get hold of the video of a particular celebratory weekend. This shows a procession, a solemn ceremony and then a parade which begins gravely and ends with the formally dressed and be-sashed men and the women in long, white frocks swaying jollily to increasingly up-beat music. Throughout, there are plenty of biblical and Williamite accessories.

Although as in Australia and New Zealand it is declining, with now fewer than a quarter of the 100,000 membership it had at its peak, early this century, the Canadian Orange Order still holds parades. 'The public image in Canada is not much different than it is here,' said its Deputy Grand Master. 'Our Grand Secretary was talking to a friend of his last night and their opinion of the Orange parade in Toronto, which was bigger than the year before, was that it was nothing but a problem for the police. There were about three thousand overall. I don't think we're a problem: it's the newspapers say we're a problem. Our parade impedes traffic, like the St Patrick's Day parade. But the Orange Order is perceived differently. All the press say is that we celebrate a 300-year-old battle where Protestant King William defeated Catholic King James.

'I got rather upset with one of the press and I said: "Do we have the right of assembly in this country?" "Oh, yes, yes." And I said: "Do you have the right to print what you like without being libellous?" "Oh, yes, yes." "Well, where do you think you got those rights? That's what William established for a press that didn't have rights. Protestants didn't have right of free assembly. That was what you gained. We don't celebrate the battle of the Boyne. What we commemorate is what it established."'

The Toronto parade has been going for 175 years and while in many places Orangepeople just have a day out or a picnic in celebration, there are several other parades across the country. 'The ladies' lodges participate and we have bands. Like Belfast, but not the rest of Northern Ireland, in Toronto we have a traditional King William leading the parade on a horse. It's getting harder and harder because of regulations. It's now a very expensive proposition to put a person on a horse on the streets of Toronto, with insurance and liability policies and the rest of it. About four years ago we had an incident when the horse got frightened and it almost went through a plate-glass window into a restaurant. Fortunately the rider was a trained horseman and got it under control.'

The temperature being around 90 degrees, only traditionalists wear bowler hats: the normal outfit is white shirt and tie and slacks and collarettes. 'We're informal, like here. Kids join in. Towards the end of the parade, more will be joining their fathers or grandfathers; my daughters used to join me when they were young. But some think it's a horrible thing to have kids running in and out of a parade area. We used to have four to six mounted police ahead of King William, so that would be a problem, with little children frightening the horses. But the parade is a family tradition and gives kids some sense of being part of what you are.'

Otherwise, the Canadians follow the same traditions as in Northern Ireland. 'We more or less end up in a park and then several lodges go back to their own halls and have do's or functions in the evenings – barbecues and dances throughout the whole country.' In Providence, in Newfoundland – the only province where the Twelfth is a holiday – their big event is a church parade which takes place when Grand Lodge sits.

'I love parades,' said Betty, the wife of an American delegate. 'I did the whole Belfast one. Another woman I know from New Zealand and I wanted to be with our men but we couldn't walk with them because they were dignitaries. Mary and I went all the way out and back.' 'Fourteen miles!' said her husband, Fred. 'Our longest parade in Pennsylvania is probably three miles. We go to a picnic area and amusement park.'

The consumption of alcohol in Belfast had shocked them both; their lodges are dry, even for socials. 'We don't drink beer in public in the US,' observed Betty. 'Most of the time we have open-container laws. And you won't find them drinking beer on the sidewalk unless you're in a place like New Orleans. And I saw an awful lot of beer-drinking in Belfast. But still, I had an awfully good time.'

The Scots bands, of course, made their contribution. Said one Scots delegate: 'Some of the Scots coming over for the parade terrify me on the ferries. I think Belfast is where some of our more ferocious bands go. And they tend to go to the harder areas. Our bandspeople see the trip to Belfast as two or three days holiday, get stuck into the beer on the way down. Go on the ferry and you suddenly find yourself surrounded by these obnoxious people and you say, "Who are these people?" And find that they are your friends, supposedly.'

'Scarva's more like ours than Belfast – more family-orientated,' said Fred. 'Scarva was marvellous,' said Betty. 'I've never seen so many people in my life. And you know there was no controlling presence, no policemen. They must have been somewhere. It just seemed like everybody was having a good time and it was a very family occasion.'

'At the most there are couple of parades a year in Pennsylvania,' said Fred. 'Normally the Twelfth, and in our case, Labor Day. We'd have in our area about seven lodges, counting some of the women's lodges. Our route has got shorter and shorter because the police don't want the commercial area blocked even for a short time.

'There are three pipe bands in the area: the Ulster Pipe Band, which a number of years ago was North American champion, the Washington Pipe Band and the Cameron Pipers. And they're all quite good. So on Labor Day they'll come and generally put on concerts. And they can really make things swing: they're mainly young people. Once there were five, but now three are more than enough with the number of lodges.

'We have banners for each lodge. One is historical: George Washington. The rest of them would be more biblical. Pretty old banners now. Some of them have been renewed over the years and if they're not out to many parades and are well taken care of it's not too bad.

'We have probably as many women in the Orange Order as men,' he added, 'and they're an indispensable part. Interestingly, when we went to Scarva we marched with them right behind the lead men. And there were a number of women who had come over – international visitors – and they marched and I was right behind them. And they got the most applause. There were about four or five ranks of women in front of us marching, so maybe there might have been twenty or so. But all of a sudden I realized that you're not used to seeing women marching. But in the States the women, as I remember it, always marched and they would always wear white dresses and hats and gloves. They would carry their own banners.'*

Scotland has managed to slow its decline. Numbers are disputed, but a conservative estimate is that they are down from perhaps 60,000 twenty years ago to 50,000 now. They have in the region of 150 bands, of whom two-thirds are flute and the rest accordion. To allow maxium participation in the Northern Ireland Twelfth, their four separate parades are held on the two Saturdays before it. 'Orangeism in Scotland, certainly in modern times, is almost completely working class,' observed one delegate. 'There isn't the same cross-class perspective you get in Ireland.'

---

* A few months before I interviewed Betty and Fred, I read in the *Irish People*, the Irish American NORAID weekly, the following column by Father Des Wilson, a devout Belfast republican:

> The Orange secret society is led by clergy. Its marches are processions to and from Episcopalian and Presbyterian churches. Protestant churches in America, particularly the Presbyterians, have encouraged these religious secret societies that march through areas where their drunkenness, obscenity and abuse are offensive to their neighbours, who may be Catholic or Jewish, or Muslim, or other faiths or none . . .
>
> There are a thousand marches a year in the northeast of Ireland. More than nine-tenths of these are by loyalists, who use the whole summer to flaunt rudeness, ignorance and their loyalty to church and state.
>
> In many cases, heavily armed RUC riot squads escort them through areas where democrats want to live in peace without such hatred and are not allowed to. Presbyterian, Catholic and Episcopalian church leaders in the United States and other countries should surely be asked now once again whether their approval of these obscene rituals can be tolerated any longer. Church leaders and others who have supported the most appalling secret societies for years must some day leave their port and come to their senses. It is particularly unacceptable that church leaders in the United States and other countries should uphold from a safe distance religious societies which hurt our people with such viciousness.

'I'm not sure parading is ownership,' said another Scot, musing on the contentious parades issue. 'It's as much rooted in the British perspective of a free society, of the right of free assembly and the right of free passage down the Queen's highway. I'm not saying there aren't some who go out saying, "I'm going to show them," but for the most part the institution's view is there should be no no-go areas – in the same way that back at the time the Provos were setting up no-go areas against British troops and police it was important to remind them that this is society and there should be no no-go areas.

'If that is seen to be confrontational I don't think that's where it starts out from. It's simply this desire to show that the highways and byways are for free passage, which is considered to be a question of British liberty. And of course the right of free assembly is something that is almost enshrined within British society. If you go back to the Chartists, the right of free assembly, of protest, was there. The government tried to suppress that at its peril. There were certain times they almost provoked revolution by taking a very hard-line attitude.

'I can see why people find it occasionally intimidating, but it's not just as simple as that.'

In parts of England the decline is being reversed: the membership is holding at around 6,000. All the English provinces have their own traditional parades. In Liverpool there are many local parades, but the biggest is the Twelfth, when they go through the city to Southport and walk back in the evening, arriving home around 9.30. Only Liverpool walks on the Twelfth itself: other parades are staggered through the year.

'Sometimes there are objections,' reported the English Grand Secretary, 'from the me-too lefties that idolize Sinn Féin – the people they'd like to be if they had the bottle. And they've got to go through this mating ritual of opposition to Orange parades: they're usually bussed in from some polytechnic.

'It varies from area to area how the locals view us. Some are quite positive: Portsmouth are very, because of the naval tradition, I think, and the idea that you walk behind the union flag and you show a modicum of discipline. Some people look at us and wonder where we've come from but that's because there's not the awareness of Orangeism in England – because of the media to some extent. I remember, for instance, being in Scotland about twenty years ago. Meself and me wife were on our way to take part in the Lanarkshire parade which had about 25,000 people on it and as we passed through Edinburgh where we were staying, we encountered a demonstration by Gingerbread – the single parent group – of less than 100 people. When we got back to the hotel at night and watched the TV in our room, the Gingerbread demonstration was covered by the local TV; the Orange didn't get a mention.'

What makes Liverpool parade stand out most from Ulster parades is that there are vast quantities of participating children and very striking clothes. Women strive more for smartness than respectability and girls are dressed in long elaborate white frocks just like those worn by their Catholic counterparts for their first communion. And as well as that there are forty or so Williams-and-Marys walking hand in hand amid the parade. Almost all are girls: only a handful of boys are prepared to risk being laughed at for parading in fancy dress. In the video I saw, there was a black, female William: about 10 per cent of the Liverpool membership are black.

It was fortunate for my researches that, as critics of the workings of the Council complain, very little business gets done, mainly because the hosts are always trying to out-do each other and give delegates an even better time than did their predecessors three years previously: 'The excursions and socials have to keep up with the Joneses of three years ago,' a business-oriented Orangeman remarked tartly.

Add to this tradition the almost fanatical hospitality of the Northern Irish and the domestic skills of the womenfolk and you face a serious challenge. The private business meetings took three hours a day maximum during the week of the Triennial Council: the rest of the time was spent on coach trips, on parading on the Twelfth and Thirteenth, on sightseeing and on food, food, food. Jim Molyneaux talks of how in his travels as Imperial Sovereign Master of the Royal Black Institution he has to beg his hosts to spare him the sightseeing. 'I can look at pictures of the places. I don't have to go and look at them. Just leave me by myself.' This could be one of the reasons why Molyneaux is very slim for an Orangeman in a sedentary occupation, for sightseeing is always accompanied by food.

Hospitality was laid on in church halls, Orange halls and other places with fraternal links. I remember the 'spread' in a Church of Ireland hall in County Fermanagh, prepared by the ladies of the parish for around 150 people. Hundreds of hours of work had gone into making sausage rolls and cakes and mounds of sandwiches and puddings and there were, of course, vats of tea and jugs of orange squash. ('The hospitality is wonderful,' said a delegate. 'But what I wouldn't do for coffee! And as for a beer!') And at the end, as always, there was the warm and unpretentious speech from, on this occasion, Bobby Saulters, the Grand Master. Like all such speeches, it was along the lines of: 'I must thank you on behalf of us all for being so kind as to welcome us into your hall, and I must say a heartfelt thank you to the ladies for their kindness in laying on such a lovely spread.' I observed to the minister afterwards that I couldn't imagine many churches in England where the 'ladies' would be prepared to put in this kind of work, and he said anxiously, 'Please don't tell them.'

It was, I think, about two hours later that we were decanted into Warren House at Donaghadee in North Down – a holiday house primarily for members of the Junior Orange Association – where we were offered tea, orange squash and lots of biscuits. The *pièce de résistance*, though, was tea in County Tyrone at Greenmount Lodge, a guest-house owned by the then County Grand Master, Tom Reid, which is renowned not just through the Orange community but far and wide as a place where you get good food and plenty of it. You don't get alcohol, although you can bring your own, for although Tom is not teetotal, as principled Presbyterians he and his wife Louie think it wrong to make money out of alcohol.

So about 160 of us arrived in the great courtyard where four barbeques were manned by various Reids, relations and friends, all of whom I knew, so I wandered about inspecting the expanses of beefburgers, steaks and sausages. 'What would you do if some of them proved to be vegetarian?' I inquired of George. He grinned. 'We considered the possibility, but thought it too unlikely to cater for. We *are* talking about Orangemen and women after all. Though we have chicken for the faint-hearted.'

Used as I was by then to Orange catering, I reeled when I discovered that everyone was being given a three-quarter-pound sirloin steak, a large beefburger and two sausages before being ushered inside to help themselves to baked potatoes and salads. 'Seven steers died for this coach trip,' said Henry. And I won't go into details about the forty-two salvers of sweets, for which Louie Reid is famous.

It was on the second coach trip with Council delegates that I got hit by a simple truth about the Orange Order, which is also true of the Black. These organizations – routinely denounced as bigoted, fascist and the rest of it – are in a completely unselfconscious way both international and non-racist. When they talk in their literature about the worldwide 'Orange family', they mean it. The trouble is that, as usual, in ordinary speech their language is so old-fashioned and politically incorrect that a casual observer would think their views are racist: it does not help that in some rural parts people still talk about 'darkies'. Yet I realized that when it comes to members of the brotherhood, Orangemen see only the colour Orange. If ET were to walk into an Orange gathering wearing a collarette, he would be greeted with: 'Come on in, brother. You are very welcome. Do you know now, we never realized there was a lodge on Mars.' And if that sounds too fanciful, consider the story of the black American soldiers who arrived in Northern Ireland during the war. Isolated because their white comrades-in-arms would not socialize with them, they were elated when one of them saw an advertisement for a Black Ball. The entire platoon presented themselves at the Orange Hall on the appointed night. Despite their absence of sashes, the hospitable Black brethren welcomed them in; they made the lodge their social HQ for the rest of their tour of duty. Of course, being black Americans, the odds are they were Protestant.

Not surprisingly, one of the accusations that most bewilders Orange or Blackmen is that of being racist. 'How can they think we're racist?' asked an aggrieved Australian. 'We've never been racist in New South Wales; we've had Aborigines, Maoris, Solomon Islanders and we had lodges in Papua New Guinea at one time, but they've now gone out of existence. Everyone's been welcome.' New Zealand has Orange Maoris too, and when the Canadians came over for the Glorious Revolution Tercentenary Celebrations in 1989, the stars of their delegation on the great parade were the Mohawk Indians – even more improbable Canadian brethren than the Italians of the Giuseppe Garibaldi Orange Lodge. 'They compare us to the Ku Klux Klan!' said Martin Smyth. 'The Order never developed in the southern states, because they did not want to appear to be anti-black and didn't want to work the fertile ground of what would have been the Bible belt where there was slavery. They did have occasional blacks, but they were in the northern states.' And it is believed that what finished off Orangeism in South Africa was its refusal to operate a colour bar.

Like the inter-class relationships in the lodge, the international relationships are conducted on a simple principle: your brethren are your brethren, whoever they are. 'English-speaking and French-speaking, black and white, employer and employee all call themselves brothers,' is the slogan all Orangemen agree on. If your brothers or sisters come from somewhere abroad they may have strange ways, but that's all right, because that's just their way. When for instance, the Scots women on the coach, who had an earthy line in urban humour, produced a few witticisms redolent with sexual innuendo, men from County Fermanagh who would never tell such a joke themselves, and who certainly never would have heard a lady do so, merely smiled benignly, for that was the way of the Scottish sisters.

There were communication problems with the two delegates from Ghana, because, as it was explained to me early on, and as I confirmed for myself, 'They're a bit hard to make out.' A Ghanaian accent is as impenetrable to the Northern Irish as must be most Northern Irish accents to Ghanaians. But where they could communicate they did and where they couldn't, they just smiled at each other.

I sat beside the Ghanaian Grand Master on the coach trip back home after a day of eating and sightseeing. Our host decided we should have a sing-song. He chose, rather bizarrely, to start the ball rolling with 'The Wild Rover', a song about various kinds of excess which could hardly have been less appropriate to people with such blameless pleasures. But he sang it with verve, and the locals and the English and Scots joined in enthusiastically. Few of the other delegates seemed to know it, so the next choice was part of the *lingua franca* – songs of the First World War. The Ghanaian Grand Master seemed to know 'Pack up Your Troubles in Your Old Kit Bag' and 'It's a Long Way to Tipperary' as well as any of the rest of us.

There was a pause at this juncture as a failure of inspiration hit everyone on the coach. I searched around my mental songbook for something appropriate and came up with 'Daisy, Daisy, Give Me Your Answer, Do', which was a great success with 95 per cent of the delegates, but was clearly not big in Ghana. However, by the end, Cephas had learned the tune and some of the words.

'I always find this group very welcoming,' said Betty from the USA. 'They let me go out and do my own thing and they're always there to welcome me back when I return.' For Betty, like most of the delegates and their wives, the great joy in these trips to meetings of the Imperial Council is the fellowship of ordinary but like-minded people from differ-ent countries. Many of the foreign delegates I met had barely a clue about what was going on in Northern Ireland. They were just conscious that these people they liked so much were unpopular for reasons they couldn't quite grasp; the more reflective concluded that the gap between perception and reality was so great that the institution was clearly failing to put its case across to the media. 'As an organization,' said someone from mainland Britain, 'we're awful at PR. Ours is a most peculiar organization in many people's minds, but it doesn't deserve to be demonized the way it has. We're just very bad at selling ourselves. In some ways it's a reflection of our extreme religious commitment: justice will prevail, good always triumphs over evil. It's all very comforting, but sometimes justice comes too late. They should appoint a full-time spokesman.'

'This is the crazy thing about the way the media treat this place,' said an Australian delegate, who had left Northern Ireland as a very young man and whose eighty-eight-year-old mother still lived in County Fermanagh. 'I went to a small church parade in my home village last Sunday week. We're on a farm. Now if the media could only encapsulate what happens in my tiny little area. For instance, the weather's been unfavourable in Fermanagh, but there were a couple of days during the week that were brilliant. The sun was shining, it was about 26/27 degrees, and even my son and I could put shorts on like we normally do. My brother had these two big fields of hay that needed doing at a great deal of knots. A guy had been hired to wrap up the hay and one by one neighbours turned up with their tractors and trailers because we had to put it in the shed in case it rained again. There were ten tractors there – five Catholics and five Prods – all pitching in because we'd better get this in. They were putting these big bales on trailers, racing them back up to the home farm, stacking them in the shed (the milking time's coming and that's a critical time on a dairy farm – they're all dairy farms). They're racing against the clock, they're racing against the weather, they're racing against everything. And in the middle of it all my sister-in-law comes down there and she's got tea and sandwiches and cakes to keep them going. And I thought this is great. There are Orange people there, there are nationalist people there – all working for the common good of helping their neighbour. I look back at that and I think: "Isn't this what it's all about?" But we get evil people on both sides and that is not in their agenda. And it's not good copy.

'And these people thought nothing of it. "Oh, that's nothing. Davy (who's Catholic) has a field of hay for tomorrow so we'll be there." And at the end of the week Davy'll go into one church and my brother into another. Nothing antagonistic.'

Ian's wife is Australian. 'Three years ago on holiday we were here, the first time we had all the family together. And she said the same thing: "Oh, the Irish are so generous and so kind. They'll give anything of themselves. And to see what they do to each other.'' And if she can't understand it and she's married to me, for goodness sake, how *can* it be explained? What I think is the root of it all is power. The poor people who are caught in the middle are the innocents with little say. They're the ones who get hurt, unfortunately. They're not nice people, those who use Drumcree as an excuse to create havoc and mayhem. And they do not help our cause in any way whatsoever.'

What all the visitors were clear about was that Orangemen have essential shared values: a belief in God, in the truth of the Reformed religion, in civil and religious liberty, in loyalty to their state, in the importance of family life and in their mutual brotherhood. It would be the normal thing to look up a local lodge when travelling abroad. 'If you've someone with local knowledge, they'll show you round. You can make instant friendships which might take you so much longer to generate otherwise. At home, we'll sometimes get a call from someone through a contact. Some kid from overseas is hitchhiking or whatever. You just give some guidance and a meal and maybe a bed for the night. All this friendship thing and the family thing that we emphasize, it's a great help to people who are worrying about their children. You call and say: ''They're fine, and a credit to you.'' '

There are, of course, many differences of emphasis between countries. 'Look at the word Protestant,' said an Australian. 'Lots think that means we've got to protest all the time, but from my understanding of either the Greek or Latin background, ''*pro*'' means ''for'' and the ''test'' part is ''testes'' or ''testus'' which means ''testify''. If you look on it in that sense, it's testifying ''for'' Protestantism. And this is what we try to do in New South Wales. Rather than saying: ''We're agin this, that or something else,'' we say, ''What are you for?'' If you can come up with some positive things, then you're looked upon in a much kinder light by a lot of people: ''at least we know what they're for.'' '

'Over the past number of years,' said an American delegate, 'we've changed a number of things that were in our constitution, in our rules and regulations. Basically we've gone to a pro-Protestant stand and taken out all the anti kind of stuff that has been there for years. We have a multi-religious country so we're not faced with a Catholic–Protestant problem. What we now push is: ''I am now and always have been and always will be a Protestant.'' You're still not supposed to marry an RC, but it's been taken out of the rules.'

In Scotland, which is still predominantly Catholic and Presbyterian

[Church of Scotland] rather than multi-cultural, a delegate had high hopes for the Orange Order. 'As the Church of Scotland adopts a more ecumenical* perspective, there is obviously a reaction; some people take up other attitudes and want to ally themselves with the Orange Order to make clear what Protestantism is.' There is a problem. 'There are too many mindless bigots around us, perhaps because folk like myself have failed in their duty to educate them properly. When I was young I was caught up in that.

'I now understand fully my Protestant heritage and it's confirmed me in my Orangeism. I've left behind what was the inherited family background and I'm doing it as a matter of conviction. And it was through communication with well-versed Orangemen who were in it for all the right reasons. I pay tribute to them. They at least in part led me to my call to the ministry and they developed in me a sense of my Christian faith that was very much rooted in Protestantism, because I had some of that from my own family. My mother wasn't a church-goer, but I was sent to Sunday School and Boys' Brigade and Bible class.

'But the Orange Order, I think, honed that. The lodge I joined, the master was a Baptist, the secretary a Salvation Army retired officer, the treasurer was a Free Churchman, the man who took me under his wing was an elder in the Church of Scotland, David Bryce, the past Grand Secretary, who was also an elder in the Church of Scotland, was a member of that lodge. And all these forces worked together to let me know the Christian basis of this organization I had joined and what was expected of me. You'd have to talk to them, but I think they'd say it worked. There are the two sides.'

'My lodge found its role finally,' said an Englishman, 'in being a body of Protestants in the true religious sense who wanted to look at Protestantism, its doctrines and its history and to try to say, "What does

---

* Many liberal Catholics and Anglicans believe that anyone who is not ecumenical is a bigot, a view which is itself bigoted. To the evangelical, ecumenism represents an attempt to dilute religions by searching for the lowest common denominator. 'The ecumenical movement is a sort of "hurray" world: everyone says "hurray", observed an English Orangeman. 'I am not ecumenical,' says Brian Kennaway, a Presbyterian clergyman who works closely with his Catholic counterpart to achieve communal harmony. 'I will not share religious services with non-Protestants. But I am tolerant of all religions and will utterly support the right of any man to go to the place of worship of his choice.' Kennaway was one of a delegation of Orangemen who went to Harryville to challenge a group of demonstrators – mainly from the break-away Independent Orange Order – who were harassing Catholics as they went to mass, in revenge for a parade ban in a nearby village.

this actually mean?'' rather than being in reaction to something else. ''What are we?'' If there were nothing external as a threat, ''What would we still be?'' '

To these religiously-minded delegates, as to so many observers, it was clear that what had kept Ulster Orangeism from moving beyond anti-Catholicism was the ever-present threat posed by republicans. As a Northern Ireland Orangeman put it: 'We'd abandon our siege mentality, if they'd lift the bloody siege.' The republican movement continues to be the driving force in keeping the Orange Order defiantly conservative. Some Orangemen want the Grand Lodge of Ireland to change its rules in line with those of the USA, but frightened people do not make radical leaps and the pace of change is slowed by the enemy.

'We don't have the same problems as all the other jurisdictions have,' remarked Fred. 'The African lodges are lucky they have survived their governments. Australians and Canadians have their problems. Generally, if you don't have any problems, you don't have any great reason for membership outside of being rather social and keeping an eye on things. We have a very strong section of our constitution on the separation of church and state and are very strong in favour of the public school system. America is much less polarized than here, for instance, because of the strength of the public schools.'

'I would think at this particular time in history if you said in company in the US that you were an Orangeman, very few people would actually know what you were talking about unless you were in particular areas. If you were in an area that was originally settled by a lot of Irish RCs, they would probably know what you were talking about. Canadians generally know what you're talking about, because they've been used to the Order. A lot of people have had grandparents and great-grandparents who belonged to the Order.' There were few members now: 'It's basically concentrated in Massachusetts, Connecticut, NY, Pennsylvania and California.

'If you go back seventy or a hundred years there were lodges all over and they were big big numbers, but as the immigration dropped and Irish Protestants assimilated, then you didn't have these people coming into the lodges. The difference between the Americans and the Commonwealth countries is that you don't pledge allegiance to the Queen, so there's a different flavour of Orangeism in the US. It was really more of: welcome the immigrant in, give him a familiar place, help him find jobs – somewhere where there was always somebody to welcome you.' It was mainly blue-collar; Fred's father, a chauffeur, had met his wife at an Orange social.

Dwindling numbers had heralded the approaching end of the US Orange Order, when the Internet came to the rescue. 'Within the last four years, we have people joining from all over the country. They're joining from places where there's no lodge – they might be 1,000 miles from a lodge – but they're picking up on the Internet. The first thing a lot of them picked up was the Grand Lodge of Ireland site. They're surfing the Internet and all of a sudden they see "Orange", and they say, "Gee, my grandfather, my great-grandfather, was an Orangeman", and then they look into it.'

A Chicago schoolteacher who said, 'I used to love to wear Orange on St Paddy's Day,' discovered from the Internet that there were still Orange people in the USA. 'He came all the way from Chicago to Boston to be initiated, went back and created a Webpage for us and he's had at least 14,000 hits. So we're picking members up that way.'

An innovation is the formation of 'what we call societies of other people who are interested'. The first were in Georgia, 'one an executive, one an attorney. They invited me to where they met and they had this room at the back of the Sixpenny Inn and they had this big portrait of William of Orange they'd commissioned and they had all Orange regalia and they met basically as a club. There weren't a lot of them to start with but they go out to all the Scottish highland games of which we have quite a number throughout the States and they're promoting the Orange society to people that have an Ulster heritage going back a couple of hundred years.' Other developments are the Tennessee Orange Cultural Society and the Californian High Desert Orange Cultural Society. 'So we're getting a sort of different brand – not a lodge. You get all these people who agree with you but the lodge system doesn't seem to be what they're interested in.'

Between proscription, enmity from the churches and accusations of witchcraft, Ghana and Togo have certainly had problems, but despite a small membership there is intense enthusiasm. 'The chap who acted as interpreter for me when I was in Togo worked with the Gideons,' said Martin Smyth. 'He was a member of the Order and he found that because I was there as Imperial Master but also was an MP, interpreting for me in different places opened doors for him and he was able to spread the scriptures in areas that he hadn't been able to get into.'

'I discovered a rather fascinating thing. There were two neighbouring villages. One was still in abject poverty. The other, not that far distant, was comparatively thriving. But the tidiness of it, compared with the other, stood out a mile. The one was the centre of a Protestant witness. The other was the centre of an RC witness – where the church comes to be the dominant centre with everything going to the church without transforming the village. So one of the reasons some people wanted to convert was when they saw this village prospering. That was market forces at work.'

(It has to be said that there are excellent practical reasons why this should be the case. First, Protestants are in favour of birth control. Secondly, the old Protestant-ethic notions of sobriety, self-reliance, hard work and thrift make for prosperity.)*

Like the Americans, the Canadians are committed to a non-sectarian public school system. They worry too about Quebec separatism and they fear an attempt to get rid of the monarch. In Australia, the Order is under pressure from ecumenically-minded Protestant churches who ban them from their church parades because of perceived anti-Catholicism. More important is the campaign to get rid of the monarchy, which both the Australian and New Zealand Orange oppose root and branch. Like Canada and Australia, New Zealand goes in for a great deal of charitable work and social activity, and manages decline, for there, as elsewhere, fraternal organizations are going out of fashion.

England and Scotland continue to hold the line on the crown and the Bible and the maintenance of the United Kingdom, but, being so close,

---

* On a personal note, for this reminiscence caused me to brood, the more time I spend with Irish Protestants the more I see the stark differences between them and the Irish Catholic culture in which I grew up. Our priests were celibate; their ministers had families to rear. We were taught to admire mystics and martyrs; they expected people to behave like normal, responsible people despite being exceptionally religious. A biblical reference my culture much appreciated was: 'Consider the lilies of the field, how they grow; they toil not, neither do they spin', whereas a Protestant would be drawn to 'By their fruits ye shall know them'. We identified with Mary, who listened to Jesus, and we laughed at poor old Martha, who was doing all the catering and earned only a rebuke. The political heroes held up to us to venerate had voluntarily died in a hopeless bid to destroy the state; theirs had fallen in a struggle to defend the crown.

Is it any wonder the two tribes have found each other so unsympathetic?

As I finished this note, a Presbyterian Orangeman rang up and I read it to him. 'Perceptive,' he said, and then giggled. 'But you should add a similarity. The nearest to the Roman Catholic Church, which produced a papal bull saying that outside its church there was no redemption, is Paisley's Free Presbyterian Church, which takes the same view of itself and opposes the fatal errors of the apostate Presbyterian Church.'

are much preoccupied with Northern Ireland and have problems with unwanted supporters. England has to exercise eternal vigilance to ward off the British National Party (BNP). In 1997 a gaggle of fascists turned up in Portsmouth in support of the Orange Order, who found themselves in the end trying to stop warfare between Sinn Féin supporters and the BNP. 'You can't stop people from standing on a pavement,' said Mike Phelan, 'but when it comes to membership, the Orange Order has been aware of the attention of these people and on the whole we do a very good job of keeping them out. If anybody's known about they're kept out or they're thrown out. And the ones who survive are those who keep such low profiles as to be ineffective anyway.' After the Anglo-Irish Agreement, rows over tactics resulted in about 10 per cent of the Orange Order – mostly the rougher element – affiliating with the Independent Orange Order in Northern Ireland, but they have almost vanished now. When the Westminster branch of the Apprentice Boys was set up, one of its founding principles was a determination to keep out neo-Nazis.

'We had one awful occasion about twenty years ago,' said the Scottish Grand Master, 'when we had a serious problem at Grand Lodge. There was a real tussle between the hotheads who wanted the institution in Scotland to be overtly connected with the paramilitaries and the others who said, "No, this just isn't the way we should go."

'The hotheads were sorted out, there was legislation put in place and it remains to this day that anybody who is in membership of the Scottish institution and is discovered to have paramilitary connections – covert or otherwise is how it's put – then he's expelled. That still happens. It's one of the reasons why there is now an independent institution in Scotland which tends to be composed of expelled members of the official institution. So yes, there are bigots, but they're not the cream of the institution. They don't rise to the top. They're not too many in my ken. I know they're there, but they don't drive the organization.

'The institution in Ireland also tries to distance itself. The problem is that when you totally distance yourself, you also take yourself out of the area of being able to wield any influence . . .

'I was quoted in the *Edinburgh Evening News* as saying that I've never approved of leaders of the Scottish institution coming to Northern Ireland, saying some inflammatory things and then going back to the safety of Scotland. If you don't live here, you really don't appreciate the whole situation. It's difficult for me to understand how there is a role or a place for any kind of Protestant paramilitary organization. If you're a unionist, it follows that any kind of paramilitary activity is pitting yourself against the police and the crown forces.'

Apart from political concerns, there are differences between jurisdictions on Orange and Black ceremonies, rituals and numbers of degrees and so on. 'I've seen rituals in Scotland, England and Ireland and they all do them slightly differently,' said a delegate. 'But most of them are biblically-oriented stories – some of them played out differently. Togo and Ghana participated in an initiation down in England in 1988. That was very funny because they had them standing there when the candidate – of course, all your candidates are blindfolded on their degrees – and when they took them off their eyes there were these black men from Ghana and Togo they weren't expecting.'

'Probably the principles and the main reason for being in the Orange hasn't altered in other countries,' said Ian. 'It's interpretation that brings a local flavour to it. Some of the workings of our lodges would be unique to Australia, because they would have no relevance to Ireland or Canada or the US. Say countries without the Queen as head of state would have a different oath of allegiance and so forth than we would in Australia or West Africa. But the basic beliefs and principles that are the bedrock of our order wouldn't change: we're a Christian organization that was founded way back in the dim and distant past.'

The biggest difference concerns the role of women in the organizations. I was sitting one day in 1997 having lunch/dinner in an Orange Hall with several other guests from England and the Republic of Ireland (for, in some respects, some good PR work is at last going on), when one of the southern journalists remarked that I was the only female guest. He suggested to Brian Kennaway, frequently denounced by brethren as a dangerous radical and modernizer, that it would do wonders for the Orange image if Orangewomen were brought on to public platforms.

Brian looked greatly alarmed: 'They have their own organization. Completely separate.' 'But hardly any of them parade and they're almost as peripheral as the juniors,' I pointed out. 'Couldn't you at least think about appearing with them on public platforms?' 'No, no, no. It's a separate organization completely. Couldn't do that.' 'Why not mixed lodges?' I asked mischievously. 'They have them abroad.' 'They have what!?'

When he had recovered, we explored the delicate subject further and then took pity on him and let the matter drop. In fact, the picture is not as bad as he feared. While heretical notions are being floated in Canada and Scotland, only in West Africa, New Zealand and Australia are mixed lodges found. 'Here, they're horrified with what we do in the Antipodes,' said an Australian. ' ' "You've ladies!?'' We've ladies in charge, for goodness' sake. They're doing a wonderful job. "Oh, we couldn't have that. We couldn't have women in the place.'' It's a 1950s mindset. If they were honest with themselves, it's that they want to get away from women. We couldn't survive without our ladies, because if a guy's got to drive two or three hours and his wife can't come and she's got to do the same to get to her women's meeting, it doesn't make any logical sense whatsoever.'

'One of the blocks on mixed lodges is the male bonding,' said a Scot. 'It's almost like that male night out. If you don't go to the pub and play darts and slurp beer, where else do you go for that male bonding? The Orange lodges and the Masons in Scotland – even more so probably in the Orange Order – is that male bonding, however you dress it up. And for that reason they're reluctant to let women in. And there's also the fear that if you let them in, the business will get reduced to teacups, which is even more boring than repairing the roof of the hall. But I think it's only a matter of time before women have a more prominent role.'

This sort of issue is not discussed at Council meetings. 'Each Grand Lodge is autonomous,' I was told, 'and the Triennial is only to promote Orangeism, to promote Protestanism and maybe to coordinate rituals. In no case would they interfere with a Grand Lodge. They don't talk through or swap ideas.' 'The Orange organization worldwide isn't effective,' said someone else. 'It's just a collection of autonomous Grand Lodges. They're not subordinate one to the other and the only real link is the Triennial Council. So they can't come up with anything very coherent. They have committees, but they are not geared to getting to grips with anything – they're much too formal. It's all very frustrating.'

Being blessed with one decision-making body – a central committee representative of all the jurisdictions – the Royal Black Institution operates far more efficiently. There is a maximum of two representatives from each jurisdiction. Where the overseas people find it inconvenient to come to Black HQ in Lurgan, they have two locals who act as their ambassadors. 'If you have a Ballymena man representing New Zealand, for instance,' explained Jim Molyneaux, 'and you're trying to alter a rule or something, he will say, "Hold on, Sovereign Grand Master, have you thought of the impact of this on New Zealand, where the distances are so much greater?'' And then people start asking, "What do you see as the logical way to tackle this as far as NZ is concerned?'' And the

Canadian representative will chime in, ''Canada couldn't wear that because you have two provincial grand chapters, one in Newfoundland and one in British Columbia, therefore they're further apart than from Brownlow House to Newfoundland.'' All of that's transmitted immediately to the jurisdiction concerned and then they have the Grand Council that meets on the same day later on and this is all reported back to them and then they finalize it.'

The Apprentice Boys are different again, being just a collection of clubs under the General Committee in Derry, which consists of the parent clubs, each of which can open branches anywhere else in the world. While in some geographically distinct areas some clubs may form a committee to liaise in order to avoid clashing events or whatever, they are informal and voluntary. 'Some amalgamated committees went through a rocky time around 1988,' said Mike Phelan, 'when there was a disagreement within the movement about applying for funds from international bodies. The people in Londonderry were examining the possibility, but some amalgamated committees were objecting to it and demanding structural reforms. And our Westminster club said, ''If you join something, you know what you're joining. If you don't like it, you don't join. Once you've joined, you've accepted it.'' And we said it's the ABs of Londonderry – not the ABs of Belfast, Glasgow or anywhere else – who live there who are the best people to make the decisions. The ABs are focused on Londonderry and Northern Ireland to the exclusion of all else.'

It is that central control that has made it possible for the Apprentice Boys, unlike the Orange Order, to deal successfully in recent years with the parades issue.

Although the Orange Order exists independently of Northern Ireland, there is within it nostalgia for the birthplace of the institution and deep sympathy for the tribulations of local members. 'I really do feel sorry for them,' said a delegate, 'because I think that lots of people looking at Northern Irish people see them as being terribly old-fashioned.' 'Protestants are very straitlaced here,' said another. 'They don't have anything but a virtuous life.' 'The Orange institution, I guess,' said the Scottish Grand Master, 'reflects the society that it happens to be in. We are different from the Irish, there's no doubt about that. I'm not saying we're an irreligious bunch compared to Ireland, but we are quite different. We do have lodges in Scotland that are pretty well social clubs. They're quite happy about it. They don't see any distinction between the Christian ideals of the organization and sitting having a beer. It would have been thought of as being very unPresbyterian at one time in Scotland, but when you go to Scotland now the shops are open on a Sunday, people are much more free. You wouldn't have hung your washing out on a Sunday and got away with it. You can now. So in that respect Northern Ireland – I shouldn't really use the term old-fashioned – but I suppose most Scots would see Northern Irish society as a bit old-fashioned. It's not necessarily bad for being that way, but it's different. The English in particular have a terrible job trying to understand Northern Ireland Protestants.'

He reminisced about a holiday in Northern Ireland the previous year; it was his wife's first visit. 'We came when it was nice and quiet. I said to Helen, "You'll immediately notice the difference as soon as we drive into the countryside. I'll not tell you. Wait till you see it." Took a little while before the penny dropped. And it was the immaculate little houses with their manicured lawns and their little bushes. You don't see that too much in Scotland. People there just aren't so particular about the property as they are here. I don't know if the reason is that life is better here or because they're more puritan in the way they live their lives: they've got spending money, therefore they spend it on their houses.'

Ian had been a frequent visitor to Ballymena, County Antrim, where he stays when over for the Twelfth. 'I'm very friendly with various families there and they are extremely hospitable to the point of being almost embarrassing. And every house is more immaculate than the other. But they're terrific people. We were here for seven days and the hospitality and the welcome everywhere – and I mean cross-community everywhere – is exceptional. They're such lovely people and the tragedy is that they're living in such a tragedy.' He shook his head. 'It'd be a fabulous place if you could just calm it down.'

5

The Wars of Religion Begin

Sure I'm an Ulster Orangeman, from Erin's Isle I came,
To see my British Brethren all of honour and of fame,
And to tell them of my forefathers who fought in days of yore,
That I might have the right to wear the sash my father wore!

CHORUS: *It is old but it is beautiful, and its colours they are fine,*
It was worn at Derry, Aughrim, Enniskillen and the Boyne.
My father wore it as a youth in bygone days of yore,
And on the Twelfth I love to wear the sash my father wore.

For those brave men who crossed the Boyne have not fought or died in vain,
Our Unity, Religion, Laws, and Freedom to maintain,
If the call should come we'll follow the drum, and cross that river once more,
That tomorrow's Ulsterman may wear the sash my father wore!

CHORUS

And when some day, across the sea to Antrim's shore you come,
We'll welcome you in royal style, to the sound of flute and drum,
And Ulster's hills shall echo still, from Rathlin to Dromore,
As we sing again the loyal strain of the sash my father wore!

CHORUS

One of several versions of 'The Sash My Father Wore'

T HE SASH WAS NOT worn at Derry, Aughrim, Enniskillen or the Boyne, for the Orange Order did not come into existence until more than a century after these battles. What is more, the anniversary of the Battle of the Boyne is actually the eleventh, not the twelfth, of July.* But no matter. To the opposing tribes in Ireland, Irish history is a but a tool in the fashioning of identity and a weapon in the long war.

---

* When an historian of the seventeenth century told me this, I was as shocked as any Orangeman. However, members of the loyal institutions will not be surprised to learn that it is all the fault of a pope. In 1582 Pope Gregory XIII announced he was replacing the Julian calendar established by Julius Caesar, for the very good reason that Caesar's astronomer had overestimated the length of the year by about eleven minutes. It took Britain until 1752 to follow continental Europe in replacing the Julian or 'Old Style' calendar in its dominions.

In the seventeenth century the Old Style calendar was ten days behind the New Style, so the Battle of the Boyne was fought on 1 July Old Style and 11 July New Style. The mistake in calculation arose because in the eighteenth century the disparity between calendars lengthened to eleven days as 1700 was a leap year under the Julian calendar but not under the Gregorian.

The Orange Order was born out of violence and has frequently been the occasion of more, but it must be seen in an intensely violent context. As the historian A. T. Q. Stewart put it bluntly in his brilliant *The Narrow Ground*,* what has been constant about the Irish people throughout recorded history 'is their capacity for very reckless violence, allied to a distorted moral sense which magnifies small sins and yet regards murder as trivial. Their kindness and hospitality are legendary, but so too is their reputation for hypocrisy and cruelty ... the frightfulness of the crimes committed in modern Ireland is to be explained by patterns of behaviour which are of great antiquity.'

These patterns of behaviour are not confined to those popularly, if erroneously, viewed as the indigenous tribe in Northern Ireland: the Catholic Gael. Protestants of English and Scots stock have perpetrated atrocities just as cruel. The tribes have learned from each other and – for all that many members of both like to think themselves of pure descent from native or planter – there has been a great deal of intermingling: Gerry Adams and John Hume, the leaders of the two main nationalist and almost exclusively Catholic political parties, bear respectively English and Scots surnames. Over the centuries a mixed marriage has operated like a kidnap, consigning one or other of the partners to cross the barrier and join the other tribe.

Most of the outward distinguishing marks of the two Northern Irish tribes are straightforward enough. Anything red-white-and-blue is Protestant/British/unionist, anything green-white-and-orange[†] is Catholic/Irish/nationalist. Outsiders are baffled as to why so much of the visible Protestant/British/unionist identity is centred round the colour orange and the unlikely figure of a seventeenth-century Dutch prince of French and German extraction.

William of Orange, King William III (or King Billy as he is known familiarly to his devoted followers), was of cosmopolitan stock. Orange is a town in the south-east of France, not far north of Marseilles. In the thirteenth century the counts of Orange upgraded themselves to princes

---

* The phrase comes from Sir Walter Scott, who wrote of Ireland in 1825: 'I never saw a richer country, or, to speak my mind, a finer people; the worst of them is the bitter and envenomed dislike which they have to each other. Their factions have been so long envenomed, and they have such narrow ground to do their battle in, that they are like people fighting with daggers in a hogshead.'

† The Irish tricolour was designed to symbolize the reconciliation of nationalism (green) and unionism (orange). These days republicans often prefer to replace the orange by gold.

and three centuries later, through marriage, became united with the German counts of Nassau (located in what is now the western part of Hesse).* King William's ancestor, William of Nassau, who became Prince of Orange, inherited and acquired through his wife extensive lands in the Netherlands, where he is remembered as William the Silent; though eloquent, he learned as a young man when to keep his mouth shut.

Appointed in 1559 Stadholder (governor and commander-in-chief) of Holland, Zeeland and Utrecht by Philip II, King of Spain and ruler of the Burgundian Netherlands, he became the spearhead of the revolt against Spanish rule that led to the Dutch Republic. During the next two centuries the seven stadholderates came to be held exclusively by a succession of able princes and counts of Orange-Nassau. There was a hiatus when the Republic collapsed in 1795, but with the setting up in 1815 of the Kingdom of the Netherlands, the Prince of Orange became king; his descendants rule the Netherlands today.

A Protestant by birth, who was brought up a Catholic from the age of eleven and reverted to Lutheranism in his thirties, William failed in his ambition to give equal rights to both religions. But though his political career required him at different times to ally himself with fanatical and intolerant Catholics and Protestants, he seems genuinely to have tried to live up to his declaration that it was wrong for princes to presume to rule over the consciences of their subjects. In 1584, four years after Philip II put a price on his head, William was murdered by a Catholic, thus entering the pantheon of Protestant martyrs; he is a very satisfying figure to have founded the dynasty that produced what some Orangemen call *our* William. What adds relevance is that Philip II was the husband of Queen Mary of England, who in her short reign in the 1550s sent almost three hundred Protestants to the stake.

I was strolling past Balliol College, Oxford, one day with an Orange friend when he spotted the memorial erected in 1841 to Hugh Latimer, formerly Bishop of Worcester, and Nicholas Ridley, formerly Bishop of London. Men of great moral and physical courage, they were burned to death in the street nearby in 1554 as heretics. On the bonfire, Latimer called to Ridley to be of good cheer: 'We shall today light such a candle by God's grace in England as shall never be put out.'

* When part of Ireland became independent, there was wholesale renaming of streets to replace British heroes with Irish. One of the names that evaded the cull was Dublin's Nassau Street, presumably because no one in authority realized its link with King William III.

My friend's excitement and emotion brought the truth of that prophecy home to me. To me this was just another memorial; to him it was of enormous significance. I had not realized to what extent the persecution of Protestants by 'Bloody Mary' is part of the folk-memory in Ulster: Latimer and Ridley are on some Orange banners today.

The perception in Catholic Ireland is that, for centuries, Protestants persecuted and exploited Catholics, who – with a few dishonourable exceptions – never let up in their heroic struggle for faith and fatherland. There is almost no comprehension of the sacrifices made for faith, and later for Ulster, by members of the biggest Protestant church in Northern Ireland: the Presbyterians. And there can be no such comprehension without some appreciation of their Scottish roots and the cosmic European clash between Protestantism and Catholicism that raged over more than three centuries.

If the Reformation in England had sprung from a revolt against papal power by that self-indulgent pragmatist, Henry VIII, in Scotland it was based on principle and a passionate belief in liberty. John Knox was the key influence in its development. A Catholic priest, Knox was converted in the 1540s by the Scottish Reformation leader George Wishart, shortly before he was burned to death for heresy by the Cardinal-Archbishop of St Andrews, then the *de facto* ruler of Scotland, who was himself murdered a few months later by Protestants. The scholarly and retiring Knox found himself pulled against his will into the public arena, where he was quickly recognized as a great preacher and the natural spokesman of Scottish Protestantism.

Captured by French allies of the Catholic rulers of Scotland, Knox spent nineteen punishing months as a galley-slave until his release in 1549 as a result of English intervention.

He became an inspiration for English Puritanism, a Calvinist* movement within the state church that believed in a more rigorous application of Reformation principles in doctrine, worship and the way of life and

---

* John Calvin (1509–64), a French theologian, was converted to Protestantism in the early 1530s and in Geneva, from 1541 onwards, put his ecclesiastical principles into practice. Where Martin Luther was a reformer, who broke with Rome only when he concluded that reform was impossible, Calvin brought new coherence and discipline to the development of Protestantism. The five points of Calvinism are succinctly summarized under the acronym of TULIP as: the total depravity of man; unconditional election; limited atonement; irresistible grace; and the perseverence of the saints. It was Calvin who created the system of congregation-based church government that was to form the basis for Presbyterianism.

aimed to purify the church of papish practice. But with the succession to the throne in 1553 of the Catholic, Mary Tudor, Knox had to flee.

In exile he became preoccupied by the fact that, by an accident of history, Protestantism was at the Queen's mercy. It led him to conclude – despite the opposition of Calvin – that it was legitimate for Protestants to resist, violently if necessary, a ruler who threatened their religion. To Knox, the Reformation's cause was God's cause; any sacrifice was worthwhile to ensure that it triumphed.

The battle in Scotland waged in Knox's lifetime between Catholicism and Protestantism was a part of the struggle that was convulsing parts of the Continent. In 1560, it was only intervention by an English army that prevented the destruction of Scottish Protestantism by the French, who wished to unite England, France and Scotland under the French king and his wife Mary, the Scottish queen and the Catholic heir to the Protestant Queen Elizabeth. The hastily-written Scots Confession of Faith, essentially based on moderate Calvinism, was agreed by a Scottish parliament. Papal jurisdiction was abolished, and, true to the intolerant spirit of the age, the saying of mass was prohibited on pain of death after the third offence. In the *First Book of Discipline*, presented to the parliament, Knox laid down the basic principles from which Presbyterianism developed; crucial was that the laity were to have a key role in helping ministers to maintain moral discipline.

There were no happy endings for any Scottish churches during the sixteenth and seventeenth centuries. Knox died in 1572, a few months after one of the most appalling atrocities in the long war between Protestant and Catholic. In the Saint Bartholomew's Day Massacre the Huguenot (Protestant) nobles of Paris were murdered by royal command and the mass murder of Huguenots throughout France by Catholic mobs followed; Pope Gregory XIII and Philip II of Spain gave retrospective approval. The inevitable backlash made it impossible for William I of Orange to prevent intolerant Calvinists from wrecking his plans for religious equality. The best he could achieve in 1573 in Holland was the recognition of liberty of conscience; Catholic worship was prohibited. And throughout Europe, the conviction among Protestants that Catholicism was intrinsically tyrannical and incompatible with freedom was heavily reinforced and therefore led in its turn to further persecution of Catholics.

In England, under Elizabeth, the fight was against the threat of conquest by Catholic Spain; in Scotland the struggle, led by Knox's followers, was ultimately against royal domination. And at her back door, in Ireland,

Elizabeth faced a succession of rebellions which had papal approval and Spanish support. By 1603, when her cousin James VI of Scotland became James I of England, though Ireland was further under royal control than it had been since the invasion of Henry II in 1172, it was potentially more dangerous than ever, for to the traditional fights over land and power had been added the poison of religious bigotry.

It was religious divisions that drew new battle-lines in Ireland. Although the temporally prosperous and spiritually impoverished Irish Church certainly was in need of renewal, there had been sullen resentment when Henry VIII declared himself Supreme Head on Earth of the Church of Ireland and dissolved the monasteries. Resistance to Edward VI's doctrinal innovations was stronger and Elizabeth's attempts to enforce attendance on Sunday at a Reformed service united in opposition the native Irish and those known as the Old English. A combination of persecution from without and the hard work of Jesuits – the shock-troops of the Counter-Reformation, who became the bogeymen of Protestants – ensured that by the time Elizabeth died Catholicism in Ireland was stronger than ever. Half-hearted attempts at settling Protestant English on Irish land to the east and south had little effect except to increase sectarian bitterness.

Yet from the earliest times until the Reformation, successive waves of invaders, including Celts, Vikings and, from the twelfth century, Normans, English and Welsh, had been assimilated. An early seventeenth-century commentator observed that 'if the people had been numbered this day by the Poll, such as are descended of English race, would be found more in numbers than the Ancient Natives'. Ulster, which at its most eastern point is only thirteen miles away, had for many centuries swapped people with western Scotland. In the fourth century, for instance, the Irish partially colonized Scotland and in the fourteenth century, Scotland's Robert Bruce tried to set up a satellite kingdom in Ireland. And Ireland's patron saint, Patrick, was a Briton captured by Irish raiders in the fifth century and enslaved.

Because orthodox Irish nationalism has successfully propagated the inaccurate claim that the Gaels were the first and then exclusive occupants of Ireland, which makes everyone else a foreigner, in self-defence some Ulster Scots have become equally certain that they got to Ireland first and were dispossessed by the Celts. Here is an extract from a conversation with George Chittick, one of the Orange Order's keenest amateur historians, who has read widely in the history of Ireland and is also, like all serious Orangeman, steeped in the Old Testament and therefore the history of ancient Israel. It is illustrative of the increasingly popular British–Israel view of early Irish history dismissed by most academic historians but treasured by many ordinary Ulster Protestants.

I was at Heathrow and I asked a man where I'd find the check-in desk for Belfast. He told me and asked, 'Have you your passport?' It was a red rag to a bull. 'I will inform you that I'm going back to the oldest part of the United Kingdom,' says I. He looked at me. 'I said, the oldest part of the United Kingdom. You'd better believe it, friend. I haven't time to elaborate on it, but if you give me your name and address I'll fully elaborate on it.' He did.

So I wrote to him about how the Stone of Destiny did not belong to Scotland. It was the stone Jacob rested his head on, which was carried to Ireland. It was Ptolemy – the Greek map-maker who lived in Egypt – who said the northern part of the islands of the west, was inhabited by a people of the Hebrew race.

The stone was brought here and the Cruthin kings of Ireland were crowned on it. Gradually the Celts moved their way up, and the kingdom became Dal Riada – which was the territory occupied now by County Down, County Armagh, County Londonderry and County Antrim. The last king was a man called Fergus MacAlpin, who had his castle at Carrickfergus and at Dunseverick up on North Antrim coast. He could look out over to his kingdom of Dal Riada, which included Argyll and the islands all round there. He was Lord of the Isles. He was driven out and he took this stone with him to Argyll and all the kings were crowned on it. And then Scotland was united under his great-great-grandson, Kenneth McAlpin, the first king of Scotland.

The stone was kept there, then Edward I, he bumped it down to London, built a chair round it and it stayed there till last year. Then it went back to Scotland and the Scottish people identified it as their nationality. I always view the stone as the stone of the United Kingdom, because it came here, went to Scotland and then went down to London and Edward I – his son was named Prince of Wales.

The people that were brought back in the Plantation of Ulster were just really the people that went six hundred, seven hundred years previous over to Argyll and the southern lowlands who were returned to Ulster again. They were only coming back to their homeland. Gerry Adams and his people, they say that's a load of bunkum, but it's not. It's true.*

---

* Professional historians would point out that the Cruthin were in fact Celts, but they were certainly in Ireland before the arrival of the Gaelic invaders.

The history war between loyalism and republicanism has latterly extended to a struggle over early Irish

There are no ethnically pure people in the British Isles and in a sane world it should not matter who was there first fifteen centuries ago, but many Ulster Scots, portrayed as illegitimate land-grabbers, feel the need to have ancient history on their side. They can legitimately call on medieval history, for many Scots mercenaries were assimilated in Ulster from the thirteenth century onwards, and throughout the fifteenth century, eastern Antrim was absorbed in the kingdom of the Scottish Lord of the Isles. For the best part of two hundred years, Scots migrated into Ulster, married the Irish – producing two varieties of Gaelic – and together formed alliances against the English. Then in the early seventeenth century, with a Scottish king on the English throne, attempts to reduce Scots influence in Ulster gave way to a policy of actively encouraging Protestant Scots as well as English to settle in Ireland, with a view to increasing prosperity by developing land and commerce, stabilizing the province and preventing it from being a staging-post for further invasions from the Catholic parts of Continental Europe.*

Elizabeth had left to James VI and I a conquered Ireland. The Nine Years War – a rebellion led by the great Ulster chiefs, Hugh O'Neill, Earl of Tyrone, and Rory O'Donnell – ended in March 1603 with O'Neill's submission. Both were pardoned and O'Donnell was created Earl of Tyrconnell. It was now possible to complete the division of Ireland into counties by shiring Ulster, which in previous administrations had been virtually a no-go area; until the seventeenth century there were only three entry routes from the south.

The first plantations came in 1606, when two Scotsmen, Hugh Montgomery and James Hamilton, secured respectively north-east and north-west Down, while the Lord Deputy in Ireland, Sir Arthur Chichester, was granted a vast tract of land in Antrim – all areas 'depopulated and

---

mythical heroes. Cúchulainn, for instance, an inspiration for romantic Gaelic nationalism, whose statue is in the Dublin GPO in commemoration of the 1916 rebellion, now appears in Belfast on the gable ends of walls in both communities; on Protestant walls he is a fighter for Ulster separatism.

∗ In 1579, about 300 soldiers, mainly Italians and Spaniards, financed by Pope Gregory XIII and Philip II, and accompanied by Spanish and English papal commissaries, landed in Kerry on what was announced as a religious crusade to help the overthrow of Elizabeth. The following year a papal force of 700 landed nearby in Smerwick. And in 1601 a Spanish force of around more than 3,000 landed at Kinsale and a few months later reinforcements followed. Although all the rebellions they were assisting failed, the unsurprising result was to increase settlers' feelings of fear and insecurity.

wasted' through war. The east coast was such familiar ground for Scots that there was no difficulty in attracting large numbers of migrants fleeing poverty or religious persecution, for, like immigrants throughout the centuries, they found comfort in going where they would find their own people. Even though Chichester established an English colony, that did not deter many Scots from settling in Antrim as well as Down.

Over the next two decades, these plantations prospered mightily through the efforts of immigrant artisans and farmers and the labour of the native Irish; commerce thrived in Bangor, Belfast, Carrickfergus and Newry.

In parallel, though less successfully, developed the plantations of James I, whose grandiose plans should be seen in the context of the contemporary colonial adventures of Holland, Portugal and Spain. James's opportunity came when, to general amazement, Tyrone and Tyrconnell, in 1607, decided – wrongly as it turned out – that they would do better to serve the king of Spain and fled the country. James thereupon confiscated their lands and the six counties of Armagh, Coleraine, Tyrconnell (later Donegal), Tyrone, Fermanagh and Cavan were escheated to the crown.

Chichester's intention had been that outsiders should be offered only land that Irish proprietors could not develop, but a rebellion in the far north of Donegal put paid to that. Short-sighted as ever, London decided on preferential treatment for English and Scots and ensured the alienation of potential Irish allies. Of the 3,800,000 confiscated acres, just 1,500,000 acres of poor and infertile land were restored to the native Irish and substantial grants were made to the Established Church, royal schools, military forts and towns. This left 500,000 acres of fertile land, which under the terms laid down in 1610 were to be divided between two kinds of entrepreneurs: 'undertakers' (high-ranking Scots or English who had to take the Oath of Supremacy) and 'servitors', mainly administrators or military men who, like the 'deserving' native Irish, paid twice as much for land as undertakers but did not have to take the Oath and were allowed Irish tenants. There were separate arrangements for the county of Coleraine, which was to be planted by London merchants.

As Jonathan Bardon describes it:

> The great migration to Ulster began, drawn from every class of British society: servitors who had long sought a share in the province they conquered; younger sons of gentlemen – such as Chichester himself . . . eager for lands to call their own; Scottish nobles like the earl of Abercorn and Lord Ochiltree, induced to plant

Tyrone for a countenance and strength to the rest', relatives, neighbours, artisans
and dependants of undertakers; rack-rented and evicted Lowland Scots farmers;
and horse thieves and other fugitives from justice. The English had more capital but
the Scots were the most determined planters.

Like all too many plans for Ulster that have emanated over the years
from London, the document laying down complex developmental and
administrative terms betrayed a lack of understanding of the place and
the people. Too much land went to undertakers and too little to those
practical men, the servitors; there were insufficient resources to colonize,
develop and fortify the land as London had instructed; and the undertakers
made little effort to bring in enough English and Scots tenants to replace
the Gaelic Irish who stayed with no security, resentfully paying high
rents. Many of those who had been dispossessed became marauding
outlaws who preyed on planters; their numbers were supplemented by
thousands of ex-soldiers of the exiled chieftains.

Nor did the plantation of Coleraine go smoothly. In exchange for
financial backing for the plantation, twelve London companies were
granted County Coleraine (renamed Londonderry) and given extra territory in Antrim, Donegal and Tyrone and the towns of Coleraine and
Derry, but progress in building was slow, expenses were high and the king
was furious because, again, it was too difficult to find enough outsiders to
replace native Irish.

There were far fewer English and far more Scots than had been envis-
aged by Chichester. Although the latter were heavily concentrated in the
east, doughty frontiersmen headed west, where Catholics were to remain
vastly in the majority. But though dissenting Scots and orthodox members
of the Church of England had no love for each other, in Ulster the Puritan
tendency prevailed among the English. This exacerbated the normal loathing between Protestant and Catholic.

In Ulster there were two extreme clashing cultures, defined by religion.
On the one hand were the vast majority of the new planters, adventurers,
frontiersmen and looters of land, who nonetheless practised austerity, hard
work, self-denial and absolute simplicity of life and worship, believed
themselves in direct communication with God and, as Calvinists, saw
themselves as the 'elect' who were assured of salvation. In doctrine and
practice, Calvinism was completely antipathetic to the traditional beliefs
of Irish Catholics and their love of tradition and mystery, deepened by
intermittent persecution and the zealous efforts of Counter-Reformation

priests. Culturally, they were miles apart too, and the natives, desolate at the loss of the old Gaelic order, bitterly resented the imposition of English laws and English methods of commerce and farming. Each side was terrified of the other. A violent clash was inevitable, but first there was business to be settled in Britain, with the clash in the 1630s between king and dissenter.

In England under Elizabeth, the Calvinist-driven opposition to a church which was organizationally little changed from pre-Reformation times met with short shrift. Puritans, seen as seditious, were as vigorously persecuted as Catholics who were seen as agents of a foreign power. Before he came to the English throne, James was doctrinally a convinced Presbyterian, though he differed with its ministers over the scope of royal authority. As King of England he behaved as was appropriate for the head of the Church of England, but made no attempt to extend Anglicanism into Scotland except by appointing bishops. But when in 1625 his son Charles acceded to the throne, his authoritarian instincts propelled him towards a disastrous confrontation with the Puritans by his attempts to impose uniformity on all Protestants in his kingdom. Whereas the Puritans, like the Presbyterians, believed that worship should be centred on extemporaneous prayer and preaching, Charles was of what became known as the High Church party, those who believed in following the prayer book and maintaining ritual. It did not help that he was married to the Catholic sister of the French king or that his religious adviser, Archbishop Laud, wanted to extirpate Puritanism.

In Ireland, Charles's lord deputy, Thomas Wentworth, who had already alienated native Irish and Presbyterians alike by fining them for non-attendance at Anglican churches, while fining planters also for failure to evict the Irish, pressed the Anglican bishops to discipline those of their ministers who had embraced Presbyterianism; many were ousted from their livings and fled back to Scotland.

One such was Robert Blair, who had resigned his chair in Glasgow in 1623 and become a minister in Bangor, County Down. Excommunicated by his bishop in 1636, he returned to Scotland and led the opposition to Charles I's attempts to impose Laud's new liturgy, based on the English Book of Common Prayer. Although the Scottish bishops had concurred, many Scots signed the National Covenant of 1638 to defend Presbyterianism. The Church's Scottish Assembly subsequently abolished bishops, enshrining as a central part of their religion the democratic principle of lay power. In Ulster, Scots signed the Covenant enthusiastically and, as

Charles mustered an army to discipline the Scots, Wentworth sent an army north to impose on all Ulster Scots an 'oath of abjuration of their abominable covenant', on pain of fines, imprisonment and excommunication. Many families were heavily punished and many others fled back to Scotland.

The good news for Ulster Scots was that Charles was defeated twice by Scottish Covenanting armies in what were known as the Bishops' Wars and Wentworth was executed at the behest of the largely Puritan parliament, which was enraged by his treatment of planters and Presbyterians. In 1641, in desperate confrontation with parliament and in need of any support he could get, Charles agreed to the full establishment of Presbyterianism in Scotland.

The appalling news was the outbreak of rebellion in October 1641. Led by Sir Phelim O'Neill and others of the native Irish aristocracy, it was intended to strike a blow for the native Irish against the Irish administration under Puritan control. Sir Phelim proclaimed his loyalty to King Charles and denied he wanted to hurt any of the king's subjects, English or Scots. Most castles, garrisons and towns fell throughout the area covered by the Ulster plantation, but bloodshed was at first at what might be termed 'an acceptable level' for those times.

Control was soon lost, though. Like so many fastidious leaders before and since, Sir Phelim and his allies could not contain the mob. Gaelic peasants – whom harvest failures had left hungry, a sense of dispossession had left desperate and rumours of Puritan massacres had made terrified – erupted and, ignoring instructions to leave the Scots planters alone, attacked every settler they could find. Of the twelve thousand or so men, women and children who died, about a third were killed by fire, sword, or hanging or drowning and the rest died of hunger or exposure when turned out of their homes. If there had ever been any doubts about it being a religious war, they were put to rest in Antrim, where some Catholic Scots joined in the massacre of Protestant settlers. The horrifying details still scar the communal Protestant memory in the north of Ireland, and as A. T. Q. Stewart put it: 'Here, if anywhere, the mentality of siege was born, and the warning bonfires blazed from hilltop to hilltop, and the beating drums summoned men to the defence of castles and walled towns crowded with refugees.'

By February 1642, all Ireland apart from part of Donegal and Antrim and Cork was under rebel control; the Old English, damned as disloyal because they were Catholic, having secured from the rebels a declaration of loyalty to the crown, threw in their lot with them. A Scots army, under Major-General Monro, arrived in April 1642 and marched south from Carrickfergus slaughtering as he went; his successes gave heart to the settlers, as did the formation of the first presbytery at Carrickfergus by chaplains and elders from the army.

King and parliament were now at war in England and events in Ireland were something of a side-show in the struggle to determine the future government of both islands. The Irish and Old English rebels, now known as the 'Confederate Catholics of Ireland', had a provisional government at Kilkenny, where as time went on their divisions became ever clearer: the Old English were loyal to the king and wanted to get the war over; the Irish wanted their lands back and were prepared to fight to the bitter end; and their respective commanders, Thomas Preston and Owen Roe O'Neill, were too jealous of each other to cooperate.

There were various peace negotiations and a long period of truce until the arrival in 1645 of the papal nuncio with enough arms for O'Neill's forces. In June 1646, shortly after Charles I had surrendered to the Scottish Covenanters, Monro's army moved south and met O'Neill's at Benburb, in County Tyrone. 'Your word,' O'Neill had told his troops, 'is *Sancta Maria* [Holy Mary], and so in the name of the Father, Son, and Holy Ghost, advance.' O'Neill was the better tactician, and won the greatest military victory of the Irish over the British before or since. He lost few men, but Monro lost between two and three thousand. The Pope attended a Te Deum in Rome and there was another mass flight back to Scotland by Protestant settlers. The Presbyterians (including Monro), blamed the disaster upon their sinful lives.

The papal nuncio saved the Ulster plantation. Utterly intransigent and determined that the Catholic Church should be the only established Church, he called on O'Neill for support in overthrowing the Catholic Confederacy, Charles' supporters. So O'Neill went south instead of north and spent the next three years in a futile war, which left his forces in poor shape to resist Oliver Cromwell.

Charles I was executed in January 1649. Cromwell arrived nine months later, intent on punishing the rebels and subduing the country, which he did with brutal efficiency and ruthlessness. At Drogheda, for instance, his army massacred around 2,600 people, including almost the entire garrison (mainly made up of English), all the clergy and some of the townspeople in retribution for the 1641 massacres with which few of them can have had anything to do: 'I am persuaded that this is the righteous judgement of God upon those barbarous wretches who have imbrued their hands with so much innocent blood.' His subsequent massacre in Wexford broke the spirit of the resistance.

Cromwell departed in May 1650, leaving his lieutenants to finish the job. In Ulster, the pro-royalist settler army and the Catholic Confederacy were routed. By the time Ireland was completely subdued, famine and disease were rampant throughout the country and the suffering was to live in the memory of Irish Catholics as keenly as did 1641 among the Ulster Protestants and to stoke the fires of inter-tribal resentment. But neither side remembers much of the suffering of the other. As the Reverend John Dunlop truly observed in *A Precarious Belonging*, his contemplative look at Presbyterians in Northern Ireland:

> It is a characteristic of communal memory to sift through the stories and remember only those parts which sustain one's own community. It seems that communities find stories of massacre and suffering to be solid material for sustaining community memory and community solidarity, provided that one's own community is the victim community. Selective memory, in turn, feeds contemporary enmity.

There was no shortage of victims. Under Cromwellian rule, hundreds were executed and thousands exiled to Europe and the West Indies. Landowners unable to prove they had supported the parliamentarians against the king were mostly fined, if Protestant, and dispossessed, if Catholic. Huge confiscations throughout Ireland replaced the Gaelic landowners with soldiers, adventurers (creditors of parliament), and those to whom they sold their entitlements. In Ulster, most of the native Irish remained on the lands of the old and new Protestant Ascendancy, though landless outlaws known as 'tories' presented an ever-present threat to the settlers. Priests were banished; Catholics who sheltered them were imprisoned and the mass was banned. It was at that time that there developed the concept of the 'mass rock' – the celebration of mass at a remote place where discovery was unlikely – which still has huge resonances in the folk-memory today.

Yet life was not easy for Presbyterians either. Naturally schismatic, they had been split between parliamentarians and royalists. And the Belfast presbytery earned the enmity of Cromwell by publishing in 1649 a declaration of support for the Solemn League and Covenant made in 1647 with Charles by the Scottish Covenanters, a condemnation of the king's murder and a litany of criticisms of parliament for extirpating laws and liberties.

The document, remarked Stewart, was 'instinct with the Presbyterian traits of independence, self-righteousness, criticism of civil government and even mistrust of religious toleration'. The declaration, and the Irish in general, were ferociously attacked by John Milton, Latin Secretary to parliament. A. T. Q. Stewart wrote:

> Allowing for the special, and very different, circumstances in which these words were written, one cannot but be struck by their similarity to the kind of things Englishmen say about Ulster now. Why should they bother to distinguish between two different kinds of Irish? One lot is as bad as the other. Papist, Protestant or Presbyterian, they are all Irish, and everyone knows what that means. [The episode demonstrated too the Presbyterian facility] for getting on the wrong side of the establishment, even a revolutionary establishment which had itself just overthrown the monarchy and the institutions of state . . . the Presbyterians were against the government.

In 1650, Cromwell demanded that those who had taken the Covenant take an oath renouncing their allegiance to Charles Stewart, heir to the throne. Presbyterians refusing were imprisoned or fled to Scotland; in 1653 their ministers were banished from Ireland. Under Cromwell's son Henry, who became Lord Deputy the following year, the persecution came to an end until the restoration of Charles II in 1660. Charles was dependent on an uncompromisingly Anglican parliament who wanted to get its own back on the Puritans, and therefore had to preside over the application of various penal laws against dissenters and Catholics. The Test Act of 1673, for instance, required any civil or military officeholder to take Anglican communion and denounce the Catholic doctrine of transubstantiation, while that of 1678 required all members of both houses of parliament to be Anglicans. Yet in Ireland life was rather better for Catholics; mass could at least be said publicly and priests began to return. For Presbyterians, it was worse, though Charles gave their ministers a royal grant. Overall, though, it was a time of great insecurity for all denominations but the Established Church, especially as the king was suspected, correctly, of having Romish tendencies. There was national hysteria in England in 1678 over fabricated allegations that there was a 'Popish Plot' to murder Charles and replace him by his Catholic brother, James, Duke of York. And the completely innocent Oliver Plunkett, the titular Archbishop of Armagh, was hanged, drawn and quartered in London in 1681 on false charges trumped up by the Anglican Bishop of

Meath of plotting a French invasion; an icon of huge importance in the pantheon of Catholic martyrs to English Protestantism, Plunkett's head has been preserved in Drogheda Cathedral and he was canonized when the pope visited Ireland in 1979.

By seventeenth-century standards, Ulster was relatively peaceful; immigrants continued to arrive from England and Scotland – where Presbyterians were having a tough time – and the absence of war as well as the industry and commercial thrust of the settlers brought prosperity. Then, in 1685, James II became king.

6

Oranje boven!*

It was when England's glorious sun in sixteen eighty-eight,
Was overcast with treason's cloud, and Popery stood elate,
That up arose her Protestants, the peasant and the peer,
And vowed the chain of perjured James that they would not deign to wear;
They sought them out a prudent chief to guide their ardent zeal,
To lead them on that victory might bless their flashing steel,
And who so fit to guide that host in all its bright array,
As William, Prince of Orange, ere he landed at Torbay.

Then up arose the mighty chief and left his native shore,
And rode upon the stormy waves our freedom to restore;
Upon his flag was blazon'd forth high fluttering o'er the main,
That our religion and our laws he ever would maintain;
'Twas then in gallant style he stood upon the vessel's prow,
With victory on his flashing sword and wisdom on his brow,
And tens of thousands greeted him upon his natal day,*
When he our glorious Orange chief first landed at Torbay.

Come brethren of the Orange bond, a bond ne'er to be riven,
When e'er we give great William's name, a bumper must be given,
For it you'd fire a feu-de-joie, to him who victory won;
Come prime and load, and see you give a good charge to your gun;
The eloquence of bumpers full, there's nothing can surpass,
There's nought expresses kindred souls, like friendship's social glass,
And thus we give our song and toast with three times three, huzza,
The memory of King William and his landing at Torbay.

'The Landing at Torbay'

'TO UNDERSTAND THE ULSTER mind, and especially the Ulster Presbyterian mind, the dissenting mind, you've got to go back to the
Covenanting† influences of our forefathers,' said an Orange chaplain to
me last year. 'It is portrayed in that remark by Andrew Melville,** who

* The lyricist was one day out: William landed in Torbay the day after his birthday.

† Covenants – sacred and solemn agreements – have their origin in the Old Testament, starting with Abraham.
The thinking behind a covenant is that if one party reneges, all bets are off. In 1557, at Knox's behest, Protestant
noblemen signed a 'band', or covenant, which pledged them to defend 'the Congregation of the Lord'.

** John Knox's successor as leader of the Scottish Reformed Church, who played a crucial role in developing
the structure of the Presbyterian Church by replacing bishops with local presbyteries. He took grave exception
to King James's interference in ecclesiastical matters, denouncing him as 'God's silly vassel.'

said to King James I and VI of Scotland: "There are two kingdoms in Scotland. There is Christ Jesus the king in his kingdom – the kirk – whose subject King James the VI is, and of whose kingdom he is not a king, nor a lord nor a head but a member." Regardless of what you think of the separation of church and state, our forefathers fought and died for the independence of the kirk. Then there was Samuel Rutherford* who, in a classic book, *Lex Rex* [which was publicly burned after the Restoration], wrote: "Power is a birthright of the people borrowed from them. They may let it out for their good and resume it when a man is drunk with it."'

Summed up here is a simple explanation of the apparent contradiction that the most loyal people in the United Kingdom are on occasion prepared to rebel against their government: their loyalty is conditional. They will put up with injustice, even persecution, and remain grimly loyal until some event makes them feel that betrayal is imminent and it is time to take a stand. In the twentieth century, flash-points have been created by the Home Rule Bill, by the Anglo-Irish Agreement and by bans on the Drumcree church parade. For a seventeenth-century Irish Presbyterian, the conditions for incipient rebellion were set by the arrival on the throne of a Catholic king.

The Protestant folk-memory is unfair to James II – a braver and more tolerant man than is commonly realized. As Duke of York, for instance, he earned a distinguished army and naval record; and New Amsterdam was renamed New York because it was at his prompting that it was seized from the Dutch in 1664. And though he converted to Catholicism in 1669 and married as his second wife an Italian Catholic princess, he was still well-disposed to Anglicanism and accepted graciously Charles II's insistence that Mary and Anne, his daughters by his first wife, be brought up Protestant. In 1677 he agreed to the marriage of Mary to William of Orange.

When James became king he had the full support of the Anglican Tories. Nevertheless, since the public agitation in the 1670s over his religion and the various attempts by the dissenting Whigs, who believed that the supreme governor of the church could not be Catholic, to exclude him from the succession, he was wary of his opponents and of the mass

---

∗ An extremist, he not only condemned the covenant with Charles II as sinful, but fell out with almost everyone. His rigorousness, fervidness as a preacher, devoutness, honesty and general cussedness earned him an honourable place in the pantheon of awkward Presbyterians.

of his subjects and determined to take control. Rebellions a few months after his succession by Charles II's illegitimate son, the Duke of Monmouth, and by the Duke of Argyll, were savagely repressed and James was determined to put into positions of power those he could trust, setting about it in a way that brought him into confrontation with parliament and lost him most of his Anglican allies. Parliament was dissolved and Catholics were appointed in large numbers to the army, to the privy council and to offices of state. And even though the dissenters were included in his Declaration of Indulgence (i.e. religious toleration) in 1687, his observation in the introduction that, 'We cannot but heartily wish, as it will be easily believed, that all the people of our dominions were members of the Catholic Church,' left only Catholics happy about his intentions. The following year the birth of an heir, who was popularly rumoured to have been smuggled into the queen's bedroom in a warming-pan, raised fears further.

It was a bad time to try to persuade Protestants that Catholicism should not be equated with tyranny. King Louis XIV of France, set on a policy of territorial aggrandisement and the eradication of Protestantism, had in 1685 revoked the Edict of Nantes of 1598, which had guaranteed toleration to the Huguenots; French refugees brought to Britain and Ireland tales of renewed persecution. And although James spoke of religious tolerance, his despotic instincts and actions inspired only fear among Protestants of all denominations. Fearing the result of an alliance between James and Louis XIV, they looked across the channel to James's son-in-law for salvation.

William of Orange, who during the 1670s had successfully resisted Louis's attempts to overrun the Dutch Republic and who was seen as the outstanding leader of Protestantism in Europe, was still faced with the French threat during the 1680s – indeed, in 1682 he had lost his Orange principality. Frustrated in his efforts to build up a coalition of forces against Louis, he jumped at the opportunity presented in July 1688 by an invitation from seven Tory and Whig peers to assume the English throne. He had two claims: as the son of Charles I's daughter Mary, he was fourth in line to the throne and he was married to James's eldest daughter, now second in line. He was driven by two primary aims: to save the United Provinces from a French take-over and Europe from French ascendancy.

His armada blown by what became known as the 'Protestant East Wind', William arrived in Brixham on Tor Bay in south-west England on 5 November, the eighty-third anniversary of what is popularly known as Guy Fawkes Day – a coincidence of great satisfaction to Protestants. For many years afterwards a service of thanksgiving was held 'for the happy deliverance of King James I, and the three Estates of England, from the most traitorous and bloody intended massacre by Gunpowder; and also for the happy Arrival of his majesty King William on this Day, for the Deliverance of our Church and Nation.'

From Brixham he went to Exeter where defectors and refugees, who included many Scots (among them extreme Covenanters), arrived to join him. As the days went on and more deserters arrived from James's camp (including John Churchill, later the Duke of Marlborough, who said he quit because he believed 'our religion and country were in danger of being destroyed'), Sir Edward Seymour, ex-Speaker of the House of Commons, conceived the idea of forming an association of English supporters of William. In Exeter cathedral they held what learned Orangemen regard as the first Orange meeting on record, at which they subscribed to a declaration whose language and sentiments are still echoed in rituals and prayers in Orange Lodges today:

We do hereby associate ourselves, to the utmost of our power, to support and defend our great deliverer, His Highness the Prince of Orange, in his present enterprise for the delivery of the English Church and nation from Popery and arbitrary power; for the maintenance of the Protestant Religion, and the establishment of a Free Parliament, for the protection of His Highness's person and the settlement of Law and Order on a lasting foundation in these Kingdoms. We further declare, that we are exclusively a Protestant Association; yet detesting, as we do, an intolerant spirit, we solemnly pledge ourselves to each other, that we will not persecute any person, on account of his religious opinions, provided the same be not hostile to the State; but that we will, on the contrary, be aiding and assisting to every Loyal subject, of every religious description, in protecting him from violence and oppression.

An Orange historian, Brother the Reverend M. W. Dewar, in 1967 wrote emotionally of William's reponse:

The closing words of the Prince's speech, which would today be termed the Worshipful Master's Inaugural Address, were: 'since God is pleased that we shall make preservation and happiness, let us not neglect making use of human means, and not expect miracles for our use of this gracious opportunity; but with prudence and courage put in execution our honourable purposes. Therefore, Gentlemen, friends, and fellow-Protestants, we bid you, and all your Followers, most heartily welcome to our court and camp.' Already, the twin foundations of Protestantism and Liberty were being laid to form the Orange Institution of today.

'The General Association of the Gentlemen of Devon, to his Highness the Prince of Orange' became known as the Orange Association; all those offering support to William were asked to subscribe to the declaration. A system of signs and passwords for recognition purposes was devised: one such was the question, 'What did you say?' to which the correct response was 'Nothing more', with the password 'Seymour' (Say more).

James fled to France and William arrived in London virtually unopposed; a new parliament declared James to have abdicated and offered the throne jointly to William and Mary subject to a Bill of Rights which included guarantees for parliament of free speech, free elections and frequent meetings. They were proclaimed in February and at their coronation in April, three-quarters of the parliamentarians present were wearing orange and blue ribbons (after the Dutch Blue Guard, William's personal bodyguards) to demonstrate membership of the Association. William III and Mary II took a new coronation oath which required them to uphold the 'Protestant reformed religion established by law'. For Protestants this was the Glorious Revolution. For Catholics there was nothing to celebrate: parliament was less tolerant than the new king, and the Toleration Act of 1689 excluded Catholics, Jews and Unitarians from the right to worship freely.

The revolution had been virtually bloodless in England; in Scotland there was resistance, but within a few months it had largely collapsed and the Scottish convention declared James expelled from the throne. The following year the Scottish parliament once again removed the bishops from the Established Church and established the Presbyterian form of church government.

Ireland, as ever, was far more troublesome, and once more gave an English monarch cause to see it as the back door for his enemies. It was there that James's romanizing policy had borne most fruit with his appointment three years earlier of Richard Talbot, Catholic Earl of Tyrconnel, as commander of the army and later chief governor. At the time of the Glorious Revolution, Anglophone Catholics were dominant in the army, the administration, the judiciary and the town corporations.

Tyrconnel was notorious among Protestants throughout the three kingdoms and was the inspiration for that most famous of all English political
songs, 'Lilliburlero'. Purporting to be a congratulatory exchange between
one 'Brother teague' and another concerning the forthcoming triumph of
Catholicism and the cause of King James, its two final verses are:

> There was an old prophecy found in a bog,
> Lilli Burlero bullen a la,
> That Ireland should be rul'd by an ass and a dog,
> Lilli Burlero bullen a la.
>
> CHORUS: *Lero, lero, lero, lero,*
> *Lilli Burlero bullen a la,*
> *Lero, lero, lero, lero,*
> *Lilli Burlero bullen a la.*
>
> And now this prophecy is come to pass,
> Lilli Burlero bullen a la,
> For James is the dog and Tyrconnel's the ass,
> Lilli Burlerlo bullen a la.

Credited in 1687 to the Whig politician Thomas Wharton, who was one of
those who flocked to William's side at Exeter, it was set to a harpsichord
quickstep so jaunty and catchy that it swept through the ranks of those,
high and low, who were disgruntled with James; Wharton was later to
claim that his 'foolish ballad' had 'whistled a deluded king out of three
kingdoms'.* But it gives an insight into Irish Protestant fears; for instance,
in its prophecy that foreigners and non-Catholics would be massacred or
expelled until 'By Christ and Saint Patrick de nation's our own'.

It was the conviction that this was what Tyrconnel intended that led
to an outbreak of panic in Derry in December 1688, set off by a letter
to Hugh Montgomery, Lord Mount-Alexander, found on the third of that
month on a street in Comber, County Down. The anonymous native Irish
well-wisher warned him that on 9 December, 'all our Irishmen through
Ireland is sworn . . . to fall on to kill and murder man, wife and child;
and I desire your lordship to take care of yourself, and all others that are

---

* That it is now the signature tune of the BBC World Service is of no political significance.

  'Bullen a lá, a corruption of the Irish 'Buallaidh ár lá,' 'our day will come,' is these days rendered by republicans
as 'Tiochfhaidh ár lá.'

judged by our men to be heads, for whosoever of them can kill any of
you, they are to have a captain's place'.

In the history/folklore of the Apprentice Boys of Derry:

> The bad writing and style, according to the historian, testified to the author being
> one of the poorer sort of natives, and the document has been described as a hoax,
> intended to frighten the noblemen and leaders of the settlers to take refuge for
> themselves and their families in Scotland or England. If this was their intention, they
> had not reckoned on the character of the settlers, who had no intention of running,
> but took immediate action to meet the challenge.*

If its origin was dubious, its effect for Jacobites was cataclysmic. A
copy reached Derry on 7 December and was actually being read out to
the citizens when word came that Lord Antrim, one of the few Catholic
landowners to have had his lands restored by Charles II, was at Tyrconnel's order about to replace the Protestant garrison with his Catholic
force, which included 1,200 Scottish highlanders, a rough lot known as
'Redshanks', a nickname allegedly given them because of their bare legs
or, in more recent mythology, because their leggings were often stained
red with Protestant blood.

Derry had been the main refuge after 1641 for terrified settlers, vulnerable though it was as a largely Protestant outpost in an overwhelmingly
Catholic area. Catholics were then banished from within the city walls
and became concentrated in what was known as the Bogside, which
Stewart describes as 'the vulnerable western flank where unsubjugated
Ireland perpetually menaced the bastion of the plantation'. Derry had
experienced a siege in 1649 when parliamentary forces under Sir Charles
Coote held it for over five months against royalist besiegers. Since it
ended with an alliance between the Puritan Coote and the Catholic Owen
Roe O'Neill to drive away the royalists, it retains no resonance among
the warring tribes of Ulster. It was, however, some kind of precedent for
resistance and relief.

The minds of the inhabitants of Derry were not on a far-distant struggle
between a foreign Protestant prince and a Catholic English king; they
simply wanted to survive. Memories of 1641 made many of them believe

* From the official brochure of the Tercentenary Celebrations of the Apprentice Boys of Derry. Commemorative
events began with a re-enactment of the finding of the Comber letter on 3 December and its conveyance
through Ulster to Derry.

– as expressed in a song by one of their descendants today – that if Antrim's forces 'get their papish way/Our faith and lives will end today'.

As the bishop of Derry, Ezekial Hopkins, pointed out to the citizens, to resist the instructions of Tyrconnel, James's representative, was to rebel against the lawful King of Ireland. What happened as Antrim's troops began to cross the Foyle is the stuff of Protestant legend. In 1826, at an event to mark the laying of the foundation stone of the memorial to Reverend George Walker, governor during the siege, James Gregg described in classic romantic form what is firmly in the Protestant folk-memory:

> while the Sheriffs and others were consulting, youthful hearts scorned debate, parleying was not their province, and tricks they did not understand; thirteen of them armed themselves, flew to the main guard, seized the keys of the garrison, and locked the city gates, at the moment their enemies were ready to enter. Never was youthful ardour so nobly repaid. The spirit of the citizens was roused – they caught the generous flame – the most of them declared for the defence of the city, and the glorious cry of 'NO SURRENDER'* echoed round its walls. Roaring Meg† was pointed at Lord Antrim's men, and they instantly retired across the river.
>
> Thus, by the youthful ardour of a few young men, who hated canting and hypocrisy, was the city saved, and, I may truly add, the Protestant religion secured – but for that heroic act, we would not be sitting here this day in the midst of a Protestant city – we would not have been worshipping in our sacred Cathedral – but have been the slaves and vassals of priestcraft, tyranny, and superstition.

There was in fact a cleavage within the city between old and young, between the elite and what some of them called 'the rabble'. The more cautious, who had no desire to commit treason and to risk the city and its citizens, wanted to do some kind of deal with the state, especially as the Jacobites** appeared to be destroying all attempts at resistance. Hopkins gave up and left the city. One who stayed was Lieutenant-Colonel Robert Lundy, the city's military governor, whose behaviour was seen by the more defiant inhabitants of Derry as equivocal at best. They

---

* Gregg is probably ahead of time here. It is thought that 'No Surrender' did not become a war-cry until Adam Murray challenged Robert Lundy on 20 April.

† A particularly noisy cannon sent by the London companies in 1642 along with provisions, clothing and other armaments.

** A variant of Jacobus, Latin for James, it was the name given to supporters of the House of Stuart.

expelled the few remaining Catholics and 'a convent of Dominican friars' from the city.

By early March, when King James arrived at Kinsale with a large French army, only the Ulster towns of Londonderry and Enniskillen were in Protestant hands. He marched straight to Dublin, where Tyrconnel had summoned what became known as the 'patriot parliament'; it had a Catholic majority, acknowledged James as king and through the Bill of Attainder (later nullified) set about the serious business of taking the land back. Bolstered by this support, James marched north to take on Derry, where Lundy and his critics were coming to the final showdown. Lundy urged surrender and began a military withdrawal, but was defied by another hero in the Apprentice Boy pantheon, Adam Murray, who called the population of the city to arms and overthrew the governor. Lundy was replaced by joint governors: George Walker, a Church of Ireland rector, and Major Henry Baker, a professional soldier. To save Lundy from the mob, he was allowed to disguise himself as a ordinary soldier carrying faggots on his back and escape from the city.

To call a fellow-Protestant a Lundy is to call him a traitor, yet there is no evidence to suggest that Lundy was a either a coward or knave, merely a cautious man who feared that resistance could lead to disaster for the city and the thousands of Protestants who had flocked there day after day as the Jacobites advanced. Every December he is burned in effigy on the walls of Derry in what Stewart describes as 'an act of ritual purgation', in which doubts and fears are swept away in the cry of 'No Surrender'. By pinning the whole blame squarely on one man, no one has to think about the other people in Derry who would rather have given in to a king who might be a Catholic but had no wish to massacre Protestants.

Not understanding the temper of the people of Derry, James arrived on 18 April to offer terms for a negotiated surrender. After some hours of listening to gunfire and shouts of 'No Surrender!' he returned to Dublin. The siege went on for 105 days and caused appalling suffering, which like the 1641 massacres burned into the psyches of Ulster Protestants. The deaths from bombardment and occasional hand-to-hand fighting were a minor aspect; it was starvation and fever that were the real enemies. In his account of the siege, George Walker gave a July price list for meat which any Derry Protestant will recognize today. A dog's head was offered for 2/6, a cat for 4/6, a rat for 1/- and a mouse for 6d; the most horrible item, at 5/6, was a quarter of a dog '(fattened by eating the bodies of the slain Irish)'. The estimate of deaths from starvation and fever is around 15,000; it was alleged that all the children died. Yet as late as the end of June, it is said, when Major Baker died of fever, Colonel John Mitchelburne, his replacement as Walker's co-governor, flew a bloody and crimson flag from the cathedral tower as an expression of Derry's defiance. (The Derry 'Crimson' flag is carried at all Apprentice Boys' celebrations.)

The conduct of General Rosen, a Lithuanian mercenary in the pay of Louis XIV, also left deep scars. At the beginning of July, returning from Dublin, he was appalled to find that the commanding officer, General Richard Hamilton, had permitted 10,000 civilians to leave the city. Rosen rounded up all the Protestants within ten miles' radius of the city and drove them under the walls to force the defenders to take them in. He let them go again after the garrison erected a gallows on the walls and threatened to hang their Jacobite prisoners. The Protestant folk-memory has not retained the information that James was horrified when he heard of Rosen's inhumanity and denounced him as barbarous, any more than it recognizes that when it came to bigotry, their revered Reverend Walker's sermons in St Columb's Cathedral during the siege would be hard to beat.*

A floating boom across the Foyle had deterred rescuers; for six weeks the agony of the defenders had been increased by the sight of the masts of English ships on Lough Foyle. At last, on 28 July, the *Mountjoy* broke the boom and with the *Phoenix* and the *Dartmouth* brought supplies to Derry. Three days later, Hamilton raised the siege.

'Valour like yours seldom occurs,' claimed Gregg, as he addressed the spirits of the dead defenders:

> I will venture to say that history records none to be compared with it. Waterloo itself, great as was the stake and momentous the consequence, must yield to it in fame . . .
>
> In the one the colossal power of Europe furnished the embattled legions – in the other a handful of citizens, almost without arms and ammunition, undertook the

---

* For instance: 'We cannot but reflect on the popish cruelty . . . in the reign of King Charles 1st, Annno 1641, when without provocation, armed with Hellish rage and the natural cruelty of the Papist, they by inhuman torments massacred no less than 200,000 English Protestants of all ages and sex . . . And what can we think at this day but a Papist is a Papist still, where even the principle of religion instills a kind of fierceness and barbarity into their nature.' Protestants, he went on, must 'become valiant for truth and bold as lions, not only for their religion but temporal interest'.

defence of the city, against a regular army of 20,000 men, furnished with every article of war. In the one there was the dense phalanx, the thick column, and the extended line; steed was supplied with steed, and a soldier stepped in where a soldier fell. In the other every man that was carried off was a loss irreparable; there was no succour near, none to fill up the melancholy chasm – each day was a battle, and each morning's sun rose to open to the view of the besieged, a scene of more misery. The hero, who in the morning took leave of his family, found them on his return sunk in the arms of death; famine and disease had consigned them to a premature grave – the infant was seen sucking the breast of its departed parent; and the emaciated citizens tottered through the streets more like spectres than like men.

There were songs, of course, of which the most beloved is 'Derry's Walls':

The time has scarce gone by, boys,
　　Two hundred years ago,
When rebels on old Derry's Walls,
　　Their faces dare not show:
When James and all his rebel band,
　　Came up to Bishop's Gate,
With heart and hand and sword and shield,
　　We caused them to retreat.

CHORUS: *Then work and don't surrender,*
But come when duty calls,
With heart and hand and sword and shield,
We'll guard old Derry's Walls.

For blood did flow in crimson streams,
　　For many a winter's night,
They knew the Lord was on their side,
　　To help them in the fight:
They nobly stood upon the Walls,
　　Determined for to die,
To fight and gain the victory
　　And hoist the Crimson high.

CHORUS

At last, at last, with one broadside
   Kind heaven sent them aid,
The boom was broke that crossed Foyle's shores,
   And James he was dismayed.
The Banner, boys, that floated,
   Was run aloft with joy,
God bless the hands that broke the boom
   And saved the 'Prentice Boys.

CHORUS.

The concept that endurance, intransigence and faith in God would bring victory to the righteous in the end had been reinforced yet again.

7

'The Orange Quadrilateral'

Some folks sing of mountains and valleys
Where the wild flowers abundantly grow,
And some of the wave-crested billows
That dash 'neath the waters below.
But I'm going to speak of a river,
And I hope in the chorus you'll join –
Of the deeds that were done by King William,
On the green grassy slopes of the Boyne.

CHORUS: *On the green grassy slopes of the Boyne,*
Where the Orangemen with William did join,
And fought for our glorious deliv'rance
On the green grassy slopes of the Boyne.

On the banks of that beautiful river,
There the bones of our forefathers lie,
Awaiting the sound of the trumpet
To call them to glory on high.
In our hearts we will cherish their memories,
And we all like true Brethren will join,
And praise God for sending us King William,
To the green grassy slopes of the Boyne.

CHORUS

Orangemen will be loyal and steady,
For no matter whate'er may betide,
We will still mind our war-cry 'No Surrender!'
So long as we've God on our side,
And if ever our service is needed,
Then we all like true Brethren will join,
And fight, like valiant King William,
On the green grassy slopes of the Boyne.

CHORUS

'The Green Grassy Slopes'

ANGLO-IRISH RELATIONS HAVE NORMALLY been central to Ireland and peripheral to Britain. That is one reason why extreme nationalists frequently conclude that only violence will focus the attention of the British government on real or alleged Irish grievances and why loyal

British citizens living in Ireland have so often felt betrayed and abandoned. But the Catholic Irish have always been sustained by the hope that the world beyond the neighbouring island would provide a saviour: over the hill would come help – in the form of arms, money or men – from France or Spain or Rome (and later Germany or the United States) which would defeat and expel the Gall (Irish for foreigner), the Saxon or whoever at the time was the resident enemy.

Such foreign incursions have always proved to be badly briefed, under-manned, under-financed or just plain unlucky, but the native optimism of the revolutionary Irish, their quasi-cosmopolitanism and, increasingly, their dependency culture, continue to triumph. Once they looked to Europe. Now they look to America for political clout and to Irish America for money.

The Protestant British living in Ireland have for centuries been terrified of such foreign enemies; the only foreign leaders to have brought them succour were the little Dutchman and, later, the unattractive Hanoverians. They have had only Britain to rely on, and it has been at best half-hearted and at worst treacherous to its loyal if troublesome citizens in its western outpost. But then Ireland has tended to be single-issue, while Britain has had a lot on its mind.

So had King William III. While his desperate followers in Londonderry and elsewhere were trying to stave off disaster, he had to deal on the Continent with the rapacious Louis XIV. From May 1689 he was using his exceptional diplomatic skills to build up around him an anti-Louis consortium, the Grand Alliance, which by 1691 would include Bavaria, Brandenburg, Hanover, Savoy, Saxony, Spain and the Pope. But first he had to deal with his father-in-law, Louis's pawn, still king in Ireland.

Two of what are called 'the Orange quadrilateral of Williamite victories' had already been won before William went to Ireland. Brother Dewar wrote:

Derry held Ireland's 'North West Frontier' for the Revolution. Enniskillen was then, as now, the gateway to the South West. If the keynote of Derry was defence, that of Enniskillen was attack. The City of the Foyle became a City of Refuge, The Castle on the Erne became a power house, radiating energy to its garrison, encouragement to its northern neighbours under siege, and death and defiance to its enemies . . . The one name 'Enniskillen' on Orange arches covers a whole series of guerrilla battles fought throughout Fermanagh, and sorties led into Monaghan and Cavan and Sligo.

On the very day that Londonderry was relieved, at Newtownbutler,* 2,000 or so Enniskilleners won a key victory over the Jacobite forces. A booklet produced for the tercentenary celebrations by County Fermanagh Grand Lodge records:

> The Jacobite foot betook themselves to the bogs, throwing away their arms, and were pursued all that night by Enniskilleners, who kept beating the bushes for the fugitives and shouting, 'No Popery, no mercy.' No bugle call could bring them back. Of the Jacobites, 2,000 were killed, 500 jumped into Lough Erne, and every man except one was drowned; 500 were carried prisoners to Enniskillen, and with them the general Lord Mountcashel, and a great many officers.

It was a perfect welcome for the Duke of Schomberg,† William's septuagenarian general, who arrived at Bangor a fortnight later: 'The shore was all crowded with Protestants', wrote a contemporary reporter, 'men, women, and children – old and young, falling on their knees with tears in their eyes thanking God and the English for their deliverance.' First losing Carrickfergus, the Jacobites had been driven out of Ulster by mid-September, after which Schomberg and his 20,000-strong army holed up for the winter. As thousands of his men died of fever, Schomberg showed himself to be of the right mettle to be a Calvinist hero: he made a punishable offence 'the Horrid and Detestable Crimes of Prophane Cursing, Swearing, and taking God's Holy Name in vain'.

Schomberg's leisurely approach to the war created problems. By the spring of 1690 Louis had massively reinforced Tyrconnel's army and William was obliged to do the same for Schomberg. Then, on 14 June, with 300 warships, William himself arrived in Carrickfergus to an ecstatic welcome from the crowds, and travelled to Belfast where the populace was similarly enthused. A Presbyterian deputation to William on his

---

* This provides yet another anniversary, 'Enniskillen Day', celebrated in County Fermanagh by the Royal Black Institution on 12 August (31 July Old Style), which technically should be 10 August.

† The remarkable career of Friedrich Schomberg, a German soldier of fortune, included a long period of service under Louis XIV which was rewarded by the baton of a Marshal of France. After the revocation of the Edict of Nantes he went back to his homeland and then served William.

The relief of Derry had been hastened because Schomberg's son was inside the walls: it was a note from the duke in London that had the ships finally sent up the Foyle.

arrival in Ulster in 1689 had secured from him, against Anglican* protests, a doubling of the £600 *regium donum*, annual grant from the royal
purse towards the upkeep of its ministers, first granted by Charles II.

In the Grand Orange Lodge's tercentenary brochure, Cecil Kilpatrick
lovingly traces the progress of King William through Ulster, the roads
that he took, the churches where he prayed (at one, the preacher's text
was Hebrews 11.33: 'Who through Faith subdued kingdoms'), the people
he met and the places where he rested. Though he was slight, pale,
asthmatic and had poor English, William had the common touch; he was
happy, for instance, to live and fight alongside his soldiers. In England,
where he was always rather looked down on by the mighty, he was
very popular with the people. In Ulster, his unpretentious, hard-working,
religious followers, who wanted to love him, loved him. In Belfast,
comments Brother Dewar, 'began a long "affair of the heart" between its
citizens and the Dutch Prince-President, whose homely virtues of thrift,
courage, and sincerity of purpose, were so similar to their own. The
Dutchman and the Ulsterman had, and have, more than a little in common.'

With his mind on Continental Europe, William wanted to sort out
Ireland quickly. Within twelve days he had left Ulster for the first and
last time: by 30 June, he was on the north side of the River Boyne, near
Drogheda, ready to take on James.

William had a cosmopolitan force of about 36,000 that reflected his
pan-European anti-French alliance: mainly Danes, Dutch, English, French
Huguenots and Germans. Cork provided two companies, but the bulk of
the Irish troops were Ulster settlers, notably 800 men from Derry and
4,500 from Enniskillen. (As ferocious as they were poor, the Enniskilleners were described thus by a contemporary: 'The sight of their thin
little nags and the wretched dress of their riders, half naked with sabre
and pistols hanging from their belts, looked like a horde of tartars.')
James's men were primarily Irish and Old English Catholics and French.

Not only did William have 10,000 more men than James,† but he had
far more firepower. He was also by far the superior strategist and had
the energy and determination as a leader that James seemed to have long

---

* One of those who protested most noisily was the Reverend George Walker, hero of the siege, who was to
fall at the Battle of the Boyne before he could take up the bishopric of Derry which he had been promised. As
Presbyterians were frequently to find, Protestant unity rarely lasted long after an emergency.

† Patriotic balladeers always like to believe their champions were heavily outnumbered. So, for instance, in
'Aughrim and the Boyne', the numbers are estimated at 36,000 troops under William and 73,000 under James.

ago lost. By nightfall on Tuesday 1 July (Old Style), James, on the advice of Tyrconnel, was on his way to France, leaving behind him an inglorious reputation with both the Irish he had led and the Irish who had contributed to his defeat. Irish nationalists branded him a traitor and a coward who had used them cynically.

To the unsophisticated Protestant he is summed up by a song called 'King James II', which includes the verse:

I'll have a bowl with James's face
Depicted in the cup;
We'll fill and empty – who would leave
That tyrant king a drop?
For Rome he would a-mass his power –
But mark what came to pass:
The bigot lost three golden crowns,
For that vain thing – a mass

Though in Ireland the war was about religion and land, in Continental Europe the issue was the balance of power: Louis had many Catholic enemies. 'History is a funny thing, you know,' observed that well-read Orangeman George Chittick: 'I amaze people by telling them that, as a matter of fact, the pope was glad he [William] won that battle because of European politics at that time. He was afraid of Louis getting too big for his boots.' (They become amazed, too, on learning that James had some Protestant and William some Catholic troops.)

Another anonymous lyricist, a composer of 'The Boyne Water', was kinder:

So, praise God, all true Protestants!
    And I will say no further,
But had the Papists gained the day,
    There would have been open murder:
Although King James and many more
    Were ne'er that way inclined,
It was not in their power to stop
    What the rabble they designed.

It was an observation true of both tribes: neither was disposed to give its enemies quarter. Indeed, the previous year, after taking Carrickfergus,

Schomberg had had to intervene to stop a massacre of the defeated Irish by the settlers. But in the Protestant folk-memory and on Orange banners, Schomberg is for ever at the Boyne, either riding across it with William or dying in action after being shot in the throat – a dramatic end for a man of seventy-four.*

The most famous images of William – in pictures, murals, on banners, tea-towels and any other appropriate surface – show him at the Boyne on a white horse. The Ulster Protestant may delude himself, but he is keen on truth, so the Orange Order has faced up manfully to those revisionists who questioned the horse's colour. *The Junior Orangeman's Catechism* includes the following:

> Q.30. What colour was King William's horse?
> A.30. Some old pictures show black, some brown. When the House of Hanover, 'being Protestant,' came to rule over us in 1714 they brought their 'White Horse of Hanover' as the badge of Loyalty to the Protestant Cause. That is probably how it came to be connected with William of Orange, but as a King he must have had a whole stable full of horses!

Though James had gone, the Irish still had leaders determined to fight on though now they were fighting *against* the English rather than *for* the Stuarts. While James in France was blaming his defeat on his Irish troops, they, under the command of Patrick Sarsfield, were earning the respect of the Williamites by stubbornly clinging on west of the Shannon. Having failed to capture Limerick, William handed over command at the end of August to Ginkel, his fellow-Dutchman, and went back to London to pursue his Continental strategies.

> Q.32. What happened to King William after 1690?

---

*   Glory illumes with holy light,
The memory of the brave;
And laurel leaves, fresh, green and bright,
Adorn the hero's grave.
For none more nobly fell in fight,
Or Freedom's sword did wave
Than William's true and gallant knight –
Schomberg, the bold and brave!'
                    'SCHOMBERG'

A.32. He passes out of Irish history, though he has never been forgotten in Ireland. He waged constant warfare against the French, even the Pope being glad of his support against Louis XIV, who cruelly persecuted the Huguenots and also quarrelled with the Pope! He died after a fall from his horse, which stumbled over a molehill at Hampton Court in 1702. The Jacobites always drank to the health of the 'little gentleman in black velvet' (the mole) who had succeeded in killing their enemy for them.

The beginning of the end of Irish resistance did not come for almost another year, but on 12 July (Old Style) 1691, the Williamite army was victorious in what was for Irish nationalism probably the most catastrophic military defeat ever. Aughrim was lost because of confusion and bad luck; among the many thousands of Irish Catholics killed were what were described as 'the flower of their army and nation'. Protestants lit bonfires when the news came to Ulster: 'The Orange Quadrilateral was complete,' said Brother Dewar. 'The first Heroic Age of Orangeism was over.'*

Although the Irish resistance continued for a few months, the only realistic issue was what surrender terms could be negotiated. Again the Williamites showed themselves merciful. The main provisions of the Treaty of Limerick signed by Ginkel and Sarsfield in October 1691 promised Catholics the same freedom of worship as under Charles II, allowed French soldiers to go home and Irish soldiers to keep their Irish lands if they gave their allegiance to William and Mary or to leave for the Continent. More than 12,000 Irish soldiers, led by Patrick Sarsfield, sailed away to fight for Austria, France and Spain; what became known as the 'flight of the wild geese' was another loss carved into the Irish nationalist consciousness. Sarsfield was to die fighting for Louis XIV against William: 'Brave men', says an Orange historian, 'deserved a better cause to fight for, in both church and State.'

As far as nationalist history is concerned, the Treaty of Limerick was another English betrayal, for parts of it were not ratified. The fault does not, however, lie with King William, or indeed with the Westminster parliament; the problem was at home. When the first Irish parliament was summoned in 1692, despite the best efforts of the king's viceroy, it

---

* 'Retreat from Aughrim' was a popular patriotic song in my youth. The battle is so engraved on my psyche as a defeat that recently, talking about a big mistake the Orange Order had made, I bewildered an Orange friend by shaking my head and saying: 'Of course, that's where Aughrim was lost.'

refused to ratify the treaty and insisted on further wholesale land confiscation. As Jonathan Bardon puts it: 'William did what he could to limit the scope of land confiscation, but if the Glorious Revolution meant anything, it meant that the monarch had to bow to the wishes of parliament.'

So polarized is Ulster that it is unlikely that many Protestants today will have thought about the effect on the Catholic psyche of that century of dispossession. In 1603, at the end of the Tudor conquest, 90 per cent of Irish land was still in Catholic hands; after the last seventeenth-century confiscation, that figure was down to 14 per cent. It would have been asking a lot to expect the landless to recognize that this was not the fault of William of Orange.

Similarly, there were no fine distinctions made about who was responsible for the next round of religious persecution. In Ireland, the two tribes always play a zero-sum game: one man's gain is another man's loss and only a fool or a traitor gives ground. The Irish parliament, which was almost wholly composed of Established Church landowners, was determined that Protestants should never again risk the annihilation so narrowly avoided in the 1640s and 1680s. To that end, from 1695 and over the next three decades, were passed the first of a series of Penal Laws banning Catholics from bearing arms, buying land, preserving their estates intact through primogeniture, entering the army, the law or any public office, voting, or being members of corporations or of parliament. Further, convinced 'that the late Rebellions in this Kingdom have been Contrived, Promoted and Carried on by Popish Archbishops, Bishops, Jesuits, and other Ecclesiastical Persons of the Romish Clergy . . . which said Romish Clergy do . . . daily stir up, and move Sedition, and Rebellion, to the great hazard of the Ruine and Desolation of this Kingdom,' priests were exiled and driven underground and the 'mass rock' once more became the main place of worship. Where they could, the governments of William and his successor, his sister-in-law Anne, held the Irish parliament back from such legislative excesses as castrating priests.

Presbyterians suffered too. Famine in Scotland led to thousands of deaths: in the 1690s tens of thousands of Scots Presbyterians survived only because they emigrated to Ireland. This was bad for Ulster Catholics, many of whom were displaced by hungry, hard people. And it was worrying for the Established Church in England and Ireland which already saw dissenters as religious competitors and feared Presbyterians might capture the Established Church in Ireland, as they had in Scotland. Their main grievance – that their marriage and burial services were not recognized as valid – paled into insignificance beside the addition to the Irish 'Prevent the Further Growth of Popery' Bill of 1704 of a clause requiring anyone in public office to take the Anglican communion once a year. Since Catholics were already barred from public office, this Sacramental Test Act was aimed at Presbyterians; one could view it as an early manifestation of the modern English preoccupation with being even-handed at all costs with various Irish factions. Among its immediate effects was that Presbyterians were forced to withdraw from municipal corporations; being driven off the Belfast Corporation was bad enough, losing ten out of twelve aldermen in Londonderry, where so many of their co-religionists had died during the siege, was felt as an outrage.

Still, neither Catholics nor Presbyterians suffered anything like as badly as a result of religious discrimination as they like to believe. The spasmodically-observed Penal Laws were irrelevant to the labouring classes; most priests stayed in Ireland; enterprising Catholics went into commerce; the Test Act was only half-heartedly enforced and during the eighteenth century, when it suited parliament, exceptions were made to allow Presbyterians to hold various offices. Yet though Catholics had far more to complain about, the Presbyterian sense of grievance was greatly exacerbated by the knowledge that they were being discriminated against by fellow-Protestants and a government to which they had given their loyalty; and their folk-memory is full of a burning sense of injustice against the Anglican Establishment, as well as bewilderment at being alleged by the Irish to be part of the Protestant Ascendancy, many of whom regarded Presbyterians as more dangerous than Catholics.

'We always hear about the Penal Laws being used against Roman Catholics,' George Chittick said to me, 'but the Penal Laws were used more against Presbyterians in many cases, for the simple reason that the landlords and the High Church feared them. Knox, as a Calvinist, believed that children should be able to read the scriptures for themselves, so therefore they should be educated, should be able to read and write. And Presbyterians carried that out and that was a fear to the landed gentry who were the only ones could read and write at that time. And there was always this fear and there was always this work ethic among them, where they'd build things and do things and it didn't go down too well with the landlords. So it was to keep them down. They weren't allowed to hold office unless they took the Test Oaths and this, that and the other.'

Shared persecution at first did nothing to bring Catholic and Presbyterian together; indeed, Presbyterians were enthusiastic supporters of anti-Catholic legislation. In a region which during the Williamite wars had once again been devastated, they were still bitter rivals in the struggle to survive. By offering land to the highest bidder when leases ran out, many landlords exacerbated mutual fear and loathing. During the first half of the eighteenth century, drought, frost and disease destroyed crops and cattle and caused widespread famine. In 1741, it is calculated that starvation and fever in Ireland killed 300,000 people and that Ulster, the poorest region of Ireland, suffered most.

While Catholics formed the majority at the bottom of the heap and therefore bore the brunt, life was terrible too for Protestant labourers, small farmers, weavers and workmen. But true to their pioneering spirit, from about 1718, Scots Irish Presbyterians began to emigrate to America in their tens of thousands; of these more than a quarter were bound by contracts of indenture of upwards of four years. Their poverty and their frontier spirit combined to send them beyond the settled land often into conflict with the Indians, as, indeed, with authority. In 1720, James Logan, a native of Lurgan and now Provincial Secretary of Pennsylvania, welcomed his 'brave fellow-countrymen'. Being nervous of Indians, he 'thought it would be prudent to plant a settlement of such men as those who formerly had so bravely defended Londonderry and Inniskillen as a frontier ... These people, if kindly used, will be orderly as they have hitherto been and easily dealt with.' Within ten years he was describing Scots Irish as 'troublesome settlers to the government and hard neighbours to the Indians'. As behoved an adventurer, Theodore Roosevelt saw them in a kinder light: 'They were a bold and hardy people who pushed past the settled regions of America and plunged into the wilderness as the leaders of the white advance. The Irish Presbyterians were the first and last set of immigrants to do this: all others have merely followed in the wake of their predecessors.'

Bitter at what they saw as their betrayal by crown and aristocracy, and passionate about civil and religious liberty, it was to be expected that the quarter-of-a-million or so Scots Irish emigrants would prove fertile ground for revolutionary ideas. So huge was their contribution to the American War of Independence (1775–83) that George Washington is believed by many to have said that if he were defeated everywhere else, 'I will make my stand for liberty among the Scots-Irish of my native Virginia.'

Here is a verse from 'Hi! Uncle Sam', a poem which illustrates Ulster
Protestant resentment at US pro-Irishness:

Hi! Uncle Sam!
Virginia sent her brave men,
The North paraded grave men,
That they might not be slave men,
   But ponder this with calm:
The first to face the Tory,
And the first to lift Old Glory
Made your war an Ulster story:
Think it over, Uncle Sam!

'They became the most ferocious fighters for American liberty,' said
George Chittick, 'but they also remembered their Orange roots. They were
also very fond of William. You got Orange county, you got Aughrim. You
go to the western seaboard, to Tennessee, to Virginia, to Maine – you'll
get the names Aughrim, Boyne, Belfast, Londonderry – an awful lot of
them. If you go to the presidential pew in Washington Cathedral, the
coat of arms carved above this pew is that of William of Orange, the
House of Nassau. I don't know if you've ever seen Trumbull's painting
of the signing of the Declaration of Independence – the Orange standard
is on the wall. The name "hillbillies" came because the people of the
mountains sang songs about William.

'Some folk wouldn't like you to say them things, but that's the truth.
They were more outgoing, they were more ferocious against George III,
the reason being because they'd been driven out by the High Church. It
was the Orange Irish gave America liberty, not the Irish Irish.

'I remember going to Texas, down to Alamo, and a tricolour was
flying. I asked, "What's that doing up there?" "Oh," he says, "they
were Irishmen." "No, friend. Oh no, no, no, no, no. They were Presbyterians. Sam Houston was a son of the manse. Davy Crockett was a
Presbyterian. So was Jim Bowie. And the man who defended the Alamo,
Travis, came from County Armagh." And I says, "The Tennessee Volunteers were Scotch-Irish to a man. And they wouldn't thank you for having
that up there if they were here. It shouldn't be up there." I couldn't
believe it.

'I'll never forget the last bit. I'd bought a Stetson to keep the sun off
my head. And this lady in a big Texas drawl says, "'Scuse me, sir.

Would you remove your hat? You're on holy ground.'' I felt like saying to her, ''You're right,'' but I said, ''I'm sorry,'' and took my hat off.'

Affection for William is as strong as ever today, partly because of his sheer humanity. 'I can identify with William,' said an Orangeman with a more exotic past than many. 'He got drunk once, threw stones at a woman's window and tried to climb up a ladder. I've never led an army into battle, but I've got drunk over a woman. I'd love a banner with King William climbing the ladder.' Orangemen are happy with their anxious hero who did his duty, lived plainly, shared the hardships of his men and – though he was emotionally stunted – loved his wife. Their only worry – which for people who take the Old Testament seriously is a big one – is the persistent rumour that William was homosexual.* There is no proof either way, but the historian and Orangeman, the Reverend M. W. Dewar, faces the issue manfully:

> The whole unfortunate rumour seems to have been based on a misunderstanding of a passage by his close confidential friend and chaplain, Dr Gilbert Burnet. The good Burnet did not always express himself very clearly, and in trying to gloss over an illicit love affair with a Court lady, spoke of William 'having endeavoured to cover' the 'disorders that are all too common to princes'. Later Burnet wrote 'he had no vice but of the one sort', which made matters worse. Like David, the Man after God's own Heart, William of Orange was not entirely sinless. But he was not, in any way, *unnaturally vicious*. But for these 'bumbling phrases' of poor Bishop Burnet no such charge is likely to have been brought against him.

Back home, however, whatever the tensions between Anglicans and dissenters, fear of the enemy close to hand could be relied upon to bring most classes and sects of Protestants together. Shared pride in the Williamite victories and a real affection for King William provided a focus for celebrations and even a vantage-point from which to look back at recent settler history. From the 1690s onwards, an Orange tradition began to

---

* The story is told that the late H. Montgomery Hyde, a unionist MP, fell out with his constituency association because he had written that William was homosexual.

By a strange irony, when I wrote a biography of that nationalist hero Patrick Pearse, the leader of the 1916 Rising, I had to deal with a similar allegation. My conclusion – that he was a non-practising homosexual who probably did not even recognize his own orientation – pleased neither his admirers nor his detractors. Nationalists are even less inclined than loyalists to acknowledge that their heroes may not be perfect.

spread, helped along by clubs. On 1 August 1714, the twenty-fifth anniversary of the raising of the siege, for instance, Colonel Mitchelburne, one of the siege heroes, hoisted a crimson flag on the steeple of St Columb's Cathedral and formed an Apprentice Boys club. Although it did not long survive him, in 1775 the Independent Mitchelburne Club was formed. Throughout the eighteenth century, descendants of the thirteen apprentice boys and other heroes of the siege attended services at the cathedral in honour of their ancestors, and there were annual celebrations of the shutting of the gates and the relief of the city, complete with processions, the firing of guns and general festivity.

Elsewhere, and widespread, there were clubs like the Boyne Men, the Glorious Order of the Boyne, the Royal Boyne Society, the Aldermen of Skinner's Alley* and, in England, the toffs' Orange club – the Loyal and Friendly Society of the Orange and Blew, founded in 1727 – which consisted of officers of the Fourth Regiment of Foot (sometimes called King William's Regiment), who sported blue and orange ribbons and celebrated, *inter alia*, the Glorious Revolution.

Except for the Royal Boyne Society, the Irish clubs were open to all classes, which tended to exacerbate their sectarianism. The charter oath of the Dublin Aldermen of Skinner's Alley, for instance, became a famous toast which was worlds apart from the exalted sentiments about liberty and peace favoured by the Orange and Blew.

> To the glorious, pious, and immortal memory of the great and good King William, not forgetting Oliver Cromwell, who assisted in redeeming us from popery, slavery, arbitrary power, brass money, and wooden shoes. May we never want a Williamite to kick the arse of a Jacobite! and a fart for the Bishop of Cork! And he that won't drink this, whether he be priest, bishop, deacon, bellows-blower, grave-digger, or any other of the fraternity of the clergy. May a north wind blow him to the south, and a west wind blow him to the east! May he have a dark night, a lee shore, a rank storm, and a leaky vessel, to carry him over the river Styx! May the dog Cerberus make a meal of his rump, and Pluto a snuff-box of his skull; and may the devil jump

---

✻ The Protestant aldermen of the Dublin Corporation dismissed by James in 1688 in favour of a Catholic body used to meet around a bust of William. After the Protestant corporation was reinstated, the Aldermen of Skinner's Alley was formed; sheep's trotters were served at their dinners to commemorate James's flight from Dublin (a Williamite medal on one side showed James running away and on the other a deer with winged hoofs).

The Lord Mayor of Dublin still sports a chain of office with a Williamite medallion; the Belfast medallion has a harp and the Gaelic inscription 'Céad Míle Fáilte' ('a hundred thousand welcomes').

down his throat with a red-hot harrow, with every pin tear out a gut, and blow him
with a clean carcass to hell! Amen.

Tony Gray, who wrote a book about the Orange Order in the 1970s,
quoted this version from *The Orange Society* (published by the Catholic
Truth Society in 1899), took it seriously as an Orange Order toast and
was duly horrified. In fact, it owes much to an Irish oral tradition which
enjoys devising hugely elaborate curses just for the fun of it. (My Irish-
speaking mother used to revel in curses such as, 'Glass legs under you'.)

Certainly it rapidly became a general Orange, and later an Orange
Order, toast. Of the later versions, probably the most common followed
'wooden shoes' with 'and whoever denies this toast may he be slammed,
crammed and jammed into the muzzle of the great gun of Athlone, and
the gun fired into the Pope's belly, and the Pope into the devil's belly,
and the devil into hell, and the door locked, and the key forever in an
Orangeman's pocket'.

Few contemporary Orangemen would know this toast. And I know no
Orangemen who would make it seriously; it is just a bit of amusing
history.

Years of fear and uncertainty brought about the establishment in 1795
of the Orange Order. There was revolution abroad, brutal sectarian violence at home and intense political debate about great constitutional issues.

Although Ulster Protestants had initially sympathized with and backed
the American colonists when the War of Independence broke out in 1775,
they rallied against the threat in 1778 of a French invasion. Fear of
foreign invasion was well-founded: only eighteen years earlier French
forces had occupied and held Carrickfergus. And early in 1778 John Paul
Jones, of the American 'navy', had captured a British vessel in Belfast
Lough. Since a severe economic depression had left the government
almost bankrupt and most regular troops had been sent to America, the
defence of the country had to be undertaken by its citizens. Volunteer
forces formed throughout Ireland were composed of those prosperous
enough to equip themselves with uniforms and arms. By 1783 they had
reached a strength of 100,000.

The Volunteers used their muscle to force constitutional and commercial concessions from the British government; from 1782 the Irish parliament was independent. By the mid-1780s, however, Volunteer numbers
and influence were on the wane. When the French Revolution broke out in
1789, many Presbyterians were enthusiastic supporters; the more radical

element were to join the United Irishmen, set up in 1791 to demand religious equality and radical electoral reform. But fearful of any resurgence of Volunteer activity, in 1793, when war broke out with revolutionary France, the British government suppressed the Volunteers and set up a proper paid militia composed mainly of peasants and artisans. Most officers were Protestant, but Catholics were in a majority of about three to one.

The anti-sectarianism of the United Irishmen was, however, way out of step with the majority of the population. Agrarian secret societies flourished: most notorious were the Catholic Defenders, who would better have been named the Aggressors, many of whom were literate tradesmen who had borrowed from Freemasonry to construct a network of lodges whose members used oaths and signs and passwords and, in reaction to them, a loose collection of Protestants known as the Peep o' Day Boys.

I well remember the frightful state of things that now prevailed in Ulster [wrote an old man in 1835 à propos the foundation of the Orange Order]. On the one hand, there was a dense mass of organized Roman Catholics, who already felt their strength, and who were united both by the prejudices of a sect, and the principles of a party, into a confederacy having for its object the extirpation of heresy and the liberation of Ireland. On the other hand, there were the Protestant peasants and farmers, not bound together in any system of association – unsupported, if not discountenanced by their own gentry, amongst whom revolutionary principles very extensively prevailed, and exposed, both by night and day, to outrages against which the laws of the land afforded but a weak protection.

Neither side had a monopoly on outrages. Defenders tended to attack Protestants from behind ditches, while Peep o' Day Boys specialized in raiding Catholic houses on the pretext of searching for arms. County Armagh, then as now, was a by-word for sectarian viciousness. As peasants fought over land, artisans fought over markets.

The traditional belief that Peep o' Day Boys founded the Orange Order after a fracas with Defenders does not bear scrutiny. As the recent research of James Wilson* confirms, the main founders were in fact Volunteers,

---

* In discussing the early years of the Orange Order, I have drawn heavily on the recent, pioneering work of James Wilson, whose kindness in letting me see in typescript his essay on 'Orangeism in 1798' I greatly appreciate.

many of whom had been involved in clashes with Defenders from the late 1780s onwards. Parades had provided the flash-point. On a Sunday in November 1788, for instance, as the Benburb Volunteers marched to Armagh Cathedral for a service, 'they were assaulted by a large body of Papists who took a bayonet from one of the lads, and pursued them with stones,' enraged, apparently, because they were 'playing tunes that were an insult to Catholics': 'The Boyne Water' and 'The Protestant Boys'.* In the ensuing mêlée, two Catholics were shot. Their funerals were attended by huge crowds. Henceforward, points out Wilson, Defenders regarded Volunteers as 'legitimate targets'; Volunteers saw themselves as the keepers of law and order.

Against the backdrop of the French Revolution and the pressure to remove the remaining penal laws, political awareness and expectations were raised and Protestant fears exacerbated. Giving evidence in 1835 to the Commons Select Committee on Orange Lodges, Lieutenant-Colonel William Verner, Orangeman and member of the County Armagh gentry, described a gruesome event which in his view caused Protestants in 1791 to reach the conclusion:

> that there existed a decided hostility upon the part of Roman Catholics towards the Protestants of the country. A gentleman of the name of Jackson died and demised his property to religious and charitable purposes, and required by his Will that a Protestant colony should be established upon his property in that part of the country . . . [and] that there should be four schools established for the purpose of the education of the children of all denominations and persuasions. In the attempt to establish this colony, the persons who came to reside there were frequently

---

* This is sung to the tune of 'Lilliburlero'. The last verse runs:

The Protestant Boys are loyal and true,

Though fashions are changed and the loyal are few,

The Protestant Boys are true to the last,

Though cowards belied them when danger has past.

Aye! still we stand

A loyal band,

And reck not the liars whatever they say;

For let the drums rattle,

The summons to battle,

The Protestant Boys must carry the day.

threatened by the Roman Catholics, and told that they should not come into that part of the country.

Defenders made an example of one of the schoolmasters, Alexander Barclay (or Berkeley), by cutting off his tongue and fingers, similarly mutilating his thirteen-year-old teenage brother-in-law and torturing his wife so badly that she died. 'The unfortunate man asked if he had ever injured them; they replied not, but this was the beginning of what all his sort might expect.' The story, in all its ghastly details, entered the psyche of rural Protestants rather as the barbarities of the Shankill Butchers were to leave their mark on terrified Belfast Catholics almost 200 years later.

As violence increased, the Defenders moved ideologically beyond simple sectarian hate: 'Their contact with the United Irishmen introduced the concept of revolution,' says Wilson, 'which was subject to a translation into a sectarian Catholic nationalism endorsed by millenarian prophecy.' The replacement of the Volunteers by the largely Catholic militia helped the spread of the secret, oath-bound Defender lodges. Simultaneously, an attempt was made to set up a respectable umbrella organization to take a stand in defence of the crown and the Protestant religion against what was being seen as a ruthless revolutionary conspiracy. Known as the 'Orange Boys', it was founded in the Dyan in East Tyrone by a Freemason, also called James Wilson.

The showdown came in September 1795; the background was escalating aggression. As an Orange historian puts it:

It was the old story – raids and counter-raids for arms, attacks on individuals and groups at markets and fairs, destruction of property, challenges between one party and another. But now things were coming to a crisis. It was no longer to be just a matter of personal grudges, or competition for farms and employment, or a continuing and obstinate social, religious, and racial dislike. All these things were there, but it was now believed that local outbreaks of Defenderism were only part of a widespread conspiracy, and evidence of a dangerous plot against the Government, and more especially against the Protestants of the County of Armagh . . . To deal with what seemed to be a deliberate, organised, violent attempt to dominate the countryside and drive out the Protestant population, there appeared to be little enough.

The occasion was provided by a local quarrel: a Defender had been badly beaten by a Peep o' Day Boy after a cockfight outside the tavern of Dan Winter at the Diamond, a hamlet at a crossroads near Loughgall in County Armagh. A couple of weeks later, shots were exchanged after a fight between Catholics and Protestants returning from a wake and a dance respectively. Arrests resolved nothing; each group continued to terrorize the vulnerable.

The Defenders had two reasons for attacking Dan Winter's tavern. That it was a meeting-place for Peep o' Day Boys made it in their eyes a legitimate target. And, strategically, capturing the Diamond and the surrounding hills would have put them in a position to dominate the neighbourhood. On the 18th, around 500 Defenders mustered on Annaghmore Hill, overlooking the Diamond; 'Orange Boys' assembled on the hill opposite. After a skirmish nearby had resulted in the death of a Defender, local gentry and priests brokered a deal. But when Defender reinforcements from Tyrone arrived on Sunday, they insisted on action. At around 5 a.m. on Monday 21 September, about 300 Defenders fell upon the Diamond and attacked Dan Winter's house. 'At the critical moment,' writes an Orange historian, 'whether fresh supplies or fresh men had arrived, a number of the Protestants who had served in the Volunteers stepped out, dressed their line according to the drillbook, and fired a destructive volley, from their commanding position and from close at hand, directly into the disorganised mob of Defenders. This won the battle.' There were up to forty Defenders killed; just one Protestant was wounded.

The victors repaired to the Loughgall inn of James Sloan and in his parlour took the decision to found an exclusively Protestant defensive association based on Wilson's Orange Boys Society. It was to be called the Orange Society; its members would be known as Orangemen.

8

'Conceived and brought forth
by humble men'

They were Twain when they crossed the sea.
    And often their folk had warred:
But side by side on the ramparts wide
    They cheered as the gates were barred:
And they cheered as they passed their King
    To the ford that daunted none.
For, field or wall, it was each for all
    When the Lord had made them One.

Thistle and Rose, they twined them close
    When their fathers crossed the sea,
And they dyed them red, the live and the dead
    In the land where the lint* grows free:
Where the blue-starred lint grows free.
    Here in the Northern sun,
Till His way was plain, He led the Twain,
    And he forged them into One.

And they grew in strength as the years went by,
    And the travail of Empire came,
And they went them forth to the ends of the earth
    With the flag of ancient fame:
Till round the world, that flag unfurled
    Pursued the circling sun,
While foremost still when the day went ill
    Were the Twain whom God made One.

Up-lifted high, that flag will fly
    Above the Ulster-born
They'll hold it dear, and guard it here,
    Unmoved by threat or scorn,
And keep the Gate, despite dictate
    As did the Twain made One.
And undismayed at the Last Parade,
    Fall in and hear 'Well done!'[†]

Rev W. F. Marshall, 1888–1959, Orangeman and Presbyterian
minister at Aughnacloy, Sixmilecross and Castlerock, 'The Twain'

---

* Lint, a material for dressing wounds, is made by scraping linen cloth on one side.

† The loyal institutions are particularly proud of their role in healing divisions between Anglicans and dissenters.

'IN ITS INFANCY,' WROTE Colonel Robert Wallace, a late nineteenth-century Orange historian, 'the Orange system had to struggle against many difficulties. It had been conceived and brought forth by humble men, who sang its first lullaby ... All things considered, the grandest feature of the Orange Society is the catholicity of its constitution. It is Protestant; but not sectarian. From the beginning the doors were thrown wide open to members of all evangelical denominations, and indeed of all political parties whose aspirations were constitutional.' It was fear that excluded Catholics. 'That No Roman Catholic can be admitted in to Our Society, by any means,' said the earliest set of rules and regulations, 'and our reason for so objecting against them is in memory of the bloody Massacre which they Committed on Our Forefathers.'

For fearful Protestants, an organization that transcended their religious, political and social differences was a tremendous breakthrough in uniting against the enemy. It was, for instance, a matter of great psychological importance that the founding group included Presbyterians from the Dyan and Episcopalians from Loughgall. Yet in the earliest days the organization almost split over what to an outsider would seem a trivial matter. When the first primitive warrants were issued by James Sloan to authorize the setting up of lodges of the Orange Society, James Wilson, creator of the Orange Boys, was given No. 1 for the Dyan in County Tyrone, causing Dan Winter of the Diamond in County Armagh to go into a long sulk from which he emerged so late that he ended up with No. 600.

Warrants and their seniority matter a great deal to Orangemen. Colonel Wallace wrote:

> There is nothing that a master prizes more than his Warrant.
>
> The tylers at the head of a Lodge in procession, carrying drawn swords, which have been displaced by deacon poles, stepped out proudly; the fifer and drummer, whose music was alone heard in former days, were proud of their performances; the bannerman was proud; the chaplain was elated to display his Bible on a velvet cushion; but prouder than them all was the Master bearing his Warrant,* the token of his superior office and undisputed authority.

However, James Sloan, the acting secretary, who received No. 28, seems to have successfully played the diplomat and recruiting went ahead speedily. Although warrants cost an Irish guinea, such was the fear of

---

* The Warrant is no longer carried in procession.

the Defenders and the United Irishmen that demand was intense. The main problem for the farmers, weavers and linen manufacturers who formed the initial membership was, said Wallace, 'to give form to the organization – to provide something simple enough for humble men to understand, and strong enough to keep them together'. There needed to be rules and rituals, oaths and passwords that were not too demanding, but would do the job of ensuring such enemies as undercover United Irishmen seeking recruits could not breach the defences; those they adopted drew on Wilson's Orange Boys, the Boyne Societies and Free-masonry.*

From an early stage, therefore, the Orange societies offered a heady mixture of attractions. First, they offered members mutual protection against known and nameless enemies. Second, there were the mysteries. As the historian James Wilson puts it, the appeal of the Freemasons – popular at the time with Catholic and Protestant alike – was that one night a month 'one could find escapism and status . . . secrets, passwords and degrees all helped create an alternative world where mundane life-styles could be exchanged for exciting – often frightening – experiences that were rewarded with the impartment of esoteric knowledge and the conferment of rank. The annual parades to church gave licence to wear sash and ribbon.' Orangeism had plenty of that. And third, they had parades and ceremonies of the kind which emulated those of the Volun-teers, which, again as Wilson puts it, 'allowed Armagh weavers and farmers to swagger along behind a flute band to the air of *The Boyne Water* and feel total fulfilment'.

From the very beginning, their secrets were based on the biblical saga of the exodus of the Children of Israel from Egypt which, as senior Orangeman Dean Waring explained to the Select Committee in 1825, was an allegory which might be construed 'as being a contest between the people of the true Religion, supposed to be under Persecution from those of a worse Religion, as the Israelites were supposed to be persecuted by the Heathens, and protecting themselves from them; I think it is likely that the Protestants might so refer.' Was this, he was asked, because they considered themselves at the time in a state of persecution? 'Yes,' replied

---

* The history of the early years of the Orange Order is at present undergoing intense re-examination by academics. The re-emergence of such primary material as early Grand Lodge minute books requires a thorough reappraisal of the work of Ogle Robert Gowan and Hereward Senior. There is no room here to get involved in this argument or in details, but I am telling the story in the light of new scholarship.

Dean Waring, 'and they do so still.' ('If it were possible to call Dean Waring as a witness in this year of grace,' commented Colonel Wallace in 1899, 'he might say, in relation to the persecution of the Protestants, particularly the Orangemen, "and they do so still". Have not the Orangemen been persecuted and prosecuted by successive Governments, their only offence being that they were too loyal?')

One of the few members of the local gentry to join in the early days was young William Blacker, who obtained No. 12 for a lodge at Carrickblacker in Armagh. He later wrote of the first meeting, held in an area 'labouring under a bad character from the superstition of the neighbours', in a newly-constructed, isolated house which yet lacked windows

> so that all was as dark within as any conspirator could desire. The proverb says 'Walls have ears'. I can only say that if these had any such organs they must have resembled those of a Newfoundland dog after a duck hunt for they were dripping wet . . . It was a scene not unworthy of the pen of a Scott or the pencil of Salvator Rosa to view the assemblage of men, young and old collected on these occasions, as far as could be seen by the light of a few small candles, seated on heaps of sods or rude blocks of wood, more standing in various attitudes, most of them armed with guns of every age and calibre . . . There was a stern solemnity in the reading the lesson from Scripture and administering the oath to the newly admitted brethren which was calculated to produce a deep impression and did so.*

Yet compared to the many initiated behind hedges or in ditches, LOL No. 12 met in luxury.

What most members of the Orange Societies wanted was protection through Protestant defensive action from sectarian violence and the feared revolution. They had early success in containing the Defenders. Yet what a contemporary called 'a deadly and irreconcilable rancour in the minds of the lower people' led to continued faction-fighting and cruelty and, in

---

* The oath was brief: 'I . . . do solemnly swear that I will, to the utmost of my power, support and defend the king and his heirs as long as he or they support the Protestant ascendancy.' This was not, said Wallace, 'conditional loyalty': 'the sole purpose, the single object of the Orangeman's Oath at any time, and in every time, no matter what form it assumed, was, and is, and ever shall be, to protect the Constitution from being altered by violence . . . The Orangeman's Oath . . . is, in fact, a concentrated expression of the spirit and letter of the Constitution established by the Prince of Orange.'

particular, to the persecution of ordinary Catholics, driven in their thousands out of Armagh and down to Connaught. William Blacker said:

> Happy had it been for the Protestant name if the Protestants had been content with the defeat of their enemies at the Diamond and the formation of a protective society. Unhappily it was not so, a spirit of vengeance and retaliation had sunk too deeply in many of their minds to be thus easily satisfied.
>
> Many it is true had a long account of wrong to suffer in this eagerness after which they totally overlooked the divine declaration: 'Vengeance is mine, I will repay, saith the Lord,' and in an evil hour they took into their own hand the mode of payment. A determination was expressed of driving from this quarter of the Country its entire Roman Catholic population. It is true a great proportion of these had taken an active part as Defenders and Persecutors of Protestants; still there were many who were 'quiet in the land', and had taken no share in such proceedings, but revenge, like love, is blind.

Individual Orangemen were among the avengers and intimidators, for, as Wallace admits: 'In some places the system spread so rapidly that local men could not keep it under proper control; in other places persons who were not altogether worthy got themselves initiated.' Yet Blacker believed

> that in proportion as the Orange organization progressed, disorder declined. The Masters of Lodges took an active and proper part, bad spirits were checked, the advice of steady men prevailed and the non-admission of any known 'wrecker' into an Orange Lodge had a powerful effect in putting an end to further outrages on the part of the lower classes of Protestants.

Still, though most of the Protestant perpetrators of violence were Peep o' Day Boys, very few of whom were allowed to join the new organization, it was Orangemen who got most of the blame: 'The enemy', wrote Wallace, 'consisted of rabid Roman Catholics and weak-kneed Protestants, whose successors do not show much sign of improvement. In addition, the most malicious rumours were circulated to the prejudice of Orangemen.' Ignorant of conditions in Ulster, in the Dublin parliament Henry Grattan identified as Orangemen those the governor of Armagh had described merely as 'lawless banditti'.

The Defenders flocked to join the United Irishmen, thus undermining its anti-sectarian character. Although it still attracted radical Presbyterians (several ministers were among those executed in the north as part of a brutal military crackdown), its rank-and-file were largely Catholic. A few of the small number of Presbyterian Orangemen sided with the rebels but, for the most part, they backed the government and tens of thousands of them joined the yeomanry that was set up in June 1796; Orange Lodges were set up within the militia.

The United Irishmen's *Northern Star* loathed Orangemen. In July 1796, for instance, a correspondent reported:

> Happening to be yesterday in Tandragee, I saw with feeling and honest indignation, a grand division or party of Orange or Break-of-day men who, on pretence of celebrating the anniversary of the Battle of the Boyne, were, in reality, celebrating their own disgrace and degradation of their country, or rather were rejoicing for the many ravages, devastations, rapes, and murders committed with unrelenting fury on the defenceless Catholics of this loyal County . . .
>
> The pious Rector of the parish was seen bringing up the rear, conversing delightfully with the most ragamuffin of them, exulting in the happy sight, and praying for their success – as much as to say, 'Go on, my boys, and prosper; fear not, I am with you, glorious defenders of the faith!' The Orange cockade denoted, as I was informed, such as had taken the Orange oath: vis. – to be true to King and Government and to exterminate the Catholics.

Writing about sectarianism, Frank Neal comments that the celebrating of the Twelfth was to be

> the single feature of lodge activities that was to provoke most physical violence. To Orangemen, they were exercising the right of free men to parade on the king's highway in celebration of events they held to be of crucial importance to the well-being of their country. To Irish Catholics, the overwhelming majority of the population, excluded from political power, almost excluded from land owning and subject to penal laws, such parades were intended to remind them of the Protestant Ascendancy.

Two hundred years later, these irreconcilable positions have changed little.

The allegation that Orangemen took an extirpatory oath took root quickly and was industriously spread by United Irishmen in order to encourage the recruitment of terrified Catholics. Widely distributed forgeries of Orange rules and regulations included resolutions barring Presbyterians, Quakers or Methodists from membership, banning the wearing of clothes of Irish manufacture, forbidding any Orangeman to 'give employment to any papist', and requiring 'that every man shall be ready at a moment's warning to burn all the chapels and meeting houses in the city and County of Dublin'.

To try to counter this propaganda and also to deter those United Irishmen who were trying to win over Presbyterian Orangemen, a meeting of lodge masters, chaired by James Sloan, was held in Armagh city in 1797 to clarify the principles of the Orange Society. In a reply to an address from the United Irishmen, they approved a policy of leniency towards anyone forsaking the revolutionary path, while calling for government measures to 'purge the land of your ringleaders'. This statement, so full of resonances today, ended:

> In future we desire you will not call us friends, as ye have done in your last address. We shall not be your friends until you forsake your evil ways, and until we see some marks of contrition for your past conduct, neither do we wish to hold any intercourse with you, for 'evil communication corrupts good manners' as well as good morals. We are satisfied in the enjoyment of what we can earn by our honest industry, and neither envy those above us, nor desire to take from them a single farthing of their property. We wish you to be of the same mind.

They published also a list of five principles of the Orange Society, the most important of which were:

> 1st. We associate together to defend ourselves and our properties, to preserve the peace of the country, to support our King and Constitution, and to maintain the Protestant Ascendancy, for which our ancestors fought and conquered; in short, to uphold the present system and establishment at the risk of our lives, in opposition to the wicked schemes of rebels of all descriptions.
>
> 2nd. Our Association being entirely composed of Protestants, has afforded an opportunity to people who undeservedly assume the appellation of Protestants, to insinuate to Roman Catholics of Ireland that we are sworn to extirpate and destroy them, which infamous charge we thus openly deny and disavow. Our obligation binds us to second and protect the existing laws of the land; and so long as we remain under the influence of that obligation, the loyal, well behaved men, may fear no injury of any sort from us.
>
> 3rd. We earnestly request that the several Members of the Administration in this

county will not suffer themselves to be prejudiced against us by the unfounded calumnies of unprincipled traitors, of ambitious dispositions and desperate circumstances, who detest us for no other cause than our unshaken loyalty; and who are using every exertion to increase their consequences and repair their shattered fortunes by plunging the kingdom into all the horrors of rebellion, anarchy, and civil war.

The flood of anti-Orange propaganda continued, as it has to this day. And then, as now, the ground was fertile. Writing in 1899, Wallace lamented that there had been created 'a deep-rooted prejudice in the minds of Roman Catholics, high and low, against the Orange Society – a prejudice which the Orangemen have not been able to eradicate, no matter what they say or do. Although again and again refuted, the calumny has survived, and is the stock argument of those who labour to malign the Institution.' He was particularly aggrieved by an 1886 pamphlet from the Irish nationalist MP Tim Healy, in which was repeated the myth of the extirpatory oath. (In a letter to *The Times* in August 1886 denouncing Healy's 'rabid and unfounded' statements, the Earl of Enniskillen wrote that in over sixty years as a member of the Orange Institution, and most of that time Grand Master, he 'never heard of the existence of any such oath. My father was Grand Master for several years before my election to that dignity, and I know that he was utterly incapable of belonging to an association bound by so atrocious an oath. I have communicated with members of the Society – the best informed on the workings and rules of Orangeism, and the oldest surviving members of this body – and none of them ever heard of the existence of such an oath.')

Wallace was equally aggrieved by Healy's statement that 'the Orange system "had existed previously as a secret society under the name of The Peep of Day Boys."': 'No statement could be more in conflict with fact. The Peep of Day Boys were never really organized; the banditti accepted the services of all turbulent Presbyterians, and their depredations were felt by Protestants as well as by Defenders. The Orangemen never sympathized with them, and seldom allowed them admission to their Society.'*

✳ The inability of Orangemen to write clearly about their history in places easily accessible to outsiders is the main reason why even an historian of the distinction and learning of Jonathan Bardon should have repeated in 1992 in his magisterial *A History of Ulster* that the Peep o' Day Boys turned themselves into Orangemen. I cast no stones: I believed the same until I applied myself recently to Orange historical tracts. The Orangeman James Wilson, presently finishing a PhD on the early years of the Order, is doing much to set the record

The 1796 French invasion and the savage military retaliation against perceived rebels helped to precipitate the 1798 rebellion. Its atrocities were to leave all the participants with terrible memories and bitter hatreds. The United Irishmen had unwittingly unleashed, in the south in particular, an orgy of sectarian cruelty from Protestants and Catholics, rebels and military, alike. Thirty thousand people died and new and dreadful memories of murders and burnings and floggings and hangings entered the psyches of all those involved on both sides.

James Wilson calculates that in early 1798 there were 18,000–20,000 Orangemen in the whole of Ireland, of whom a disproportionate number were in the militia and the yeomanry. Their strength deterred the Presbyterian-dominated United Irishmen from rising in much of Ulster and they were crucial in quelling those that did. As part of the North Cork Militia, they helped in the merciless destruction at Vinegar Hill of the Catholic rebels who had committed anti-Protestant atrocities in Wexford which horrified and broke the spirit of many idealistic United Irishmen. The widespread antipathy to Orangemen was such, however, that their role became exaggerated and distorted and they were widely accused, then and subsequently, of organizing the burning of Catholic churches.

Take, for example, the statement by a contemporary historian, Francis Plowden, that the Orangeman Philip Johnson, Vicar of Derriaghy in County Antrim, had encouraged his Orange parishioners in their 'orgies' of church-burning. In fact, along with several other Orangemen and Orange sympathizers, in August 1798 Johnson had denounced the burning of four local Roman Catholic chapels

> by some wicked person or persons unknown . . . with the intention of inciting the Roman Catholics of this neighbourhood to join in the Rebellion, or supporting the groundless calumny that Orangemen are combined to persecute their Roman Catholic brethren; whereas their great object is to preserve our excellent Constitution, and to promote the general tranquillity and happiness of the country, having always solemnly avowed that they are enemies to none merely on account of Religious opinions.

He contributed generously to a repair fund and offered a reward for information leading to the convictions of the guilty. Sixteen years later,

---

straight and to examine Orange historiography critically. However, it flies in the face of common sense to believe that there was no cross-over of membership.

when the Plowden history appeared, local parish priests gave testimony on his behalf. 'You and the Protestants of your Parish,' wrote one, 'showed themselves in the most friendly manner to the Catholics of the place, and rendered them every protection from time to time in their power, and always continued to live with them as good neighbours and friends.' It is, however, almost always easier to spread a calumny than a retraction.

Because so many Protestants were rebels in 1798, it has never rivalled 1641, for instance, in the Orange pantheon of horrors, but as the years went by and events brought Protestants closer together, it suited Presbyterians* as well as Catholics to play down the Protestant role in 1798. One of the casualties of this convenient amnesia was the truth about the nickname 'croppy', applied in the early 1790s to those sympathizers with the French Revolution who cropped their hair and soon applied to all rebels against the state. So when the rebellion was over, as the Reverend John Brown put it, 'and loyalists were exulting with the somewhat uninhibited arrogance of the age', they did so with a song called 'Croppy Lie Down'.

A month after the defeat of the Ulster rebels, there was a triumphant procession of County Antrim Orangemen with brethren from nearby locations in Armagh and Down to the Maze racecourse, near Lisburn. They marched to the music of fife and drum, carrying the banners they had borne into battle the previous month. Drawing on the description of a participant, Wallace described the scene thus:

> Firm in pace and lofty in mien, the brave men, some of whom had fought at Antrim and Ballynahinch, marched in good order, the fife and drum of each Lodge playing the new and popular air 'Croppies Lie Down'. The tune was heard at the Maze for the first time; and the words were accepted as an excellent reply to the United Irishmen's password 'Are You Up?'
>
> As the Lodge filed past, ardent Orangemen added vocal to instrumental music, singing

---

✳ In 1998, fed up with the way in which 1798 had been appropriated by Sinn Féin, the Education Committee of the Orange Order launched a counter-offensive. The high spot was a dinner (black tie, chamber music, excellent food and wine) attended by, among others, several distinguished Catholics from the Republic of Ireland, at which Professor Brian Walker movingly spoke of the need to commemorate, not celebrate, the anniversary, to recognize the idealism and self-sacrifice that had existed among the ranks of rebels and defence forces alike, while remembering, above all, that 30,000 people had died.

> We soldiers of Erin, so proud of the name,
> We'll raise upon rebels and Frenchmen our fame;
> We'll fight to the last in the honest old cause,
> And guard our religion, our freedom and laws;
> We'll fight for our country, our King and his Crown,
> And make all the traitors and croppies lie down.

> The song had a wonderful effect in restoring confidence to the community. It was the very thing that was wanted to raise the drooping spirits of the Protestants living in isolated localities; for, taught by experience, they dreaded the return of turbulence.

As ever, one tribe's confidence-booster became another's humiliation. To loyalists, a croppy was a rebel of any persuasion: Catholic, Presbyterian or Unitarian.* As sedition became increasingly an exclusively Catholic occupation, the term 'croppies' in time was to be perceived by Catholics as a sectarian insult aimed at them, and at all of them. These days, republicans use the word cleverly: when nationalists suffer a negotiating setback or a contentious parade is approved, a republican spokesman will announce that unionists/Orangemen can no longer make the croppies lie down, thus pressing a Catholic tribal button. No decent unionist uses the term publicly, but to them, like 'Fenian', it denotes those who wish to destroy the state. Between republican and loyalist riff-raff, however, it is kept in currency. Thus, when some of the dregs of loyalism produced a banner on the Drumcree front-line in July 1998 reading 'CROPPIES LIE DOWN', it was a propaganda gift for Sinn Féin.†

James Wilson's assessment is that Orangeism's decisive role in 1798 was in making loyalism attractive. 'It took the Williamite myth of 1688/90; its theme of collective persecution, affliction, solidarity, providence and eventual deliverance and it fashioned it into a system of unique

---

* Because they do not believe in the Trinity, in Ireland Unitarians are not eligible to become Blackmen.

† I have heard Orangemen talk of 'Fenians', but never of 'Croppies'; and I've not found 'Croppies Lie Down' in any of my collections of Orange songs. Yet a verse like the following was to imprint it for ever in the Catholic mind as a classic example of Orange anti-Catholicism.

> Poor Croppies, ye knew that your sentence was come,
> When you heard the dread sound of the Protestant drum;
> In memory of William we hoisted his flag,
> And soon the bright Orange put down the Green Rag.
> Down, down, Croppies lie down.

collective cultural individuality. It redefined loyalty as a holy virtue: "Honour all men, Love the brotherhood. Fear God. Honour the King." '

All this had happened haphazardly. What was to turn the Orange Society into an institution that became a permanent feature of the Irish landscape and a force abroad, was the creation in November 1798 of the Grand Lodge of Ireland, a ruling body based in Dublin. Traditionally, this has been seen as the nobs seizing control of Orangeism from the plebs but, as Wilson points out, the founders of the Orange Society were no more mainly peasants than the founders of Grand Lodge were mainly gentry; of the eighteen men who met in Dublin in March 1798, eleven were yeomen of sergeant or non-commissioned-officer rank, which strongly suggests they were middle-class farmers or traders.

Grand Lodge set up a system of county and district Grand Lodges, rationalized and made uniform the rules and rituals, and issued a declaration of what Orangeism was about:

> We associate to the utmost of our power to support and defend His Majesty King George the Third, the constitution, the laws of this country, and the succession to the throne in His Majesty's illustrious House, being Protestants; for the defence of our person and properties, and to maintain the peace of our country: and for these purposes we will be at all times ready to assist the civil and military powers, in the just and lawful discharge of their duty. We also associate in honour of King William the Third, Prince of Orange, whose name we bear, as supporters of his glorious memory, and the true religion by him completely established: and in order to prove our gratitude and affection for his name, we will annually celebrate the victory over James, at the Boyne on the 1st day of July, OS. in every year, which day shall be our grand aera* for ever.
>
> We further declare, that we are exclusively a Protestant Association; yet detesting as we do any intolerant spirit, we solemnly pledge ourselves to each other that we will not persecute or upbraid any person on account of his religious opinion, but that we will, on the contrary, be aiding and assisting to every loyal subject of every religious description.

While in matters of detail, there have been modifications along the way, in essence what was set up two centuries ago is what exists now. And although there were some turf wars at the beginning and long-running

---

* A stately way of saying Big Day.

arguments over the number of degrees,* the system was put into operation without too much pain. The appointment as Grand Master and Grand Secretary respectively of the Armagh landowner Thomas Verner, Lord Donegall's brother-in-law, and John Beresford, two members of the serious gentry, brought a new respectability to the institution. However, simultaneously, they had to deal with the divisive issue of William Pitt's proposal to get rid of the Irish parliament and unite Britain and Ireland. Verner was for and Beresford against.

Grand Lodge recommended Orangemen 'to avoid, as injurious to the Instititution, all controversy not connected with their principles' – an injunction which, of course, as they frequently do, they largely ignored. Most of their politically-conscious members were anti-Union, and many lodges, including three in Dublin, passed negative resolutions which did not endear them to the government. Yet they were largely peripheral to the debate that ended with the 1800 Act of Union.

Given the horror stories of outrages like the burning to death of more than 200 Protestants at Scullabogue in Wexford ('Remember Scullabogue' became a watchword), the rumours of what the Defenders had planned to do had they won in Antrim, as well as fears of further French invasions and the disastrous rebellion in Dublin in 1803, which constituted the last gasp of the United Irishmen, the growth of Orangeism was inevitable. Particularly in the north, landlords encouraged their tenants to join, for Orangeism was simultaneously a defensive organization and a way of constraining hotheads. And there was considerable provocation caused by the re-emergence of the Defenders in the guise of the marauding

---

* There was a long struggle between traditionalists – mostly 'the lower orders' – who enjoyed elaborate ceremonies, often frightening initiations and myriad degrees, and the modernizers of Grand Lodge, who were minimalists bent on institutional respectability who aimed at reducing the initiation ceremony to a simple catechism and abolishing all 'travel'. In 1811, for instance, as a result of tidings from County Armagh, Grand Lodge denounced the continuing 'silly, shameful and even idolatrous practices of mystically initiating into Black, Red and perhaps Green Orders'. A subsequent resolution confirmed that Orange and Purple degrees only would be recognized: 'all other colours of Black, Scarlet, Blue, Royal Arch Purple, or any other colour are illegal and injurious to the true Orange System, and if any Orangeman shall presume, after public notice of this resolution to meet in any such Black or other similar Lodges, upon due proof thereof he shall be expelled'.

Despite its best efforts, Grand Lodge failed to eradicate the embryo Royal Black Institution and block the emergence of the Royal Arch Purple Chapter: rank-and-file brethren did not take kindly to interference with their cherished customs.

These days all three institutions coexist peacefully.

Ribbonmen, many of whom were, rightly, believed to have sworn their own extirpatory oath.*

The Reverend Brown has encapsulated the point of view of the ordinary Protestant who wanted to feel

> that his own position and living, and those of his family, were secure. He wanted to go to fairs and markets without being cudgelled there, or waylaid on his return, and to use whatever roads he wished.
>
> When reports of disorder, intimidation, and 'agrarian' crime came in from the South, the northern Protestant refused to allow the slightest self-assertion to 'the other side', lest the same occur in his own neighbourhood. On the 12th of July, and on other occasions, he marched with his lodge behind its flag and drums and fifes, wearing his regalia (cockade, ribbons, scarf, or sash) and armed with his yeoman gun, to show his strength in the places where he thought it would do most good. Where you could 'walk' you were dominant, and the other things followed.

Catholic resentments were increasing, too. Their middle-classes, who had been disappointed in 1795 when Pitt had funked the removal of the law preventing Catholics taking seats in parliament, were enraged when in 1801 – through the intransigence of King George III – Pitt had to renege again on what this time had been a solemn promise; they turned steadily against the Union and viewed with unaccustomed sympathy some of the excesses of the Catholic poor. The bitter opposition to Catholic emancipation by the Orange leaders who, like most Protestants, now equated Catholicism with sedition, and the combative anti-Catholicism of the rank-and-file, increased sectarian bad blood. As Orangeism spread into England and Scotland and brethren clashed with Catholic Irish immigrants, its violent image was intensified.

The first of a series of famous clashes between Orangemen and Ribbonmen came in 1813 with what became known as the Battle of Garvagh, immortalized in yet another ballad beginning:

---

* 'I, AB, Do Swear in the Presence of My Brethren and by the † of St Peter and of Our Blessed Lady that I will Aid and Support Our holy Religion by Destroying the Heriticks and as far as my power & property will Go not one Shall be excepted . . . I Do further Swear that I will be Ready in twelve Hours Warning to put Our Glorious Design in Execution Against the Heriticks of Every Sect So Help me God By the † of St Peter.'

> The day before the July fair
> The Ribbonmen they did prepare
> For three miles round to wreck and tear
> And burn the town of Garvagh.

Garvagh was a frontier village in Londonderry. The fertile lands of the north and east were predominantly settler country; the high grounds in the south and west were largely in native hands. In 1641 the settlers had been routed by natives and in 1689 by Jacobites, and though normally reasonably peaceful, it had been the scene of several incidents that year. In May, with both sides sporting cudgels, Orangemen were defeated at the May fair by a superior force of Ribbonmen; on the June fair day, so many vengeful Orangemen with staves arrived that the Ribbonmen stayed away and towards evening drunken and frustrated Orangemen broke the windows of a Catholic house. Four hundred Ribbonmen assembled on the morning of the July fair day to attack a public house frequented by Orangemen:

> The Tory* whistle loud and shrill
> We heard it o'er the high Mourne Hill,
> Fall on, brave boys, we'll slay and kill
> The Protestants in Garvagh.

Armed with sticks and stones, the Ribbonmen set upon a group of Orangemen, who retreated. A few of them obtained firearms and, as the Ribbonmen advanced, fired over their heads. When that didn't work, they fired into the crowd and one man died and some were wounded. After many triumphant verses, the Orange balladeer goes into indignant mode:

> But mark what followed this affray:
> They thought to swear our lives away.
> To jail we went without delay,
> We had no guards from Garvagh.

> They horrid oaths against us swore,
> Such swearing you ne'er heard before.
> McCluskey swore three hours or more
> Against the Boys of Garvagh.

---

* An Irish term for 'outlaw'.

The Judge then he would us condemn
Had it not been for our jurymen,
Our grateful thanks are due to them
For they cleared the Boys of Garvagh.

Naturally, the other side saw it differently. A Catholic curate in Londonderry explained in a speech at a rally in favour of Catholic emancipation that since the laws of the country offered no protection to Catholics: '[do] not give your Orange enemies cause to drag you before Orange magistrates. You know that from them you have no reason to expect either justice or mercy – you have seen an Orange jury, in direct opposition to the charge from the bench, acquit the Orange murderer who shot your poor brother like a bleeding dog in the streets of Garvagh.'

There were plenty such incidents and they did not endear Orangemen to the authorities. Official gratitude for their role in suppressing the 1798 rebellion soon gave way to general distaste and a wish that they would go away. It was official policy to try to bring the Catholic bourgeoisie on side by offering them cautious concessions: one such was the adoption of a tough line on the cult of William.

For a large part of the eighteenth century, the statue of King William in College Green had been decorated with a scarlet cloak, an Orange sash and Orange lilies and streamers every 1st of July and 4th of November. The birthday celebration had become a great ceremony, which was attended by the viceroy and other dignitaries, for William was popular with all Protestants and liberal Catholics. The divisions of the 1790s altered all that, and by the early nineteenth century he was becoming the exclusive property of Orangemen and poorer Protestants; from 1806, the viceroy no longer participated in the procession.

After 1815, with the French defeated, there was increasing hostility in both islands to the strong Orange presence in the army and the sectarian tensions and faction fights its spread caused in cities. Daniel O'Connell, the inspirational leader of the campaign for Catholic emancipation, made eloquent attacks in Ireland on Orangeism, echoed in Westminster by radical MPs such as Joseph Hume. By 1821, local and national authorities were trying, where possible, to prevent Orange demonstrations, and a flood of hostile parliamentary questions about the institution's legality in parliament led the Duke of York, heir to the throne, to resign the Grand Mastership of the British Grand Lodge.

A ban on dressing King William's statue in July that year, although flouted, caused great resentment among Dublin Orangemen. A successful ban in November 1822 caused fury, especially since O'Connell, who loathed Orangemen ('the most depraved as well as the most despicable of the human race'), had been calling for it vociferously for some time. The following month, a few louts decided to make clear their disenchantment with the administration, and chose as the venue the Theatre Royal to which the new viceroy, Lord Wellesley, was paying a state visit. It was a perfect example of loyalism's idiosyncratic approach to public relations. Not only did they distribute leaflets which, *inter alia*, mocked the viceroy for being small, but they threw a bottle at the stage and part of a watchman's rattle at the viceregal box. O'Connell and colleagues publicly announced their abhorrence at 'the recent daring outrage offered to the representative of our beloved Sovereign' and, along with liberal Protestants, called for the suppression of all secret societies. 'If we had hired at large wages the Orangemen,' wrote O'Connell gleefully to his wife, 'they would not have done our business half so well.'

While those Orangemen charged got off (because, it was popularly believed, the jury was partisan), the consequences of the attack were catastrophic for the institution, left with almost no friends and many new enemies. Public celebrations in Dublin of Williamite anniversaries were effectively ended and the government had the chance to lump together the loyal Orangemen with the revolutionary Ribbonmen and ban them both under the 1823 Unlawful Oaths Act.

As Grand Lodge was engaged in making the necessary constitutional and regulatory changes to restore the institution to legality, O'Connell was setting up the mass-membership Catholic Association to unite Catholics behind the emancipation campaign. When a frightened government in 1825 declared it an illegal organization, it demonstrated even-handedness by suppressing the Orange Society too. The respectable Orange leaders, who were not enjoying their unpopularity, obediently dissolved the institution in March 1825, although many private lodges refused to disband.

By 1827, British Orangeism had reorganized itself so it could operate within the law and the High Tory Duke of Cumberland, brother and heir of King George IV, became Grand Master; when the Act lapsed the following year, the Irish organization came back into existence and also elected Cumberland. O'Connell, who had substituted a virtually identical association for the one suppressed, was on the brink of achieving Catholic emancipation; he had already been elected to parliament, though he could not yet take his seat.

Sectarianism was intensifying, encouraged by both Catholic and Protestant revivalism. The Jesuits were spearheading an assault on laxity; the Church of Ireland was trying to convert Catholics and the Reverend Henry Cooke, a virulent opponent of Catholic emancipation, was leading Presbyterianism away from liberal and enlightenment ideas and towards a conservative and Bible-based evangelism. Puritanism, proselytizing and temperance were in and tolerance was out; increased recruitment into Ribbonism and Orangeism and a series of the usual affrays were a consequence. In 1829, for instance, an attack on an Orange Lodge at Glenoe, near Stewartstown, County Tyrone, on the Twelfth caused five deaths. Four Orangemen were killed on the following day at Macken, near Derrylin, in County Fermanagh.

Catholic emancipation in 1829 was followed by the launch of O'Connell's campaign for repeal of the Union, which brought even more frightened Protestants flocking into the Orange Order.* A combination of O'Connell's support for the Whig government and a general dislike of Orangeism led in 1832 to the Anti-Processions Act, which banned Orange demonstrations. The gentry in Grand Lodge were not particularly troubled; the rank-and-file were desolate and defiant and in many places kept on walking for the fun of it, as well as to make sure the Catholics knew they were there.

As further concessions to Catholics dribbled out of parliament, in October 1834 the Conservative peer Lord Roden called on all Protestants to meet at Hillsborough to make common cause against Irish nationalism; Henry Cooke was the principal speaker. Seventy-five thousand Orangemen attended a meeting the following month at Dungannon. It won them no friends. In 1835, the Whig government, at the request of Joseph Hume and Dan O'Connell, who wanted to break the Orange institution and also embarrass the Duke of Cumberland, set up parliamentary select committees on Orangeism in Ireland and Great Britain. The first reported inconclusively. The second, which Hume had chaired in a breathtakingly partisan manner, gave the thumbs down; a great deal of mud was thrown at Cumberland and the suppression of the Orange institution was recommended.

MPs expressed alarm at the discovery that Orangemen controlled the yeomanry and that lodges were rife in the army, and a statement from King William IV announced that he intended to discourage anywhere in his dominions 'Orange Lodges and ... political societies, excluding

---

* By the mid-1830s there were probably in the region of 100,000 Orangemen in Ireland and 10,000 in Britain.

persons of a different religious faith, using secret signs and symbols, and acting by means of associated branches.' Having cancelled all military warrants, both Grand Lodges dissolved themselves.

The English institution reorganized itself with some speed; Ireland was much slower. Havering and ineffectual leadership meant that, for the most part, lodges did whatever they wanted to do. In effect that meant a falling away in Orangeism in the south while it remained strong, if largely undercover, in the north.

O'Connell had secured from the Whigs several concessions for Catholics in, for instance, the spheres of education and local government, but with the return of the Conservatives in 1840 he decided to launch another popular agitation. The National Repeal Association held monster meetings around Ireland, though Ulster was almost entirely a no-go area. Although the campaign failed, it exacerbated Protestant fears and encouraged Ribbonism.

By 1845, when the Anti-Processions Act expired, the Grand Orange Lodge of Ireland had been reconstituted in Enniskillen; the Earl of Enniskillen was Grand Master. Parades began again all over Ulster that year and increased markedly the next. It was only the terrible famine of 1845–48 that stopped parading from spreading south again.

Fears of another rebellion made officialdom smile on Orangemen again. As the Reverend Brown put it wryly: 'The Orangemen of Dublin received the flattering information . . . that Government, in the coming crisis, felt it could depend on them.' The fiasco that was the tiny Young Ireland rising of 1848 raised loyalist spirits and in some of the less wretched areas made for a happy Ulster Twelfth. But though the Union seemed safe again, the Ribbonmen were back in business; the privations and suffering of the previous three years had further exacerbated the loathing of the have-nots for the haves, or those they perceived as haves.

The big show-down came in 1849 on the Twelfth at Dolly's Brae, a steep road through a narrow pass, which Ribbonmen had blocked the previous year to halt the traditional march of Rathfriland Orangemen to Tollymore Park, near Newcastle, County Down, the home of Lord Roden, Deputy Grand Master of Ireland. To avoid trouble, the Orangemen had taken an alternative route and had been humiliated over the next year by songs mocking their cowardice. In the spring of 1849, several local incidents, including the murder of an Orangeman and an attack on police and Orangemen on St Patrick's Day, had put the brethren into their most bloody-minded mood. Not only were they intent on going through Dolly's

Brae, but they took a specially long route through a Catholic area.

> The sun did shine in splendour in a bright and cloudless sky,
> Our drums did beat and fifes did play and Orange flags did fly;
> Each loyal son, with sword and gun, was ready for the fray,
> Had the enemy attacked us goin' over Dolly's Brae.

Troops, police, magistrates and two priests between them ensured the safe passage of the more than 1,200 Orangemen through the hundreds of opposing Ribbonmen at Dolly's Brae.

> A splendid arch that gate did span which we all passed thru,
> And in the centre of the arch these words appeared in view,
> 'Welcome all to Tollymore, this day we gladly join,
> To commemorate and celebrate the victory of the Boyne.'

> Lord Roden gave a brief address, and then to us did say,
> 'Beware, my Orange brethren, going home by Dolly's Brae,
> Give no offence to any man as you're returning home,
> But don't look shy when passing by those pagan troops of Rome'.

By the time the Orangemen arrived back at the pass, more than a thousand well-armed Ribbonmen were on a hill a mile beyond. The Orangemen were under instructions from their leadership to maintain discipline, but a squib went off, two shots were fired – probably from the hill – and a gun battle began.

> The battle it raged loud and keen along the mountain-side,
> To save ourselves, as best we could, our ranks we opened wide;
> The volleys from the rebel guns had no effect at all,
> For not a man among our ranks fell by a Papish ball.

> As fearlessly we charged them, their terror it was great,
> Thru rocks and whins, to save their skins, they beat a fast retreat.
> The Coolagh tykes threw down their pikes and boldly ran away,
> And cursed the day they came to fight at fatal Dolly's Brae.*

---

* A strange version of this song, called 'Dolly's Brae No More' is an appeal to Ribbonmen to see sense. Thus the Orangemen were marching to the tune of 'Croppies do give o'er', and after the story of the battle has been finished, the lyricist makes this handsome appeal:

Left out of the song was the role of the police in storming the hill and their fruitless appeals to Orangemen to stop firing once the enemy were fleeing. At least thirty Ribbonmen were killed and Orange stragglers burned some Catholic houses and attacked one of the owners. Lord Roden was among the Orange gentry dismissed as commissioners of the peace.

The Party Procession Act passed the following year decreed that

> all Assemblies of Persons in Ireland who shall meet and parade together or join in procession, and who shall bear, wear, or have amongst them or any of them any Fire-arms or other offensive Weapons, or any Banner, Emblem, Flag, or symbol, the Display whereof may be calculated or tend to provoke Animosity between different Classes of Her Majesty's subjects, or who shall be accompanied by any Person or Persons playing music or singing any Song which may be calculated or tend to provoke Animosity between different Classes of Her Majesty's Subjects, shall be unlawful Assemblies.

Not only was the reputation of the institution now at rock-bottom, it was attracting violent people and there were deep divisions between the gentry who led it and many of the rank-and-file. The leadership accepted the ban on parades and sought to make the institution a disciplined and efficient force to be reckoned with electorally and, should there be another rebellion, militarily. Few ordinary Orangemen, however, were prepared to accept that it was the fault of their brethren that they had been banned from processing down the Queen's highway. Instead they burned with resentment at the ingratitude of government to its most loyal citizens and sometimes defied the law. 'Sandy Row were a law unto themselves,' observed George Chittick. 'In 1864 there was a whole debate as to whether they should march or not march. And the County Grand Lodge of Belfast said to tell us: "Don't youse go marching now." So the six lodges said: "Who do they think they are? Take themselves off."

'They formed up, down Sandy Row they went, over the Saltwater bridge that's now the Boyne Bridge, into the city, into the town centre. And at the town centre the leading citizens came out and said, "Who are these ruffians?" And Dr Henry Cooke, the famous divine, he was

---

Come all you blind-led Catholics, as long as you do live,

Never depend on Pope or priest, or they will you deceive;

Never bow down to wooden gods, or images adore,

But join our Orange heroes, and cry Dolly's Brae no more.

standing at the side of the road and these citizens prevailed upon him to speak out against these men that were walking down the road with these bands with the Orange favours on. And Cooke turned round and said: "Gentlemen, you see today the pride of Belfast and don't you ever forget it." And from that day our district is always called the Pride of Belfast No. 5, because it was given by Dr Cooke.

'And if you come up on the Twelfth morning to Clifton Street, I'll walk up to the County Grand Master and I'll say – as my predecessors over the last hundred years have done – "County Grand Master, the Pride of Belfast is in position. The Twelfth of July can begin." And as we go by Henry Cooke's statue on the Twelfth morning, the district officers all take off their hats.'

Sectarian riots occasionally broke out in traditional flash-points like Derry, Lurgan and Portadown, but they became a serious problem in Belfast. The 1857 riot lasted ten days and, like those of 1864, 1872 and 1886, led to serious loss of life.

A. T. Q. Stewart has written an account of sectarian rioting in Northern Ireland over the past few hundred years which is so wise and witty and true that I quote it here in full.

These periodical outbursts of violence follow a complex internal logic of their own, which is unaltered by the current political circumstances, the ululation of politicians and clergy, or the military strength used to suppress it. The 'troubles' (to use the Irish term which is more comprehensive than rioting) go through well-defined stages. The first is usually confined to provocation of the opposite party, intense and often prolonged over weeks and months. This provocation, which is not the cause of the ultimate outbreak, but appears to be a ritual part of it, may take the form of marching, jeering, waving flags and singing party songs. Where a main road divides Catholic streets from Protestant the displaying of flags and hurling of insults may go on all through the summer, slowly building up to the inevitable clashes and bloodshed. The first stage is followed by physical violence, fisticuffs, stone-throwing, forays into enemy territory by men armed with clubs, the smashing of windows and the starting of fires. This automatically introduces the police, who must take the routine steps to preserve the peace, apprehend troublemakers and, if possible, separate the two mobs. The violence is then re-directed by one side or the other towards the police, who are accused either of partiality or over-reaction. It is not unusual for both sides to attack the police, or for one side to cease hostilities in order to enjoy the spectacle of the other fighting it out with the police.

The police begin to sustain casualties; reinforcements are called in, and the conflict is aggravated. If really serious disorders develop, the police will lose control of the situation and be obliged to call for military aid. At some point before this stage is reached, the whole character of this ritual dance of provocation and aggression will have been changed by the use of firearms. The firing of weapons at night, from a quarter which is predominantly of one religion, may often be simply a signal to the other side that the inhabitants mean business; but it usually begins unexpectedly and dramatically when someone emerges from a jeering crowd and deliberately fires a weapon into the opposing crowd. The reaction is total shock, and bitter recrimination, conducted on the basis that no one in the long history of Ireland has ever seen a gun, let alone used one, and that the other side have broken the rules, in the most treacherous manner, which is all one can expect from them.

The first use of firearms is always by the other side, and there is invariably a sensation of shock and anger at the elevation of the conflict to a more lethal plane. This creates a momentary pause, followed by indiscriminate retaliation. Death and injury initiate the vendetta, and if it has been caused by police or troops, then they are fired on also. Actual contests between Protestant and Catholic mobs do not last long. Some of the worst, like the 'Battle of the Brickfields' in 1872, have been over in twenty minutes, but sporadic rioting, cowardly assassination and attacks on the police and troops may continue for days or weeks. A 'flashpoint' usually cools in three or four days. The rioters seem to tire of the activity, no doubt because of extreme physical exhaustion, and the rioting may be transferred to another locality, where the able-bodied men are fresh for combat. Riots die away for no apparent reason, or for reasons which seem illogical; for example the prolonged fighting of 1886 ended because of three days of continuous rain. That is to say, the rioters were more demoralized by rain than by rifle fire.

What is more, Stewart points out: 'The army is almost totally ineffective as a means of restoring order, simply because it is never allowed to operate *as an army*.'

Of course each side blames the other, but Protestants, and especially Orangemen, always feel particularly aggrieved at being blamed by the representatives of the crown to which they are (normally) so loyal. There was outrage at the new restrictions imposed by the 1860 Party Emblems Act which was passed after a serious riot at Derrymacash, near Lurgan, County Armagh, and which forbade the playing of music or the display of any banners, emblems, flags or symbols anywhere in public. There were Orangemen, including one Captain William Johnston of Ballykilbeg, head of the Black institution, who believed that Ulster MPs had not fought it hard enough. Johnston lived and breathed Orangeism, defended it eloquently and was well in tune with the feelings of the rank-and-file. Like them, he became enraged that in the early 1860s the authorities turned a blind eye to parades by nationalists and even by Fenians in the south and west of Ireland.

In July 1863, eight County Down millworkers were charged with having paraded behind pipes and drums when leaving work on the 14th. Later that summer they were sentenced to three months' imprisonment. A week later, 60,000 people wearing green emblems and sashes and with other nationalist accessories, including pikes, marched with bands through Dublin to attend the laying of the foundation stone of a monument to Daniel O'Connell. The authorities took no action.

After a petition on behalf of the millworkers organized by Johnston and signed by two MPs and fifteen magistrates was rejected, Johnston announced that 'the time for quiet endurance has gone by, and private remonstrances are useless'. He began a tour of Orange halls whipping up anti-government sentiment:

> Every wrong is put upon us, because it is supposed we will submit to anything. We shall not submit to this any longer. We have not got fair play, and we must have it. We must have the right of publicly meeting in any way we please. We have been deprived of this through popish conspiracies. But we are firmly resolved, under God, to obtain again the freedom we once had, to commemorate the deeds of glorious and immortal William.

In another speech he warned the government that Orangemen would not 'move hand nor foot for the government of England till we are recognized fairly and treated as Orangemen' – a potent threat when there was much alarm about the Fenian threat. An attempted rebellion by the Fenians in March 1867 was the final provocation, though it was swiftly crushed. On the Twelfth, Johnston marched at the head of an Orange parade from Newtownards to Bangor. In the course of a powerful speech, he addressed the accusation that flags and banners and sashes were childish things. He was reported as saying:

> They were not. Were they childish things when they were carried before William at the Battle of the Boyne? Were the banners of the British army childish things when they were carried before Wellington at the Battle of Waterloo? Were such memorials as they possessed, and were proud of, to be given up as childish? No, no, no! They

were not so ungrateful to Almighty God, or so forgetful of the mercies of the past,
to put up a grave-stone on the victory of the Boyne.

He reminded his audience of the principles of Orangeism in regard to
religious toleration. 'The man who would shout ''To hell with the Pope''
was no Orangeman ... They would accord to their Roman Catholic
countrymen full liberty, but they would, at the same time, demand that
their feet should no longer be kept upon their necks.'

In September Johnston and several other Orangemen were charged.
The government had no desire to make an example of him but, since he
refused to plead guilty or give sureties of good behaviour, he ended up
serving a two-month sentence. In jail he wrote such songs as 'Let Recreant
Rulers Pause', which included the lines:

For wearing a ribbon of Orange and Blue,
The prisons were filled with the loyal and true.
  But, though they thus proved us,
  We were, as behoved us,
Still true to the Protestant Queen on the Throne.

Shortly after he was released, he won a Westminster seat as an Independent Orange candidate in South Belfast and was a crucial voice in the
campaign that finally, in 1870, had the offending Acts repealed. But that
did little to calm the nerves of Ulster Protestants. The Disestablishment
of the Church of Ireland and the ending of the payment of the Royal
Bounty to the Presbyterian Church helped the recruitment of clergy into
the Orange Order. On a political level, there was the threat posed by the
extremism of the Land League and the electoral success of the Home
Rule Party. Events were strengthening Protestant loyalty to the union.

9

A Century in the Life of a Lodge

When lodges meet our brethren greet
The Master in the chair;
All hand in hand, in order stand,
And bow their heads in prayer.
In duty next the Bible Text
Our chaplain doth supply,
To the love of King and Brotherhood,
To the fear of God on high.

CHORUS: To God above we give the praise,
With heart and hand we join,
To celebrate the glorious days
Of Derry and the Boyne.

No treason binds our honest minds,
No rancour moves our arm;
We weave no rope for Priest nor Pope,
We aim at no man's harm.
We fain would give to all who live
A freeman's heart and home;
We fain would free from slavery
Benighted sons of Rome.

CHORUS

We ponder on our brethren gone
To dwell with God on high;
We speak of those our country's foes,
Of perils great and nigh.
For King we and for Fatherland
We raise our boven cry.
For Freedom's right we're bold to fight
To conquer or to die.

CHORUS

Who wouldn't stand for England's land,
The valiant and the true?
With fife and drum we boldly come:
The Orange and the Blue.
And may each gallant Orangeman
Be as he's ever been –

The traitor's foe, the good man's friend,
And loyal to his King.

CHORUS

Ye men of the North come boldly forth,
A winsome sight to see;
And let us join our glorious Boyne
To the waters of the Lee.
Let hills and dales tell thrilling tales
Of heroes passed away;
But Orangemen will march again,
And nobly win the day.

CHORUS
Brother the Reverend Dr Drew
(father-in-law of Captain William Johnston)
'The Orangeman'

I N 1895, JOSEPH HOPE, secretary of Loyal Orange Lodge No. 152, based in Lisburn, County Antrim, embarked on an ambitious venture.*

As the year that has closed has been the first of a new century in the history of our Lodge, I thought it would be interesting to try to give a short sketch of the preceding century from facts supplied to me by Bro James Innes at present a member of No. 152 whose Great Grandfather was one of the men who took out the Original Warrant of this Lodge; and also from the Minute books of the Lodge dating back to the year A D 1805.

The Orange institution, he explained, which had been born after the battle of the Diamond, was

an Association in which the Protestants of Ulster banded themselves together for the mutual protection of their lives and property against the Celtic inhabitants of the country who looked upon them as confiscators of and intruders on the ancient possessions of their forefathers who were foreigners in race and heretics to the religion which they professed.

In an age when the laws of the land were not so ably and uniformly administered

---

* The manuscript contains about 17,000 words and is in the keeping of the Grand Lodge Archivist.

as in the present, no doubt the Orange Association proved very useful in preventing those periodical outbursts of massacre and bloodshed which have often blotted the history of our Island. In those days though there were neither Telegraphs, Telephones nor Railways yet it is wonderful how quickly in those exciting times the news spread over a large extent of country.

When the news of the Order's foundation reached Lisburn, 'we can imagine the excitement it would create amongst men of whom a great number were the descendants of the Huguenots who fled from France in the 16th century on account of the persecution which culminated in the Massacre of St Bartholomew in the year 1572'. It was, explained Brother Hope, the period when William the Silent,

the ancestor of our own Illustrious William 3rd of Glorious and Immortal Memory, was fighting the cause of civil and religious liberty against the Inquisitors of Spain headed by the Duke of Alva in whom the Church of Rome never found a more cruel and bloodthirsty representative who drenched the Netherlands with Protestant blood during the early years of the Reformation because they dared to worship God according to the dictates of their own conscience.

A local Lisburn association known as the Old Twenty Five, which existed 'for mutual defence and protection', commissioned some carters who traded between Lisburn and County Armagh to bring them a warrant on their return,

but the journey being long and the carters needing refreshment the money was spent before they arrived at their destination and so the Warrant came not.

At last after waiting several days it was decided to commission Mr James Innes and John Coburn to proceed to Armagh and bring back with them the long looked for Warrant. They started on their way and having arrived safely they obtained the Warrant and proceeded on their homeward journey but in the meantime a heavy downpour of rain having swollen the River Blackwater over which they had to cross into a raging torrent there was nothing for them but to try to get over as best they could. James Innes taking the Warrant in his mouth to save it from getting wet plunged first into rushing water but the strength of the current swept him off his feet who in the excitement of the moment let the Warrant drop out of his mouth which went quickly floating down the raging stream. When both had safely reached the other side of the river they bethought themselves of the Warrant which they saw floating a little farther down the stream stopped in its mad career by some

projecting bushes. James Innes plunged in swam to where it was and brought it
safely again to land after which they arrived in Lisburn without any mishap.

The new warrant 'first found its home in a small house in what is
known as the Sandy Loaning'* and on the first Twelfth 'on which the
Brethren walked I am informed by Bro Innes they were the only Lodge
that turned out in Lisburn on that day. On arriving at the Market Square
they were attacked by the Roman Catholics when I think we may rest
assured the members . . . gave a good account of themselves.'

As ever, there was the distinction betwen 'decent' and 'seditious'
Catholics. In 1798, 'during the troubles with the United Irishmen a Roman
Catholic in the employment of Bro Innes and who appreciated the kind-
ness of his Master having heard of an attack about to be made on the
Lodgeroom took the box belonging to the Lodge and buried it in the
garden.'

He notes the lodge's first surviving authentic record of business in
which was confirmed on 25 January 1800 that

> our true and wellbeloved Bro John Matthews was legally admitted into our Lodge
> and has regularly received the most loyal and invincible Orders (being the first and
> second degrees) of a true Orange Man and hath with due fortitude and becoming
> zeal justly supported the same. We therefore recommend him as a worthy Brother
> and request all the regular Orange Associations of the Universe to recognize and
> admit him as such.†

Dated 'the year of our Lord 1800 and of Orange 110', it was signed
among others by the two procurers of the warrant, James Innes and John
Coburn, respectively Master and Assistant Master, who were still in post
in 1806 when the lodge treated itself for its Twelfth celebrations to eight
loaves, twenty-three pounds of cheese, three gallons of whiskey and new
colours.

---

* In 1809 a suggestion that the lodge should move to the town of Lisburn was defeated: Brother Hope found
no record of when the move eventually took place.

† The modern travelling certificate is slightly more prosaic, certifying that the brother in question 'has been
duly admitted a Member of the Loyal Orange Institution of Ireland, and regularly received the Degree of a true
Orangeman and [other degree if appropriate] therein; and that he is a Member of this Lodge in good standing;
and has paid all Dues in advance for the space of – months.

'We therefore request that all the Loyal Orange Institutions in the Universe do recognize him as such.'

Money was a constant problem, hence a complicated system of dues and fines and penalties for defaulters was developed, discussion of which occupies more space than any other issue. Finally they agreed on:

Private rules and byelaws of Lodge No 152
To be read on every night of Meeting immediately after the general rules.

1st That this Lodge shall regularly assemble at the hour of seven o'clock in Winter and at the hour of eight o'clock in Summer.

II That each Member shall pay sixpence half-penny per month subscription; to be appropriated towards defraying the expense of the Night the remainder to go the stock purse.

III That no member shall presume to speak or leave the Room while business is going on without permission from the Worshipful Master or person presiding for him.

IV That every Member shall be duly obedient to the Worshipful Master or person presiding for him in his lawful commands under a penalty of Tenpence for the first transgression, of Two Shillings and Sixpence for the second and of exclusion for the third.

V That any member cursing or swearing or using indirect language shall for the first offence be fined in the sum of Fivepence for the second be fined in the sum of Tenpence and for the third be excluded for the space of three months.

VI That any Member attending intoxicated or giving abusive language to another shall be fined in the sum of two Shillings and Sixpence for the first offence for the second be excluded for the space of one year and for the third be expelled.

VII That any Member who shall be guilty of riotous behaviour or who shall create any disturbance in this Lodge shall for the first offence be excluded for the space of one year and for the second be expelled.

VII That any Member who shall have wilfully absented himself for the space of three Months shall be fined in the sum of Ninepence.

IX That the Secretary shall on each night of Meeting make a return to the Worshipful Master of the names of those Members who have absented themselves for a longer period than three monthly Meetings; that the Worshipful Master shall then issue his summons to those persons to attend the next night of Meeting and to discharge their arrears; and if they contemn this Summons unless they render a sufficient reason for such contempt they shall be excluded for the space of nine months and shall not be readmitted after the expiration of such period until they shall have satisfied their Lodge.

X That any Member appearing intoxicated at the Procession on the Anniversary of the Battle of the Boyne shall be fined in the Sum of Five Shillings and that any member who shall be guilty of riotous behaviour on that Day shall be excluded for the space of Twelve Months.

XI That any Member who being fined shall refuse to pay the sum herein annexed to his offence shall be excluded.

XII That every offence against these Private Rules and Byelaws shall upon motion of the Worshipful Master or of any Officer or of any private member be ascertained and determined by the majority of the Lodge.

XIII Any member being an Office bearer of this Lodge and not being present at the time of opening the Lodge shall be fined in sixpence half-penny and not to sit as an Office bearer till it be paid unless he give a sufficient apology for his absence.

That did not settle all the tricky issues or financial problems. An 1820 committee meeting, for instance, decided 'that the members of this Lodge do pay 10 pence on each night of meeting and only to have two quarts of spirits each night until every demand on this Lodge is settled'.

The most important matter, of course, was the Twelfth. In 1805 a resolution about turning up 'in decent apparel' showed, explained Brother Hope, 'that No. 152 have always taken a lively interest in their members turning out respectable'. On 19 June 1808 the following rules were agreed for the Twelfth:

1st each member to pay 1s.1d each, 2nd to walk in coloured clothes 3rd to meet in the Lodge-rooms at 9 o'clock all not coming at that time to pay 1s.3d, 4th all members not coming on that day to be fined 1s. 7½d on not paying the fine to be excluded, 5th any person coming at any time through the day in drink to be put out of this Lodge without exception.

In 1832 they decided to restrict themselves to one glass of spirits each night in order to save up for 'collars' for the Twelfth.

Here is a typical account of the festivities on the big day:

On the 12th July 1822 the Lodge opened at nine o'clock in the morning in commemoration of the Battle of the Boyne – there were 32 members present the Lodge closed at ten o'clock when the whole proceeded to Lisburn to join the general procession which having been composed of the most numerous and most respectable body of men ever seen in Lisburn on such an occasion with the Grand Master and many other distinguished Officers of the Grand Lodge at their head. The whole procession composed of the 32 Lodges of the Lisburn District went to the

Maragall church when a very excellent sermon was preached by the Grand Master the Rev Doctor Cupples after which they returned to Lisburn and then to their Lodge rooms where the members of this Lodge spent the evening in great harmony and brotherly love and the entire members were very much delighted with the proceedings of the day all declaring they had never spent a more pleasant day and at a late hour they separated to their respective places of residence in a regular and sober manner.

The end of Brother James Innes's reign as Worshipful Master in 1829 moved Brother Hope to sentimental and poetic flights:

The records of the Lodge have been very well kept considering the state of education in those days and there is no doubt but that Loyal Orange Lodge No 152 owes a deep debt of gratitude to him. And I am sure we all feel proud to have still amongst us his direct representative in the person of his Great Grandson another Bro James Innes who still takes a lively interest in the Lodge of his forefathers.

So here's to James Innes, who took out our Warrant
Who I wish, with his comrade, was with us alive
To tell how they stemmed the storm and the torrent
In Seventeen hundred and ninety and five
When homeward returning and bringing the charter
Beneath which we meet as Brethren and Men
Determined to ne'er sell our Rights nor to barter
The Freedom our forefathers won for us then
For o'er thirty years he ruled as her Master
Our men to her principles loyal and true
And her records proclaim those men in the past sir,
Were all worthy members of one fifty two.

Some Orangemen were in trouble in August 1834, when 'it was resolved that all the Brethren be summoned to attend to assist in defraying the expenses of the brethren who were summoned for walking on the 12th July. It was also resolved to put 6 pence by in the stock purse and spend 3 pence'. The following April the minutes reported tersely and somewhat perplexingly:

Lodge opened at 9 o clock the following sums have been appropriated to the said purposes:-

	s	d
To Carrickfergus	5	3
To drink on return	7	0
To defend the Brethren against Gilmours prosecution	15	0
To an Orangeman	1	0
Total £1	8	3

The records came to a stop on 9 September 1836 and resumed on 30 September 1843 when all the lodge members were summoned to a meeting in October. 'Thus for seven years it seems as if the members of the Lodge had fallen asleep and suddenly awoke to summon the members for the next meeting as there is no break in the minutes but they continue as if nothing particular had happened. The cause was this', said Brother Hope, quoting from a *Belfast Weekly News* article of July 1896 which told how the 1835 Report of the Select Committee

bears testimony to the falsehoods hurled against the Orange Society from the beginning, while impartial historians have acknowledged the importance of such a loyal organization existing in the midst of a disaffected population incapable of being reconciled to British Protestant Government . . . It is probable that the aim of Joe Hume and his base confederates . . . was to discover an excuse to impeach the Duke of Cumberland who was then Grand Master; the wicked attempt failed; the Prince resigned, the society was dissolved, but it soon recovered from the shock and has been going on prosperously ever since.

While Brother Hope regrets that the dissolution of the Grand Lodge deprived the Society 'of a great deal of the lustre which it unquestionably enjoyed in consequence of the noble men that were then identified with it', he found local evidence that the institution had not been dissolved, for lodge records include a certificate dated 1839 from a Dromore lodge, 'which shows that the institution was still working though 152 kept no minutes in deference perhaps to the wish of the Grand Lodge'.

There was the occasional reference to charitable activity. John McIlwrath died on 9 March 1846 and was buried on the 11th in Lambeg: 'there was a numerous attendance of the Brethren there was also assistance for the funeral and other help for him.' Important decisions were taken: at the same meeting in October 1845, for instance, it was decided that 'each man pay 1s 6d for the 5th November event, that ham and bread and apple pie be provided for supper' and that 'each candidate for initiation in our Lodge shall be five feet six inches fully and of good character'.

Members, even officers, were occasionally disciplined. On 17 March 1847, the Master, Brother Michael McCombs, was suspended till the regular election night and excluded from the lodge for three months 'for wilfully going contrary to the 7th rule in the byelaws of said Lodge also the 23rd in the regular regulation book and striving to create a disturbance on the street after leaving the Lodge it being fully proved by more than the majority of the meeting'. (He was not re-elected.) The following year Andrew Hill was charged by the new WM, James Stanton, 'with being at John Belshaws, at a Papist Ball'. He was later 'excluded for the space of two years, not to be readmitted till he satisfies the Lodge'.

> On the 7th April 1863 there was a charge brought against John Farrell that he did on Monday night being the time of the Canvass during the Election join an unlawful mob who did beat and abuse harmless people on that night. William Dunwoody was summoned to answer a charge of disobeying orders in the Lodge and also for intoxication. Edward Hull was summoned to answer a charge of disobeying orders in the Lodge. Conway Leathem was summoned to answer a charge of endangering the honour and dignity of the Institution.
>
> By the foregoing paragraph it will be seen that the members of 152 always like true Orangemen not only respected themselves but also the persons and feelings of their neighbours while always zealous for upholding the dignity and honour of the Orange Institution. The proceedings of the district do not seem to have always been in harmony with the feelings of some of our members as we find by the following, May 5th Lodge 152 Bro McCamby says that there is no fair play in the District Lodge and that he was ordered out before he got a hearing. As we were not there to judge we cannot say who was wrong but Bro McCamby seems to have had the courage of his convictions who was not afraid to speak the thing he thought.

There is an account of the period after the riots of 1857 when 'the Orange men of Ulster were treated rather like rebels than as loyal men'. The source quoted by Brother Hope contends that the riots had come about because 'a Roman Catholic evidently with a malicious intention attempted to induce a Protestant to show an Orange lily in a part of Belfast inhabited by Roman Catholics'. Having failed, the Catholic donned a lily somewhere he was not known and stirred up 'discord . . . Offence was taken at the obnoxious display and party feeling were aroused which resulted in riot and bloodshed', leading to the Party Processions Act.

I am sure some of us can remember when it was a crime to be seen on the public road with either a banner or a drum on the 12th July. Let us be thankful to God that the lines have fallen to us in pleasant places enjoying the glorious heritage of civil and religious liberty when we can march with our music and our banners waving fanned by the free breezes of heaven chiefly through the instrumentality of Bro William Johnston of Ballykilbeg whose name was once a household word not only to the Orange men of Ulster but in the heart of every Orange man upon the face of the globe when he along with many others suffered bonds and imprisonment to gain for us that liberty which we enjoy today. Well indeed may we with Colonel Blacker raise our voices and sing:

Hurrah, Hurrah for liberty
For her the sword we drew
And dared the battle while on high
Our Orange banner flew
Woe worth the hour woe worth the state
When men shall cease to join
With grateful hearts to celebrate
The battle of the Boyne.

Minutes of a meeting on 7 October 1879 give an insight into a typical evening's business:

The Lodge having been opened as usual by the WM Dr St George the dues etc having been duly collected the Lodge numbering 15 members proceeded to transact business as follows:
   1st That Bro Capel B. St George Secretary provide proper minute and register books for next Lodge night. The Lodge paying for same
   2nd Bro Wm Patterson gave notice of resigning
   3rd That this Lodge meet again in their Lodge room Orange Hall on Tuesday November 4th instead of Wednesday 5th to commemorate that day being King Williams Birthday [14 November under the new calendar] by the usual social tea decided that 2/6 be the fee for each single member or 3/6 for each couple. The following were selected as committee of management

Bro George McClure ⎤
Bro Robert McClure ⎦   Chief Committee

Bro Capel B. St George   Decorator

Bro Dr St George ⎤
Bro J. Innes ⎦   Assistant Committee

Also that all names be given to Bro J. J. Harvey Market Square on or before 25th October 1879

	£	s	d
Box in Hand	2.	7.	0
Income		4	
	2.	11.	0
Outlay			7
Bal	£2.	10.	5	Signed Geo St George

Another rare example of lodge accounts comes from July 1880 and concerns a new flag. In 1868, its predecessor had cost £1 6s 6d: 10s 9d for scarlet material, fringe and binding and 15s 9d to Miss Curran for sewing. In 1880 unspecified subscriptions were collected at the March meeting and a special meeting was then convened to discuss the new flag. Although it was ready and presumably paid for by July, some strange ancillary costs cropped up in a tantalizing Twelfth-related account

	s	d
Bro Hill Mercer got for drums	6	0
For drinks flying home flag	7	2½
For the Fifer on the Saturday the flag did not come ½ pint of whisky	1	2
Painting flag and deacon poles*		3
Day of funeral – drinks	2	6
District dues	1	6

* There was a drama about the deacon poles the following year: 'On May 2nd a conversation arose about the deacon pole heads which were lost coming from Portadown on Easter Monday. The W Master said he had written about them but as he did not get a satisfactory reply he had given it into the hands of Mr Wellington Young solicitor . . . On June 7th a vote of thanks was passed to Mr Wellington Young for recovering the money for the deacon poles lost on Easter Monday.'

Fare to Belfast to see after flag	1	6
Crape for flag and postage	1	6
For fifer for the 12th	8	

£1	9	7½

The lodge under this WM seems to have been more charitable and more social than in the past, possibly because Dr St George was comfortably off. In 1881 Bro. John Best was appointed tyler at two shillings per night 'which allowance was granted by the Lodge up till his death in 1896 when he was buried at the expense of the Lodge'. In 1882 'a deputation appeared before the Lodge from L O L No 141 to solicit aid concerning some fighting as which some of their members had been drawn into and were given 5/-'; the same amount was voted to 'the distressed farmers in County Donegal'; and ten shillings was voted to the Ward testimonial fund 'which was raised to one pound ten shillings by W Master and subscribed in the name of the lodge'. In 1884 the lodge voted one pound ten shillings which was raised to two pounds by the Worshipful Master 'all to appear in the name of the Lodge to the memorial which the Lisburn district wishes to raise to the memory of our late Bro the Rev Dr Hudson'; in December a brother was introduced who asked the brethren for some assistance for Bro. Connor who was both blind and unable to work – 'the W Master also supported what he said as he was under his (the WMs) medical care in the Infirmary' – and the Lodge voted five shillings. Then, in 1885, the Worshipful Master raised the matter of a cork foot for Bro. Albert Smyth, 'whose foot had been taken off in the infirmary':

He [the WM] said he would give 10/- towards it and thought he could get some fair subscriptions from others that he knew. He also said that he did not wish any brethren to go round the different Lodges as it would tend no doubt to hurt the feelings of Brother Smyth, all of which the Lodge was in favour of. In April the W. Master was absent on account of sickness when Bro Charles Maginnes took the chair. A subscription list was opened for Bro Smyths foot and a committee appointed to go round the brethren in order that the foot might be purchased as soon as possible. In May the W. Master said he was glad a subscription list had been opened for Bro Smyths foot and also that he had asked the district lodge for a subscription and they had promised the sum of one or two pounds if the funds would permit.

It would seem that as a temporary expedient Bro. Smyth was given some employment by the lodge, for which in August they voted him seven shillings and sixpence, 'with which Bro Smyth was dissatisfied and said it was not a brotherly action and laid his charge before the brethren viz 15/-. After a rather hot discussion Bro Smyth allowed he had wrought 4 days at 2/6 per day which only amounted to 10/- and had to be paid.' Despite that altercation, the Worshipful Master was able to announce the following month that the subscription for Bro Smyth's foot amounted to eight pounds, seventeen shillings and sixpence.

In 1882, a typical year, the social highlights were the Twelfth, when the Worshipful Master entertained his lodge at home (in this case in his barn); committee-election night, when he bore the expenses of refreshments and 'songs and speeches were delivered by several of the brethren and at a late hour a happy evening was brought to a close', and on 7 November the celebration of the anniversary of the Gunpowder Plot:

in the County room of the Orange Hall it being beautifully decorated for that occasion after a good tea fruit cake having been served by Mrs Leatherdale of the Refreshment Rooms Market St, the Lodge took this opportunity to present to the W. Master a beautifully illuminated address and to Mrs St George a silver inkstand as a small token of their esteem for their valuable services to this Number for the past eleven years. After a most enjoyable evening the Lodge broke up at an advanced hour.

In 1884, at the Twelfth evening festivities in the Worshipful Master's barn, 'they partook of the good things prepared for them by Mrs St George. The W. Master with his usual kindness provided some nice rhubarb pies.' And on gunpowder plot night a supper was held in the Orange Hall, followed by singing and dancing, 'some humorous readings being given by the W. Master'.

There were still occasional problems among the brethren. In March 1880, for instance, there was the curious matter of Bro. Hill Mercer, summoned to answer at the next meeting a charge brought by Bro. W. Cooper for slander of No. 152. When he turned up in May, Bro. Cooper alleged that that Mercer

threw him back both his own and his brothers summonses and said he would not sit with such a pack of dirt. Bro Mercer denied the charge and said he never said the words. After they both went out, the Lodge (the committee not being present) decided that Mercer apologize for saying 'cods' and as they could not swear them Mercer got the benefit of the doubt. Being brought in the decision was told them and Mercer refused to apologize and on being told he was suspended for two years for defiance of Lodge authority replied 'you may for twenty two'. But he afterwards stood up and apologized.

It must have been a matter of some satisfaction to Bro. Mercer when the following year Bro. Cooper was found guilty of being drunk and disorderly on the field on the Twelfth and suspended for a year and fined five shillings.

In the same year, in December, an unspecified charge was preferred against Bro. Charles Duncan by Bro. McClure that was so serious that the committee expelled Bro. Duncan for life. One can only infer that the charge involved alcohol at the gunpowder plot ball, since Bro. McClure was charged with repairing 'both the box and the chair'.

In 1882, there was concern about the state of the drums which a member had borrowed without leave; it was agreed that no member in future should be allowed to contract a drink account; and – stark evidence that some members were falling into serious depravity – in August 'there was an investigation held about some members who pawned their sashes'.

A more serious mood was creeping into the lodge. In June 1884 the Worshipful Master gave to his newly enfranchised brethren 'an address as to how Orange men should stick together and vote at the General election and try as far as lay in their power to return Conservative Candidates to Parliament who would uphold the Bible and Constitution'. Then came two major innovations which, according to Brother Hope, resulted in the lodge making more progress 'than in the preceding ninety years of its existence'. The first was educational: in 1886 at Worshipful Master St George's suggestion, they embarked on a programme of quarterly lectures; quarterly biblical readings were added in 1888 at the suggestion of Bro. Robert Patterson, and three years later debates were introduced. The lectures given over the next ten years by brethren of the lodge were fairly predictable: they included, 'Home Rule meaning Rome Rule', 'The Principles of Orangeism: the Public and Private Duties of Orangemen', 'The Spanish Armada', 'The Life of St Patrick',* 'William of Orange', 'Martin Luther', 'The Decorating of Churches', 'Education', 'Perseverance', 'Tact', 'Example' and 'Habit'.

---

* Then, as now, Protestants were fighting to reclaim St Patrick from the Catholic church.

Biblical readings and addresses included: 'The Prodigal Son', 'Choose ye this day whom ye shall serve', 'Brotherly Love', and the life and times of Abraham, Moses, Gideon, Elijah, Jacob and St Paul.

And the debates: 'Should the State compensate Publicans?' (No); 'Would an extended form of self Government benefit Ireland?' (No); 'Should Capital punishment be abolished?' (No); 'Is Temperance or Teetotalism the Scriptural rule of life?' (Verdict not recorded); 'Is Sunday travelling Justifiable?' (Verdict not recorded); 'Is compulsory education necessary for the Good of the nation?' (Verdict not recorded).

In 1887 had come another major innovation: 'a very important step . . . in the right direction when Bro Robt Patterson proposed that this Lodge become a total abstinence Orange Lodge and that it be entered on the byelaws. On the vote being taken 18 voted for the motion and 4 against it.'

A paragraph summarizing the other highlights of these years included in 1886 the decision being taken 'that no half Protestants be initiated into this Lodge'; in August 1889 the ordering of a new tablecover, cushions and collars, and in December the according of 'a hearty vote of thanks' to Bro. St George 'for his kindness in presenting the Lodge with a new stamp and also with a beautiful likeness of Lord Arthur Hill':* the Worshipful Master returned thanks 'for the kind expressions of opinion'; in 1894 a new chest and ballot box were acquired and the Worshipful Master photographed the members of the lodge in the grounds of the local castle; and the following year it was decided that, after considering several estimates, the lodge should have a new banner 'made by ladies interested in the Lodge the centres to be painted by a lady in town'.

In 1892 an Orphan and Sick Fund for lodge members was set up and inaugurated the same evening with a presentation to the lodge by the Worshipful Master 'of a beautifully wrought purse the gift of Mrs Hudson and also a subscription: a hearty vote of thanks was passed to her for her kindness.' On the Twelfth that same year the lodge held its first tent† on the field and earned seven guineas for the Orphan and Sick Fund.

Another sign of confidence was some brethren taking out the warrant of a new lodge in Belfast 'to be worked on the same lines as No 152

∗ The local MP and youngest son of a local landlord, the Marquess of Downshire. Deference was creeping in.

† Fund-raising tea-tent, presumably.

and to be called Star of Hope No 479'. Innovative recruitment methods resulted in the award of a medal and a collar to the brethren who had introduced the greatest number of new members during the year.

The war against alcohol was on the collective mind of what was now called Royal Independent Temperance LOL No. 152 Lisburn: in December 1889 a committee was appointed 'to visit other Lodges of the District in order to induce them to adopt temperance principles'; 'in July 1890 Bro St George W. M. mentioned Bro George Briggs in commendable terms for having given Bro Hamilton his support at the District meeting against strong drinks being allowed into the field on the 12th July'; in October 'an arch-purple meeting was held under this warrant which was very successful 140 members and friends being present 8 members and one stranger received the degree it being the first of its sort held without strong drink'; in 1891 'this Lodge celebrated the discovery of the Gunpowder plot by holding a service in the Temperance Institute. Tea and cake and fruit and lemonade were served in good style.'

Politics crept in occasionally: 'In December 1880 we are reminded of the great Land League crises when outrage and murder were rampant in the land. The Orangemen were now as always found on the side of law and order and willing to support the hands of government.' On 7 December we find the lodge subscribing to the Boycott relief fund, 'also Bro the Rev W. D. Pounder Dist Master and Captain Smythe Dep District Master visiting the Lodge when a volunteer list was started'. A decade later Protestant concerns were uppermost: 'In Feb 1891 the Sec read a Petition about to be presented to the House of Commons against the disability bill allowing Roman Catholics to be Lord Lieutenant of Ireland & Lord High Chancellor of England it was resolved that it should be signed by the members'; in January 1892 'it was resolved to request Bro W. E. McCartney MP to be in his place in the House of Commons to support the Sunday closing and early closing movements'.

Anti-Home Rule fever gripped the lodge rather late in the day, in March 1893, when it was resolved that its members

hereby declare at this momentous crisis in the history of our country as loyal and patriotic Irishmen our unswerving loyalty to her most Gracious Majesty Queen Victoria and our unalterable attachment to the Constitution of the United Kingdom of Great Britain and Ireland as at present established by law.

And we most emphatically protest against any attempt on the part of Parliament to hand us over to a rebel majority; as a Parliament and executive of such a character would undoubtedly be placed and maintained in power by the influence of the Bishops & Clergy of the Church of Rome with an illiterate electorate. This party has been well described by the members of Her Majesty's present government as steeped to the lips in treason and as marching through murder and rapine to the dismemberment of the Empire.

They agreed to send copies to 'Mr Gladstone, Mr Morley, Marquiss [sic] of Salisbury, Mr Balfour and Mr Macartney M. P. also to the Press'. And the lodge met a few weeks later 'to make arrangements for the reception of Mr Balfour in Belfast and take part in the street demonstration'.

Early in 1894 the lodge expressed 'our warmest disapproval of the conduct of the Roman Catholics of the city of Cork in their brutal attacks on our fellow Protestants & loyal subjects of her most gracious Majesty Queen in the exercise of their religious and civil liberty under the British Constitution and we also condemn the authorities and R. I. Constabulary for not affording that protection to which they are justly entitled.' And in happier mood, in September 1895 a committee was appointed to draw up a letter of congratulation to Lord Salisbury 'on being returned to parliament with such a large majority of supporters'.

In 1893 LOL 152 had exhibited its new gentility by celebrating the discovery of the gunpowder plot with a *conversazione** in the Cathedral School: about 150 were present including members of LOL No. 479 Star of Hope and the Worshipful Master was presented with an illuminated address, entrée dishes and a dessert service. In the light of what was to follow soon after, the poem read to him by Bro. Hope[†] takes on a melancholy air:

Address to Bro Geo St George M D 21 years master of 152
Worshipful Sir

---

* Many Orange lodges around this time borrowed middle-class terminology and called evening functions with tea and entertainments *conversaziones* and *soirées* without realizing the words came respectively from Italy and France, those hotbeds of Catholicism.

† Clearly Bro. Hope, the author of this centenary sketch, was the lodge poet laureate. He records that in June 1894 'Bro W. J. Greene D. M. made a statement to the Lodge in reference to a Poem that Bro Joseph Hope had written for the benefit of the sick and orphan fund and concluded by moving a vote of thanks to Bro Hope the subject of the Poem being A Short History of the Siege of Derry in verse.'

With gladsome hearts we greet you here to night
Acknowledging your worth your record bright
For twenty years and one beneath your sway
Our Lodge had held its onward, upward way
Firm yet gentle with all a masters arts
You ruled our Lodge you also won our hearts
With friendly hand with kindly heart and true
Each member felt he owned a friend in you
So may you rule for one and twenty more
And guide us as you've guided us before.

But let us go one moment back in thought
And mark the changes 'neath thy guidance wrought
And trace the path we try to reach the goal
To train the mind and elevate the soul
England's St George the deadly dragon slew
And our St George has slain a dragon too
The dragon drink beneath his sway took flight –
Oh is he not a true and noble knight –
And from our Orange escutcheon wiped the blot
That deadly mark for every foeman's shot
By prayer and praise by reading and debate
Drove ignorance the monster from our gate
What nobler thoughts can human minds inspire
Than training souls to seek with pure desire
The fount of knowledge and from thence to bring
True pleasure from Eternal Wisdom's spring
Each height attained us onwards helps to spur
And wave our banner with Excelsior

Nor all for self the good we seek to share
The widow and the orphan claim our care
We by our tent and several other ways
Seek for their need a helping fund to raise
Right willingly each brother gives a hand
So far as he can time and purse command
Each feels within his sympathetic breast
In blessing others he himself is blest
For Jesus said that inasmuch as ye
Do it to them ye do it unto me.

Also to night with all a parent's pride
We welcome here at our fraternal side
With 'caed [sic] mile failte'* for Auld Lang syne
To Star of Hope young sturdy 479
May she reflect her mother's glorious past
And blessings shed on loyal old Belfast

Nor yet do we perfection's virtue claim
We fan the spark to kindle it to flame
So we to night with heartfelt words and true
Acknowledge Sir that fan is waved by you
Long may you live to over us preside
Pride of our Lodge our Institution's pride
May choices blessings rest on yours and you
And every member loyal good and true
And each well wisher hoping they're not few
Who wish good luck to good old One five two

Disaster struck in May 1895, when at a meeting in Bro. St George's house, after a discussion about their MP's conduct *vis-à-vis* the Sunday closing bill, 'the Committee then drew the WM's attention to some letters which had appeared in the local papers bearing upon his vote in the Church Synod. The W Master then went into the Question and gave a full explanation of his conduct and stated he would willingly do the same in the Lodge and also that he would abide by their decision.'

At the June lodge meeting, he 'made a statement regarding his vote in the Church Synod which was discussed at some length by the members', who decided to hold a special meeting.

On June 11th 1895 a special meeting of this lodge was held the Dep Master Bro Greene presiding. There were 48 members present. The Lodge being called together to consider the action of the W. Master in voting for the Cross in the Dublin Synod and other alleged Romanizing practices in the Church the matter was very fully discussed. The first vote taken was on – Should the W. Master have a majority or two thirds majority: 30 voted for the former and 17 for the latter.

The next vote taken was – Should the W. Master continue in the chair: 22 voted

---

* The capture by Irish nationalism of the Irish language was not yet complete.

Royal Black Preceptory No 800, Clogher, County Tyrone, circa 1930.

Tom Reid (as baby) at his first Twelfth, Fivemiletown, County Tyrone, 1934.

Banter at 'The Field', Ballymoney, County Antrim, August 1989.

The annual reenactment of the Battle of the Boyne at Scarva, County Down.

Making lambeg drums in Belfast.

Three generations of the Brownlees family, Ballymena, County Antrim.

Henry, Erin and Thomas Reid outside the Orange Hall in Glenageeragh, County Tyrone, 1995.

Gerard Rice of the Lower Ormeau Concerned Community.

Donncha MacNiallis of the Bogside Residents' Group.

Martin McGuinness and Brendán MacCionnaith walk the Garvaghy Road.

Robert Saulters, Grand Master.

Press Conference at Craigavon, County Armagh, 27 June 1997, *left to right*: David Jones, David Burroughs, Denis Watson, William Bingham, Harold Gracey.

Garvaghy Road, County Armagh, 6 July 1997.

Apprentice Boys Pageant, Londonderry, August 1997.

RUC versus loyalists in Derry, aftermath of Apprentice Boys Parade, 1997.

Right: Gerry Adams and Martin McGuinness at rally following Belfast anti-internment march, August 1997.

Opposite: Chinook picking up British soldiers from field above Drumcree church, 10 July, 1998.

Below: Joel Patton (*centre*) and his supporters occupying the House of Orange in protest against the leadership, December 1997.

Protest march in Sandy Row, 6 July 1998. (George Chittick, *third from right*)

Funeral of Jason,
Mark and Richard Quinn,
July 1998.

Harold Gracey in his caravan at Drumcree, January 1999.

for him and 25 against him. The Secty was instructed to inform the W. Master of the result and the following letter was sent:

'Worshipful Sir

'It was proposed and passed by a majority of 25 people to 22 that for the peace and harmony of the Lodge you should absent yourself until September next being election night.'

In July the district master, district secretary and district committee visited the lodge 'to make a settlement of the difference existing between the Worshipful Master and members.

The Dist Master Bro Canon Pounder stated his views on the case, Bro G. H. Clarke, Bro Lavery & Bro Gillespie also spoke. The members of 152 then asked to be heard but were refused. The Dist Master stated that he came in the interest of the W. Master and he would not hear anything from the members. After a good deal of debate no settlement was arrived at and no time was left for making arrangements for the 12th so a committee was appointed to make arrangements. On Sunday 7th the Brethren attended divine service in Christ Church when there were 44 members present. On the 8th a committee was held in the Lodge room to make arrangements for the 12th but as the brethren refused to walk none were made. It was then arranged the tent should be held on the field as usual.

Although that is a less than fully enlightening explanation of how the matter was resolved, there is no doubt that Bro. St George became the third of the seven Worshipful Masters of 152 to have been fired by his brethren: James Spence (1829–32), the second master, had been replaced because he failed to turn up to meetings; Michael McCombs (1846–47) had been excluded for stirring up trouble in the street; and now, the lodge he had put on the path to puritan righteousness had kicked out for having Romish tendencies the Worshipful Master who in his time had given them lectures on 'Some of the errors of the Church of Rome' and 'The Inquisition'. The following month Bro. Greene became Worshipful Master and Bro. Hope secretary.

Thus ends the sketch of No 152 for 100 years, [concluded Bro Hope] and we hope they may long continue to prosper and carry out the principles of Orangeism which are very fully set forth by the Grand Master of Scotland in the following words.

1st An open Bible and the right of all to read it.

2nd The doctrine that justification is by faith alone of grace and that man's salvation is to be ascribed to the finished work of Christ and to the power and love of Christ now glorified and living in heaven not in whole nor in part to any works of man himself; good works flowing from grace received and necessarily flowing from it but not in any degree contributing to procure grace or to merit any of the blessings of salvation.

3rd The doctrine that in consequence of the fall all men are by nature sinful; and that no one can enter into the kingdom of Heaven without being regenerated by the Holy Ghost, by whom also all true believers in Jesus Christ are sanctified and so fitted for the fellowship of God and kept through faith unto salvation.

4th The only proper object of worship is God Himself Father Son and Holy Ghost and prayer is to be made to God alone and all prayer to the Virgin to saints angels and the like with all veneration of images and relics is to be abhorred as idolatrous.

5th The only Priest of the Christian Church is the Lord Jesus Christ Himself our Great High Priest who has passed into the heavens; who having made one and all – sufficient sacrifice for our sins the sacrifice of Himself hath entered in by his own blood into the Holy Place not made with hands there to appear in the presence of God for us and ever liveth a priest upon His throne making continual intercession for His people; and under Him all His true people have equal and full access to God in prayer and all other exercises of worship.

6th Confession of sins to be made to God alone who alone can forgive sins; and auricular confession is to be rejected as having no authority in the Word of God and indeed contrary to it.

7th The pretended sacrifice of the mass is impiety, being plainly inconsistent with the all sufficiency of the sacrifice of Christ once offered for the sins of many.

8th The doctrine of purgatory so fruitful a source of gain to the Popish clergy* and a most powerful instrument for binding the souls of the people in slavish subjection to them is to be detested as a virtual denial of the all sufficiency of the sacrifice of Christ and of the free and full forgiveness of sins for His sake.

9th The Holy Scriptures of the Old and New Testament are the only rule of worth the traditions of the Roman Catholic Church and the decisions of the Pope being of no authority.

10th Loyalty to the Sovereign and to the British Constitution is the duty of every one in this land – a duty plainly taught in the Holy Scripture.

The same authority defined the duties of Orange men in the following terms which we heartily endorse. Such sentiments appropriately close this sketch.

Our duties like our principles are summed up in the two words: Protestantism and

---

＊ A reference to the selling of indulgences which was believed to give the buyer time off in purgatory. In fact such sales were contrary to Catholic teaching and indulgences could be used only on behalf of others.

Loyalty. I have explained these words already – that Protestantism is pure
Christianity – that Loyalty is not mere attachment to the person of the Sovereign
nor a particular Royal Family but it is such attachment subordinated to a regard for
the constitution of the country; let us seek then to be good Protestants – not mere
haters of Popery but true Christians believers in Christ walking by faith walking in
love rejoicing in hope adorning the Gospel. May God make us so and make us all
more and more to abound in every grace so that our lives may be lives of piety and
holiness and active obedience to all God's commandments. May our protestantism
be that genuine and pure religion which manifests itself in the family circle and in all
the intercourse of society and in all the occasions and affairs of ordinary life. Let us
be zealous against popery; and let us also be in all things zealous Christians. Avoid
intemperance and honour the Sabbath day by attending your places of worship. And
as to Loyalty let our whole conduct show that we are faithful subjects of Queen
Victoria; that we feel ourselves bound by that law which is above all laws to respect
the laws of our land living quiet and peaceable lives in all godliness and honesty;
and that we in the highest degree esteem and prize and are thankful to God for the
civil and religious liberty secured to us by the British Constitution that admirable
Constitution which was established let us hope for all coming time at the glorious
Revolution of 1688.

So Mote it be. J. H.

Postscript

'What a boring time the poor devils had,' I said on the telephone to an
Orange friend, reporting on the activities of LOL 152. 'And then having
to become temperance on top of it all. Seems really unfair.'

'Boring?' he said. 'Boring? I'll tell you what boring is. Do you know
what we discussed at my lodge for two hours the other night?'

The issue was the annual outing for wives and children. Should they
go to the same place as last year? Should the charge be higher? If they
hired a larger coach, could they fill it? After two hours, no decisions had
been taken.

10

Villains and Heroes

Their webs shall not become garments, neither shall they cover themselves with their works: their works are works of iniquity, and the act of violence is in their hands.

Isaiah 59.6.

The dark eleventh hour
Draws on and sees us sold
To every evil power
We fought against of old.
Rebellion, rapine, hate,
Oppression, wrong and greed
Are loosened to rule our fate,
By England's act and deed.

The Faith in which we stand,
The laws we made and guard –
Our honour, lives, and land –
Are given for reward
To Murder done by night,
To Treason taught by day,
To folly, sloth, and spite,
And we are thrust away.

The blood our fathers spilt
Our love, our toils, our pains,
Are counted us for guilt,
And only bind our chains.
Before an Empire's eyes,
The traitor claims his price.
What need of further lies?
We are the sacrifice.

We asked no more than leave
To reap where we had sown,
Through good and ill to cleave
To our own flag and throne.
Now England's shot and steel
Beneath that flag must show
How loyal hearts should kneel
To England's oldest foe.

We know the wars prepared
On every peaceful home,
We know the hells declared
For such as serve not Rome –
The terror, threats, and dread
In market, hearth, and field –
We know, when all is said,
We perish if we yield.

Believe, we dare not boast,
Believe, we do not fear –
We stand to pay the cost
In all that men hold dear.
What answer from the North?
One Law, one land, one throne.
If England drive us forth
We shall not fall alone.

Rudyard Kipling, 'Ulster 1912'

IT WAS A LONDONDERRY Presbyterian solicitor, the Young Irelander and revolutionary, John Mitchel, who said of the famine: 'That million and a half men, women and children, were carefully, prudently, and peacefully *slain* by the English government.' To nationalists, the Union was the source of all Ireland's ills; to Ulster unionists, it was the source of its prosperity. Compared to most of the south of Ireland, Ulster was very prosperous indeed; Ulster had had more crops than the potato and because of fast-growing industrialization, it suffered less during the famine than most of the rest of Ireland.

During the second half of the nineteenth century, Belfast was the fastest-growing urban centre in the British Isles. (It would become a city in 1888.) In 1841 its population had been one-third that of Dublin; fifty years later, with over a quarter of a million, it had edged ahead. Workers flocked from the country to work in engineering and textile factories and in shipyards, and exporters blessed the empire that took their goods.

In agriculture, too, Ulster was relatively thriving. The Ulster Custom, which gave tenants security of tenure and some compensation for improvements made on their land, was the envy of embittered tenants elsewhere. Yet many Ulster Protestants as well as Catholics were dissatisfied with their largely Church of Ireland landlords, and as the agricultural depression of the late 1870s took hold, their militancy increased. Many were happy to join the Irish National Land League at its inception in 1879 and campaign for the 'three Fs': fair rent, fixity of tenure and free sale. 'Most of the Presbyterians, the younger Methodists, and I may say all the Romanists go in the "whole length of the unclean animal" with the Land League,' observed a worried clergyman.

Among these were Orangemen, though others were utterly opposed. When in 1880, Captain Boycott, a Mayo land agent who had refused to reduce rents, was subjected to the 'moral Coventry' proposed by League and Home Rule party leader, Charles Stewart Parnell, it was Cavan and Monaghan Orangemen whom a Grand Lodge emergency committee sent to save his crops. The following summer the emergency committee sent more than 300 Ulster labourers to work on boycotted farms throughout Ireland. And after the Irish Land Act of 1881 granted the 3 Fs, Protestants began to fall away, unhappy with the League's extremism and the ancillary violence. Nor did the vast majority want any truck with the Irish nationalism with which it was becoming inextricably linked. As the Reverend Brown put it: 'Parnell and Home Rule were now identified in the loyalist mind with the "moonlighter", the assassin, the boycotter.'

Nationalism was an ideology that developed in the nineteenth century and did not appeal to Ulster Protestants. Instead they continued with their tradition of conditional loyalty, taking what the historian David Miller has described as the 'contractarian' view: subjects owe allegiance to a sovereign if he protects and does his duty by them. And when it came to the threat of Home Rule, the sovereign and her government were to be found wanting. This was to be the issue that rapidly transformed the Orange Order from the convivial plebeian organization it had become to a potent Protestant political force that crossed all class divides: the richest landlord and the poorest peasant could now find common cause again.

From the perspective of most Protestants, politics took a turn for the worse when in October 1882 the Land League was replaced by the Irish National League, the constituency organization of Parnell's Irish Parliamentary Party, aka the Nationalist Party, with 'national self-government', aka Home Rule, replacing land reform as its primary aim. When Parnell's lieutenant, Tim Healy, a Corkman, won a by-election in County Monaghan in 1883, it was clear that all Catholics had voted Nationalist and all but a handful of Protestants Conservative; the practice of sectarian voting that had for so long dominated urban areas was now spreading to the countryside.

Blithely ignorant of the realities of Ulster life, southern nationalists exacerbated the fears of Ulster Protestants with the slogan 'All Ulster is ours'. An announcement by Parnell a few months later that he would speak in Dungannon, County Tyrone, enraged local Orangemen. 'Are you prepared to allow Parnell, the leader of the enemies of our united empire, the champion of the principle, Ireland for the Irish . . . meaning Ireland for the Romanists,' was an Orange appeal. 'Are you prepared to accept the doctrine of the English radicals that the Protestants of Ireland are aliens in their land and should be swept out of it by fair means or foul?'

And when nationalists called on men from Fermanagh and Monaghan to attend a public meeting in October in Rosslea, County Fermanagh, to demonstrate 'your unalterable devotion to the cause that your fathers fought and bled and died for – the cause of Irish nationality', Lord Rossmore, Grand Master of County Monaghan, summoned brethren from three counties to a counter-demonstration. Their numbers boosted by his provision of free railway travel, 7,000 Orangemen faced 5,000 nationalists across a providentially swollen river. Rossmore was reported as having said that nationalists were 'rebels and scavengers, whom the Orangemen could easily vanquish, and that the Brethren could also, if they thought fit, eat up the handful of soldiers in a few seconds'. Threatened with arrest by the resident magistrate, Rossmore called his bluff: 'On you and you alone will rest the blame of having transformed this orderly body of men into a leaderless mob.' He then refused a re-routing order and police and troops had a tough time keeping the belligerents apart. Despite the banning of demonstrations, there was subsequently a similar defiant exhibition of political muscle at Dromore, County Tyrone, led by Colonel Knox, another pillar of the establishment.

By the early 1880s, just over a quarter of the population were Protestant, three-quarters of whom lived within the nine counties of Ulster. The 1884 extension of the franchise trebled the size of the Irish electorate, massively increased the proportion of Catholic voters and further exacerbated the religious polarization of Irish politics. In June 1885, taking revenge for various coercive measures, Parnell and his thirty-eight MPs joined the Conservatives in bringing down Gladstone's government and colluded with them so effectively during the subsequent election as to wipe out Liberal representation.

That same election was a triumph for Parnell's party. Through ruthless suppression of dissidents, disciplined organization and the bringing on board of the Catholic clergy, nationalists won eighty-five seats in Ireland, including seventeen in Ulster. Only five of their MPs were Protestant – none of them from Ulster. Of the eighteen Conservatives returned, all but the two representatives of Dublin University came from Ulster, and, except for three Presbyterians and one Methodist, all were members of the Church of Ireland and ten were Orangemen. Most of the defeated Liberals were Presbyterians.

Like the nationalists, the Irish Conservatives had been energetically developing a new party organization, particularly in the north-east of Ulster. The Orange Order was a vital instrument in bringing the new working-class voters into the new divisional associations. E. S. Finnigan, the Conservatives' Belfast-based, full-time organizer, successfully pioneered the appointment of the local district master and officers to Conservative local committees in Counties Antrim and Down. In Counties Armagh, Londonderry and in Belfast, however, recalcitrant Orange labourers complained they had insufficient influence and forced the adoption of their preferred candidates or, in some cases, ran their own independent candidates. Like the Catholic clergy, who were very visible in National League branches, their involvement stirred the sectarian pot.

In the new parliament, Parnell's party held the balance of power. Gladstone, who seventeen years previously had said his mission was to pacify Ireland, turned his back on his failed policy of carrots and sticks (conciliation and coercion), announced (sincerely) his conversion to Home Rule and became prime minister for the third time at the end of January 1886. Orangemen and Ulster Conservatives began a frenzied anti-Home Rule campaign and organized huge demonstrations all over Ulster, the most famous of which was the February Ulster Hall meeting addressed by the maverick Lord Randolph Churchill. No lover of 'foul Ulster Tories', Churchill had taken a deliberate decision to attack Gladstone by playing 'the Orange card . . . Please God it may turn out the ace of trumps and not the two'. It would be neither the first nor the last time that a mainland politician would cynically make use for his own ends of the fervent loyalty of the United Kingdom's most faithful tribe.

'Ulster will fight and Ulster will be right', was the rallying cry with which Churchill enthused the cheering crowds on his arrival at Larne and in his speech in Belfast. 'We are prepared to take the Bible in one hand and the sword in the other,' announced the MP and Orange hero, William Johnston of Ballykilbeg: 'We will defend the Protestant religion and our liberties won at the Boyne with our rifles in our hands.' And though most of the Orangemen who then began drilling were armed only with wooden guns, there was no doubting the seriousness of their commitment.

Though defiant unionists needed no encouragement from mainland British statesmen, there was plenty forthcoming. The Conservative leader, Lord Salisbury, was one of those who declared that loyalists would be entitled to resist Home Rule by force. 'The word "Resist! Resist!" was on the lips not merely of Orangemen,' reported an Ulster liberal unionist journalist, 'but of Liberals, of those who by their profession were men of peace, merchants, manufacturers, bankers, medical men, and even clergymen.'

The Orange card proved to be an ace. The Liberal Party split and Gladstone's Home Rule Bill was defeated in June. Like Parnell, Gladstone had no understanding of the strength of feeling in Ulster, which had been whipped up to new heights of excitement and sectarianism. Rioting had begun a few days before the Home Rule vote and intensified thereafter as rejoicing Protestants and enraged Catholics attacked each other, drove each other out of workplaces and attacked each other's strongholds. In the increasingly ghettoized Belfast, about fifty people died that summer as a result of vicious riots, many of them shot by the largely Catholic police force (whose officers were, however, almost exclusively Protestant). To the more paranoid Protestants, this was evidence that their own government was persecuting them. As the inflammatory Presbyterian preacher, the Reverend Hugh Hanna, put it: 'The armed servants of that Government are sent to suppress rejoicing loyalty by the sanguinary slaughter of a people resolved to resist a wicked policy.'

Liberal unionists became part of what was now known as the Conservative and Unionist Party which won the July election. The Irish voting pattern was once against distinguished by religious polarization. In 1890 the split in the Irish Parliamentary Party over the citing of Parnell in a divorce case gave unionists a respite, but the return of Gladstone to power in 1892 led to another attack of nerves, for Gladstone was still convinced that Protestants could be persuaded to become nationalists and was determined on pushing ahead with another Home Rule Bill. Like so many of his successors, he could never appreciate the genuine fears of Protestants who believed that government by Dublin would mean government by Rome, the confiscation of land that had been legitimately in settler hands for many generations and the destruction by feckless Catholics of the prosperous industries of the north-east built up by the Protestant ethic.

At artisan level, Protestants feared the loss of their disproportionate share of better-paid jobs.

An enormous Ulster unionist convention held in Belfast in 1892 symbolized the extent to which northern unionism was developing its own strong identity as it came to realize that the electoral battle in the rest of Ireland had been lost to Catholic nationalism. As unionists in the south of Ireland accepted they were beaten, 'southern politics', as David Miller puts it, 'gradually ceased to resemble a zero-sum game'. Ulster was completely different, for there the two communities stayed locked in electoral and territorial struggles. Gladstone dismissed the anti-Home Rule fervour of the 300,000 or so demonstrators and pressed ahead with another Home Rule Bill, but, after its defeat, with his resignation, the threat receded for a decade of Conservative rule.

Irish nationalist historians liked to blame the British for creating the conditions that were to bring about partition. It was not until 1959 that this premise was seriously challenged in a pamphlet by a young lawyer, Donal Barrington, who wanted a United Ireland but believed it could come about only by facing reality and building trust. 'It is true,' he wrote, 'that Tory leaders came over to Ireland to wake up the Orangemen to the dangers of Home Rule, but the Orangemen did not need much waking up, and little is to be gained by counting all the Tory leaders who came to Ireland to speak to the Orangemen and ignoring all the Orange leaders who went to England to speak to the Tories.'

There was, of course, a vast range of opinion across the unionist political spectrum from Catholic-hating bigots to highly civilized and non-sectarian liberals, from social conservatives to labour agitators and land reformers. And although the Orange Order was enjoying a renaissance in numbers and range of membership, it too suffered from serious divisions. In the sectarian heartlands of Belfast, allegations such as 'Romanist' tendencies and 'ritualistic practices' in the Church of England that had riven LOL 152 were among those leading to a serious division. More important was a widespread perception that the British government, with the connivance of unionist MPs, was appeasing Roman Catholics and their Church.

Brother Thomas Sloan, Worshipful Master of St Michael's Total Abstinence LOL No. 1890, trade unionist and leader of the Belfast Protestant Association, complained in 1902 at his district lodge about the conduct of Colonel Edward Saunderson, the witty and popular leader of the Ulster unionists and a member of the General Synod of the Church of Ireland.

A Liberal MP in 1865, Saunderson had crossed the floor to the Conservatives over disestablishment and had joined the Orange Order in 1882
because he feared that Home Rule would bring Rome Rule. Sloan had
been outraged by a misleading report that Saunderson had voted with the
government to exclude convent laundries from its Workshops Bill.

The complaint was overruled by the District Master and Sloan's anger
intensified when an Orange parade scheduled for Rostrevor on the Twelfth
was banned and the Chief Secretary of Ireland said the decision had
been taken after consultation with the Orange leadership. Sloan was the
ringleader of a large crowd who began to heckle Saunderson, the County
Grand Master of Belfast, at the Twelfth demonstration in Castlereagh.
Proceedings degenerated when Sloan climbed on to the platform to
interrogate Saunderson.

A few days later, William Johnston died and Sloan decided to stand
as an independent against the unionist candidate. Belfast Grand Lodge
passed a resolution condemning Sloan's conduct and supported the unionist candidate, but the majority of Orange lodges backed Sloan, who won
the seat after a rough campaign. He was subsequently summoned to a
Grand Lodge meeting, charged with unbecoming conduct and, along with
some of his supporters, was suspended for two years. Angry at what
they saw as political vengefulness, Sloan and other dissidents set up the
Independent Orange Order, which became popular with radical Presbyterians who resented the Church of Ireland gentry who dominated
Orangeism and unionism.

The Independent Orange Order had grown to sixty-eight lodges by
1906, mostly in Belfast and North Antrim. There was bad blood and
occasional violence between members of the two orders. The new institution's working-class orientation led to a brief and loose alliance with
the Belfast Labour Party and even the Ancient Order of Hibernians in
support of striking dockers, but though it still exists, it lost its political
clout in 1910 when Sloan lost his seat. By then the Orange Order proper
had been given formal recognition within unionism with the allocation
of fifty seats on the 200-strong Ulster Unionist Council which was constituted in 1905.

The new opportunities and enhanced equality offered to Catholics by
land reform and industrialization engendered increasing self-confidence,
further demands and new sensitivities. As Frank Wright puts it, 'in an
ethnic frontier, as forces become balanced, distrust becomes circular and
self-reinforcing. Any hint of an assumption of superiority, any hint of

Protestant efforts to keep control over Catholics, even a suggestion that equality for Catholics would be *given* by upright Protestants, could infuriate Catholics'. Increasingly, Catholics were setting their own agenda and Protestants were feeling ever more insecure.

The 1896 riots, the worst of the nineteenth century, had been bloody proof of Catholic advance. As Wright explains:

> As the two communities became more alike, the boundaries between them hardened and the dangers of tension between them affected ever more people. It is not a sign of degeneracy that fewer and fewer Protestant Liberals supported Catholic perceptions of each successive riot in Belfast. What happened was that Catholics rivalled more and more thoroughly with Protestants in each riot. That meant that the riots became more and more lethal, and that the two sorts of rioters became more and more alike. Eventually, when their differences expressed themselves as opposed national differences, they had become total rivals.

On the British mainland and in the USA, where in the mid-nineteenth century anti-Catholicism and fear of papal pretensions had caused riots and had been reflected in discriminatory legislation*, sectarianism was diminishing steadily. In Ireland, with the religious polarization of Irish politics around the Home Rule issue, it could only get worse. Ian Paisley's present-day rants against the pope would have raised few eyebrows in London during the reign of the young Victoria, but would have been thought to be over the top by the time she died. In Glasgow or Liverpool, of course, such rhetoric can still be heard. The distaste shown by successive British governments for Ireland has much to do with a growing alienation from expressions of religious fervour: fundamentalists, whether Catholic or Protestant, were seen as throwbacks to an earlier and more ignorant age. The Chief Secretary, George Wyndham, who believed in killing Home Rule by kindness, was seen by unionists as an appeaser of nationalists. For his part, he railed against 'Orange uncouthness' and Ulster parochialism. Although he managed to remove the land question from politics, the hunger for Home Rule could not be assuaged.

The promulgation of papal primacy and infallibility which emerged from the first Vatican Council of 1869–70 had confirmed the worst fears of a people who believed that the only authority was the Bible. The 'Ne

---

* 'When an Englishman sees anything in religion which he does not like, he always, *prima facie*, imputes it to the Pope,' wrote Walter Bagehot in 1854.

Temere' decree issued by Pius X in 1907 might have been expressly designed to stoke the fires of Protestant paranoia by its requirement that a marriage in which one of the parties was Catholic would be invalid if not solemnized according to Roman Catholic rites. As interpreted and put into practice by the Irish Catholic hierarchy, this meant that the children of mixed marriages had to be brought up Catholic.* It was to be a cause of heartache and bitter resentment among Irish Protestants for almost a century.

'Wee Joe' Devlin, who became ghetto boss and Nationalist MP for West Belfast in 1907, energetically encouraged Catholic sectarianism for political purposes. It was Devlin who turned the Ancient Order of Hibernians into a major force. Founded in the United States in 1838, allegedly by Ribbonmen, branches of the AOH were established in Ireland, but by the turn of the century it had only about 8,000 members, largely because it was condemned by the Catholic Church as a secret society. Its development as a mass movement was made possible when the episcopal ban was lifted in 1904 and Devlin, as Grand Master of the Board of Erin, its ruling body, registered it as a friendly society; at its peak, in 1915, it had more than 120,000 members.

By now Orange parades had been enriched by accordion, flute, pipe and silver bands and an immense variety of painted banners. The railways had made massive demonstrations possible, while the Home Rule crisis had brought in recruits from all classes, including many previously standoffish Presbyterians. It was now the norm for political as well as religious resolutions to be passed at the 'field' and for senior unionist politicians there to address the assembled paraders. The AOH, whose motto was 'Fidelity to Faith and Fatherland', was the mirror-image of the Orange; its Twelfth was St Patrick's Day, when members paraded with green regalia and bands playing nationalist tunes.

Many Protestants resented being tainted with the Orange label, which was frequently used by their opponents to portray unionism as synonymous with religious bigotry. Yet unionism relied heavily on the loyal institutions for platforms, votes and shows of might. When the liberal

---

∗ I asked a devout Presbyterian friend how he would feel if his son married a Catholic. 'It would be OK if she wasn't a Fenian,' he answered first. The next time we spoke, he added: 'But the children would have to be brought up Presbyterian.' 'So you're issuing a Presbyterian version of "Ne Temere",' I said. Being hot on civil and religious liberty, he agonized over that, but his conclusion was that it is reasonable for an individual to hold such a view, but not for a church to impose it. In any case, he knew his son would make up his own mind.

government elected in 1910 found itself dependent on nationalist support, the prime minister, H. H. Asquith, committed his government to Home Rule, now possible since the removal of the veto of the House of Lords. The Ulster Unionist Council now secretly decided to arm and prepare for resistance.

On 25 September 1911, unionism publicly flexed its muscles with the launch of the anti-Home Rule campaign at Craigavon, the estate of the Boer War veteran and unionist MP Captain James Craig. More than 50,000 members of Orange lodges and unionist clubs marched thither to be told by the new leader of Ulster unionism, the MP and distinguished lawyer Sir Edward Carson, who had been Solicitor-General from 1900 to 1906, that he was entering a compact with 'every one of you, and with the help of God you and I joined together – I giving the best I can, and you giving me all your strength behind me – we will yet defeat the most nefarious conspiracy that has ever been hatched against a free people'. They must all be prepared 'the morning Home Rule passes, ourselves to become responsible for the government of the Protestant Province of Ulster'.

Six months later, at Balmoral in Belfast, the new Conservative leader, Bonar Law, whose father had been a Presbyterian minister in Coleraine, and who knew Ulster very well, with seventy other mainland MPs joined a crowd of 100,000 and spoke their language:

> Once again you hold the pass, the pass for the Empire. You are a besieged city. The timid have left you; your Lundys have betrayed you; but you have closed your gates. The Government have erected by the Parliament Act a boom against you to shut you off from the help of the British people. You will burst that boom. That help will come.

Carson, a Dubliner and graduate of Trinity College, loved Ireland passionately but regarded the Union as his 'guiding star'. He had only reluctantly come to accept that Home Rule for most of Ireland was now inevitable and therefore, though he knew Ulster and its people hardly at all, and was himself non-sectarian, he was prepared to throw himself into a crusade to save what could be saved from a gross betrayal. 'A precedent has yet to be created to drive out by force loyal and contented citizens from a community to which by birth they belong,' he declared at Balmoral.

If unionists are given to paranoia, nationalists are given to wishful thinking. Although John Redmond, the leader of the Irish Parliamentary Party, was more sympathetic to the Protestant viewpoint and more conciliatory by disposition than most of his colleagues, he shrugged off expressions of Ulster unionist defiance as a 'gigantic game of bluff and blackmail'. And as usual most people in England found the apocalyptic language of Ulster Protestantism incomprehensible and absurd. The Protestant Dubliner, London-based George Bernard Shaw, was one of the few with the acuity to note that when Protestants sang 'O God, Our Help in Ages Past', they should be taken seriously.

As was frequently the fate of the Orange Order, it was in many respects an embarrassment to its allies. Paul Bew identified a three-pronged unionist strategy to combat the Orange mud critics used to throw at the anti-Home Rule case. First, unionists insisted on the limited role of Orangeism within the Irish unionist coalition. In February 1912, with the support of Orange Grand Secretary Colonel Wallace, the Ulster Unionist Council issued this statement:

> That we, the Standing Committee of the Ulster Unionist Council, desire to call public attention to the gross mis-statements that are constantly being made by members of the Government and their supporters in the Press, in which they assert that our opposition to Home Rule proceeds solely from the Orange Order. We consider it right to point out that the Ulster Council is representative of every shade of Unionist opinion, and includes not only the Orange Society, but every other Unionist organization in Ulster – Conservative, Constitutional, and Liberal Unionist – all of whom send duly elected delegates to the Council.
>
> We have, in addition, the support of large numbers of men who hold Radical views on general politics, but who are determinedly opposed to the imposition of Home Rule upon our country.

The second prong was an insistence 'that Presbyterians, at least, had a tradition of co-operation with Catholics and of a certain coolness towards Orangeism'. And the third:

> and probably the most important and revealing one – claimed the Orange Order was in any case basically a positive force in Irish society, at any rate when compared with the heartless activities of nationalists . . . 'When did Orangemen forfeit their rights as citizens?' asked a commentator who wrote as 'Southern Presbyterian'.
>
> Are not Orangemen worthy of being heard in Irish affairs? It is true they are a secret society: but they have never been charged with hanging horses or cutting

the udders of milch cows. They have never blackened their faces and butchered on a winter night peaceful households around the family hearth. They have never organized boycotting, hounded lonely defenceless women to death, refused persons of a different faith the necessities of life, and prevented the village carpenter from providing a coffin for the dead. No, Orangemen may have their faults but these faults lie in an excess of loyalty to the Crown and the Constitution, lie in too vivid a memory of the glories of Derry and the Boyne, in too sincere a devotion to the Dutch William who at the Revolution established our liberties and gave us our present Royal House.

However, there was no disguising the extent of Orange influence. On a Twelfth platform, an Orange clergyman crowed in 1912 that 'there was not a single member of the Irish Unionist party in Parliament but owed his seat largely to the influence and practical support of the Orange society, nor were there any who more sincerely acknowledged that practical help than the members of that party themselves'. The closing of ranks between Orangemen and their traditional Protestant opponents was symbolized for Paul Bew by the career of Peter Kerr-Smiley, MP, 'an Eton and Trinity Hall man who emerged in politics under the tutelage of Professor Richard Smyth, MP, one of the most gentle, scholarly, and intellectual adherents of traditional Ulster Presbyterian liberalism'. Yet by 1912 Kerr-Smiley, chairman of the liberal unionist *Northern Whig* newspaper, was endowing Orange halls. The Orange Order's faithful shadow, the AOH, was also by now of tremendous political significance in the Irish Parliamentary Party.

It was hard for Orangemen, let alone Ulster Protestants in general, to tolerate being called bigots during a period in which nationalism was being infused with a spirit of Gaelic exclusivity and Catholic revivalism. There was no longer a welcome for Protestants like the Gaeltacht-born County Grand Master of Belfast who taught Irish classes on the Falls Road at the turn of the century. The Gaelic Athletic Association demonstrated the new contempt for and rejection of aspects of British culture dear to many Protestants by excluding from membership police, soldiers and those who played 'foreign games' like cricket or rugby. The Catholic Church showed itself as evangelical about the Gaelic revival as it had become about religion; in March 1912 declared the *Catholic Bulletin*: 'The time has arrived for action. The day of Ireland's missionary heroism is at hand ... To bring into the bosom of Holy Church the million of our separated brethren is a most attractive programme.'

The summer of 1912 saw more sectarian outrages, including an AOH attack on a Presbyterian Sunday-school outing which triggered expulsions of Catholic shipyard workers. In mid-September, an all-out battle between supporters of Celtic Park and Linfield football clubs left sixty injured; the trouble had been provoked by a vast crowd of Protestant Linfield supporters who waved Orange banners and chanted obscene versions of Orange songs. That same month, Carson embarked on a series of loyalist demonstrations which began in the far west in Enniskillen and moved east. The climax came on Saturday 28 September, 'Ulster Day', with the mass signing by Ulster Protestants of Ulster's Solemn League and Covenant – a formal bond of mutual obligation:

> Being convinced in our consciences that Home Rule would be disastrous to the material well being of Ulster as well as the whole of Ireland, subversive of our civil and religious freedom, destructive of our citizenship and perilous to the unity of the empire, we, whose names are underwritten, men of Ulster, loyal subjects of His Gracious Majesty King George V, humbly relying on the God whom our fathers in days of stress and trial confidently trusted, do hereby pledge ourselves in solemn Covenant throughout this time of threatened calamity to stand by one another in defending for ourselves and our children our cherished position of equal citizenship in the United Kingdom and in using all means which may be found necessary to defeat the present conspiracy to set up a Home Rule Parliament in Ireland. And in the event of such a Parliament being forced upon us we further solemnly and mutually pledge ourselves to refuse to recognize its authority. In sure confidence that God will defend the right we hereto subscribe our names.

After morning services, all day, to stirring band music, men and women dressed in their Sunday best queued up to sign in Belfast and in towns throughout Ulster. By the end of the day the Covenant had been signed by 237,368 men and a similar declaration by 234,046 women.

In January 1913, as the Home Rule Bill continued on its way through parliament, the Ulster Unionist Council finalized its scheme for creating a provisional government of Ulster and set up an Ulster Volunteer Force (UVF) with recruits from signatories of the Covenant. By the end of the year, 90,000 were training and drilling throughout the province – with far more enthusiasm being manifested in the east than the west. Orange Halls were used for UVF meetings and for 'shindigs' to raise funds. There was plenty of loyalist violence, often centring round parades. In Philip Orr's words, 'the atmosphere in Ulster, always tense, was becoming

increasingly manic'. But as Carson intended, disciplined protest and training contained potential violence.

Asquith and Bonar Law were prepared to agree a compromise to avoid
civil war, but the Irish Parliamentary Party rejected any form of permanent
partition. When in March 1914 Redmond reluctantly agreed to allow each
Ulster county the opportunity to opt out of Home Rule for six years,
Carson denounced a 'sentence of death with a stay of execution' and left
for Ulster. Sixty cavalry officers at the Curragh army camp in County
Kildare announced they would not lead their men against Ulster loyalists
and the following month there was a massive importation of arms at
Larne. In Dublin, nationalists emulated unionists by setting up the Irish
Volunteers and running guns, and the Irish Republican Brotherhood
moved into positions of influence. Ulster was an armed camp, with both
sets of volunteers busy drilling almost side by side. An RIC officer in
Londonderry reported that there was 'no doubt that many of the lower
element of the Orange Order' had joined the UVF and that there were
fears that they were prepared 'to proceed to extremities'.

Asquith was prepared to exclude Antrim, Armagh, Down and Londonderry; the Ulster Unionist Council would have settled for those plus
Fermanagh and Tyrone; Carson refused to contemplate abandoning the
covenanters of Donegal, Cavan and Monaghan and insisted on all nine
counties; many Ulster Catholics would have preferred no Home Rule to
exclusion; and most of nationalist Ireland refused to contemplate any
form of permanent partition.

A popular verse of the time, like Kipling's 'Ulster 1912', summed up
the sense of bewildered betrayal of most ordinary Protestants as the Home
Rule Bill received the Royal Assent:

> She had pleaded and prayed to be counted still,
>   As one of our household through good and ill;
> And with scorn they replied,
>   Jeered on her loyalty, trod on her pride,
>   Spurned her, refused her,
>   Great-hearted Ulster,
>   Flung her aside.

With the outbreak of war with Germany on 4 August 1914, Ulster –
and indeed Ireland – showed its great heart. 'Our first duty as loyal
subjects is to the king,' said Carson. 'The armed Catholics in the South

will only be too glad to join arms with the armed Protestant Ulstermen,'
said John Redmond. It was some months before Redmond was seriously
weakened when the Home Rule Bill was suspended for the duration of
the war with a promise that amending legislation would then make special
provision for Ulster.

'TYRONE'S FINE EXAMPLE. NATIONAL AND ULSTER VOLUNTEERS
MARCH TOGETHER. ROUSING SCENES' was the headline on 10 August
in the nationalist *Irish News* over a report of Ulster Volunteers marching
side by side through Omagh with the National Volunteers.* There were
already 58,000 Irishmen in the British army: about 150,000 more volunteered, with the highest rate of recruitment in Ulster. It is reckoned that
a disproportionate 43 per cent of recruits were Protestant and that of the
27,000 who died, about half were Catholic. Because of the effect on the
nationalist psyche of the execution of the leaders of the Easter Rising of
1916 and the subsequent Anglo-Irish war, Catholic members of the British
army would for generations be virtually written out of nationalist history.
(In the 1950s, my grandmother O'Sullivan summoned my brother to her
bedroom to show him our grandfather's British Army commission from
1916. She insisted the door be kept shut and no one be told. Her particular
terror was that Sinn Féin grandmother Edwards upstairs might find out
and we'd never hear the end of it). But for Protestants, and particularly
Ulster Protestants, the enormous sacrifices made during the Great War
became a central sombre part of the tribal folk-memory.

It was a matter of great jubilation to Carson and Craig that the UVF
was allowed stay together to form the 36th (Ulster) Division,† which
after a long period of training in Northern Ireland was sent to Seaford
in Sussex in the summer of 1915. Early in the morning of the Twelfth,
an officer was awakened by the skirl of bagpipes playing Orange tunes,
and from his window saw the whole battalion, minus the officers, marching around the parade ground led by a soldier on a white horse. The
townsfolk watched a procession through the town with banners later in
the day and in the evening a London Orangeman told a large crowd that
he hoped that 'when July 12th came round again he would have the

---

* The Irish Volunteers split. About 11,000 of the 170,000 stayed with the Irish Parliamentary Party to form
the National Volunteers. Joseph Devlin was very active in the recruiting drive.

† It was a courtesy and a comfort not extended to the National Volunteers, who were dispersed among many
different regiments.

privilege of addressing them on their own beloved soil and that Germany would have received a sound thrashing by then'.

Parent lodges back home gave birth to military offspring, recorded Philip Orr, with a special wartime charter for meetings at the front. In France, where the division was sent in the autumn, there were lodge meetings where

> men encountered old friends, made new ones and caught up with what was happening at home. They talked openly at these meetings without fear of disciplinary proceedings, and so the lodges may have been a valuable vent for feelings stirred up by the miseries of war. Officers and men met on an equal basis, much to the displeasure of some HQ staff, and yet this allowed the officers to know – much more accurately than in many other divisions – just how the men were feeling.

Orr quoted an Orangeman recalling a lodge meeting in a French village:

> You couldn't get a pint of porter, but the wine was cheap and there was always a hunk of French cheese and long loaves of French bread and we had these after the meeting was over. There was little or nothing to do at times, and it broke up the night for you . . . now and then we had officers present and it did your heart good to see them respect the Worshipful Master and maybe him a private. It was just like home at some of those meetings . . . you felt the better of them for a week afterwards.

'I could not turn down an invitation to go and meet again men who stood with me on the quayside that Friday night we brought the guns in,' said another. 'It is difficult for the English to understand the loyalty we have for each other and the comradeship we enjoy as Orangemen.'

Yet another recalled a meeting when 'we sung all the old favourite Orange songs, them that goes with a swing. Out comes the pennies and the tin whistles; we really got it going.' As they left they saw a few officers and artillery men from London standing outside.

> Now a few days after this I saw one of the artillery men and he pestered me to give him the words and tunes of some of the songs . . . we were digging in some of the French artillery just before the Somme and some of the London men were helping us. Do you know, a couple of gun crews were singing 'The Sash' with all the get-up-and-go you'd hear on the Twelfth night in any Orange Hall.

Orr records too that the Ulster Division was noted for its passion for order and neatness: the divisional depot near Harfleur was 'one of the showplaces behind the lines, with its bright gardens and trim paths lined with whitewashed stones'.

At the end of June 1916, just before the division was due to go over the top at Thiepval Wood, an ex-teacher expressed the feelings of many of his brethren when he began a letter to the secretary of his Orange Lodge near Portadown:

> Dear Br. Secretary,
> There is no doubt that when you receive this note I shall be dead. There are all the signs that something bigger than has ever taken place before in this war is about to be launched . . .

As the men of the Ulster Division emerged from their trenches on 1 July, some wore orange lilies and a sergeant wore his sash. By any standards, they acted with both efficiency and bravery, but they never stood a chance. In only two days, 5,500 were killed or wounded. Some companies were virtually wiped out.

Back home, Orange lodges were in a state of shock and grief. On the Twelfth, instead of parades there was a five-minute silence right across Ulster at noon: work stopped, trams, trains and other traffic came to a halt, blinds were drawn, flags flew at half-mast and people stood still in the street in the pouring rain. One Orangeman recalled:

> On the 14th night, we arranged a meeting in the school house and we had members from all the local lodges present . . . each lodge represented at the meeting then stood and gave out the names of their members killed, wounded or missing in fighting in France . . . there was over 150 names in all . . . We sang 'Shall We Gather at the River' and the women made tea and cakes for us all.

The ground the Ulster Division had so bloodily won was soon lost again. The only small consolation was that it had gained a fine reputation for courage, as well as four posthumous Victoria Crosses. The bereaved clung for comfort to the accolades from the outside world including this eulogy from an English Staff Officer: 'The Division has been through an ordeal by fire, gas, and poison. Our gallant fellows marched into a narrow alley of death, shouting "No Surrender!" and "Remember the Boyne!" I wish I had been born an Ulsterman, but I am proud to have been associated with these wonderful men – the most gallant in the world.'

A war correspondent reported:

Just as calm and controlled as on the parade ground, the men moved forwards. One or two, remembering the ancient watchwords, sang out 'No Surrender' or 'Dolly's Brae', but for the most part they kept the stiff upper lip and the clenched teeth which meant death or victory.

As in the past when dangers and difficulties confronted them, so now the Covenanters were led to their high trust. Sheets and flashes of flame swept the terrain . . . the air was 'stiff with shot'. The hail fell thickly upon these brave advancing Ulstermen, and they paid the penalty with set, firm faces. There was no thought of giving way, merely duty to be done, a task to be completed. Into the very furnace heat of the German fire our gallant lads went, and as shot and shell raked their ranks others pressed forward to take their places. From both flanks the machine guns enfiladed them, and amid the hail of death, as they merged from the Thiepval Wood, they fell in hundreds. The German fire at this point was protracted and perfect. The tops of the trees were slashed clear, clean as sabre cuts, and the stumps stood up gauntly, behind which the Ulstermen formed their line and held firmly, while the Teutonic wave of men swept towards them, protected by a curtain of artillery fire.

But there was less chance of the waves of our own North Channel making an impression upon the basaltic rocks of Ulster than of these German hordes beating down the Ulster defence. When the counter attack had spent itself, amid roar and spume of dead and wounded, the line formed out of apparent chaos and with a steady, rhythmic clatter flung itself headlong into the enemy's position. The constant click of the machine guns, the roar of the heavy artillery, and the sound of rifle fire mingled in the air, but now the blood surged in the veins, and the proud traditions of a brave ancestry impels these gallant fellows to the onset. They falter not.

With broad sweeps and widespread movements they penetrated the enemy's third line, and prisoners by the score were taken. Even then they were not to be stopped, for though they were losing men in hundreds they swept on, and the sadly thinned ranks reduced to the merest semblance of the brave khaki line which had set out came to and occupied the fourth and fifth lines of the German positions. But these advanced points could not be held further than the time necessary to kill or capture the enemy. The place had developed into a narrow and dangerous salient, principally because the Ulstermen had carried everything before them in an impetuous rush. Right and left of our men the troops had been held up by insurmountable obstacles and the necessary consequence was that the men of the

Imperial Province were singled out as the centre of the fire of the hostile guns, while
they had also to contend with a hot flanking fire.

Now the position was terrible. Before our men the enemy had suffered fearfully,
and those who had not been captured or slain had beaten a quick retreat, but the
guns were playing sad havoc in our ranks. The order to advance had to be
countermanded, and the retire given. It was not too soon, for the toll of life which
had to be paid. From cunning hiding-places and concealed positions the machine
guns were splattering their deadly missiles and the wondrous valour of the
Ulstermen was like to prove their doom. With their faces to the foe, back came our
brave lads, and as the Germans were driven forward to the counter-attack they
were met with a steady, persistent fire. As the 'contemptible little army' fought the
most splendid rearguard action in all history, from Mons to the Marne, so on a
more limited terrain did our brave Ulster boys live up to the traditions of the British
Army.

Reckless individual courage was chronicled in local papers too. Two
of the most incredible among those listed in the *Tyrone Constitution* were
Private Thomas Gibson, of Coalisland, who 'saw three Germans working
a machine gun; he attacked them single-handed and killed them all with
his clubbed rifle, thereby saving many lives'. And 'Private Robert Monte-
ith of Lislap, Omagh, had his leg taken off above the knee; he used his
rifle and bayonet as a crutch and continued to advance. It is feared he
succumbed later.'

'All the accounts of the division in action,' said my friend Henry, after
perusing the *Tyrone Constitution*, 'absolutely sum up what we are when
our backs are to the wall. If we're in a war in impossible circumstances
we shout "No surrender", plunge in and don't give up. It's our cussedness, it's our strength, it's our essence. It's our good side and it's our
bad.'

Their essence was well summed up in a *Tyrone Constitution* account
of the annual Orange anniversary service in First Omagh Presbyterian
Church:

the seating accommodation of the sacred edifice was taxed to its utmost, every
available seat being occupied. There was but a small turn-out of the members of the
local Orange lodges, a fact which bore ample testimony to the number who have
volunteered in their country's service and many of whom are to-day either lying in
hospital or sleeping their last sleep in a Flanders grave, after covering themselves
with glory on the memorable 1st July.

The congregation wore crepe rosettes and 'the praise portion of the service consisted of the well-known psalms and hymns, the latter including an intercessory one for the fighting men.' The preacher said:

It has been my custom for the last 23 years to say something from this pulpit on the Sunday before the 12th, that I thought bore more or less directly upon your great anniversary, and on many occasions during this period I have been asked to conduct special anniversary services for you, but we never met for worship before at a time like this. These are solemn times and they are also rousing times. We are passing through a crisis fraught with momentous issues for weal or woe, not only for our own Empire but for all the nations of the earth. Never since history began has God caused the people to pass through such a horror of darkness as we have been passing through for the past two years, and never before have I found the same difficulty in the effort to get a message suitable to the occasion.

When I was thinking what I should take as my guiding thought these words from 2nd Chronicles seized me, 'Be ye strong, and let not your hands be slack, for your work shall be rewarded.' One of the great needs of the present is calmness and strength both in men and women, and if we betake ourselves to the true source of these, and go on steadfastly in the path of duty, we shall have assurance of the fulfilment of the promise that our work shall be rewarded.

Through your history there is one principle to which you have always been true, true as the needle in the pole, and that is the principle of loyalty to the King and constitution. Whatever weaknesses either friends or enemies have been able to detect in your order, even your bitterest enemy could never accuse you of being weak or wavering in your loyalty: you have been loyal all through your history. Even when your loyalty seemed to stand in the way of the interests of the vast majority of your members. Yes, and spite of all the strain that has been put upon your loyalty during the last quarter of a century.

Those dreadful few days were to become part of the mental and spiritual furniture of Ulster Protestantism. 'I was brought up in the Cregagh Road in Belfast close to an estate whose streets bore the names of Flanders,' recalls James Hawthorne, former controller of BBC Northern Ireland. 'Somme, Albert, Bapaume, Hamel. There was a small cenotaph at its centre. My father was inordinately proud of his wartime service in the Ulster Division and on Remembrance Sunday we watched him take part in the ceremony from the corner of Thiepval Avenue.'

Eighty-one years after the horrors of Thiepval Wood, I sat in the House of Orange in Belfast listening to two elderly men talk about what the

Somme meant to them. One of them had lost four great-uncles there; both of them, after decades of attending commemoration services for fallen brethren, had become distressed that there was no public awareness of the huge sacrifice thousands and thousands of Orangemen from many parts of the empire had made in the Great War – particularly the Canadian Orange Order, which had lost more men than the Irish.

Young people had been their inspiration for creating a memorial: 'One of the things that led me to a greater understanding of what happened at the Somme was during the International Year of Youth when we brought kids from Tallaght* in Dublin and from the Shankill to France in a joint project. We were taking them around showing them the Eiffel Tower and the Arc de Triomphe and it wasn't until we were coming back – we were early to the boat – that Ian Adamson says: "Have you ever heard of the Ulster Tower?" We took them there, and both the kids from Tallaght and the kids from the Shankill, you couldn't move them away from the place, it was so emotional for them. They simply wanted to stay, they wanted to see more. They were relating to the names on the stones and that's basically how that whole thing started.'

So Tommy Doyle, who is almost blind, and his friend Jack Hewitt had set about organizing a memorial. Tommy met Martin Smyth, then Grand Master, at a Last Saturday and secured his approval, and with Jack and a handful of other brethren embarked on the project. 'There seemed to be a reluctance in government circles to accept the part that the Orange did play in the whole development of the United Kingdom, the defence of the United Kingdom and all the rest of it. They said that we couldn't build our memorial within the grounds of the Ulster Tower because the charter that they had agreed with France allowed only one memorial in there. Which was basically a lie.'

After conversations with various British and French authorities, the Orangemen struck up a friendship with the local mayor, bought a plot of otherwise useless ground from her son, found a French architect and successfully surmounted the language barrier. Donations came from individual brethren, lodges and districts throughout Northern Ireland. 'We got money from Togo and Australia, New Zealand, Canada and the US and a powerful lot of small amounts of money from Scotland all totalling up to a worthy sum [close to £20,000], enough to get the memorial made here in the North of Ireland and shipped across by the contractor and put

* A sprawling, deprived estate on the outskirts of Dublin.

in its place. We put a capsule underneath the memorial containing a lot of bits and pieces that we thought would be of interest to posterity if and when this was dug up: coins of the realm, artefacts of the institution, badges etc, a copy of the Holy Writ, a copy of the *Belfast Telegraph*, though why we ever brought that I cannot understand: it'll go amouldering in the grave long before the rest.'

It was 1993: 'We started to get a memorial service together and expected a couple of hundred. But word got about. I wonder what a stranger would have thought to see roughly 500 men in collarettes walking down in their Sunday togs with a band playing 'Killaloe' on a Sunday afternoon. We got permission from the authorities for the band: we were legally there. And there were passersby there and people we met on the Saturday before the Sunday who were there paying homage. And you felt sort of in a kind of a way proud. Even though there was a bit of a tear and even though somewhere along the line the tear was also a raincloud, but you could still withal feel the feeling when the flags were flying.' There were flags from all the jurisdictions as well as an original UVF flag. And from England came a Portsmouth accordion band. 'There was a chap from here, lost both his legs, but he had to come. And he struggled from that chair to put his wreath down. Terrible hard.'

The following year, 'We took about forty ladies from West Belfast over, Orange ladies, and when we were there we had a good time there. They thoroughly enjoyed it. I heard just a few days ago that two of the ladies died a short time afterwards and they had said that they had enjoyed themselves and were glad to have been there.' On the way home in the bus with the ladies, Jack Hewitt suggested to Tommy Doyle that they should have a lodge to oversee the memorial, 'to make sure that in another ten or fifteen years time when I won't be there and he won't be there that this will be maintained.' And that is how LOL 1916 was formed.

We approached the Belfast County officers and told them what was in our mind. We sent a formal letter in. They accepted that, put it through the Central Committee and the Grand Lodge. And we got the warrant, which is the authority to sit as a lodge and we actually opened our first lodge meeting in this room, Grand Master in the chair, Grand Sec beside him, Assistant Grand Master and County Grand Master from Cavan, with officers from each of the six northern counties. We had a great night.

'Now we've got our first non-Northern Ireland members. We've got members from Ayrshire about to join – maybe four or five. And if we start here we certainly will advise the Imperial Council of our activities.

And we could have a 1916 lodge in Canada, Australia etc. We all have the same objective.'

'We didn't want anyone offended by anything we did', said Tommy Doyle. But they had reckoned without the Protestant intelligentsia. The poet Michael Longley, not a man needlessly to upset anyone, wrote in *The Twelfth* a piece later reproduced in the press.

As a boy watching the Twelfth of July procession on the Lisburn Road I used to wait with particular commitment for the banners commemorating the Battle of the Somme. In March this year my wife and I visited some of the First World War battlefields and cemeteries in Northern France. We did not detect a wrong note until we arrived at the memorial to the 36th (Ulster) Division close to the place where they made their heroic attempt to reach Thiepval and take the Schwaben Redoubt on 1 July 1916.

Outside the front wall, however, and close to the entrance gate a black and mean-looking obelisk commemorates the Orangemen who died in the Great War. This recent effort to improve on the 36th (Ulster) Division memorial contradicts the tenderness and nostalgia with which, in 1921, Helen's Tower was reproduced among the wounded fields of France. Aesthetically a disaster, an ugly lump of prose that detracts from the poetry of its setting, the obelisk is appropriately kept outside the enclosure of remembrance, beyond the pale. Out of touch, out of proportion, this monument to bad taste affronts Lutyens' profound vision and the unobtrusive, attentive, fastidious management of the cemeteries from day to day and over the years. Whereas desolation on an unprecedented and multi-national scale produced the cemeteries, tribal assertion thrust the obelisk onto the scene. Our present Troubles lurk behind its inadequate cover. It seems to be an attempt at tit-for-tat commemoration, a reply to Padraic Pearse's claim: 'The Fools! The Fools! The Fools! They have left us our Fenian dead.' Veneration for the dead of the Somme has degenerated into a necrophilia that mimics the necrophilia of political enemies. Two graveyard cultures vie with one another.

A failure of the imagination, the obelisk symbolizes much that has gone wrong with Orange and Unionist culture. Those who trampled on the graves in Drumcree churchyard last year trampled on the graves in France. Those who march on the Twelfth of July this year should ask themselves to what extent they are in danger of destroying the values they ostensibly seek to maintain.

It was the year of Drumcree Two. Michael Longley was endowing a simple, heartfelt tribute by ordinary people with a significance it did not possess. His essay caused a lot of distress.

11

Ourselves Alone

Each thought it had good reason to fear the other. As Namier says, the irrational is not necessarily unreasonable. Ulster Unionists, fearful of being isolated on the island, built a solid house, but it was a cold house for Catholics. And northern nationalists, although they had a roof over their heads, seemed to us as if they meant to burn the house down. None of us are entirely innocent.

David Trimble, Oslo, 1998

UNIONISM IS EASILY PARODIED by friends and foes alike. All I knew about Northern Ireland as a child was the verse:

Sir Edward Carson had a cat,
It sat upon the fender
And every time it caught a rat,
It shouted: 'No Surrender!'

Yet for unionists, the years before partition were a period when Ulster Protestants demonstrated courage and principle in the face of violence and betrayal. They watched helplessly as Irish nationalism turned militant, as the Irish Parliamentary Party began to disintegrate in the face of Sinn Féin electoral successes and as Lloyd George, who had replaced Asquith as prime minister in December 1916, pressed for unionist concessions; he wanted the United States in the war so Irish America had to be kept sweet.

Like many another British prime minister, Lloyd George attempted in Ireland to reconcile the irreconcilable. He assembled an Irish Convention which sat in Dublin from July 1917 until April 1918, but not only was it disabled by a Sinn Féin boycott, its major distinguishing feature was to show up the cleavage of opinion between northern and southern unionists. An Ulster Liberal unionist wrote of southern unionists to his wife: 'They want to capitulate & make terms with the enemy lest a worse thing befall them. They are a cowardly crew & stupid to boot. We shall do all we can to stiffen them & keep them in our ranks.'

Southern unionists, like northern nationalists, had every reason to be frightened of partition: each – quite rightly as it turned out – feared they would be abandoned by their natural allies on the other side of a border. The British government was prepared to ditch the Ulster Unionists should nationalists reach a deal with southern unionists, but Redmond was too weak to deliver. Scenting that Lloyd George was prepared to go back on earlier promises not to coerce Ulster, Carson saw no point in offering any concessions. In January 1918 he resigned from the Cabinet and James Craig from the government and they returned to Ulster to concentrate on saving it from Home Rule. Sinn Féin rhetoric stiffened Ulster Protestant resolve. Unionists were 'a rock in the road' to an Irish settlement, said Eamon de Valera in South Armagh in February 1918, which nationalists 'must if necessary blast . . . out of their path'.

Demonstrating culpable ignorance about nationalist attitudes, the British government announced in April its intention of imposing conscription in Ireland and destroyed constitutional nationalism at a stroke; they had conspired, said John Dillon, who had succeeded to the leadership of the Irish Parliamentary Party the previous month on the death of Redmond, to leave nothing in Ireland but 'Republican separatists and Ulster loyalists'.*

As Sinn Féin gained ground through organizing a successful anti-conscription campaign, the mood among northern unionists became ever more apocalyptic: 'Nothing has more disgusted me with the filth of politics,' thundered Carson to Belfast Orangemen on the 1918 Twelfth, 'than to find men going back on their word to those who have given their lives to the British cause.' And although Ulster Unionists did well in the north-east in the general election that came in December 1918, a few weeks after the armistice, Sinn Féin's destruction of the Irish Parliamentary Party boded ill for any agreement between nationalism and unionism. Refusing to take their seats in Westminster, Sinn Féin set up an independent parliament, Dáil Éireann, on 21 January 1919, the day which saw the first murders in what became the Anglo-Irish war by members of what would be called the Irish Republican Army.

At Westminster, the British government attempted to solve the Irish problem pragmatically. 'It is quite misleading to say that Partition was forced on Ireland by the British Government against the wishes of North and South,' said Donal Barrington pithily, countering in 1959 a view which is still steadfastly held in republican circles.

∗ 'John Redmond found all appeals in vain,' wrote Shane Leslie, 'whether to Ireland or to Ulster. Cursed by his own followers at home and abused by the English; cursed by one for getting nought for all he had given, and abused by the other for not giving more: broken and battered and bleeding at heart he left Ireland like O'Connell and Parnell at their ends and died away from an ungrateful country.'

Probably the most traduced leader in Irish nationalist history, John Redmond has only recently begun to receive the recognition he richly deserves for his decency and his commitment to his country.

It would be more correct to say that Partition was forced on the British Government by the conflicting demands of the two parties of Irishmen. It is true that both North and South were dissatisfied with Partition but that was because the North wanted all Ireland for the act of Union and the South wanted all Ireland for Home Rule. Both demands could not be met, neither party was prepared to give way, and the inevitable result was Partition.

The Government of Ireland Act of 1920 repealed the 1914 Home Rule Act and separated Ireland into two: Southern and Northern Ireland. To the great distress of unionists in Donegal, Cavan and Monaghan, Northern Ireland was restricted to six counties, though realists accepted that a unionist majority in the nine counties no longer existed. There were to be two separate parliaments and a Council of Ireland designed to provide a mechanism which might ultimately lead to unity by agreement. Sinn Féin contemptuously rejected the compromise, but the Ulster unionists settled for it as the best that they could get. As Jonathan Bardon observed: 'Thus it was that the part of Ulster that had fought hardest against Home Rule was the only part of Ireland to get Home Rule.'

The Act became law in December 1920 and came into force on 1 May 1921. In the ensuing election the two communities voted predictably, returning to the Northern Ireland parliament forty unionists, six Sinn Féin and six nationalists. Carson, who in February by his own wish had been succeeded by James Craig, gave the Ulster Unionist Council a last piece of advice: 'From the outset let us see that the Catholic minority have nothing to fear from the Protestant majority. Let us take care to win all that is best among those who have been opposed to us in the past. While maintaining intact our own religion let us give the same rights to the religion of our neighbours.'

Any chance that unionist politicians would approach government in that spirit had long been dashed by the appalling violence of the previous two years. Jonathan Bardon summed up the context in which Irishmen murdered and maimed each other:

The cult of violence in Ireland thrived in fertile soil before the war: it had been fostered either by stirring tales of imperial adventure or by romantic nationalist writing . . . and then it had been boosted by the exhilaration of gun-running and drilling in rival volunteer armies. Now men returned from the front, many inured to violence by the horrors of trench warfare, to renew their fighting in Ireland. Robert Lynd . . . reported that 'soldiers who fought for the Allies as they return home are becoming converted by the thousand into Sinn Féiners', some, like Tom Barry, to become leading men in the IRA. Returning soldiers played a crucial role in reviving the UVF, particularly in Derry. 'I had thought my soldiering days were over', wrote Captain Sir Basil Brooke, the Fermanagh landlord awarded the Military Cross during the war; '. . . I was to become a soldier of a very different sort . . . but I had the added stimulant of defending my own birthplace.' As IRA attacks spread northwards Brooke took a lead in organising Protestant resistance, while, at the same time, Lloyd George recruited ex-servicemen to revive the demoralised RIC and thus unleashed the notorious Black and Tans, and the Auxiliaries, on the southern Irish countryside.

In July 1920, as IRA attacks intensified in the north-east counties and terrified border Protestants, Brooke asked the British military authorities to give recognition to his vigilantes, otherwise the 'hotheads will take matters into their own hands and threaten retaliation'. He was refused. 'We in Ulster will tolerate no Sinn Féin,' Carson told Belfast Orangemen in Finaghy Field on the Twelfth. To the British government he added, 'if, having offered you our help, you are yourselves unable to protect us from the machinations of Sinn Féin, and you won't take our help; then, we tell you that we will take the matter into our own hands. We will reorganize.'

The 'hotheads', aka vicious loyalist thugs that embarked the following week on terrible anti-Catholic pogroms in Belfast and beyond, were under no one's control. Lloyd George tried to solve the problem by setting up three categories of Ulster Special Constabulary, of which the largest was the 19,550-strong part-time, unpaid B Specials. With no effort being made to persuade Catholics to join, the B Specials rapidly became seen as an official Protestant paramilitary force, yet without them the IRA would have had almost a free rein in their campaign in the border areas. Over almost half a century, while the B Specials were seen by frightened Protestants as their brave defenders, Catholics mostly viewed them with loathing. Like so much in Northern Ireland, the truth was much more complex: there were many decent people in the B Specials and some who should have been behind bars. Republican propaganda, however, ensured that they were seen as bogeymen by Catholics in Northern Ireland and as sectarian brutes by the world outside.

In July 1921, a month after King George V had opened the Northern Ireland parliament in Belfast and begged Irishmen 'to stretch out the hand of forbearance and conciliation', Lloyd George negotiated a truce with the IRA. It made little difference in the north. Bardon wrote:

> In Belfast one horrific incident followed another; twenty were left dead after three days of fighting north of the city centre in August; on 18 September troops opened fire on loyalist rioters and killed two women near York Street; on 24 September a youth was shot dead as he left St Matthew's Church in Short Strand; next day a bomb thrown by Catholics in Seaforde Street killed two people and a bomb thrown by Protestants into Weaver Street left one man dead and four children under the age of six seriously injured; and a few days later Catholics opened fire on a Protestant funeral, killing one person.

With that genius Irish republicans have consistently shown for putting extra obstacles in the path of a United Ireland, the Dáil's contribution was to order a boycott of Belfast goods and Ulster-based banks. Originally a protest against shipyard expulsions of Catholics in July 1920, this, in Winston Churchill's words, 'recognized and established real partition, spiritual and voluntary partition, before physical partition had been established . . . it did not secure the reinstatement of a single expelled Nationalist, nor the conversion of a single Unionist. It was merely a blind suicidal contribution to the general hate.' The IRA sent resting southern commanders to help their northern colleagues.

In December, Dáil representatives signed a treaty agreeing the setting up of an Irish Free State with dominion status. To many Ulster Protestants, this truck with terrorists was the ultimate betrayal. The following year, in his maiden speech in the House of Lords, Carson, full of what A. T. Q. Stewart described as 'the hopelessness of irredeemable defeat and betrayal', flayed the British political establishment. 'There is not a noble lord in this House,' he said, probably justly, 'who believes for a moment that these terms were passed upon their merits. Not at all. They were passed with a revolver pointed at your head. And you know it . . . You know you passed them because Sinn Féin with the army in Ireland has beaten you.'

Carson produced a devastating quote from an ex-Chief Secretary of Ireland, Augustine Birrell: 'It is a British characteristic, though not an amiable one, that once we are beaten we go over in a body to a successful enemy, and too often abandon and cold-shoulder and snub, both in action and in writing, the suffering few who adhere to our cause in evil and difficult times.'

Referring to the near-universal pressure on unionism to join a United

Ireland, he asked: 'What has Ulster done? I will tell you. She has stuck too well to you, and you believe because she is loyal you can kick her as you like.'

It was a speech which most Ulster unionists would regard as equally valid today.

When the IRA split over the treaty early in 1921, the violence in Northern Ireland was exacerbated by IRA raids from the south which provoked further vicious loyalist retaliation against vulnerable Catholics. It was only the outbreak of civil war down south that prevented a total collapse into anarchy up north: from August 1922, pro- and anti-IRA-men abandoned the north and went to fight each other in the south, leaving Northern Ireland in comparative peace.

Between July 1920 and July 1922, there were 557 people killed in Northern Ireland, 82 of whom were members of the security forces. The Catholic minority had borne the brunt: 303 Catholic civilians dead to 172 Protestants. Although Catholic civilians made up just a quarter of the population of Belfast, 257 of them had died as against 159 Protestants; in the region of 10,000 Catholics had been driven out of their jobs, more than 20,000 out of their homes and around 500 had their businesses destroyed.

In the Free State things were worse. Perhaps as many as 4,000 people had been killed, the country was financially crippled and the bitterness was to last for more than half a century. The task of trying in such circumstances to construct a stable democracy ensured that few Irish politicians would henceforward do other than pretend to care about the nationalists of the north. Instead, the two parts of Ireland steadily grew further and further apart.

'The fact that a third of the population was so hostile to the six-county state that it hoped for its downfall,' commented Jonathan Bardon, 'would have taxed the ingenuity of any government of the region. Now Ulster Unionists felt embattled and isolated. Few were disposed to conciliation and yet the restoration of peace in 1923 gave the Northern Ireland government a unique opportunity to attempt a healing of wounds and to woo at least some of the minority into an acceptance of the new regime.' That they failed to do so was mainly because they were frightened, because they lacked imagination and because the Ulster nationalist leaders were no better than they were.

Ireland, north and south, was bedevilled by the double-minority syndrome. Catholics were the frightened minority in the north and Protestants the frightened minority in the whole island. Neither majority treated its minority well, but each looked at the mote in the eye of the other rather than the beam in its own.

The average Ulster Protestant believes that between terror and Rome rule, Protestantism was virtually wiped out in the south of Ireland. The statistics back this up. Between 1911 and 1926, the Protestant population fell by 34 per cent, from 327,000 to 221,000, at a time when the Catholic populations in both north and south fell by just 2 per cent. This 'catastrophic loss was unique to the southern minority and unprecedented,' said Peter Hart in his essay, 'The Protestant Experience of Revolution in Southern Ireland': 'it represents easily the single greatest measurable social change of the revolutionary era. It is also unique in modern British history, being the only example of the mass displacement of a native ethnic group within the British Isles since the seventeenth century.' In addition, thousands of Free State Protestants on the run from the IRA left home for long periods and thousands more stayed away from home for weeks and months on end sleeping in barns and fields.

Hart's horrifying description of persecution during the period 1920–23 graphically shows why most rural and small-town Protestants were 'in a constant state of anxiety, waiting for the next knock at the door'. Thousands of Protestant families had guerrillas billeted upon them for days or weeks, even on and off for years. In County Cork, for instance, where Protestants made up 7 per cent of the population, 36 per cent of the 200 civilians shot by the IRA were Protestant and 85 per cent of the 113 houses burned belonged to Protestants. Admittedly, there was a strong class element in the arson attacks: big houses were mainly in Protestant hands. But when it came to murder, the sectarian element was strong.

The excuses were the same as those one still hears today from IRA apologists: those shot were dismissed as having been 'spies' or 'informers'. Indeed, on the good old no-smoke-without-fire principle, the fact that an apparently innocent man was shot could be used as evidence that he must have been guilty.

Because republicans always believed that sectarianism was a Protestant phenomenon, excuses had to be found for persecuting the other tribe, which was never, of course, identified by its religion.* 'As a result of

* A blackly funny example of such Irish Catholic double-think cited by Hart comes from 1914, when in response to reports by resident magistrates that there was widespread Protestant apprehension that fighting in the north would bring about reprisals in the south, the furious response to this slur from members of Limerick County

the treatment of the Catholic population of Belfast and other northern towns by the Orange gunmen there', said one typical IRA communication to a Galway landlord in the spring of 1922, 'thousands of men, women and children are homeless and starving and their immediate needs must be supplied ... The executive committee of the IRA have decided that the unionists and freemasons of the south and west be compelled to supply their needs. You are ordered to leave your residence at Woodlaw which with your entire property is confiscated.' Admittedly, there was nothing sectarian about the persecution of the members of the Royal Irish Constabulary: Catholic or Protestant, they were fair game for murder or expulsion, but they were the exception. In Hart's view:

> All the nightmare images of ethnic conflict in the twentieth century are here: the massacres and anonymous death squads, the burning homes and churches, the mass expulsions and trains filled with refugees, the transformation of lifelong neighbours into enemies, the conspiracy theories and the terminology of hatred. Munster, Leinster and Connaught can take their place with fellow imperial provinces Silesia, Galicia and Bosnia as part of the postwar 'unmixing of people' in Europe. We must not exaggerate. The Free State government had no part in persecution. Cork was not Smyrna, nor Belfast. Nevertheless, sectarianism was embedded in the Irish revolution, north and south. Any accounting of its violence and consequences must encompass the dreary steeples of Bandon and Ballinasloe as well as those of Fermanagh and Tyrone.*

Protestant nervousness and Catholic amnesia prevented until quite recently any public recognition in the south of the scale of violence towards Protestants in the early years of the state. And for most of the Protestant population, happily adjusted to modern Ireland, past wrongs can be forgotten. But in the border counties people still tell stories of IRA terror and the flood of refugees. Here is a typical story which I

Council was to condemn Munster Protestants for failing to contradict such reports and to warn: 'The worm may turn ... and those people who may remain silent now may have reason to regret it.' It is reminiscent of the present-day IRA argument that people who doubt their commitment to peace are responsible for driving them back to war.

* In parliament in 1922, Winston Churchill spoke of Europe post-war: 'The modes of thought of men, the whole outlook on affairs, the grouping of parties, all have encountered violent and tremendous change in the deluge of the world, but as the deluge subsides and the waters fall short we see the dreary steeples of Fermanagh and Tyrone emerging once again.'

heard in County Tyrone recently from Johnny: 'I was a couple of months old in October 1921. They come along. As far as I understand the situation, a neighbour of my father's had a son in the police. He was away in Belfast or something. And because of that, the IRA burned his family out. The dwelling house was in the middle of outhouses, byres, stables and all in a long row – thatched houses. So they come in the middle of the night and they lit the place and they put them out in whatever nightclothes they had on and the whole place went up in flames. So my father he went down then and shared what we could with them.

'A night or two after they come and burned him out because of what he had done. He had nowhere to live then. He left and went over to Scotland, for he had a sister over there. I wasn't doing too well when I was a baby and the doctor said that he thought I'd have a better chance of surviving in Ireland. So they brought me and they left me with an uncle and aunt near Letterkenny.

'My people weren't big farmers. Ordinary arable farmers, growing potatoes, as well as some cattle. When my father was burned out, an uncle living further down near him – the one I was brought up with – he geared up the neighbours and they went up and carted the corn down and threshed it and handed on the money to my father. They were loading the corn onto a cart and a bullet came along and shot the horse. They really wanted us out.'

While the serious violence ceased in 1923, attacks continued on manifestations of Protestant culture. Orangemen, with their halls and their parades, were an obvious target. Before the Great War there had been eighty Orange Lodges in the twenty-six counties, thirty-eight of which were in Donegal, Cavan and Monaghan. Even before independence, the county grand lodges of Cork, King's County and Longford had collapsed, and those of Dublin City, Dublin County and Sligo went in the next few years. It was fortunate for the Order that they moved Orange HQ to Belfast on 1 January 1922, for in March republicans took over their building and stayed there until driven out in June by Free State forces in a battle that badly damaged the building.

The attitude of Orangemen in the Irish Free State was summed up in a resolution passed by the County Monaghan Grand Lodge in 1922: 'That we are bound to be loyal to the Government under which, against our will, we are placed, and are determined to be so, as resistance to the powers that be is forbidden by our religious teaching.' Although they stuck to that, the destruction or vandalizing of Orange halls went on. An

Orangewoman from the Republic told me the story she had heard from her father of the last parade in her grandfather's lodge. As a little boy in the 1920s he had gone excitedly with his father to the Orange hall where the brethren were to gather for refreshments before setting off. When they got there they found the sandwiches the ladies had provided had all been stolen, the plates had been smashed and the furniture had been wrecked. They never tried to have a parade again.

July parades continued in Donegal, Cavan and Monaghan until 1931, when republicans at Cootehill blocked a Black parade despite the efforts of police and soldiers. While the prime minister, William T. Cosgrave, agreed with the right to march, he told a delegation that he could not guarantee their protection. From then onwards, Orangemen congregated every Twelfth at Rossnowlagh,* County Donegal, or went to parades across the border.

Essentially, southern Irish Protestants kept their heads well down and those that stayed cooperated with the new state. The élite continued to prosper: Protestants owned such key businesses as Guinness, Jameson and Powers along with some of the biggest shops. But their numbers continued to decline: from 10 per cent in 1911 they were down to just over 3 per cent seventy years later. It was the very smallness of the population which helped speed its decline, for while in Northern Ireland there was little need for intermarriage, in the Free State the pool of Protestants was so small that inevitably many married out and had no choice but to have their children brought up Catholic. Then, too, because under new rules no one could join the civil service or become a lawyer without an Irish-language qualification, a disproportionate number of Protestant professionals emigrated. And there was discrimination – particularly in the provinces. R. B. McDowell quotes an Orangeman's daughter from King's County saying, 'No Protestant will ever get fair play in the Irish Free State,' and a small farmer in Cork saying that when it came to jobs, 'it is all priests and the Irish language'. Typical would have been a story told by Johnny about how the Protestant postman in his village was sacked to make way for a Catholic.

Though most discrimination was petty and local, it combined to make many ordinary Protestants feel that they were not regarded as truly Irish. 'There was very little existence for me in Donegal,' said Johnny, 'so I come up to Tyrone. A lot of others came up in the '50s because times

---

* These, too, were suspended for several years.

weren't too good down there. A lot of them had families come up [that] were doing better up here. Some left better land to come to worse land just to live in the north. And that time land was worth twice as much here as it was worth in the Free State.'

Successive Irish governments genuinely wanted to reconcile Protestants to an independent Ireland. There was nothing they liked better than demonstrating their tolerance by giving the occasional high-profile job to a nationalist Protestant. Yet their good intentions were undermined by their tendency to kow-tow to the Catholic Church. An enduring image was of the taoiseach and members of the Cabinet sitting in cars outside a Protestant church because the Catholic hierarchy forbade them to attend the funeral service for Douglas Hyde, first President of Ireland. Another occurred in 1957, when the parish priest of the Wexford village of Fethard-on-Sea successfully ordered a boycott of Protestant businesses and neighbours in an effort to force the Protestant wife of a mixed marriage to send her children to a Catholic school. And it was divisive that the Archbishop of Dublin prohibited Catholics on pain of excommunication from attending Trinity College Dublin, 'a danger to faith and morals' because of its Protestant ethos.

In the Free State – which in 1949 became a republic and left the Commonwealth – there was rampant and narrow nationalism and anti-Britishness, repellently manifested in the attitude to those who had fought in two world wars. As an example, one hundred or so people died in Kerry in the fight for independence and the civil war and thirty times as many died in the First and Second World Wars; there are about seventy memorials to the former and none to the latter. Hostility to the marking of occasions such as Armistice Day was defended on the grounds that they commemorated the former British presence. And though there were excellent pragmatic reasons for remaining neutral in the Second World War, the failure to show any recognition of the idealism of the many thousands of Irishmen, Catholic and Protestant, who joined the British army to fight nazism, rankled.

What has distorted the perception of what happened in partitioned Ireland has been that the bad treatment experienced by Protestants in the south until recently was virtually ignored by historians and commentators, while the story of the oppression of Catholics in Northern Ireland was exaggerated out of all proportion – helped by a combination of republican propaganda and the damage done to the image of Northern Ireland Protestants by the bigoted ranting of Ian Paisley.

The violence of Northern Ireland's early years terrified Protestants and Catholics alike and made the government fearful that there was a Fenian under every bed. 'Ulster unionism was by its nature defensive,' observed Jonathan Bardon, 'tending to throw up leaders who were dogged, reliable and conservative, rather than imaginative and innovative.' There were few who were prepared to face down paranoid Protestant deputations complaining that Roman Catholics were being given preference in public appointments. It was particularly unfortunate that the Minister for Home Affairs, Dawson Bates, was convinced that Catholics were the enemy.

Even where the government theoretically wanted to encourage Catholic recruitment, it lacked the vision to put theory into practice. Though one-third of places in the Royal Ulster Constabulary were reserved for Catholics, they took up only one-sixth, and that proportion fell steadily as ex-members of the RIC retired; Catholic police believed they were discriminated against when it came to promotion. Terrified of socialism, the government abolished proportional representation in local government and ensured the triumph of the sectarian headcount, which was further strengthened in the mid-1920s by wholesale gerrymandering of local government boundaries. It was, as Bardon points out, a recipe for political ossification.

Nationalists and Sinn Féin leaders were culpable too. Unlike the Free State Protestants, they were terrible losers and refused to play any part in making Northern Ireland a warmer house for Catholics. Their objective was to make the state unworkable, even though it meant sacrificing the well-being of their tribe. They let the nationalist case go by default and allowed unionists a free hand both by refusing to take their seats in the Northern Ireland parliament * or to meet the commission that was charged with redrawing the boundaries. The plans of Lord Londonderry, Minister for Education, to provide all children with a non-sectarian education were scuppered by both sides. 'Religious instruction in a denominational sense during the hours of compulsory attendance there will not be,' said Londonderry, only to fall foul of the Catholic Church's view that 'Catholic children [must be] taught by Catholic teachers under Catholic auspices' and the demand of many Protestant clergy and numerous Orangemen that Protestant teachers teach Protestant children and that Bible study be made compulsory in state schools. Between them, they ensured that every

---

* Nationalists, but not Sinn Féin, went into Stormont in 1925 but did not agree until 1965 to become the official opposition.

child had a sectarian education and that Catholic children ended up in schools with poorer facilities than the state equivalents.

Belfast had been enriched by the Great War, but slid into economic depression in the 1920s. The consequent fall in agricultural prices brought about great hardship in rural areas and a rise in sectarian aggression. There were Orange resolutions in 1931 about 'the insidious propaganda of the Roman Catholic Church' and a robust declaration by Cardinal MacRory that the 'Protestant Church in Ireland – and the same is true of the Protestant Church anywhere else – is not only not the rightful representative of the early Irish Church, but it is not even a part of the Church of Christ.'

An Anglo-Irish economic war precipitated in 1932 by de Valera's government increased sectarian tensions in Northern Ireland in the very year when Rome came to Ireland in the shape of the Eucharistic Congress. Enraged by the visit of the Cardinal Legate bringing the papal blessing to Newry in June through a forest of papal flags, the Twelfth was dominated by resolutions about 'the unchanging bigotry of Rome' and 'the arrogant, intolerant and un-Christian pretensions fulminated by Cardinal MacRory'. Craigavon's contribution was to announce in his Twelfth address that 'Ours is a Protestant government and I am an Orangeman'. Sir Basil Brooke, later Lord Brookeborough and prime minister, told Orangemen the following year that 'he had not a Roman Catholic about his place . . . He would point out that the Roman Catholics were endeavouring to get in everywhere and were out with all their force and might to destroy the power and constitution of Ulster.' Craigavon defended Brooke and later explained: 'I have always said I am an Orangeman first and a politician and Member of this Parliament afterwards . . . in the South they boasted of a Catholic State. They still boast of Southern Ireland being a Catholic State. All I boast is that we are a Protestant Parliament and a Protestant State.'*

Craigavon's contention about the Free State was borne out by de Valera's explanation in a St Patrick's Day broadcast in 1935 that Ireland had been a Christian and Catholic nation since the time of St Patrick and remained 'a Catholic nation', and by the articles in de Valera's 1937 constitution acknowledging 'the special position of the Holy Catholic

---

* Most politically-inclined nationalists know Craigavon talked of a Protestant state for a Protestant people; hardly any known that he did so in the context of talking of the Free State as what it was – a Catholic state for a Catholic people.

apostolic and Roman Church'. Still, de Valera was much less sectarian than most of his countrymen, and the constitution enshrined tolerance of other religions. Craigavon had no objection to the religious provisions, he said, for 'while the Government of the South is carried on along lines which I presume are very suitable to the majority of Roman Catholics in that part . . . surely . . . the government of the North, with a majority of Protestants, should carry on the administration according to Protestant ideas and Protestant desires.'

The trouble was that while the Protestant minority in the south was small and resigned to its fate, the Catholic minority in the north was large and encouraged by its politicians and its clergy to hope for the downfall of the state in which it had ended up. Protestant unionists in the south gradually surrendered their sense of Britishness, but Catholics in the north treasured their religious and national identity as a mark of their differentness from the majority. Northern unionists who would have considered themselves Irish at the beginning of the century, accentuated the Britishness of Ulster in reaction to the nationalist threat manifested in, for instance, the claim in de Valera's 1937 constitution of jurisdiction over the whole island and in the ineffectual IRA offensive of 1956–62.

Life was made difficult for those Catholics who were prepared to cooperate with the state. For those who decided to join the public service, for instance, it was not only that they experienced discrimination at the hands of unionists who doubted their loyalty but that, as Patrick Shea, who eventually rose to become Permanent Secretary of the Ministry of Education, recalled: 'It was my experience that some Catholics, and especially those in Belfast where, I had been told, the Bishop had advised them against seeking government employment, looked with suspicion on Catholic civil servants. We had joined the enemy; we were lost souls.'

The Orange Order, so visible and so loud, was a predictable focus for Catholic resentment. With nearly 100,000 members, around a third of the Protestant male population, it was perceived as running Northern Ireland, dismissed by propagandists as 'the Orange state'. But while it was true that unionist politicians as a matter of course joined the Orange Order, this was more a matter of anti-nationalist solidarity than anything else. Unionist leaders kept their grassroots and electoral cannon-fodder sweet by turning out in collarettes and making defiant speeches about Bible and crown in muddy fields on the Twelfth. The intensely respectable and conservative leaders of the Orange Order had little influence on unionist politicians since they were all in agreement on most issues anyway and saw the loyal institutions as primarily an expression of Protestant solidarity in the face of external religious and constitutional threat. True, many unionist politicians emerged from the Orange Order, but the reason for that was primarily that ordinary people had gained from being office-holders, experienced in speaking and handling meetings and consequently had a head-start in local politics.

At their best, Orange lodges were benign manifestations of the fraternal spirit. But from the perspective of those who wanted to mobilize a Labour vote, the genial relations between employers and employees in the loyal institutions was a confidence-trick to keep the poor in their place. 'If you took all the Orange sashes and all the Green sashes in Belfast and tied them round a ticket of loaves and threw them in the Lagan,' declaimed a socialist orator in Belfast, 'the gulls, the common ordinary sea-gulls, they'd go for the bread, but the other gulls – yous ones – yous'd go for the sashes every time.' Of course they did and they showed off their allegiances proudly.

For the Orange Order, the Twelfth, which in 1925 had become a bank holiday, was still the biggest day, but for all the loyal orders remembrance services were of great emotional significance. The Ancient Order of Hibernians followed the lead of southern politicians and distanced itself from such commemorations, continuing to concentrate their attention on St Patrick's Day and on the 15th of August, the Feast of the Assumption of the Blessed Virgin Mary. But the AOH were a declining force: gradually over the century their parades dwindled to almost nothing and by the mid-1970s their membership was down to fewer than 10,000. These days, the AOH is important only in New York, where this exclusively Catholic organization still controls the St Patrick's Day parade.

Parades, and particularly Orange parades, still provided flashpoints at times of sectarian tension: from time to time they were banned, and during the war the Twelfth parades were suspended. But the vast majority of parades, processions, marches and walks were peaceful and many were enjoyed by members of both traditions. Many Orangemen in rural areas remember wistfully the days when Catholic neighbours looked after their cattle on the Twelfth and they looked after theirs on the 15th of August. There was much more harmony than appeared on the surface. Relative poverty in the 1920s and 1930s, 'made us all very close-knit,' said James Molyneaux, who became leader of the Ulster Unionist Party. 'Slightly before my time, a family lived beside us at the crossroads, where you had Aldergrove chapel, the inevitable pub, the parochial house, the little

[Catholic] school which I attended.* And this Catholic family were a bit involved with the church. They would have been regarded as working class and they sacrificed a great deal to educate the eldest son to pass the vital degree or whatever it is at Maynooth. He wasn't actually ordained a priest yet but he'd passed the examination.

'The station master, John Russell, after the lodge meeting when they were having a cup of coffee, said: "This is great news about young White, isn't it?" And they all said it was, bringing distinction and honour to this wee area of ours, a remote rural area. And somebody else says: "Shouldn't we be doing something about it?" And then Russell, the secretary at that time, said, "Why couldn't we do what we did for the retirement of the local doctor two years ago?" And that was to go around with the collecting card and make a presentation.

'Father said, "Yes, but I think it would be tactful if we had a word with the local priest just to make sure we know where we are." And the priest gave it his blessing and on occasions went around with him. So there you had the DWM and the Secretary of the lodge and the priest all in the priest's car touring round all the well-heeled farmers and the working class and everybody else – a diameter of a circle about two miles at most. And I remember they had a whale of a social presided over by the parish priest in the little school that I was attending. And my sister was picked to make the presentation, which was something very appropriate like a wallet of notes, which in those days would have meant a lot to the family that had sacrificed such a lot.

'It didn't seem to be odd. It struck everybody as natural. Yet nowadays if you tried to tell that to some English people they'd say: "But you've been at daggers drawn since day one", and all that kind of rubbish. But it was because of the social pattern of things in those days – the degree of poverty, the feeling of being together, helping each other. It was that kind of thing that conditioned me. And the Order was about the only effective organization in the country at that time – in the rural parts anyway.'

Even in Belfast, relations were often better than appeared on the surface. George Chittick remembered occasions in the 1950s: 'I was in the Prince of Orange band and we got a new uniform. And because I had a new uniform I had to sell the old uniform. And the music pouches, we

* When Aldergrove church was burned down by loyalists in 1997, James Molyneaux was one of the first to contribute money towards its restoration.

had to sell them too. We got the new uniform but didn't get the new music pouches. So coming up to the Twelfth, we didn't know what to do. Ardwell Dunning, who taught James Galway play the flute, Ardwell says, "I'll go up and see Paddy Mays up in the Falls. He looks after St Peter's Brass and Reed band."

'He went up and seen Paddy and Paddy says, "Oh, right. No problem. Only thing's wrong, Averill," he says, "all these pouches have big Irish harps on the back of them." "Ah, we'll take them off." "Ah, that's all right." So we marched up the road with St Peter's Brass and Reed pouches on our back playing away.

'They had no drum. They got a lend of the Prince of Orange big drum. And they stuck paper over the name and the number of the lodge and marched up the Falls Road on the St Patrick's Day parade with it.

'Them things happened. But Gerry Adams wouldn't like you to say that.'

At their worst, unionist leaders and the leaders of the loyal institutions were mean-spirited, dreary, hide-bound and – like their nationalist counterparts – too bigoted, unimaginative and timid to take on the worst of their own tribe in the interests of the whole community. (Sir George Clark, Grand Master of the Orange Order, deserves a special mention for responding in 1959 to the proposal by the chairman of the Unionist Party that Catholics be allowed to join the party and represent it in parliament by explaining at Scarva that it was 'difficult to see how a Catholic, with the vast differences in our religious outlook, could be either acceptable within the Unionist Party as a member or, for that matter, bring himself unconditionally to support its ideals'.)

If discrimination at a local level, particularly in housing, was a fact of life, it was not a one-way street: where nationalists had the opportunity, they discriminated against unionists with enthusiasm. Considering the threat from violent republicanism, the regime was restrained and justice was administered fairly and temperately for the most part. Yet between the Irish nationalist genius for propaganda and the inability of Ulster Protestants to explain themselves in a way the outside world could understand, a completely distorted picture of life in Northern Ireland was to become conventional wisdom. (In a classic overstatement, John Naughton wrote in the *Observer* in July 1997 in an article on David Trimble and the Ulster Unionists that 'their heroes – and in many cases, their current members – ran the nastiest, most repressive little statelet outside of Verwoerd's South Africa. Northern Ireland under the Craigs and the Taylors and their farce of a parliament at Stormont was a vicious place in which a substantial ethnic minority was systematically disenfranchised, discriminated against and terrorized, in which a sectarian and heavily armed police force maintained a brutal semblance of order and in which civil liberties were available only to those of the right religious and racial stripe.')

In fact, by the 1960s, though many Catholics still felt like second-class citizens, they were mostly far better off than their co-religionists in the Republic. At at time when education was free for everyone in Northern Ireland up to and including university level, in the Republic schools other than primary were fee-paying* Northern Ireland also had a free health service, generous benefits and better housing than the Republic. A significant part of the Catholic population had come to accept that Northern Ireland was here to stay and many Protestants had come to realize that the Republic was far more interested in itself than in a United Ireland. When in 1965, the taoiseach, Sean Lemass, visited Belfast at the invitation of Prime Minister Captain Terence O'Neill, there was good ground for hope that Catholic and Protestant, nationalist and unionist, might grow towards greater mutual understanding.

Yet, as John Darby puts it, 'the traditional Ulster values, which would have been threatened by reconciliation, may have been in temporary hiding, but they soon emerged with banners flying.' The main credit for dragging the province into more than three decades of blood and degradation goes to the IRA, which hijacked the civil rights movement of the late 1960s. But a special mention must go to the Reverend Ian Paisley, who has played to the worst instincts of loyalism and has riven Presbyterianism, unionism and Orangeism along the way.

During this period, the loyal institutions for the most part behaved true to form, stuck their corporate heads in the sand, passed a lot of resolutions, said no to anything new and demanded the right to parade down traditional routes however dangerous the timing: the Apprentice Boys' parade on 12 August 1968 has the distinction of having set off the Bogside riots that led to the British army being sent to Northern Ireland to keep the peace. Although their skills in this regard were still in their infancy, by

---

* I remember vividly the feeling of disbelief followed by irritation when I discovered that a Northern Irish student at University College Dublin, who had been complaining bitterly of discrimination against Catholics, was studying in Dublin at the expense of the British taxpayer. At the time I had come across only two working-class students in UCD; both of them financed themselves by canning beans in England during the summer holidays.

the early 1970s the Provisional IRA were using Orange marches as a pretext for burning down the Northern Ireland house. They also were firmly convinced that if they could destroy the Orange Order they could destroy the state – hence the strategy that led to the Drumcree confrontations of the 1990s.

Throughout the years of violence, there have been thousands of unflattering images and millions of unflattering words written about the loyal institutions, which could always be relied upon to behave mulishly and stupidly towards journalists. What was little covered outside the unionist press were the sufferings endured – for the most part stoically – by thousands of members of the loyal institutions. In the border areas in particular, many of them became part-time soldiers or policemen to protect their communities from the IRA and thus became prime targets for assassination. Brethren were stabbed, shot and blown up. There were mass atrocities like the INLA gun attack on the Guiding Star Temperance Lodge in Tullyvallen Orange Hall in September 1975, which killed Brothers Herron, Johnston, McConnell and James and Ronald McKee. The following year the IRA stopped a bus at Kingsmills in County Armagh, told the Catholic bus driver to stand aside and machine-gunned to death ten Protestants, of whom four were Orangemen. There was the murder by the Provisionals in 1981 of two members of Derryhaw Boyne Defenders, the eighty-six-year-old Sir Norman Stronge, a former Speaker of the Northern Ireland Commons, and his son James, and the burning down of their home. And so on and so on.

When I think of the strengths of the loyal institutions, of the courage, decency and simple faith that mark the brethren at their best, I often think of Roy Kells, now Grand Master of County Fermanagh. Like so many other ordinary people in Northern Ireland, he has been faced for decades with extraordinary physical and emotional demands that he has met with stoicism and grace.

Roy inherited a family business and has three draper's shops in Fermanagh. Reluctantly he joined the Ulster Defence Regiment to defend his home village of Lisnaskea, since bombs were being left on the main street almost every week and he thought it unfair that the burden of defending the community be left to local farmers. He hated having to be away so much from his wife and four children. 'This is one of the things that any security force man will tell you – that he missed his family. You were out four or five nights a week. You just had to get up and leave your family. That was the sad part of it. That's what I missed most.'

In twenty years, Roy's Lisnaskea shop was burned three times, bombed a dozen or so times and completely destroyed once.

The IRA have always made Catholic policemen and soldiers their number one target, so almost no Catholics were prepared to join the UDR when it was set up in 1970. In consequence, it was easy to represent it to nationalists as a sectarian force, which in turn made the murder of its members more acceptable. Eleven of Roy's company were shot or blown up over the years and he himself survived three assassination attempts. The last time, when he had fallen wounded to the ground, he recognized the gunman, Seamus MacElwain, who stood above him and did not fire – because of the intervention of God, Roy believes. MacElwain, who is thought to have committed at least eighteen murders, was later shot by the SAS: a memorial eulogizing him was recently erected by local republicans nearby.'You learn to live with it . . . I couldn't have gone through the whole thing without faith in God. That carried me through . . . I've been in some very dangerous situations, but I trusted him.'

Roy has been in the Orange Order since he joined it in Portadown in 1954: 'I was always interested in it, because I felt from a traditional point of view it was good, but I was interested in it from a spiritual point of view too because I believed in the open Bible and the Orange were basically based on the open Bible. I came back in 1958 and joined the lodge here. I love pipe bands, so I joined the lodge there was a pipe band attached to and I was involved in the pipe band for twenty-five years. We won three all-Ireland contests.

'When it came to 1970 most of our band and lodge joined either the police reserve or the UDR, so therefore our band hadn't time to contest. About 65 per cent of our lodge would have joined the security forces then and we had three members of our lodge – which would have had about 40 members – killed in the security forces; two of the three murdered Graham brothers were in our lodge *. . . You'd wonder how people do it. The Graham brothers would have been known to them and have worked with them in the factory and so on. It's so hard to understand.'

In 1998, Roy was on holiday in Scotland when he heard that the centre of Omagh had been blown up, that there were seven bodies in his shop

---

* Albert Graham, Hilary, one of his daughters, and three of his sons joined the UDR. Hilary died of injuries sustained when a car crashed through a checkpoint; Ronnie was murdered by masked gunmen when delivering groceries to an isolated farmhouse, Cecil was killed when visiting his Catholic wife's parents and Jimmy was shot while waiting in a bus outside a primary school for the children he was to take swimming.

and that his entire staff was traumatized. When I rang him a week or so later, he was intending to drive to Donegal to commiserate with the parents of Catholic children who had been killed. He was tormented by the fear that his shop had been chosen as a target because he was an Orangeman and that this made him somehow responsible.

Yet Roy Kells considers himself a fortunate man: 'I can assure you there's no bitterness in my heart. I pray for those that commit the atrocities, for those that orchestrated the boycotts and I don't pretend to be a saint, but I believe from my Christian teaching that that's the way to live. There's no bitterness in my life towards any of them. Yes, atrocities like Enniskillen you certainly feel bitter toward it, but that's only a natural reaction. But from an individual point of view, no, there's not.'

Roy Kells is no longer in the UDR, but for the rest of his life, he will remain what the IRA call 'a legitimate target'. His is a typical story, but one largely ignored by the world outside Ulster Protestantism.

So too are the grievances of southern Protestants. 'Many Catholic friends tell me that Protestants have been treated eminently fairly here since 1922,' wrote Robin Bury early in 1999 in the newsletter of the Reform group, which campaigns to win recognition in the Republic for the British contribution to its culture, 'When I look at them quizzically or in amazement, they are upset, because they really believe it. The story of the shameful treatment of the minority ethnic Anglo-Irish community since 1922 has been glossed over. A narrow, nationalist Catholic state was calculatedly established after 1922. It was based on the silly myth of a pure, Celtic, Gaelic-speaking race living in an Arcadia in the West. Deeply Anglophobic, the new state vigorously pursued a policy of de-Anglicisation. The Anglo-Irish were wrenched from their culture overnight, and made to feel unwelcome in a theocratic state. They were denied divorce and contraception and had to put up with extreme forms of censorship. Their religion was rubbished by the Roman Catholic Church. The Land Commission and Ne Temere . . . set about ethnic cleansing . . . In this environment Protestants emigrated to pluralist countries where they felt at home . . . The tide is turning at last . . . Just as nationalists seek an apology for the famine and Bloody Sunday, the ethnic minority here has impeccable grounds to seek an apology from the Roman Catholic Church and from An Taoiseach, who is, fair play to him, trying to construct a more inclusive, less Anglophobic society. To use David Trimble's words, this country has been "a cold house" for Protestants. It still needs the central heating turned up.'

12

The Rise of the Residents' Groups

'Do you know what Irish Alzheimer's is?'

'You forget everything but the grudges.'

Prologue

ON THE MORNING OF Wednesday, 10 December 1997, Tom Reid, Grand Master of the County Tyrone Grand Orange Lodge, and Denis Watson, his County Armagh equivalent, left their homes to find that nearby lampposts were sprouting posters which read 'FIRST JUDAS THEN LUNDY NOW REID/WATSON'. Two Presbyterian ministers, Brian Kennaway, Convenor of the Orange Order's Education Committee, and Warren Porter, one of the two Assistant Grand Masters of the Grand Lodge of Ireland – in counties Antrim and Down respectively – were similarly honoured, though in their case the insults were simpler: 'FATHER KENNAWAY' and 'FATHER PORTER', read their posters. 'Why didn't they add "SJ"?'* I asked the Orange friend who rang me about the latest developments. 'Too stupid,' he answered.

From 1996 onwards the moderate leadership of the Orange Order had been subjected to relentless and bitter attack from fierce internal critics, whose most vociferous spokesmen were part of the pressure group, the Spirit of Drumcree, popularly known as the SODs. What the maligned Orangemen had in common – apart from the fact that the SODs were strong in their areas – was that they were well known for their determination to communicate the Orange case rationally to the outside world and to encourage their brethren to avoid unnecessary confrontation. They had enraged their critics for being among those whose influence helped to bring about voluntary re-routing of contentious parades on the previous Twelfth of July at a time when Northern Ireland was once again staring into the abyss of civil war.

When the County Grand Masters and the ministers arrived at the House of Orange, the institution's headquarters, they found that they and the rest of the delegates to the biannual meeting of the Grand Lodge of Ireland, the Order's ruling body, were locked out. Under the leadership of the highly articulate and passionate Joel Patton, the building had been occupied by about two hundred SODs. Their objective was to prevent the re-election that day of the Grand Master, Robert Saulters, and his allies and to force upon the Orange Order a leadership with a mandate

---

* Society of Jesus, signifying Jesuits, whom extreme Protestants see as evil masters of such black arts as deviousness and manipulation.

to brook no compromise on parade routes. The two-centuries-old organization dedicated to Protestant brotherhood was facing a vicious split in the full glare of the media.

The conflict between Orangemen and nationalists over the right to walk down a few hundred yards of road on the way from a church service at Drumcree has since 1995 produced scenes of violence and devastation which played on screens across the globe, polarized opinion on the island of Ireland, further alienated the British public from the most patriotic citizens of the United Kingdom, brought sectarian hatreds in Northern Ireland to a new high and turned brother against brother within the Order itself. The members of an organization mainly composed of decent, Christian, law-abiding people have been represented around the globe as violent bigots.

The responsibility lies mainly with the Provisional I R A and its subsidiary company, Sinn Féin. But in its stubbornness, inarticulacy, indecisiveness and (frequently) stupidity, the Orange Order was to prove the Provisionals' greatest ally.

The Campaign Begins

Ten years or so ago, at a conference about Northern Ireland, the Irish nationalist journalist Tim Pat Coogan remarked that unionists had no culture. It was a breathtaking comment that caused panic among the English and Irish liberals who predominated in the audience. 'What about Louis MacNeice?' cried one. He was contemptuously dismissed by Coogan: MacNeice, like many other Ulster Protestant poets, had turned against his own tribe and therefore didn't count.* The well-meaning frantically tried to come up with representatives of what they considered to be culture – artists, novelists, composers, ballet dancers – and, to avoid further embarrassment, the chairman changed the subject.†

No one, to my recollection, mentioned the outward and visible culture

---

* By the same logic, of course, Irish nationalism has no right to claim James Joyce, Frank O'Connor and many more of the greatest Irish literary names.

† This demonstration of ignorance about Ulster Protestantism is typical. As Paul Bew pointed out in a review of Joseph Lee's *Ireland 1912–1985: Politics and Society,* Lee was highly impressive except where it came to his ignorance and prejudice about Ulster unionism. 'He is scathing', wrote Bew, 'about the "sterility" of the Ulster Protestant "imagination" – this in the very period when C. S. Lewis, E. R. Dodds, Louis MacNeice and Ernest Walton were flourishing: everything from *Narnia* through brilliant Greek scholarship, outstanding poetry to Nobel prizewinning work in atomic energy!'

of the majority of the Ulster Protestant people: their bands and their parades. The few unionists present were middle-class. But even had any Orangemen been present, it would not have occurred to them to call what they do on the Twelfth of July 'culture'. It is only recently that, at long last, they have begun to learn from republicans the importance of getting the language right.

The chief strategist of the republican movement, Gerry Adams, is smarter and better informed than Tim Pat Coogan. Around the same time, in 1986, he showed he understood something of Protestant culture, and wanted it eliminated. In a speech to an internal Sinn Féin conference, he explained: 'To understand our struggle it is worthwhile starting with this basic proposition. To use [James] Connolly's phrase, our main objective, our destination, is the reconquest of Ireland by the Irish people. This means the expulsion of imperialism in all its forms, political, economic, military and cultural.' The final objective was 'an Ireland, free, united, socialist and Gaelic'.

In the same year, in his book, *Free Ireland*, Adams addressed Protestant culture more specifically:

> The Loyalists have a desperate identity crisis. They agonize over whether they are Ulster-Scotch, Picts, English or British. When they go to England they are Paddies. They express a massive rejection of a very rich Irish culture, despite the fact that this heritage cannot in any way reasonably be regarded as exclusive. Instead, they waste their time trying to work out some kind of obscure notion of Ulster Protestant culture.

In a televised interview with Adams in 1995, the psychiatrist Anthony Clare quoted that passage and remarked: 'Your conclusion really is: "The loyalists are Irish" . . . It seems to me with respect that there's something quite fascist about someone from your tradition and your background telling other people what is their culture or what is not their culture.'

Adams seemed genuinely baffled by this. In republican terms he would see himself as a liberal – someone who rather than aiming to run all unionists out of Northern Ireland would welcome them seeing the light and calling themselves Irish. 'Loyalism is part of the British way of life in Ireland,' he explained in his presidential speech to the Sinn Féin annual conference early in 1994. 'It, like unionism, is a child of the British connection. Its extremists will be redundant when that connection is severed and when the Protestant section of our community can shake off the shackles of unionism.' That offers little scope for a culture that Protestants have centred on their Britishness and their religion.

In his 1986 speech Adams had addressed himself to the means of achieving republican aims: 'What will make a movement like ours revolutionary is not whether it is committed to any particular means of achieving revolution, for example street agitation or physical force, but whether all the means it uses – political work, propaganda and mass education, armed struggle, projects of economic resistance – are conducive to achieving the revolutionary end.' This was the period when Adams was coming to realize that, despite the best efforts of the IRA, Northern Irish unionists had too much courage and too great a capacity for endurance to knuckle under to force. Republicanism therefore needed to take a more political path, while retaining the capacity of the IRA to inflict damage where it would be productive. Behind the scenes, on and off, Adams and other republicans were in secret talks with representatives of constitutional Irish nationalism and the British government.

Gradually the methods became more refined and the language smoother. As Adams put it in 1992 in an interview with *An Phoblacht/ Republican News*, the strategy was to ensure that the issue of 'Irish national self-determination [code for a United Ireland] is on the overall political agenda here at home and internationally. We need to define and project our aims in a manner which will be most clearly understood by the broad base of Irish national and international opinion.' More and more the IRA avoided obviously sectarian targets and cut back on civilian murders, while Sinn Féin played down socialism, let alone revolution. The propaganda machine worked hard to sell the message that republican paramilitaries killed for reasons of principle, while loyalist paramilitaries killed because they were sectarian. This was as untrue as it had ever been. At the end of the twentieth century, extremists in the two tribes in Northern Ireland still hate each other equally and kill for equally prejudiced reasons: at their worst, they still regard each other as sub-human.

The late Cardinal Ó Fíach, a hate-figure for many Protestants because they perceived him as a republican apologist, once remarked quite rightly that most of the religious bigotry in Northern Ireland was Protestant while most of the political bigotry was Catholic. But since the chief distinguishing characteristic between the tribes are the labels of Catholic and Protestant, such fine distinctions do not really matter. They are all bigoted; the only difference is that Protestants are much readier than

Catholics to admit to bigotry. 'We're all bigots in Northern Ireland,' observed an Orangeman to me once. 'But beware the ones who don't admit it. They're the worst.'

The republicans marketed their message well. They had been smart enough apparently to transcend sectarianism by developing the classification of 'legitimate'* targets: these amounted to perhaps half the Protestant, and a fair sprinkling of the Catholic, population of Northern Ireland (anyone who was or ever had been full- or part-time in the security forces, civil servants, construction workers, caterers or anyone else providing the security forces with any services and so on). Thus in 1992 when the IRA, at Teebane in County Tyrone, blew up eight Protestants for the crime of doing construction work at the Omagh security base, they explained it was political. They did not take the credit for the vandalizing of the memorial erected on the site the following year.

Loyalists had as 'legitimate' targets only republican terrorists. If, as they occasionally did, loyalists killed a policeman or a prison warder because they felt they were traitors, they were turning on the agents of the state to which they were fanatically loyal. If they killed a politically-uninvolved Catholic, they were sectarian.

If a republican who wanted to get Protestants off their farms killed a border farmer, he had done so because the victim had once been a part-time policeman; and even if he hadn't, the excuse was 'mistaken identity'. If a loyalist killed someone he believed but could not prove was a violent republican, the murder was denounced as sectarian. And the loyalists' reputation was further blackened by the bigots among their ranks who believed all Catholics were republicans and therefore deserved to die. When Martin McGuinness, the IRA and Sinn Féin leader,

---

* In an article in the *Belfast Telegraph*, the ex-communist and peace campaigner Bert Ward wrote: 'Anybody trying, for their own purposes, to force political change upon an unwilling or unsuspecting population will start to interfere with language. Using language in a way that obscures the real meaning in order to render the unacceptable acceptable, is usual. It is then necessary, by repetition, to instil the distortion into the public consciousness. The term "take out" illustrates the point. I was travelling in a car one day with a top-ranking official of the British Communist Party. "The Americans have hydrogen bombs targeted on the Soviet Union that could take out Moscow," he said.

'"Take them out where?" I enquired. "Dinner? A dance? The pictures?" He got quite shirty . . . Another example is "legitimate targets". In a democracy that has rejected capital punishment the human mind cannot take in the notion that working men and women can "legitimately" be put to death. So people have to be conditioned and language is moulded to make the inconceivable, acceptable.'

announced smugly in 1993, 'Our republicanism has ensured that the only sectarian murderers in Ireland today are loyalist bigots aided by their British masters,' few commentators were astute enough to reveal this hypocrisy for what it was.

By 1995, the year of Drumcree One, republican strategists had succeeded politically beyond all but their wildest dreams. A few years earlier they had been international pariahs, banned since 1972 from the airwaves of the Republic of Ireland (in Britain, absurdly, they could appear, but their words had to be spoken by an actor), performing badly in elections and short of money to fund their politics – let alone their army. Now, after the ceasefire of 31 August, there was in place a pan-nationalist alliance consisting of John Hume's Social Democratic and Labour Party (SDLP), the constitutional nationalist party in Northern Ireland, the government of the Republic of Ireland and Irish America; the republican leadership was all over the British and Irish media, making mincemeat of interviewers; Sinn Féin was riding high in the polls; and there was the prospect of lucrative fund-raising in America.

Republicans wanted the British government to ditch unionists and push them into a United Ireland. And unionists themselves were confused and increasingly paranoid. When they were being bombed and murdered they knew where they were. Now they were convinced that sell-out deals were being done behind the scenes. Why else, they speculated, would the Provos have declared a ceasefire? And anyway, why had they not said the ceasefire was permanent? In their wariness about greeting a ceasefire as good news, it became easy to label unionists as anti-peace.

To keep republican foot-soldiers happy, to apply pressure on the British and Irish governments for more and quicker concessions and to upset unionists, the leadership had adopted the tactic of encouraging street agitation of various kinds. From parades to riots, that had always been a part of republican tactics. In August 1993, for instance, with bands and Irish flags, they had held the first of their annual marches to Belfast City Hall to mark the anniversary of the introduction of internment in 1971. (It had ended in 1975.) Flanked by representatives of the Basque terrorists, Martin McGuinness had told the crowd of 10,000 or so: 'We are a risen people and we will not be still. We have come here today to demand nationalist rights and to demand back our country.'

Quasi-military parades were common in nationalist areas. One planned to be particularly provocative was held in Belfast in October 1994, a few weeks after the ceasefire, when hundreds of people and six bands honoured the memory of Thomas Begley, a nineteen-year-old IRA Volunteer who had died along with nine Protestant civilians when his bomb went off prematurely in a fish shop in the Shankill Road.

Early in 1995 Gerry Adams called for a wave of protests in support of 'parity of esteem' for Sinn Féin: 'If the British refused to listen to reasoned and reasonable argument, then let them listen to the sound of marching feet and angry voices.' The only difficulty was that most of the inhabitants of even the republican heartlands seemed strangely uninterested in protest marches; without a good issue, they simply didn't come on the streets in large enough numbers to form an effective pressure group. The decision was taken to step up normal levels of opposition to parades by the loyal institutions and make them the focus for republican discontent, which, with careful management and clever propaganda, could be made to spread to the wider nationalist community. The strategy was that this in turn would lead to the loyal institutions coming into conflict with the state and thus lead to destabilization. Unionists would destroy themselves.

Being in an increasingly paranoid state – as so often in their history – the loyal institutions were their enemies' unwitting accomplices. Jonathan Bardon wrote in the *Irish Times*:

> More than ever before in this century, the Orangemen march to assert their territorial imperative. All around they see their territory being eroded. The Catholic population of south Belfast is rising fast; Ardoyne, once a beleaguered Catholic island, is now connected by broad corridors to the Antrim Road; swathes of rural borderland have been abandoned; and save for the cosseted Fountain protectorate, Protestants in Derry have decamped to the Waterside. If the Protestants move any further east, a Catholic colleague observed, they will topple into the Irish Sea.
>
> Outside the leafy bourgeois suburbs, Northern Ireland is made up of distinct territories of one sect or another . . . Protestants can see only that their enclaves are contracting or being lost.

Sinn Féin admitted no contradictions in holding ever more parades themselves while trying to stop those of the other side. 'Ours are about freedom, equality and justice,' explained a Sinn Féin spokesman. 'Orange marches are about intimidation, supremacy and triumphalism.'

The beauty of this approach was that it enabled republicans to target the Protestant population in the name of anti-sectarianism. Repeating over and over again the incontrovertible truth that the Orange Order was sectarian was one of Sinn Féin's twin propaganda tactics. The other was to seize on any misdemeanour by an individual Orangeman, flog it for all it was worth and use it to smear the whole Order. And, of course, having stirred-up nationalist protests, the next objective was to force the police to face down either paraders or nationalists. Whichever happened, the RUC had to fence off the disputed territory to stop one lot of thugs getting at the other lot so, either way, the residents could complain about being hemmed in.

The Lower Ormeau Road in Belfast provided a testing-ground in the summer of 1994. It is a wide commercial thoroughfare, off a few hundred yards of which lead narrow streets which have changed from mainly working-class Protestant to working-class Catholic in less than a genera-tion; parades do not actually pass any Catholic houses.*

The *Guardian* journalist David Sharrock later wrote of the emotional resonances of the contentious route:

> The first parade of the season – in what has become a modern tradition – has already been banned by the police. It would normally take six minutes for the 25 members of the Apprentice Boys Belfast Walker club, based in Ballynafeigh Orange Hall, to cross the Ormeau Bridge and walk along the lower section of the Ormeau road on Monday morning at 7.30 [on their way to the main Easter Monday parade]. They have been walking the route for a century. The naked eye would not see it, but this has been twisted into fiercely contested territory.
>
> The parade passes the spot where senior loyalists Joe Bratty and Raymond Elder were murdered by the IRA in the summer of 1994, within weeks of their ceasefire announcement. The killings were interpreted as a settling of old scores but also a deliberate provocation to ensure that loyalists would continue their operations and therefore provide the IRA with a blameless escape route out of their own ceasefire if political events went against them.
>
> Once over the bridge the marchers pass the Sean Graham bookmaker's shop, where five Catholics were murdered by the Ulster Freedom Fighters in 1992. This

---

* In mid-April, a *Belfast Newsletter* columnist examined the lay-out in detail and found on the disputed area only a dozen occupied houses: 'So. Only a tiny few, if any, Roman Catholics live in houses fronting on to the main Ormeau Road. It is those in the side streets who are objecting.' He looked at the nationalist enclave of six side streets and found 'the outward and visible signs . . . [of] a hotbed of Irish republicanism': posters for 'Saoirse', a front organization that demands the release of 'political prisoners'; and Gaelic street-names.

attack was itself in retaliation for the IRA murder of seven Protestant workmen at
Teebane in County Tyrone.

During what is known as a 'Mini-12th' parade which went down the
Lower Ormeau Road on 8 July 1992, there had been angry exchanges
between people on the parade and protesters waving tricolours; fifteen
people were arrested and eight charged. Cameras were there to record at
least three men raising five fingers and a woman dancing as they passed
the bookmaker's shop. Apologists suggested that the woman was simply
dancing along with the whole parade and that the men were acknowledging friends on the pavement, but the Orange Order did not accept this
version of events. The Belfast County Grand Master, John McCrea,
immediately condemned those Orangemen involved and later visited them
personally to suspend them from membership.

News of their suspension would have gone a long way to counter the
appalling publicity the incident attracted that year and has attracted ever
since, but it was kept private to the Order. Discipline is seen to be a
family matter and, as ever, there was to the fore that feature of the Ulster
Protestant psyche that is inimical to explaining, excusing or publicly
apologizing. It was a great propaganda coup for the opposition.

Despite a failed legal attempt to block a parade in 1992, protesters
were successful in 1993 and 1994 in having several parades re-routed.
An *An Phoblacht/Republican News* report of 7 July 1994 about a small
parade began:

> A large force of RUC and British army personnel were in evidence in the nationalist
> Lower Ormeau Road area of South Belfast on Wednesday evening, 6 July. An
> Orange parade, scheduled to pass the small streets of the Lower Ormeau
> community was once again aimed at totally disrupting life in the beleaguered
> community.
>
> However, local people angry at not being allowed onto the Ormeau Road which
> links the community, organized a rally in protest at seeing Orange bands bearing
> loyalist death squads insignia (such as UVF and UDA)* protected by the sectarian
> RUC.
>
> The local protest has gradually grown in size, particularly following the brutal
> slaying of five local men in the Sean Graham bookmaker's shop in 1992. Following

---

* Unsavoury bands of a kind deeply disapproved of by the hierarchy of the loyal institutions sometimes turn
up in parades either at the invitation of a rogue lodge or without any invitation at all.

this slaughter by a UDA death squad Orange bands playing sectarian tunes raised five fingers as they passed the spot where the men were cut down. As on other occasions the nationalist community were hemmed in by RUC vehicles despite an RUC pledge that they would not be unduly affected by the coat-trailing procession . . .

For nationalists across the Six Counties, imprisonment in their homes and streets will be the rule of law over the next few weeks.

Post-ceasefire, the protests became better orchestrated. In November 1994 *An Phoblacht/Republican News* quoted 'resident Gerard Rice'* as saying apropos of another 'coat-trailing Orange parade': 'This decision to march along the Lower Ormeau once again highlights the sectarian and triumphalist nature of both the Orange Order and the RUC. The Orange Order, by continuing with its policy of marching past the scene of UFF massacres, causing grave offence to this community, has demonstrated to the whole world its true anti-Catholic and anti-nationalist nature.'

If Gerry Adams's memory is accurate, it was at this time that Sinn Féin began organizing residents' groups in promising areas across Northern Ireland. On a tape secured by a journalist, he was heard telling an internal Sinn Féin conference in November 1997, after the third massive confrontation at Drumcree:

Ask any activist in the north, did Drumcree happen by accident and they will tell you 'no'. Three years of work on the Lower Ormeau Road, Portadown and parts of Fermanagh and Newry, Armagh and in Bellaghy and up in Derry. Three years of work went into creating that situation and fair play to those people who put the work in. They are the type of scene changes that we have to focus on and develop and exploit.[†]

* Rice, who claimed to have no involvement in politics, had stood beside Gerry Adams the previous week in Milltown Cemetery at the Sinn Féin celebration of the 1916 Easter Rising.

† Adams may no longer claim to be a traditional Marxist, but he and his colleagues certainly learned from communism: 'It is impossible to exercise the dictatorship [i.e. dictatorship of the proletariat],' stated Lenin in 1920, 'without having a number of transmission belts from the vanguard [i.e. communist party].' Trade unions, youth movements, peace movements, agricultural organizations, writers and cultural societies were all potential 'transmission belts'.

In Irish republicanism, the IRA is the supreme policy-making body, the 'vanguard'. Sinn Féin, through its organizational structure, is a transmission belt, as are front organizations representing prisoners and their

Gerard Rice, a publicly-funded community worker, was the driving force behind what became the Lower Ormeau Concerned Community (LOCC)* – the pioneering residents' group. By April 1995 the LOCC was begging for assistance from outsiders as 'they remained deeply apprehensive about Orange marchers tramping through their community'. The terminology used in the *An Phoblacht/Republican News* report was to become increasingly familiar over the next months and years. Orangemen banned from the route 'waved fists and union flags in a paroxysm of fury'; they had wanted 'to go out of their way just to be provocative and triumphalist'. It was the duty of the state to make it clear 'to the bigots that they cannot parade through nationalist areas'. The 'forces of peace and the future will triumph over those of sectarianism and the past'.

'Somewhat ironically,' it ended, 'the Orange parade on the Springfield Road yesterday marched to the tune of "The Carnival is Over". The carnival of reaction so vividly predicted by James Connolly is coming to an end. And no one will ask for an encore.' It was in his capacity as 'main spokesperson' in June that year that Rice rejected a suggestion by an Orangeman that members of the Order lay a wreath in front of the bookmaker's. He had, Rice told *An Phoblacht/Republican News*, 'sought the opinion of the victims' families, who felt the offer was not acceptable and should be seen for what it was, an "attempt to march down the Ormeau Road".'

Statements like that also covered a depressing reality. For residents of the Ormeau Road to stand up to the forces that Gerard Rice represented required enormous courage: intimidation is rife in areas dominated by republicans (or, of course, by loyalists). Rosalind Hughes, an extraordinary woman who lived within the LOCC area, went public in 1995 when Rice produced an anti-Orange march petition signed allegedly by 92 per cent of the inhabitants. Every household, she explained, had been visited by several men demanding signatures; signing seemed the only option.

Malachi O'Doherty, a Belfast journalist, attended an LOCC meeting a few months later and 'smelt fascism' in the use of the word 'community': 'I hear someone claiming to represent people like me or unlike

---

relatives, youth groups, women's groups, promotional groups for the Irish language, and, of course, community groups. Since 1995, residents' groups have been the most powerful transmission belt.

∗ It was reported in the *Belfast Newsletter* in April 1996 that Rice and the LOCC had received, through the Northern Ireland Voluntary Trust, £60,000 of Euro money emanating from the Delors 'Peace Fund'.

me, and inviting me to decide whether I am in or out.' The meeting debated whether to allow the Orange parade on the Twelfth to pass through the Lower Ormeau Road. One-third of those present were in favour, 'but the two-thirds who roared, whistled and stamped their feet in support of protest were represented to the excluded media as representing the whole community', and Rice announced afterwards that the decision to block the parade had been unanimous. The result was, said a dispirited O'Doherty, that those who had gone to the meeting to call for an end to protests not only might as well not have gone at all, but were now by association anti-Orange agitators.

> All the people who had gone to the meeting to try to soften the resistance to the parades had taken the risk that they would be publicly exposed as supporting the very position they contested, and once exposed they would be at risk of a beating or worse from supporters of the Orange Order. Why would they bother again? Vociferous machine politics like that simply leaves such people behind, or it uses them to swell numbers. It ropes them into a notion of a consistent community, beleaguered and at odds with the rest of the world, or it shuts them up.

To have challenged the Rice line publicly would also have had its dangers. As the experience of people like Vincent McKenna – beaten up for challenging the party line on the Lower Ormeau Road – has shown, a public challenge to republicans can attract intimidation and violence.

The equivalents of Rice to emerge subsequently in the two other major flashpoint areas, Derry and Drumcree, were Donncha MacNiallais (hibernicized from Denis Nelis), another community worker, and Breandán MacCionnaith,* who brought into being respectively the BRG (Bogside Residents' Group) and the Garvaghy Road Residents' Association (GRA). Like Rice (and many other residents' spokesmen who were to appear over the next few months and years), MacNiallais and MacCion-

---

* MacCionnaith is genuinely an Irish-language enthusiast, but there has been a deliberate policy to encourage high-profile republican spokesmen to hibernicize their names so as irritate unionists and exaggerate for the benefit of the outside world the importance of the Irish language in nationalist culture; in reality, only about 4 per cent of Northern Irish people can speak the language fluently. Gerard Rice made an effort to change his name, but was already too well-known to succeed. Efforts to go Gaelic by such prominent members of the republican leadership as Gerry Adams had earlier failed for the same reason.

There is a reverse process. When John Stephenson, who as Seán MacStiofán became Chief of Staff of the IRA, blotted his copybook, republicans disparagingly downgraded him back to his original name.

naith are convicted ex-terrorists, chosen as frontmen because members of the loyal institutions would almost certainly refuse to talk to them. As in the case of Rice, too, the claims of MacNiallais and MacCionnaith to be democratically selected spokesmen were bogus. The BRG, for instance, was formed at a public meeting which had not been advertised. The fifteen people present elected a committee of eight, with MacNiallais as chairman. Suddenly and mysteriously, the Garvaghy Road Association emerged in May 1995; it stated that it had come into being to articulate 'the opposition of the vast majority of the residents in this predominantly Catholic/nationalist area to the routing of Orange marches through the area'.

While all the residents' groups which spread rapidly to contentious areas were to be important in exacerbating sectarian tension and bringing nationalist feet on to the street, it was Drumcree, at the Mecca of Orangeism, that was to become the centre of the IRA/Sinn Féin strategy of setting not just Protestant against Catholic and unionist against nationalist, but the loyal institutions against the state to which they were so fervently loyal.

13

The Background to Drumcree

In sixteen hundred and forty-one, those Fenians formed a plan,
To massacre us Protestants down by the River Bann,
To massacre us Protestants and not to spare a man,
But to drive us down like a herd of swine, into the River Bann.

Brave Porter fell a victim, because he did intend
To help his brother Protestants, their lives for to defend;
The blood did stain the waters red, their bones lay all around,
As they drove them down into the Bann, that flows through Portadown.

A lady living in Loughgall, and with her children five,
She begged for the sake of them, to let her be alive,
That she might go to England, her husband there to see,
And to live in peace and unity and far from Popery.

But, oh, they would not hear her cry, they placed her on the ground,
And after having tortured her, the six of them they bound,
They said, 'You are a heretic, the Pope you do defy,
And it's from this bridge in Portadown, this day your doom to die.'

And after having tortured her to a pain she could not stand,
Down through the streets of Portadown, they dragged her to the Bann;
O'Shane appointed as her guard, to guide her on her way,
And the thought of five young children was leading her astray.

At least ten hundred faithful souls, in Portadown were slain,
All were the deeds of Popery, their wicked ords to gain;
But God sent down brave Cromwell, our Deliverer to be,
And he put down Popery in this land, us Protestants set free.

King William soon came after him and planted at the Boyne,
An Orange Tree there, that we should bear in mind
How Popery did murder us, Protestants did drown,
The bones of some can still be seen, this day in Portadown.

'Portadown.'

A FEW YEARS AGO, I mentioned to a good friend of mine that I was going to write a book on the Orange Order. 'If you do, I'll never speak to you again,' he said. George had always seemed to be unusually free of Northern Irish hang-ups. He used to laugh over the fact that as a Catholic with a father in the RUC he had regularly been beaten up by both sides and was therefore impartial. He had gone to Oxford, married an English wife and since then had lived in Scotland.

When the conversation became sensible, it emerged that George was afraid that I'd make Orangemen seem less bad than they were. 'But they are much less bad than they seem,' I protested. 'In fact, lots of them are good.' What I had forgotten was that George came from Portadown, which is regarded as the most sectarian place in Northern Ireland.

The bitterness is evenly spread. An elderly Orangeman of great seniority and experience told me recently that he had never seen anything as hideously sectarian as anti-Catholic graffiti in a public lavatory in Portadown. It is no coincidence that the most vicious battlefield of republicans vs Orangemen is at Drumcree, in Portadown.

There is an Irish phrase; 'There's two of them in it', which is appropriate in any discussion of inter-communal discord in Northern Ireland. When it comes to issues concerning marches, parades, processions or walks (there are subtle differences in terminology: at Drumcree, for instance, the paraders think they walk, their enemies say they march), throughout history neither side had a monopoly of intransigence or hooliganism. The history of parades in Portadown in particular is full of violent incidents provoked by one side or the other which set off riots into which members of both communities plunged enthusiastically. Along the way people have been killed and injured, property has been destroyed and grievances have been stockpiled for the future. The losers, almost every time, are the police, whether they handle the situation well or badly.

Portadown in County Armagh, a seventeenth-century plantation settlement, is known as the 'Orange Citadel' or, less respectfully, as the 'Orange Vatican'. It is an area full of bitter folk-memories: Orange banners commemorate the massacre of Scots Protestant planter families during the 1641 rebellion of the native Irish, when eighty men, women and children in Portadown were driven off the bridge and drowned; those who tried to reach the shore were knocked on the head or shot.

Then there is the close geographical link with the foundation of the Orange Order. 'Due to its proximity to the site of the Battle of the Diamond,' say Orange chroniclers proudly, 'Portadown was quick to embrace the ethos of Orangeism and throughout the nineteenth century played a prominent role in establishing and moulding the Order. The rebellion of 1641 . . . must certainly have encouraged participation in the fledgling Orange Order for Protestants saw it as a bulwark against any future repetition of the massacres.'

Over the two centuries since then, although the names of the combatants change, the sectarian passions in Portadown at best lie dormant. Some of the worst atrocities perpetrated on Orangemen – like the Tullyvallen and Kingsmills massacres – have happened in this county. And in Portadown itself, with its big Protestant majority, violence against Catholics has been a constant. It is a town that gave birth to and nurtured the bitterly sectarian Loyalist Volunteer Force.

In Portadown, parades have frequently provided a flash-point. The Ulster artist Sir John Lavery, who saw and painted his first Orange parade in Portadown in 1928, wrote in his diary:

> I have seen many processions and exhibitions of intense feeling, but nothing to quite equal the austere passion of the Twelfth in Portadown. The colour was more beautiful than anything I have seen in Morocco, black and orange predominating with every other colour except green adding to its beauty and the dozens of big drums beaten with canes by drummers whose lives seemed to depend on the noise they were able to make, their coats off, their shirt sleeves rolled up, their rists [sic] bleeding and a look in the eye that boded ill for any interference.

So Portadown parades have often provided a focal point for sectarian conflict and the police have usually been caught in the middle. Notable nineteenth-century riots occurred over a Catholic parade in 1880, a Salvation Army band parade in 1885 and an Orange parade in 1892. A newspaper report of the 1884 Twelfth gives a flavour of the mood of near-collusion between enemies intent on confrontation that prevailed even in comparatively peaceful times:

> During the day some lively proceedings occurred. It was market day, and the Roman Catholic party flocked into town with their 'goods' for sale. Of course, the usual quantity of 'John Jamison' was imbibed, and with the flow of the spirits came the flow of the 'fists', and several 'shindies' occurred of a harmless and amusing nature. It reminded the observer of Donnybrook fair, where one friend knocked down the other for 'love', but Mr Smith D. I., and Head Constable Egan did not seem to enjoy the 'sport' and at once put an end to the row.

Until the late 1960s, although there were occasional incidents, most parades went off peacefully, Catholics watched Orange parades and some musical instruments were shared amicably by Catholic and Protestant bands. But once the 'Troubles' started, communal bitterness flared up more viciously than ever. By 1972 Portadown was suffering from IRA and UDA violence, and parades and parade routes became the main inter-community battleground.

By then, most of the Catholic population of Portadown – about 30 per cent of the population – lived in two adjacent areas near the town centre: Obins Street and the Upper Garvaghy Road. The first, Obins Street, has been Catholic for over a century and there had been sporadic protests over marches through that part of it known as the Tunnel which is as unappealing as the rest of the most hotly disputed territories in Northern Ireland. It is 'nothing to write home about', wrote Tim Cooke in the *Belfast Telegraph* in 1985:

Turning off the main High Street, Market Street shopping area into Woodhouse Street you eventually encounter a 20ft long, 9ft high subway which allows pedestrians to pass under the busy Northway road. After 30 yards of open sky, passing the train station entrance, it's under the railway bridge and into Obins Street which leads in turn to the bottom of the Dungannon Road. The end of Obins Street nearest the town centre is rather run down. Some of the terrace houses are lying open and derelict and many others are bricked up.

Inevitably, it was the 1,000 metre run-down area – which these days houses about seventy families – that was contentious.

Annually, Orangemen used the Tunnel twice: to parade to Drumcree Church on the Sunday before the Twelfth and, like the Royal Black Institution the following day, for the journey to their assembly point at Carleton Street Orange Hall on the morning of the Twelfth itself. The first known account of anti-Orange violence in the Tunnel dates from 1873, when the *Portadown Times* recorded a 'most wanton and unpro-voked ... assault ... of the most dastardly and despicably sneakish description' made upon eighty-six Orangemen coming home from the County Armagh demonstration:

from the backs and windows of the houses with stones, brick-bats, large pieces of broken crockery and every conceivable description of missile, all of which were thrown with a violence and continuity perfectly compatible with the skulking poltroonery that dictated such a plan for waylaying a number of peaceable men whose only crime was that they were Protestants and loyal subjects.

On leaving Obins Street, the Drumcree Church parade went down the Dungannon Road, turned up Drumcree Road to the church and, after the service, went home by the Garvaghy Road, down which they had paraded since 1807.* The Upper Garvaghy Road was then bounded with fields and a rose nursery. In the late 1960s public housing estates were built there. Garvaghy Park, Churchill Park and Ballyoran were integrated at first, but Protestants were intimidated out of the estates and replaced by Catholics intimidated out of Protestant areas. The Lower Garvaghy Road estates have always been exclusively Protestant.

The road is very wide and the estates are built off it. Only sixty-six out of 900 houses in the Catholic area have a window from which the parade would be visible; fewer than ten houses have addresses on the Garvaghy Road itself. As with the Ormeau Road, and indeed the Bogside, most residents have to go well out of their way to be offended; three-quarters of the houses are between 100 and 600 metres away from the road. Still, during the 1970s and early 1980s there were sporadic protests against the Drumcree Church parade, including a silent protest from young people on the Garvaghy Road and the placing of two bombs in Obins Street; routinely the police had to put up barricades to separate Orangemen and protesters. As year after year murder and violence became a familiar part of the landscape in Northern Ireland, sectarian tensions in Portadown worsened steadily. The effects were visible in parades, with more young recruits coming into the Orange Order and the emergence of the 'blood-and-thunder' bands: by 1979 the Portadown Old Boys Silver Band had disappeared, to be replaced by the Portadown Defenders and the Portadown True Blues.

Rumours in 1985 concerning meetings of the British and Irish governments about the future of Northern Ireland precipitated serious violence. Unionists were aware that the leader of constitutional nationalism, John Hume, had access to governments that they were being denied and were convinced that betrayal was in the air. The view among Portadown Orangemen was that 'the Eire government wanted [the Tunnel] declared out of bounds to the Orangemen of Portadown. They were insistent on proof from the British government that they were prepared to face down

---

* Portadown Orangemen speak of having paraded to and from Drumcree since 1807, but the history of the period between then and 1822 is unclear and for some time afterwards the parade took place in November. What is certain is that the July church service has been an annual event for over 150 years and the route home has been via Garvaghy Road.

unionist opposition to the forthcoming Anglo-Irish Agreement. Where else could the government choose as a symbol of loyalist Ulster, than Portadown, the "Orange Citadel"'*

In the spring that year in Portadown, after a loyalist protest, police stopped a nationalist band and a Sinn Féin parade from going past Protestant areas. Nationalists threatened to retaliate. Orangemen were not mollified; from their perspective, their parades were legitimate because they were traditional, while republican parades were illegitimate because they had deliberately changed their routes to be provocative. Bans on loyalist band parades in June in nearby towns caused confrontations.

Not for nothing is Northern Ireland known as a rumour factory, with Portadown having a reputation for being a mass producer. Among the rumours rife in the town were that the RUC were bringing in riot police staffed with 'hand-picked' Catholics and that gardaí (police from the Republic of Ireland) would be on duty at parades wearing RUC uniforms. When Hume's deputy, Seamus Mallon, said in an interview that the Dublin government had the right to make representations about parades, Harold McCusker, the local MP, claimed that the RUC was acting on instructions from Peter Barry, the Irish Minister for Foreign Affairs. Ian Paisley's DUP, the UDA and the UVF came in to stir the pot.

A big but peaceful protest rally of Orangemen organized by the Parade Action Committee was held in Portadown on 3 July. Local Orangemen offered the RUC some concessions. In the event, on 6 July, John Hermon, the Chief Constable, announced that the Drumcree Church parade could go through the Tunnel but the Twelfth and Thirteenth parades could not. Twice or three times the usual number of Orangemen turned up for the church parade, which was led by the Grand Master of the Grand Orange Lodge of Ireland, Martin Smyth, and his fellow-MP, Harold McCusker. The RUC had to clear a sit-in protest from Obin Street at a cost of injuries to several police and protesters and form a barrier of police and Land Rovers between Orangemen and protesters, some of whom shouted IRA chants as the parade returned home via Garvaghy Road.

A summary of subsequent political reactions has a timeless quality:

---

* Politicians and public servants in Ireland were at the time even more ignorant about Ulster Protestants – not to speak of Orangeism – than they are now; it is hard to imagine that in 1985 they knew anything about Portadown. But one of the manifestations of Protestant paranoia is the belief that Dublin is full of well-informed Machiavellis.

A Sinn Féin councillor criticized the 'outright thuggery' of the RUC on the Obins
Street Residents who were attempting to hold a peaceful demonstration. Seamus
Mallon MP demanded John Hermon's resignation for an 'abject climb-down' on the
original re-reouting plan, while an Alliance councillor was pleased that the march had
been relatively peaceful, but was concerned that prominent people in the community
were making matters worse. Paisley attacked Hermon over the expense of the
policing, as apparently 500 RUC officers had been needed. Molyneaux [then leader
of the Ulster Unionist Party] suggested that the Northern Ireland Office had
blundered into making Portadown a test case, but hoped things could be sorted out
in a civilized manner. The RUC issued a statement that re-routing decisions were
being made in the light of IRA and UVF plots to stir up trouble . . . [Douglas] Hurd
[Secretary of State] repeated his assurances that there was no political involvement
in the policing of parades.

The Parade Action Committee then announced that no compromises
or re-routings would be accepted, while Walter Williams, the Grand
Secretary of the Orange Order, accepted the re-routings and asked
Orangemen not to confront the police. Various Orangemen and members
of the Royal Black Institution fell out with each other.

The Portadown No. 1 District decided that rather than be re-routed on
its way to join the main Armagh parade at Tandragee, it would stay in
Portadown for the Twelfth and conduct a peaceful protest. Instead there
was a violent confrontation with the RUC at the Tunnel end of Obins
Street amid shouts of 'SS RUC'. Young thugs ignored appeals by
McCusker and senior Orangemen and throughout the day attacked the
police; as a side-show, there was a fight between nationalists and bandsmen. The yobs and the drunks dispersed towards evening, but returned
the following day when the Blackmen, after a peaceful protest, had left
Portadown.

The two days of rioting left many police and civilians injured, around
fifty Portadown shops damaged and more than fifty people charged with
Public Order offences. Loyalists complained of police brutality, Danny
Morrison of Sinn Féin recommended that 'no one should be fooled by
such cosmetic gestures of alleged impartial policing' and the usual sus-
pects made the usual allegations. There were clear splits in both the
Orange Order and the Royal Black Institution between conservatives and
radicals, which manifested themselves all summer, as bandsmen, loyalists
and republicans used disputes over parades as an excuse to attack the
police and each other. A serious riot followed a band parade in Portadown.

Behind the backs of unionists, and largely at the dictation of John Hume, in November Margaret Thatcher and Garret Fitzgerald signed the Anglo-Irish Agreement, which gave the Irish government influence without responsibility in the running of Northern Ireland. The sense of betrayal gripped unionism. More than 200,000 people – about one in four of the Protestant population – demonstrated against the agreement in Belfast one week later, but were ignored. The 1986 marching season became the focus for discontent.

The Apprentice Boys of Derry got the year off to a bad start by deciding to hold their Easter Monday parade in Portadown and to go down the Garvaghy Road, though not through the Tunnel. Hermon banned the parade the night before because he believed the Boys had been infiltrated by paramilitaries. The subsequent chaos included the outnumbered police having to allow 3,000 people to parade down Garvaghy Road in the middle of the night and riots in Portadown throughout the day; one young man hit by a plastic bullet later died. Unionists blamed the violence on the ban and the ban on the Dublin government. The Orange Order and the Royal Black Institution condemned violence and backed the police.

Parading disputes went on over the next few months, and in June Portadown No. 1 District announced: 'Our resolve for the preservation of our civil and religious liberties has been strengthened by the implementation of Dublin rule in our beloved Province. As our district will not accept any re-routing we are obliged, should any take place, to oppose it.'

Nevertheless, in 1986, the RUC took the same decision on parades through the Tunnel as they had the previous year. Obins Street residents issued a statement attacking the Orange Order, the RUC and the Anglo-Irish Agreement (which, among nationalists, only republicans opposed) as 'not being worth the paper it is written on'. The police had to clear protesting loyalists and keep Obins Street residents hemmed in to let the Drumcree Church parade through. Serious trouble broke out as they tried to stop non-local Orangemen from going through the Tunnel: as the police tried to pull the offenders back, along with some journalists, they were attacked by Orangemen. When the locals had walked though, holding a banner saying, 'TUNNEL SAYS NO TO ORANGE PARADE', Obins Street residents threw bottles at the police. At Drumcree, during an altercation between police and some Orangemen, a police Land Rover was overturned. Deploring this as unfortunate, Orange chroniclers blamed it on a policeman who in the middle of 'a highly volatile situation . . .

stepped over the parameters of his professionalism by seeking to taunt Orangemen by use of a physically obscene gesture'.

For the return journey, police and soldiers lined both sides of the Garvaghy Road on which was being held a tea party organized by the Drumcree Faith and Justice Group, which had been set up to oppose loyalist parades. From the Orange perspective: 'Protesters ran on to the road in an attempt to block the path of the Orangemen; however, the police quickly moved in to remove them. As the Orangemen proceeded on their way they were taunted by sectarian outbursts by the on-lookers. Verbal abuse was hurled and many physical attacks were made on the dignified parade. Even though they had come under severe provocation, the Portadown Orangemen continued on their way without breaking ranks.'

In total, twenty-seven policemen and three civilians were injured. Bríd Rogers of the SDLP complained that it was 'simply intolerable that the nationalist population of Portadown should be held prisoners in their own homes for most of the day in order to allow a totally unnecessary exercise in coat trailing and deliberate provocation by loyalists'. Everybody blamed the police and the police blamed everybody. A rumour that two senior Dublin civil servants had been present did not help.

While the Grand Master of the Orange Order called for strict discipline and reminded Orangemen from outside the district that they could not go to a Portadown demonstration without permission from their private lodges, loyalist fringe groups were geared up for trouble on the Twelfth and Thirteenth. The Orangemen who usually walked to the assembly point at Carleton Street Orange Hall via Obins Street agreed to walk down the Garvaghy Road, playing no partisan tunes.

'Although the Portadown Orangemen had enjoyed their day in Armagh,' recorded their chroniclers, 'there was much apprehension about the situation awaiting them when they returned to the town.' They got off their coaches and paraded into the town to find themselves in the middle of a battle between loyalist youths and the police. Although the Orangemen stayed out of it, one of the brethren collapsed with a heart attack.

The Thirteenth began with some members of the Royal Black Institution having to use their umbrellas to fight their way through loyalists who wanted to stop them taking the Garvaghy Road compromise route rather than Obins Street, which was now blocked off. A few broke ranks and helped loyalists try and pull apart the barricade. There was a mainly peaceful protest on Garvaghy Road and a parade in the afternoon by a nationalist band through Obins Street. During the day, loyalists tried to destroy the barricade, even trying to ram it with a hijacked bus.

When the Blackmen came back in the evening from Scarva, their parade was marred by continuing clashes between police and loyalists; the RUC later praised the dignified way they had comported themselves. But the widespread rioting of the two days had done great damage to relationships between loyalists and police, some of whom were subsequently intimidated out of their homes. Politicians reacted predictably, and Peter Barry, the Irish foreign minister, in Garret Fitzgerald's government, fuelled unionist paranoia by condemning the RUC for allowing the parade down the Garvaghy Road, using identical language to John Hume when he claimed that the RUC had 'backed down in front of bully boys'. Unionists were furious. 'It is a sad day in Ulster's history,' said one Paisleyite, 'when the RUC enforces the directions of Peter Barry to ensure that a legitimate expression of loyalist rights is suppressed.' And even the leader of the liberal Alliance Party described Barry's remarks as 'irresponsible, inflammatory, and totally one-sided'.

The gradual subsiding of violent opposition to the Anglo-Irish Agreement and the introduction of the Public Order (NI) Order 1987, which required detailed information in advance about parades and gave the police time to negotiate routes, helped defuse the situation. In 1987 Portadown District held its annual service at the end of Obins Street rather than in Drumcree Church, but in subsequent years the Orange accepted the inevitable and gave up on the Tunnel. The Drumcree Faith and Justice Group held its final 'tea party' in 1991 and the following year, after the murder of four local people by the IRA, it called off a protest. According to independent observers, the Portadown Defenders and the Portadown True Blues swaggered during the 1992 church parade, but other bands behaved properly. In 1993 and 1994, only inoffensive bands participated in the Drumcree Church parade and the Orangemen were considered by independent observers to have behaved with decorum. This showed impressive restraint, since in 1993 Portadown town centre had been devasted by an 2,000lb IRA bomb which had caused many injuries. Though the Drumcree Faith and Justice Group kept up protests at a modest level, the heat seemed to be off.

Then, in May 1995, another IRA transmission belt came into the picture.

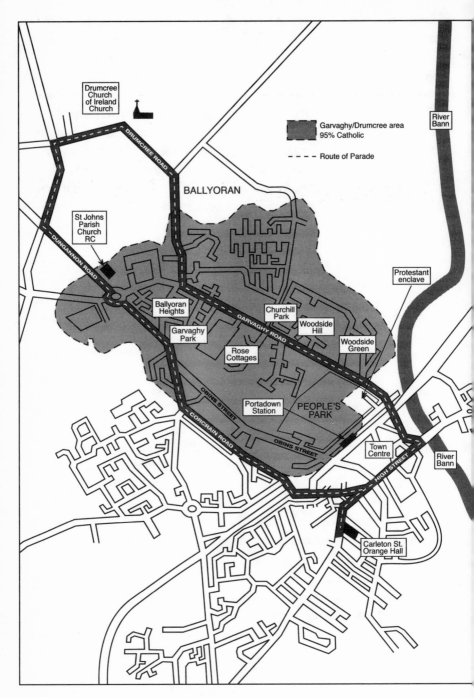

Route of Orange Order Parade, Portadown.

14

Drumcree One, 9–11 July 1995

It was a quiet Sunday
As brethren left for prayer
But one thousand RUC men
Were waiting for them there

Anon, 'The Siege of Drumcree'

B Y 1995, THERE WERE no longer any parades by the loyal institutions through Obins Street, and only two passed along the Garvaghy Road: the Drumcree Church parade on its way home and the county Orangemen en route to Carleton Street Orange Hall on the morning of the Twelfth. The number of bands going down Garvaghy Road was strictly limited, they were confined to hymn* or march music and they did not play when passing the Catholic church. These were small but telling manifestations that Protestants felt themselves to be in a state of permanent retreat.

> They have experienced [wrote Jonathan Bardon] the loss of Stormont; the collapse of traditional and multinational firms which employed them; the most draconian fair employment legislation in western Europe which stops them being 'spoken for' when seeking work; the imposition of an international 'diktat' in 1985, when despite loyalist protest the Anglo-Irish Agreement gave the Republic a say in Northern Ireland's affairs; John Major's statement that Britain no longer had a strategic or economic interest in the region; and Tricolours and street signs in Irish no longer torn down by the RUC.

To those elements were added the conviction that the Anglo-Irish framework document outlining a possible political settlement was a sell-out by their own government, fury at the lionizing of Gerry Adams in the Republic of Ireland and the United States, outrage at such concessions to nationalism as the abandonment of the national anthem at graduation ceremonies at Queen's University, and the anxiety and bitterness caused by the constant rows over the Ormeau Road route. The Portadown Orangemen were fearful yet defiant when they read in the *Portadown Times* on 26 May that a committee had been set up of Garvaghy residents 'to express the opposition of the vast majority of the residents in this predominantly Catholic/Nationalist area to the continued routing of Orange marches through the area'. The Garvaghy Residents' Association (GRA) requested meetings with the RUC and the Orange Order.

---

* Bands in Protestant Sunday parades play only hymns.

On 9 June, the GRA described as 'totally unacceptable' the RUC explanation at a meeting that they could re-route parades only if there was a threat to public order under the Public Order Order; on 30 June they announced that they would hold 'a peaceful public protest on Sunday July 9 and on the morning of the Twelfth to coincide with the Orange marches through the area'. Garvaghy Road residents 'simply don't want the Orange parades coming through'.

The situation was exacerbated by the release on licence on Monday 3 July of Private Lee Clegg, who had served only four years of a life sentence for the murder of a Catholic joyrider in 1990. Clegg had fallen victim to the law which decreed that members of the armed services can be charged only with murder, not manslaughter. That benefits some soldiers, but was seriously to Clegg's disadvantage: the charge against him was that he had fired lawfully on a suspect car three times, but that his fourth shot was unlawful. A member of the Parachute Regiment, he was a persecuted hero to tabloid readers in Britain who thought the law an ass; the *Daily Mail* alone collected two million signatures in support of his release, and since the forensic evidence was in doubt and he was appealing against the verdict, the Secretary of State bowed to pressure. The republican reaction was that the release of the 'para-killer' was 'a kick in the teeth to the peace process' which proved the British government's contempt for nationalist lives: rioting that week caused about £8-million-worth of damage. Government and RUC alike were terrified of exacerbating the situation.

On Tuesday, the GRA held a press conference to announce that on Sunday they would parade from the Garvaghy Road through the town centre to Carleton Street Orange Hall with a letter to the Orangemen; they would then hold a protest on the road against the parade: 'We're determined to put a stop to this yearly triumphalism, through our area.' Their choice of high-profile spokesmen had a touch of genius. First there was the chairman, Breandán MacCionnaith, imprisoned in 1981 for firearms offences, hijacking and kidnapping a local Protestant as part of his contribution to blowing up the Royal British Legion Hall – a particularly holy spot – in Portadown. He was not a resident of Garvaghy Road. Next there was the Jesuit, Father Eamon Stack, originally from the Republic of Ireland. Energetic, fanatical, selfless and gullible, Stack stalked the Garvaghy Road hunting for state injustices.

Tension rose on Wednesday, when the Ballynafeigh District Lodge was banned from the Ormeau Bridge and was later offered by the Lower

Ormeau Concerned Community (LOCC) a deal which would permit them to walk through the Ormeau on the Twelfth on condition that no loyalist parades took that route again during 1996. The Orangemen described this as blackmail. On Thursday, the editorial in *An Phoblacht/ Republican News*, said: 'Marching feet and angry voices – those were the words of Gerry Adams at Easter, and that has been our path since . . . Marching feet will be heard throughout this summer.'

On Friday, apprehensive about the coming Sunday, the Portadown District Lodge published a statement headed 'Challenge for Peace and Calm at Annual Church Parade to Drumcree'. 'For almost 200 years,' it said, 'the Orangemen of Portadown have paraded with dignity to and from the mother church at Drumcree causing no offence. As a religious organization we believe in civil and religious liberty. The anniversary church parade to Drumcree Parish Church is the oldest recorded Orange Service in the history of the Orange Institution.'

It sketched the history of the parade route. 'Always conscious of the feelings of the local residents of the Garvaghy Road, the Orange Institution has been at pains to avoid confrontation and to conduct themselves with the utmost decorum as befitting a religious organization parading to and from divine worship.' The lodge was sure, it ended hopefully, that the majority of Garvaghy Road residents would not welcome the 'aggressive confrontation approach' being displayed by a minority. 'Discipline and determination not to give offence despite extreme provocation has been a feature of the Orange parades to and from Drumcree with no breach by those on parade ever having been committed.'

By the standards of Orange communications, this was conciliatory, but there was no thought of compromise where the bottom line was concerned. As ever, when pushed to the limit, what governed Orangemen's conduct were traditional cherished principles like Martin Luther's 'Here I stand. I can do no other,' or King William's, 'I will maintain [the liberties of England and the Protestant tradition]'. As far as Portadown Orangemen were concerned, the parade was on. They had given due notice to the police, asking, as always, as a formality, to walk the old route of Obins Street to Drumcree and had been informed that, as usual, they would be re-routed via Northway. No objection was made about the return journey down the Garvaghy Road.

The Drumcree parade was due to leave Carleton Street at ten o'clock. The GRA turned down the RUC's suggestion that they parade to Carleton Street before 8.30 a.m., and three people, led by Breandán MacCionnaith, were stopped at a police line outside the town centre at 8.45. Told by Assistant Chief Constable Freddie Hall that their march was banned under the Public Order Order, MacCionnaith asked that the Orange parade be likewise banned and led his group back to Garvaghy Road.

In bright sunshine, just before 10.30, Portadown No. 1 District – the first-ever Orange district lodge – set off from Carleton Street along with their guests on the two-mile walk to Drumcree Church. Portadown Ex-Servicemen's LOL No. 608 provided the colour party, and at the head of the parade was the District Master, Harold Gracey, his officers, Denis Watson, an Assistant Grand Master of Ireland, and David Trimble MP. The total number on parade was just under 1,000. The music was provided by two accordion bands. In a show of solidarity, the crowd watching the parade was the largest for many years.

The service began at 11.15. In his sermon, the Rector of Drumcree, the Reverend John Pickering, spoke of Jesus Christ as the only real hope for the world: 'That makes all the difference – Jesus Christ is alive. This hope is what Orangeism, the Reformation, Protestantism and Christianity is about . . . The answer for Northern Ireland and for its people is for people to have renewed spiritual life.'

> Freddie Hall, he had the choice
> That day in Portadown
> He told his men, go to Drumcree
> And face the Orange down.
>
> They won't protest to us, he said,
> We've done all this before.
> What Freddie didn't realise,
> The Prods could take no more.

By the time the Orangemen had filed out and formed up for their fifteen-minute walk back to Carleton Street, on the road at the bottom of Drumcree Hill was a line of grey police Land Rovers blocking the route to the Garvaghy Road, where there was a sit-down protest.

The parade was not banned and nothing was said about re-routing, but the RUC explained it could not go ahead because of the presence of protesters. If ACC Hall had hoped that the Orangemen would disperse and go home the way they had come, he was quickly disappointed. 'The brethren of Portadown will not be moving. Let it be hours. Let it be days.

Let it be weeks,' announced Harold Gracey. 'We are for staying until such time as we can walk our traditional route, down the Garvaghy Road.' Or, as the anonymous poet described it:

> Harold Gracey said, 'We're here
> And here we're going to stay
> We have the legal right to walk
> Down any Queen's highway.
>
> So go back to Garvaghy
> And clear the road for us
> We'll walk with pride and dignity
> And we won't make a fuss.'

From the Orange point of view, it was a matter of simple justice. The Drumcree parade was legal, the Garvaghy Road sit-down protest was not; the police should simply uphold the law by removing the protesters. The police, however, had to take public order into consideration and were also undoubtedly aware that in the background were politicians frightened of giving republicans another excuse to riot. They knew, too, that there were several active IRA men among the Garvaghy Road protesters and the police seemed genuinely fearful that they could not guarantee the safety of the Orangemen if they took them down the Garvaghy Road. As with most decisions concerning parades, they were going to take the line of least resistance. At one stage of the negotiations, Freddie Hall tried a somewhat surreal appeal to the Orangemen's respect for the law: since notice had been given for a parade down the Garvaghy Road at one o'clock and it was now much later, he explained, the parade was no longer legitimate.

Not for the first time, the RUC underestimated the extent of the latent anger and frustration among Ulster Protestants as well as their sheer stubbornness. As soon as the news was out, loyalists began blockading roads in Portadown. And 'within an hour of the standoff beginning,' wrote one chronicler, 'provisions began to arrive at the church hall and under the management of a team of ladies a "field kitchen" was soon in operation . . . A seemingly tireless band of ladies continued to provide refreshments for the Orangemen both by day and during the long hours of the night.'

The Drumcree Church parade comes under the aegis of Portadown

District No. 1, so the master, Harold Gracey, was in charge. As ever, it was beyond the understanding of outsiders that democracy ruled in the Orange Order. Even had the Grand Master and officers of County Armagh or of the Grand Lodge of the Order itself wanted to, they could not have prevented Gracey from playing it his way; the Worshipful Grand Master and his officers were in charge of their own event. David Trimble had a high profile throughout the stand-off, but he was there in his capacity as the local MP. Although he has been an Orangeman since he was a schoolboy, he has never held office in the Order and is not even a member of Portadown District; his lodge is in Bangor, County Down. He had influence, but no control. Had he urged Portadown District No. 1 to forget about the Garvaghy Road and go back the way they had come, he would have been ignored and that would have been the end of any influence he might have had.

Not that there was ever any likelihood that Trimble would want the Orangemen to back down. Convinced that capitulation would be disastrous for the morale of the Protestant community, he was as determined as anyone that they sit it out. Early on in the stand-off, when he was worried that people might drift away, he said to Gracey: 'If this goes badly, you and I have to be the last two people to leave.'

There are many sides to David Trimble: alongside the often pedantic academic lawyer is an activist who enjoys what a university colleague once described as 'prancing around the streets'; he is quite proud of his two minor convictions for offences related to illegal parades. Completely opposed to violence, he nonetheless recognized that his community had to be allowed to let off steam. At Drumcree, he saw his job as two-fold: to help negotiate a satisfactory solution and to keep the protest peaceful.

'Be it days, hours or weeks,' announced Harold Gracey (an untutored but natural master of the soundbite), 'we will stay until we walk our traditional route.' His plea to Orangemen to show solidarity was ignored by almost all the broadcast media, but via mobile phones, the word went out. By evening, there were Orange protests in Belfast, Antrim and Derry as well as Portadown, and thousands of Orangemen were en route to Drumcree. The police were taken aback. Hall had apparently believed that Portadown District would drift away to attend their annual evening service at Seagoe Parish Church and, thinking themselves redundant, the Garvaghy Road protesters had virtually packed up by late afternoon. Shortly afterwards, however, it was clear the Orangemen were going to stay put.

> But Police put on their riot gear
> Preparing for a fight,
> And the siege of Drumcree Churchyard
> Began that Sunday night.

There was some violence in the evening. After an elderly man was hit with a baton as he tried to push between two Land Rovers, a few members of the crowd threw stones at the police; later a hedge near the Land Rovers was set on fire. These episodes were followed by a very Orange event: Orangemen assembled in the church hall, formed up and paraded down to the police lines where the County Armagh Grand Chaplain conducted a service, everyone prayed and then they sang 'O God, Our Help in Ages Past' and 'Abide With Me'.

> They came from every County
> As word was passed around,
> The countryside a sea of Orange
> Prepared to stand their ground.

> The support for loyal Portadown
> It really was immense
> Food and drink came pouring in
> Some even pitched their tents.

Morale rose as reinforcements arrived and it was announced that a mass rally would be held the following night. Although he had resigned from the Orange Order in the 1960s, the MP, MEP Ian Paisley turned up. He was in responsible mood: in conversation with the RUC he backed David Trimble's compromise proposal that a parade restricted in numbers be let down the road. Hall's counter-proposal that a dozen or so Orangemen be driven down the road in police cars was dismissed by everyone as a joke. In a speech Paisley managed a side-swipe at Cardinal Daly, the Roman Catholic Archbishop of Armagh who had supported the Garvaghy Road protest: 'The Cardinal has lined up with his militant republican flock.' But he was calm and he strongly urged the crowd to be restrained and not to allow themselves to be provoked. He then raced off to Belfast to argue with the Deputy Chief Constable and returned to Drumcree in the small hours to announce that the police intention was to face down the Orange Order.

While many Orangemen went home to sleep, about 500 or so stayed at Drumcree. 'During the night,' wrote Graham Montgomery and Richard Whitten, 'the site of Drumcree had a surreal atmosphere – a mixture between a military camp and a Scout jamboree.' Spirits were good as people met up with those they hadn't seen for some time, discussed past times and pondered future prospects. The graveyard was occupied by sleeping Orangemen in suits still wearing their collarettes, even a tent was pitched. The church and church hall were open; the hall was a hive of activity as local women made sandwiches and tea throughout the night while the church provided a serene contrast where Orangemen slept and prayed throughout the dark hours. In the early hours of the morning the crowd at the Land Rovers dwindled away as the brethren returned to the hall to sleep. The RUC took this opportunity to advance their Land Rovers and news of this brought the crowds quickly back to the 'front' where they remained all night.

During the night, Trimble's attempts to sleep in his car were interrupted by sounds of trouble at the Land Rovers. The second time he managed to defuse a potentially violent encounter between the RUC and those convinced there was a plan to clear Drumcree Hill of protesters.

Those Orangemen who believe that the Vatican is behind republicanism had their pananoia nicely fuelled on Monday morning: Father Eamon Stack was quoted as saying that it was 'not humanly possible for nationalists to tolerate these parades', and Cardinal Daly confirmed on radio that he 'wrote to applaud their efforts [the GRA], and any peaceful efforts to resolve the problems that arise at this time of year and I'm glad to say that they have, it seems, according to reports, acted in a very responsible and peaceful way'. In fact, as two independent mediators brought in later that day were to find out, the GRA line as expressed through Breandán MacCionnaith was that the church parade was 'history'; Portadown Orangemen could walk down the Garvaghy Road only if preceded by a nationalist band and with an Irish tricolour alongside the union flag.

During the day, in addition to Gracey and Trimble, those negotiating with the RUC included Jeffrey Donaldson, an Assistant Grand Master, Norman Allen, County Grand Master of Armagh and James Molyneaux, the leader of the Ulster Unionist Party. On the RUC side, Freddie Hall was left in charge: Sir Hugh Annesley, the Chief Constable, never appeared. Sir Patrick Mayhew, the Secretary of State, refused to get involved in what he said was purely a matter for the police under the Public Order Order. Meetings during the day were inconclusive: a hardening of Orange rank-and-file opinion led Gracey to come out against the Trimble compromise of a restricted parade.

At seven that evening, Jeffrey Donaldson went to a meeting with Brendan McAllister of the Mediation Network, set up to help resolve conflicts through negotiation, and Joe Campbell, a Presbyterian who belongs to Evangelical Contribution to Northern Ireland (ECONI), an organization which tries 'to promote a greater understanding and application of Biblical principles to the Northern Ireland situation'. They were asked to find out what the GRA wanted.

The Drumcree rally was held in a field behind the church, far from police lines. It had been scheduled for seven o'clock, but had to be postponed for an hour to allow time for the bands and the crowds of Orangemen and loyalists to assemble. People had come from all over Northern Ireland and even from Scotland; numbers were somewhere between 30,000 and 50,000. There were other demonstrations elsewhere, including in loyalist areas of Belfast and Derry, a protest by Orangemen and Orangewomen outside Carrickfergus police station, and the blocking of all main roads in the ferry port at Larne harbour. Donaldson and Trimble went down to the police lines before the rally started to try to persuade the thousand or so people there to go to the field. A few hundred, some of whom were Orangemen, stayed on; they were abusive towards Donaldson and Trimble as well as the police and were clearly in an ugly mood. Gordon Lucy, the chronicler of Drumcrees One and Two, reports that such has been the antipathy between the police and extreme loyalist elements in Portadown since the riots of 1985 that they refer to the RUC as 'the green slime' (their uniform is bottle-green) or, with surprising erudition, as the *milice* – the French fascist anti-Semitic militia who rounded up Jews and members of the resistance for deportation to concentration camps.

The Drumcree rally was like a super-Twelfth, without the hot-dog stalls. It passed what is known as the Drumcree Resolution:

We, the Orangemen assembled at Drumcree, loyal subjects of her Majesty Queen Elizabeth, do hereby resolve that we will maintain and defend our civil and religious liberty.

We will not accept a ghetto system. As free-born Britons we demand equal treatment with every other British citizen.

We repudiate the slander of those who accuse us of triumphalism and intimidation in the expression of our cultural and religious identity.

We totally condemn the tyrannous and unnecessary interference with the peaceful procession returning from a Protestant place of worship on the Sabbath Day.

We re-assert that the Queen's highway belongs to all law-abiding citizens. No faction, under any pretence whatsoever, can claim it as their own exclusive territory.

We call upon the police to uphold this fundamental principle. That is their duty to the citizens of this land.

Those on the platform included the Grand Master of Scotland – who told the audience that Scottish Orangemen were whole-heartedly behind them – and four MPs. Gordon Lucy described Trimble's speech as 'impeccably moderate'. He and Donaldson called for a peaceful protest, but even before the speeches were over, news came of violence erupting at the police lines. Gracey and Trimble left the platform while Paisley was speaking.

Paisley was later blamed for stirring up the trouble, but though the timing exonerates him, his language was certainly inflammatory. The Secretary of State was Pontius Pilate and Drumcree was the Orange Order's last stand: 'There can be no turning back on this issue – we will die if necessary rather than surrender. If we don't win this battle all is lost. It is a matter of life or death. It is a matter of Ulster or Irish Republic. It is a matter of freedom or slavery.'

'The speech was vintage Paisley,' reported Lucy, 'a blend of politics and early-twentieth-century music hall. Humour is an essential ingredient in that tradition of populist rhetoric of which Ian Paisley is such a master practitioner. Many of those present cringed with embarrassment. Others enjoyed the speech as superb entertainment.' While Paisley was performing, Trimble was appealing to the crowd for calm and restraint and getting abuse in return. 'Things could have got an awful lot worse,' Trimble said to me later. 'Someone came and told us they had just found several crates of petrol bombs – not near the Land Rovers, but further up behind this hedge. The man who reported that wasn't too keen to do anything more than just tell us. I remember going back right into the field and seeing a responsible Orangeman – an Ulster Unionist councillor. I went straight up to him and said, "Look, get a couple of reliable fellows and go with this man who will show you where these petrol bombs are and get rid of them, take them away somewhere else, or if you can, break them or whatever. Just get rid of them."'

He decided then that the crowd might calm down if told that negotiations were going on with senior RUC officers, and two policemen let him through. A yob chased after Trimble, and, as the police stopped him, a fight began, followed by stone-throwing. Being the only person behind the lines without riot gear, Trimble had to take shelter in a Land Rover until the trouble petered out.

By then the rally had finished and most of the crowd, along with the bands, paraded down to the police lines. Trimble and Donaldson went to the church hall to meet the mediators, who reported that there seemed to be no basis for negotiation. Then a few hundred loyalists and Orangemen tried to get to the Garvaghy Road via the field beside the police and a running battle followed; rioters hurled missiles and police fired plastic bullets.

> As the siege approached its second night
> The Police Chiefs they all knew
> The only way to keep the peace
> Was to let the parade pass through.

Worried by the size of the increasingly angry crowd at Drumcree and by the belligerent loyalists massing in Portadown – led by Billy Wright, a local paramilitary hero – the RUC asked for a meeting at a police station, where with Donaldson, Gracey, Paisley and Trimble they began to work out a compromise. It was provisionally agreed that Portadown District could go down Garvaghy Road. Trimble and company went back to Portadown to persuade the crowd to go up to the church where the Portadown contingent could be sorted out. At the bottom of Drumcree Hill, as had been agreed, the police started to remove the Land Rovers.

After Trimble had told the crowd of the agreement, Paisley intervened. Through a loud-hailer he addressed the crowd at length, and led them in singing 'O God, Our Help in Ages Past' and 'God Save the Queen'. The singing and the cheering were carried to the Garvaghy Road. Either because of this or because of media stories, protesters were summoned by bin-lids and by 2 a.m. there was a sit-down protest on Garvaghy Road. Youths were roaming around, many of them allegedly armed with clubs, hurley sticks and iron bars. The parade was off again.

Negotiators and Orangemen became angrier as the night went on. Many shouted abuse at Paisley and Trimble when they came back to Drumcree after another futile meeting with the police at 4 a.m. Portadown District were threatening to stop all negotiations and to go down Garvaghy Road at whatever time they chose. But in Portadown, Belfast and elsewhere, phone-calls and meetings went on all night.

> So on the Tuesday morning
> The 11th of July
> The Orange walked Garvaghy Road
> With head and colours high.

Eventually, at 10.30 a.m., Harold Gracey led 800 members of Portadown District down Garvaghy Road, while eighty or ninety protesters stood on the pavements holding placards with a picture of a faceless Orangeman and the caption 'NO SECTARIAN MARCHES'. There was no music; the only sound was that of shoes on road. As the Orangemen arrived at the Protestant part of town and were seen by the waiting crowds, there were cheers and flag-waving. The emotion was intense. One Orangeman recalled 'people crying, ex-servicemen who had gone through the war and they were in tears'. The Protestant people of Portadown were out in force and many followed the parade, now joined by bands and other Orangemen, as they made their way to Carleton Street Orange Hall.

At Carleton Street, the Orangemen lined the street and Harold Gracey went up and down the lines, shaking hands. He was followed by Paisley and Trimble (neither of whom had walked down the Garvaghy Road but who were wearing collarettes) with their hands linked above their heads. It was a moment which the television cameras caught and which will haunt Trimble for ever. Yet to those present it was a natural expression of euphoria after all the tensions and disappointments of the previous forty-eight hours. Trimble had little media sense. Exhausted, delighted by the outcome and relieved that everything had gone off peacefully, he was in the middle of a happy crowd of brethren and gave not even a passing thought to the television cameras, which sent around the world an image that came across as triumphalist and was interpreted as a deliberate attempt to rub salt in the wounds of nationalists.* Indeed, assiduous propaganda ensured that it became universally believed that Trimble and Paisley had danced a victory-jig in the middle of the Garvaghy Road.

There is no agreement on who gets the credit for what unionists claimed

---

* Months later, Trimble laughingly reminded me that I'd written in a London newspaper that he and Paisley looked like the principals in a gay wedding.

was a solution and nationalists claimed was a compromise, but in addition to the politicians (including Molyneaux who, from London, was lobbying the Chief Constable), Ronnie Flanagan, the Acting Deputy Chief Constable, who was to be heavily involved with Drumcree in the future, played some part and the RUC and the GRA publicly praised the work of the Mediation Network.

As a concession to the residents, the Twelfth and Thirteenth parades were re-routed. But the fundamental message that Drumcree One had sent out to loyalist and republican paramilitaries alike was that decisions like this were taken not on the basis of what was legal or just, but according to the police view of which side was likely to cause most public disorder.

'No more calls for compromise,' warbled Anon, 'Or trying to appease/ The Protestants of Ulster/ Have got up off their knees.' What he did not appreciate was how brilliantly the republican leadership would turn Drumcree further to their advantage.

15

The Road to Drumcree Two

'WHILE SENIOR POLITICIANS SPEND much of their time discussing framework documents,' wrote the authors of the pamphlet *Political Rituals: Loyalist Parades in Portadown* in July 1995, as a last-minute post-Drumcree update, 'the majority of people understand their politics through parades, flags, anthems, sports and cultural events. Policy makers should therefore not view these things as ephemeral, for it is around such issues that future solutions can be won or lost.' Yet the pamphleteers were optimistic about what had happened at Drumcree, where they believed that skilful negotiation had brought about a resolution that could offer 'a blue-print for other areas of contention'.

The reality was very different. Republicans were determined to step up the pressure. They were in a powerful position. Most coverage of Drumcree had been strongly pro the residents, for the Orangemen had been as inept and unfriendly in their dealings with the media as the Garvaghy Road residents had been clever and cooperative.

The republicans' main propaganda sheet got to work. 'For two days this week,' wrote an *An Phoblacht/Republican News* commentator, 'the Orange Order did exactly what it was formed to do, threaten, intimidate and tramp through nationalist areas.'* Trimble had demonstrated 'his undisguised triumphalism as he held hands with Ian Paisley at the head of the "victory" procession into Portadown'. And there was condemnation of an Orange parade held the previous week in Bellaghy and described by a local Sinn Féin councillor as 'a carnival of sectarianism with the purpose of ensuring the disruption of residents' normal activities'.

For the moment, though, Drumcree, like Bellaghy, was still playing second fiddle to the Lower Ormeau Road. An agreement made with Orangemen on Monday 10 July had been rejected the following night at an LOCC meeting, where 'a peaceful protest' was decided upon. At 5 a.m., hundreds of police and 150 jeeps had arrived to make it possible for Ballynafeigh District Orange Lodge to parade down the road in the morning and back in the evening. 'HEMMED IN LIKE ANIMALS' was the front-page headline of *An Phoblacht/Republican News*, under a photograph of Gerard Rice gesticulating angrily at a police line. Inside were accounts – under the heading 'RUC SHOWS TRUE ORANGE COLOURS ON LOWER ORMEAU' – of the 'military curfew' and RUC brutality towards the 500 protesters trying to reach the Ormeau bridge.

---

* Republicans at this period became keen to strengthen the pan-nationalist alliance by describing protesters as 'nationalist' rather than 'republican'.

'The bigots were back again,' wrote Meadhbh Gallagher in the same issue. 'And they were being backed again. At Garvaghy Road, on the Ormeau Road, they claimed their right to trample on the notion of equality. And the British forces, their "brothers in arms", granted it to them. Again.' Nationalist residents had been placed 'under siege . . . After Portadown, the RUC were happy to be keeping the Taigs down once more, their lines of Saracens like rats moving in for a feed.' It was British policy that 'the right to march must be afforded to sectarian bigots no matter what the cost to the people who are the targets of their bigotry'. Gerry Adams described it thus: 'In Portadown, the Garvaghy Road was put under siege by Orangemen; on the Lower Ormeau Road the RUC has done the job for them.'

In public relations terms, the LOCC had a walkover. There were televised scenes of protesters being batoned and residents complaining about being 'under siege'. And as other residents' groups learned to do, the LOCC had commissioned videos to back up their case. Condemnations of the RUC from Dublin put pressure on the British government and enraged loyalists. But Sinn Féin, too, was annoyed, for the Irish prime minister, John Bruton, had called on republicans to stop the street protests which had increased in number and intensity since the release on 3 July of Lee Clegg. While residents' groups were winning sympathy for their opposition to Orange marches, other IRA front organizations were also providing 'angry voices and marching feet' by engaging in such activity as a sit-down protest in Belfast city centre on a Friday lunchtime followed by a march up Royal Avenue. An editorial in *An Phoblacht/Republican News* on 3 August fulminated about requests to republicans 'to call off a campaign of marches, street protests and pickets. Nationalists and republicans again being asked to lie down, take the kicks and then polish the boots that kicked them.'

That same issue covered a counter-demonstration by loyalists against a Sinn Féin march which led to violence and also to another misleading and widely-used television clip of David Trimble. He was in fact gesturing at an angry policeman and saying 'calm down, calm down' but succeeded in looking threatening; he has a great capacity to look crosser than he is and flushes when annoyed in a way which makes him look positively choleric.

There was a bumper crop of new grievances in *An Phoblacht/Republican* News on 17 August. First was the account of how hundreds of protesters who sat down on the Ormeau Road at 5 a.m. on Saturday 12

August, were moved by 8.15 by the RUC to allow eighteen Apprentice Boys down their traditional route to join the coaches to take them to Derry; there were dozens of victims of 'state violence', injured by batons, fists and plastic bullets. An American observer had said: 'It's like the Klu [sic] Klux Klan being allowed through a Black American district.' It was alleged that Apprentice Boys had played 'The Sash' in front of Sean Graham bookmaker's and that one had mimicked spraying the bookies with gunfire. Rice was pictured carrying blood-soaked towels and a plastic bullet and saying: 'All this so a handful of Orangemen can walk where they're not wanted.' Injured residents had appeared at a press conference at midday, and in the afternoon there had been a protest rally joined by 'nationalists' from throughout the city.

Then there was 'BLIND BIGOTRY IN DERRY' where, for the first time since the Battle of the Bogside of 1969, the Apprentice Boys were allowed to walk along the walls despite protests by the Bogside Residents' Group. Those residents sitting peacefully on the disputed section of the wall from 3 p.m. on Friday had been subject during the night to 'sectarian abuse and taunts from loyalists' who later became drunk and abusive and threw bottles and insults without intervention from the RUC. At dawn, the RUC and armoured cars had blocked streets to stop more protesters arriving: 'However, residents circumvented this tactic and scaled the wall with ladders.' They were later dragged or lifted away, 'kicked and punched, trampled on . . . every single protester was assaulted'. Eventually, as the Apprentice Boys made their way along the wall, protesters reacted to the 'triumphalist parade. In complete silence, they turned their backs and made victory and clenched-fist salutes as the bigots marched overhead.'

The RUC, Donncha MacNiallais of the Bogside Residents' Group said afterwards, 'must accept full blame' for the riots that followed: 'The Apprentice Boys and the RUC have ensured that the normally tense situation in the city, caused by the annual parade, will now become a yearly stand-off on Derry's walls, which will no doubt lead to further strife within the community.'

On that same Saturday, the Royal Black Institution had been commended by Roslea nationalists for re-routing their march through the town. 'Roslea is 98 per cent nationalist and its residents have been forced to endure the coat-dragging antics of the Black Preceptory for countless years.' It was the first re-routing since the 1920s. 'Fermanagh Sinn Féin spokesperson Brian McCaffrey believes that the loyalist institute [sic] only reluctantly rerouted the march after nationalists took to the streets and blocked their route through Lower Main Street in the town. People from Clones, County Monaghan [in the Irish Republic], supported the Roslea residents' action.' 'Why', asked McCaffrey, 'could the marches on the Lower Ormeau Road and Derry not have been re-routed?'

Republican (aka nationalist) marches were, of course, different. More than one hundred Mid-Tyrone 'disgusted and outraged' protesters carrying flaming torches had held a demonstration on the night of Monday 14 August at Carrickmore's 'heavily-fortified RUC barracks', where they 'were met by a line of baton-wielding RUC personnel, taking their cue from their forces' actions in Belfast. A senior RUC officer then began to shout to the marchers that their presence was 'illegal'. Local Sinn Féin representative Barry McElduff reminded the imported unionist militia that if anyone in that area was 'illegal and unwelcome', it was them!

McElduff ended by 'calling for everyone to attend local and nationally-organized demonstrations demanding all-party talks. "Movement by the British government should not mean the firing of plastic bullets, the splitting of skulls by RUC bigots, or the use of military curfew on nationalist communities."'

There was, too, an ecstatic two pages about the 11 August anti-internment rally at which an estimated 20,000 with tricolours and banners with messages like 'DISBAND THE RUC NOW' had marched from north, south and east Belfast to the City Hall, to be greeted by Gerry Adams welcoming them 'to our city centre and outside our city hall'. He regretted the failure of the British government or the unionist leadership 'to grasp the hand of friendship', and then saluted the people of the Ormeau Road 'and all those residents' groups who have resisted Orange terror in their areas. "Most nationalists in this statelet have a tolerance for Orange parades and we object to them only when they go into areas where their behaviour is clearly unwelcome."' Turning to the RUC, he simply said: 'For some long time we were told that the RUC can be reformed. It cannot be reformed.'

It was at that rally that someone shouted 'Bring back the IRA', and Adams responded: 'They haven't gone away, you know.'

The police were rebuked in the course of coverage of the anti-internment march, because 'despite RUC claims that 1,500 extra officers had been drafted in the city' (to protect the marchers from loyalist attacks), some loyalists had broken through on one part of the route and started a fracas and the RUC had been tardy in reaching them and pulling them away. Provocation from RUC Land Rovers on the marching route had been dealt with 'by marchers climbing on RUC jeeps and hoisting the Tricolour'.

The marching season sputtered to a close with the RUC and the British government always in the wrong with republicans and sometimes with loyalists too. When on 29 October, for instance, a seventh parade was blocked by the RUC from going along the Ormeau Road, an Orange chaplain accused the Northern Ireland Office of blocking the parade, while the LOCC claimed credit for the ban on the grounds that the previous week they had threatened to take the Secretary of State to court.

An unforeseen bonus for republican propagandists, at least in the short term, was the election of David Trimble in September as leader of the Ulster Unionist Party, just after he had been publicly presented by Portadown Orangemen with a medal to mark the 'Siege of Drumcree'.* They attributed this result mainly to the votes of Orangemen intent on punishing their Grand Master, the Reverend Martin Smyth, because he had failed to turn up at Drumcree.

> Once again the winner was the man who rallied the troops to the Orange banner and the Lambeg drum, who catered to the need they felt to dominate their nationalist neighbours and to believe that things could be again as they always had been. Rather than being led by someone prepared to face the future and the need for political and constitutional change, the unionists have a man whose most dramatic act this year was to strut down Garvaghy Road, hand in hand with Ian Paisley, saying he was 'delighted we came home down our traditional route'.†

Most commentators in Britain and the Republic of Ireland agreed. Those who knew Trimble mostly disliked him: he is shy, short on social skills and uninterested in popularity. And almost all of them believed

---

* Five thousand of these were produced to raise money for Carleton Street Orange Hall and were inevitably seen from outside as triumphalist. The image of Orangemen was not helped by 'siege' being spelled 'seige' on the medal.

† The *Irish People*, the US organ of NORAID, whose readers are unsullied by any knowledge of Northern Ireland, can go further with propaganda than *An Phoblacht/Republican News*. Trimble, it explained to them, 'led some ten thousand loyal "Ulstermen" in repeated attacks on the RUC last year at the nationalist Garvaghy Road'.

him to be a dangerous, irresponsible rabble-rouser.* I was at a conference which included leading players on the Anglo-Irish scene the weekend he was elected, and almost everyone present joined in a chorus of what in Northern Irish terminology is described as 'Woe, woe and thrice woe'. They failed to see that while his high profile at Drumcree played a part in Trimble's election, so too did his intelligence, education, articulacy and comparative youth as well as the work he had put in, from 1985, as founder and chairman of the Ulster Society for the Promotion of British Heritage and Culture, which through its publications and its lectures has done a great deal to give the ordinary Orangeman and the ordinary unionist a sense of cultural identity. After a long period of losing the media war, Ulster unionists were desperate to have an effective spokesman.

The Orange Order, too, was showing signs of grasping that the parades issues was a public relations disaster, thus giving a boost to those of its members who had been for some time putting forward the revolutionary notion that you had to make a coherent and well-argued case if you wanted to be understood. Under Brian Kennaway, the energetic and combative convenor of its Education Committee, some steps had already been taken to present a rational case through publications and discussion. One example was *The Orange on Parade*, a booklet written by two history teachers; it explained what parades were all about, tried to remove misconceptions and made suggestions for accommodation on the biblical basis of St Paul's injunction to the Corinthians to 'Give none offence', with the reminder that love is 'not quick to take offence'. After Drumcree One, members of the Education Committee and others began to talk to journalists and to address organizations outside the Orange Order; four even took the unprecedented step of going to Dublin to address a public meeting about Drumcree. Most Orangemen, however, continued to carry on like a particularly stubborn and stupid defendant who keeps silent in court on the grounds that he knows himself to be innocent. Others became militant.

Within the Order, Drumcree One had caused tremendous polarization and radicalization. Recruitment was sharply up, particularly in Portadown, and, as responsible Orangemen were to note ruefully later, many of these

---

∗ David McKittrick, for instance, in the London *Independent*, wrote that Trimble 'has built a reputation as an ill-tempered, unalloyed hardliner. Northern Ireland's largest political grouping has just elected a figure whom most non-Unionists regard with something close to horror.'

newcomers were joining for political rather than religious reasons. The militant element found a leader in Joel Patton, Worshipful District Master of Killyman District No. 1 in County Tyrone, who, with a few like-minded, mainly rural, brethren, brought into being the pugnacious and intransigent group they called the 'Spirit of Drumcree'. It hit the headlines when on 14 November they held a rally of about 1,500 Orangemen in the Ulster Hall in Belfast. Journalists were expelled early on,* but a group of moderates who had infiltrated the meeting took copious notes of an event that horrified them. The Orangeman who sent me a copy of the notes added:

> My immediate reaction was that I now know what it was like for the Germans in the 1930s to attend the Rallies in Nuremberg.
> Remember, Ruth, all of this upsurge in the institution came about in just a few seconds on Sunday 9th July. I wonder did A. C. C. Freddie Hall the moment he gave his units the command to seal the arranged route realize that he just might be waking a slumbering giant. Now it has awoken, it might be a little bit more difficult to rock it back to sleep again.

On the basis of these notes and comments, I wrote an article that began: 'As if the Orange Order did not have enough enemies, it is now facing a split in its own ranks precipitated by its militant tendency – a gaggle of hot-heads parading their prejudices under the title of the Spirit of Drumcree (which for the sake of brevity I shall call SOD).'† I tried to explain that there had been good reasons why many decent Orangemen had flocked to Drumcree and that there were within the institution both moderate and immoderate people.

> Now the sinister SODs have hi-jacked Drumcree, to take advantage of the widespread bewilderment and fear that exist among the mainly decent people in Orange ranks and to push an agenda of aggression and bigotry.

---

* On being asked to leave, they were allegedly encouraged on their way with cheers and the injunction from the floor: 'Get out, youse bastards.'

† My claim to a footnote in the history of Orangeism is that apparently I was the first person publicly to use the abbreviation SOD. A Sunday Times sub-editor gave the piece the inspired title, 'Tell the Orange Bigots to SOD off', and at the Grand Orange Lodge meeting in December, the Reverend Martin Smyth told them in those words to do just that. Nowadays some of the SODs use the term as a badge of pride, rather as did the 'Old Contemptibles'.

Among other intentions, the SODs want to oust the Reverend Martin Smyth, the Orange Order Grand Master. This is because: a) he failed to turn up to Drumcree, b) he once said in principle he would be prepared to talk to Sinn Féin, c) he makes ecumenical* gestures and d) he is an Ulster Unionist MP while most of the SODs are DUP or worse.

Essentially, they think him a wimp but, as an anguished anonymous Orangeman wrote in a letter to the *Belfast Telegraph* last Wednesday, at least 'nobody is languishing in Ulster's jails because of any inflammatory speech or call-to-arms by Martin Smyth' . . . However, the SODs want a demagogue and for that reason are pressing for the introduction of one-Orangeman-one-vote rather than the representative democracy that exists at present.

The Grand Lodge of Ireland re-elected Martin Smyth in December and faced down the SODs, but they were not going to go away. As an Orangeman who wrote to me in response to my article put it, because the media had not realized

that there might actually be an extreme wing to the Orange Order being kept in check by the moderates . . . there is a growing feeling among some that there is little point in responsible behaviour as it earns no praise. Within the Orange Order many people who now feel that responsible behaviour achieves nothing have found themselves supporting the dangerous and radical elements that have surfaced through the 'Spirit of Drumcree'.

During the summer I stood at Drumcree because I believed there was a vital point of principle at stake and that those who broke the law and in some cases intimidated their fellow residents into helping them should not be rewarded by having the traditional parade rerouted. I attended the Ulster Hall rally as an observer and was startled, shocked and saddened by the bigotry and violence espoused.

Most Orangemen are ordinary decent people who have jobs to do, businesses to

---

* 'Ecumenism' is a tricky concept in Ireland. Mainstream Presbyterians, for instance, would say they were pro-tolerance but anti-ecumenical, i.e. they would defend everyone's right to freedom of worship but oppose any dilution of their own religion. Hence Martin Smyth would (as he did) attend an inter-denominational prayer breakfast. Orangemen are forbidden to attend a Roman Catholic mass – though many do in the case of weddings or funerals – and certainly none would take communion there. Until Vatican II, Roman Catholics were not permitted to attend a Protestant service; these days, canon law still forbids taking communion in a Protestant church. When President Mary McAleese took communion at a Church of Ireland church shortly after taking office, she was strongly criticized by the Catholic Archbishop of Dublin, whom liberal Catholics condemned in turn for intolerance and anti-ecumenism.

> run and hobbies to pursue. They believe in the doctrines of reformed Christianity
> and the Union with Great Britain, they enjoy the social occasions and the pageantry
> of the parades but they also have Roman Catholic friends, neighbours and
> colleagues with whom they mix on a daily basis. It is my experience that most
> Orangemen do not accord with the inflammatory sentiments expressed (albeit
> articulately) by the speakers on 14th November.

He concluded gloomily that, though in a minority, the SODs had the potential to do much damage.

The intransigents were already in the ring: in the green corner was Breandán MacCionnaith, demanding that the Garvaghy Road be ruled off-limits for 1996; in the Orange was Joel Patton, declaring that Orangemen should never voluntarily accept the re-routing of traditional parades. In the shadows behind both of them were respectively the IRA and the mid-Ulster wing of the UVF, under the leadership of Billy Wright. And cheering on both protagonists were vast audiences that included the wicked, the angry and the 'useful idiots'.

The IRA contribution to making everything worse was twofold: first, they ended the ceasefire on 9 February 1997 with the huge blast at Canary Wharf in London that killed two civilians and, second, their transmission belts continued to seize every opportunity further to harass the police, exacerbate sectarian tensions and, where it worked to their advantage, bring bloodshed to the streets.

The marching season kicked off on Easter Sunday with around eighteen republican parades to memorials and gravestones throughout Northern Ireland honouring the old and new IRA. In Armagh and Belfast, masked volunteers read out the IRA leadership's Easter message and were thanked by senior members of Sinn Féin. But media attention was focused on the twenty-five or so members of the Ballynafeigh Apprentice Boys Walker Club who had offered to ensure their band played no partisan songs and to avoid any provocative behaviour, and who at 8 a.m. on Easter Monday refused to accept being re-routed and were prevented by a barricade of RUC Land Rovers from walking the Ormeau Road; in protest they decided to stay put. The police admitted privately that they had acted in fear of a mass sit-in on the road organized by the LOCC and were once again taking what they hoped was the line of least resistance.

Most other Belfast Apprentice Boys went on to their Portadown rally, but a few bands stayed behind. As the travellers returned in the early evening and joined their brethren, tension rose. Although the leadership had called for a peaceful protest, there were others of a different mind. Jonathan Bardon watched from his house 'as youths gripping their off-licence carry-outs spilled out of a van ... to join others racing towards the Ormeau bridge. By engaging the RUC in conflict they were getting the same kind of buzz they would find in a football ground fracas.' That, he added, was not true of the Apprentice Boys 'who vainly demanded a right of passage down their traditional route towards the city centre. The blocking of the bridge was yet another outward visible sign that they had lost ground.' The violent young loyalists – many of them drunk – launched bottles, glasses, cans and even petrol bombs at the police. The riots went on until 1 a.m.

The Deputy Chief Constable, Ronnie Flanagan, blamed the trouble on 'outsiders'; David Ervine of the Progressive Unionist Party blamed 'beer-drinking hangers-on'; but a Sinn Féin spokesman said 'the Apprentice Boys were involved in violent confrontations'. It was all gleefully recorded in *An Phoblacht/Republican News* under the heading CLASH OF BIGOTS. Now that their two sets of enemies were pitched against each other, there was no need for republicans to organize protests. There was a colourful 'blow-by-blow' report:

'People are staying off the main road,' says Gerard Rice, spokesperson for the Lower Ormeau Concerned Community. 'Nobody wants to do anything to make the situation any more difficult.'

The RUC are snapping. 'We cannot be intimidated by force of numbers or threats of violence,' says RUC Deputy Chief Ronnie Flanagan, but on the ground the RUC resent confronting loyalists. 'Where's your Daddy now,' yells one RUC man at Gerard Rice's young son. 'We're doing Rice's dirty work for him.' The child runs away in tears amidst a barrage of threats and abuse.

The newspaper piously drew no comfort from the ban: despite it, 'the local nationalist community is again faced with months of tension':

There is no reason to believe that the main loyalist parades down the Lower Ormeau will be prevented ... What is unchanging and unyielding is the attitude of the Apprentice Boys and Orange Order, which refuses to respect the wishes of local people, or even to meet them ... nationalists object to only a tiny handful of loyalist parades which – on part of their routes – pass through their districts. But defying the wishes of nationalists seems to make these parades the most important of all to the Orange organizations.

Their two accusations were accurate in so far as they went. *The Orange on Parade* had discussed both. It said that negotiations with local residents were to be welcomed: 'However, Orangemen must not be given the feeling that the community groups are just fronts for the IRA. If these groups are serious about reaching accommodation they should consider carefully who they appoint as their spokesmen . . . there are some people with whom [Orangemen] cannot in conscience discuss these matters.' That recommendation was, of course, a non-starter, since the residents who wanted accommodation were in most areas being intimidated into silence.

The authors made an attempt to explain the psychology of the loyal institutions. Giving examples of occasions when lodges voluntarily re-routed themselves to avoid inconveniencing residents or causing traffic and security problems for the RUC, they went on:

> Important lessons should be drawn from these re-routings. The Orange Order is not intransigent and is not unable to adapt itself to changing circumstances – nor is it prepared to be bullied and pushed around by a small group of militant Republicans.
>
> Coercion and bullying are NOT ways to change parade routes, rather they are simply perceived as orchestrated attacks upon Protestantism. To quote the Centre for the Study of Conflict in their paper 'Loyalist Parades in Portadown', '*Since it is part of the participant's identity, opposition to the ritual becomes an attack upon both the individual and his or her community.*'
>
> It is a fact of life that attacks on any group serve only to increase fear and hostility and therefore do nothing to advance community reconciliation, rather attacks push the day of reconciliation further and further away.
>
> When Orange lodges can hold their traditional parades in an atmosphere of mutual tolerance and respect for diversity and not in the teeth of fierce and unrelenting opposition they are able to reach dispassionate decisions about parade routes to benefit the whole community.

It was, of course, their sophisticated understanding of these arguments that was informing republican strategy; appeals from well-meaning people broke on the rocks of their leaders' cynical intransigence. Jeffrey Donaldson, Assistant Grand Master, said Orangemen were prepared to compromise if there was movement on both sides. The deputy mayor of Belfast, a well-respected doctor and long-time SDLP councillor, Alasdair McDonnell, took a delegation of party colleagues to meet the Ballynafeigh Orange Lodge and reported that it had been made very clear 'that there

was no intention of giving offence and that they were terribly keen to
reach reconciliation and stability on the Ormeau Road'. There had to be
compromise, he told the BBC,

> because the vast majority of people want to live in peace. Certainly, there are
> protagonists in terms of the marches but they are not in the majority.
>
> The majority of people don't want Orange marches and they are not particularly
> enamoured with the Orange Order, or certainly what they perceive the Orange Order
> and the marches to be representing.
>
> But, nevertheless, there is a realization on the part of the people that life is about
> give and take, about tolerance and about putting up with something, even though
> you don't like them.

McDonnell's comments were 'an insult to the people of the area', said
the South Belfast Sinn Féin spokesperson. The LOCC demanded he
substantiate his claims: 'We have no doubt the overwhelming majority
of people in the area want to see a complete end to all sectarian, triumphalist parades along the Lower Ormeau Road. This is only the latest in
a long line of silly remarks by this maverick councillor.'

The moderates on both sides were becoming increasingly desperate.
Not only were the extremists determined on confrontation, but with each
bloody episode more and more decent people became hard-liners. Loyalist
mobs stirred up vivid memories of anti-Catholic pogroms; republican
propagandists succeeded in representing their own violent protesters as
innocent victims of police brutality; and there was increasing resentment
by ordinary residents of the restrictions imposed by a heavy police
presence.

A letter to the Dublin *Sunday Independent* in April from Sister Laura
Boyle, a minor player in what was now called the Garvaghy Road Residents' Coalition (GRRC), complaining about an article in which I had
argued for nationalist tolerance at Drumcree 1996, explained that what I
had described as a fifteen-minute parade 'means 12 hours of police satu-
ration (up to 1,000 officers), six hours of riots, 2 hours of severe restriction
and a growing resentment in the hearts of our children that is timeless'.
A response from an Orangeman pointing out that if the illegal protests
were replaced by peaceful legal protests policing could be drastically
reduced went unanswered. 'Does Sister Boyle believe that race relations
are better in South Africa today because of apartheid? If not, how can

she possibly expect community relations to improve with cultural apart-heid?' And when at my request – for in addition to complaining publicly she had complained in a private letter to me that Orangemen refused to meet Garvaghy Road residents – this Orangeman rang her, she was not prepared to meet him privately. The diktat had been laid down: no meet-ings with Orangemen except with Breandán MacCionnaith present. As Charles Fitzgerald, a unionist commentator, put it, people with a long-standing hatred of the loyal orders did not want to recognize any signs of what had occurred in recent years of 'a massive, soul-searching, traumatic change for the better, a desire for good-will'.

It was becoming increasingly difficult for the moderate Orangemen to make their voices heard in either community. Gerry Adams made it harder, by publicly offering to meet Martin Smyth to discuss measures to reduce tension in the months ahead and by explaining kindly to the Orange Order that it should 'accept that residents in the Lower Ormeau bear them no ill-will, but do withhold their consent for any Orange march through their area. The unionist and Orange leaderships, like the rest of us, have a moral responsibility to give positive leadership to our people. We all have a responsibility to instil confidence and not fan the flames of division and hatred.'

When it comes to effrontery, Adams is a master. Yet somehow, the Ballynafeigh Orangemen, banned from walking the Lower Ormeau Road on Sunday 27 April on their way to a widows' service at the Ulster Hall, kept their cool and resisted loyalist calls to summon Orangemen to join them for a Drumcree-style siege. The district secretary, Noel Liggitt, who was to come to greater prominence the following year, insisted that any protest should be 'dignified and lawful'.

For the lodge members, this took the form of a service at police lines, with a furious sermon being preached by their chaplain, the Reverend William Hoey, a Church of Ireland cleric who can sometimes out-Paisley Paisley (and whom I was to hear in action a few weeks later at a church service in Tyrone; see Chapter 1). The Chief Constable, Sir Hugh Annes-ley, he told his audience, 'is more and more perceived as worthy of the title of chief of staff of the republican movement in Belfast'. Disgrace-fully, he added that the RUC would have 'nowhere to run and nowhere to hide' when Protestants 'rise as one'. The brethren at the Ulster Hall, led by Smyth and Robert Saulters, who was to become his successor, unsuccessfully tried to join the Ballynafeigh brethren after the service, but all ended peacefully. While this was going on, when Gerard Rice was not to be found playing football with local children, he was chatting with a visiting nun from the Irish Missionary Union's Justice and Development desk, who had come as an independent observer: the residents' groups were busy at the time searching for suitable well-meaning people to join them at the scenes of confrontation.

Despite a few attempts to block some band parades, little happened on this front in the next few weeks. During that period, in the Forum elections of 30 May, the Sinn Féin vote increased from 12.5 to 15.5 per cent, Adams and McGuinness began a massive campaign against their exclusion from the Stormont talks, an IRA unit disobeyed standing army orders and killed a garda in Limerick during an armed raid, and the IRA blew the heart out of Manchester. A week later, what *An Phoblacht/ Republican News* called 'a peaceful, sit-down protest against a sectarian parade' was organized by 'the Cliftonville–Antrim Road Concerned Residents' Association (CARCRA). Among the 400 or so protesters were a very large number of fit young men who energetically resisted being moved, along with a sprinkling of grannies and a clutch of high-profile Sinn Féin councillors, all of whom claimed to have been injured. CARCRA accused the RUC of orchestrating violence in the course of forcing 'the loyalist coat-trailers through an area that is predominantly nationalist', called for 'all those injured or verbally abused by the RUC or Orange Order to contact the residents' committee or their local residents' association', and demanded a full independent inquiry.

It was now a week before Drumcree, which was of crucial importance because of David Trimble. Trimble had proved to be a disappointment to the republican leadership. Within a week of becoming leader he had gone to Dublin for the first meeting for thirty years between a leader of his party and an Irish prime minister; he had proved to be a modernizer, who wanted to cut the links between the Orange Order and the Unionist Party as part of an attempt to attract Catholic unionists; and he had visited Washington and had a meeting with President Clinton. He had internal party troubles, often annoyed people by his bluntness and made enemies and mistakes, but he had won plaudits in Dublin and London for constructively engaging in talks with nationalists despite opposition from more hard-line unionists like Ian Paisley and Robert McCartney (of the UK Unionist Party). To the republican movement, excluded from the talks, there was a real fear that Trimble might be able to make some sort of deal with constitutional nationalism. The hope was that his credibility would be completely destroyed at Drumcree in July.

Trimble had been aware throughout the year that a trap was being baited. If the parade was allowed, the RUC would have to move protesters off the road and the ensuing bloody scenes would be blamed on the insistence of Orangemen on walking where they were not wanted. If it was banned, there would be another stand-off and Orangemen would be seen as the aggressors. That Portadown District would re-route themselves was not an option; Harold Gracey and his brethren were doggedly standing on principle and there was no chance of moving them.

'Will you be at Drumcree?' I asked Trimble in May 1996. 'I can't duck it,' he said. 'But I'm trying to sort something out behind the scenes through intermediaries.' He was not the only person involved in that vain exercise: clergymen and mediators and police and politicians had all been working to find a way of bridging the gap between the Portadown Orangemen and the Garvaghy Road Residents' Coalition. But the stumbling-block remained: the GRRC would meet no one without Breandán MacCionnaith, and him the Orangemen refused to meet. What was more, the message was coming through loud and clear that, meeting or no meeting, MacCionnaith would not agree to any parade, even if small, silent and with its banner furled.

Sophisticated Orangemen knew that, whatever happened, they were heading for a public relations disaster. And Garvaghy Road residents who didn't care about the parade one way or the other and just wanted a quiet life read the leaflets the GRRC pushed through their letter-boxes requesting that they provide accommodation the weekend of Drumcree and realized with dread that coachloads of republicans were heading towards Portadown to provoke a massive confrontation. It was inevitable that blood would be shed over Drumcree. The question was how much and whose.

16

The Drumcree Disaster, 7–11 July 1996

Young Seamus from Garvaghy Road found an abandoned Orange sash among the debris from Drumcree. Fascinated by this relic of a foreign culture, the fourteen-year-old put it on and went home. He met his mother, who was scandalized: 'Go you and put that thing in the bin, I don't want to see it in our house'. He was doing her bidding, heading for the bin, when he met his father. 'Take that thing off this minute, and put it on the fire', his dad roared. Seamus turned round, took two steps and met his granny. 'Wherever did you get that?' she exploded. Seamus explained and Granny said: 'You take that right back to where you found it.' At this point, Seamus burst into tears. 'There, there,' said Granny, 'things aren't that bad.' 'Not that bad?' sobbed Seamus. 'I've only been an Orangeman for five minutes, and I've been re-routed three times.'

1996 joke*

I WAS IN LONDON WITH no intention of going to Drumcree when the phone calls started. Until then it had not occurred to me that, with the ceasefire over and the residents' groups carrying out the Sinn Féin agenda, the RUC and/or the British government would not have realized that the church parade at Drumcree had to be allowed go down the Garvaghy Road. Ulster Protestants have a very slow fuse: I knew a ban would light it.

From time to time I read statements from Dublin which showed that ministers and officials had not the faintest understanding of the state of mind of Ulster Protestants, let alone of Orangemen. Anxious to bring the IRA back into the peace process, they were following the Sinn Féin lead on the parades issue and swallowing the line that the problems were caused by provocative parades which hurt nationalist feelings and by the failure of the leaders of the loyal institutions to talk the problems through with local residents and reach sensible compromises. Suggestions from me and a handful of like-minded commentators that the residents' groups were IRA front organizations were dismissed as nonsense.

To keep Sinn Féin happy and put pressure on the British government, Irish politicians like Dick Spring, the Minister for Foreign Affairs, came out with frequent statements intended to placate nationalists; every time, they pushed Protestant paranoia to new levels. Those of us who were

---

* I like, too, the one about the dyslexic Orangeman who sat alone for a week in July in the middle of Duncrue Street, wondering where everyone was hiding.

behind the scenes assuring Orangemen that Dublin did not wish to see them mown down in the Garvaghy Road or anywhere else but simply didn't understand the situation, were losing the battle. Most Orangemen saw a clear scenario: the hated Gerry Adams, frontman of a terrorist organization that had resumed bombing and murdering, was using John Hume as a messenger to the Irish Department of Foreign Affairs, who were in turn instructing their men in Maryfield (the headquarters of the Anglo-Irish Secretariat, the visible sign of the infamous Anglo-Irish Agreement) to lean on their British counterparts to instruct the RUC to sell out the Orangemen at Drumcree, even though everyone knew Breandán MacCionnaith was an agent of militant republicanism.

I know how hard the English find it to understand Celts, particularly those on the neighbouring island. They are quick to be seduced by the charm and fluency of Irish nationalists and are repelled by the truculence and intransigent language of loyalism. The loyal institutions are the last straw. 'Why do these ridiculous people insist on putting on those silly sashes and awful bowlers and making idiots of themselves in public?' is what the average English person always asks, and when I mention patriotism or religion they look at me as if I were mad.

So I did not expect the Secretary of State for Northern Ireland to have learned to love Orangemen, but the rights and wrongs of the issue and the alienation of the Protestant population were so clear that it seemed obvious that he and the Chief Constable would agree that the Garvaghy Road should be closed off before protesters were bussed in, so as to make it possible to send down the road as small and quiet a parade as possible. It would get a bad press, there might be a few bloody encounters with militant local protesters, but it would be manageable. But then I was not very well-informed about the Chief Constable: I had not, for instance, been aware that his nickname within the force was the 'Eternal Light', because he never went out.

It was only later that I realized that Sir Hugh Annesley was a living example of how the English passion for compromise can wreak havoc in Northern Ireland. He had been given the job on the grounds that as a Protestant from Dublin he would be acceptable to both sides: the most sensitive police job in the United Kingdom had therefore been given to someone who understood neither tradition and was suspect with both. And as three well-informed journalists were to tell me at Drumcree, Annesley was believed to dislike David Trimble a lot and Orangemen intensely.

During the week, talking to friends within officialdom, I learned that the decision was very finely balanced. Yet knowing what Orangemen were saying, I knew there was no possibility the Portadown District or Orangemen in general would accept a ban. Calls from two Orange friends were alarming: one was as close to hysterical as I had ever heard him; the other was in a state of almost terminal gloom. They were despairing about the apparent inability of those in charge of Northern Ireland to grasp that the mood of the average Orangeman was one of absolute defiance. Although the loyalist ceasefire was still in operation, they were apprehensive that the dissident Portadown section of the UVF (Ulster Volunteer Force), led by Billy Wright, might resort to violence. An organization calling itself the Portadown Diamond Loyalist Action Group had said it would 'act' if the Drumcree parade was re-routed.

I was roped in to make a call to Harold Gracey suggesting that he try going above the heads of the GRRC to the residents. I immediately spoiled any chance I had of getting through to him by using the fatal word 'compromise'. To many Ulster Protestants, the word has to do with sacrificing principle: they will accommodate; some, though not many, will even negotiate; but hardly any will compromise. It was clear from the conversation that Harold Gracey, a retired store keeper, was a decent man completely out of his depth. A devout member of the Church of Ireland and Portadown District Master for a decade, he was well-liked by his brethren but he was not the man to outflank Sinn Féin strategically, tactically or in dealings with the international media. Yet because Portadown District had complete autonomy, he was on the front-line and it was he who would make the decision that was to pull into dangerous confrontation with the state not just the Orange Order but the bulk of the Protestant population of Northern Ireland. Increasingly depressed, I booked my ticket for Saturday.

With three days to go, *An Phoblacht/Republican News* announced that on Garvaghy Road 'nationalists are bracing themselves for a repeat of last year's loyalist "siege" when they will be curfewed in their homes by the RUC and Orange Order'. The residents' association 'has made repeated attempts to find a solution but they have failed to get a response from the Orange Order. The residents view this parade as an attempt by Orangemen to stamp their influence and supremacy on Portadown nationalists.'

The following day I was invited on to a breakfast radio programme in London. I sat in the studio as the two young presenters finished the previous items and during the news looked at their briefing on Drumcree. They were laughing. 'Ghastly people,' said the young woman to the young man. 'Imagine marching around with those stupid hats.' And without time to find out how I felt about it, she responded to the flashing green light and asked me to explain what Drumcree was all about. I did my best. 'And what do you think should happen?' 'They should be let go down the road,' I said. As one, they gaped at me. It simply hadn't crossed their minds that anyone they regarded as half-way civilized could have such a strange view. (It was after the interview and a subsequent tabloid article that I began to receive hate mail of a kind that brought home to me that however sectarian are the worst Orangemen, the other side has nothing to learn from them.)

While Breandán MacCionnaith addressed the television cameras of the world piously about his desire for dialogue with Orangemen, Portadown District LOL made a great leap into the world of public relations and on Friday issued a press release.

> The Orangemen of Portadown District have almost since the foundation of the Loyal Orange Institution, held an Annual Church Parade to Drumcree Parish Church to worship and give thanks to Almighty God. In so doing they witness for their faith, at the same time accepting that all others have the right to worship according to their conscience.
>
> There is no element of triumphalism or attempt to offend in this. Merely a desire to, with dignity and decorum, involve themselves in an act of public worship as their fathers and forefathers have done through successive generations.
>
> In parading to and from the Churches a circular route is used along the main arterial roads in that area of Portadown. The Garvaghy Road is not only such a road, it is the traditional route for the return journey and the most direct access between Drumcree Parish Church and Carleton Street Orange Hall.
>
> Portadown District rejects any concept of a ghetto mentality and reiterates its belief in the right of lawful parades along traditional routes.
>
> We regret that there are those who consider Protestants walking to and from Church to be 'sectarian'. This speaks volumes of their attitude to our community whose Faith, culture and traditions they would deny.
>
> We are, however, conscious that this view is not shared by many of the residents of the Garvaghy Road whose desire is to live at peace with their neighbours.
>
> On Sunday, 7 July the Brethren of Portadown District will as usual participate in this Annual Church Service. They will do so with their usual discipline and respect for others. They merely seek that others will respect their rights.

This did not do much to change the tone of the media, whose reporters and cameramen were pouring into Portadown in ever-larger numbers.

Before I left London on Saturday I wrote an article predicting that all hell would break loose if the march were re-routed because of the threat of nationalist violence. As I was on my way to Northern Ireland, Annesley, who had reason to believe that up to 3,000 republicans would be bussed in to Portadown, announced that after extensive consultation he had concluded 'that to allow the Orange Order Parade along the Garvaghy Road would be likely to occasion serious public disorder'. He had therefore ordered 'that conditions are to be imposed on the organizers to prohibit this part of their proposed route'.

I drove down the Garvaghy Road that afternoon and looked at the gable ends of the Catholic housing estates. Bearing in mind that even the vast majority of the residents who had no view of the road would allegedly be offended by a silent parade, I was reminded of the story about the maiden lady who calls the police to complain that a man is exposing himself in her vicinity. When they arrive at her house she takes them upstairs and shows how if you climb on a cupboard and look through a telescope you can see a naked sunbather in a walled garden half a mile away.

I spent the evening with Orange friends and acquaintances speculating fruitlessly and morosely on how bad it was likely to be, before being ferried to stay with friends of a friend.

I was collected after breakfast early on Sunday by Graham. Wearing a three-piece suit to set off his bowler hat, orange collarette and white gloves, he was somewhat improbably driving a red MG Midget sports car. When we reached Portadown he groaned as he waved at the outbreak of new red-white-and-blue stripes on the kerbs and the lampposts – a sure guide to the rising levels of militancy. He had been appointed press liaison officer – an unprecedented breakthrough for the Portadown District. The previous year, I'd been told, journalists had been greeted with hostility. This time, some lessons had been learned and a few people had been appointed to be civil and try to help.

Graham installed me in Carlton Street Orange Hall to await the press conference. At nine o'clock there arrived Harold Gracey, Denis Watson, County Grand Master, and David Trimble, in his capacity as the local MP. The message was clear: the ban was unfair and brought about by republican threats. Portadown District would not be re-routed; they would stay at Drumcree for as long as it took. Trimble had to jump in a couple of times to try to avert the public relations disaster that threatened every time Gracey opened his mouth. Gracey was in an apocalyptic mood anyway: this was not a stand for Portadown, he explained, but a stand for Ulster, 'and I'm sure that people of Ulster will agree – the Protestants of Ulster, for Catholics won't agree with me when I say that this is not a fight for Portadown alone but a fight for Ulster'. He had also become affronted when asked by a journalist why he refused to compromise. The language of the three Orangemen came across as blunt and intransigent when compared with the politically correct language of Breandán Mac-Cionnaith and his associates on the Garvaghy Road.

I was talking on the pavement outside the hall with the Belfast-based journalist Hugh Jordan, when I saw Harold Gracey talking to someone I recognized from photographs as Billy Wright, the legendary 'King Rat'. Jordan and I knew that Wright was believed to be behind many sectarian murders and was a byword for intimidation and murky drug-deals. He was strange company for Gracey, but then the Portadown view of Wright was more benign than ours. There, in many circles, he was seen as a defender of the law-abiding against the rebels. Both tribes are adept at seeing their own terrorists as maligned freedom-fighters.*

I introduced myself to Gracey and he introduced us to Wright, and we talked to him for twenty minutes. I wrote afterwards:

> Among the leaflets I was given at Drumcree was one which purported to be the Sinn Féin oath; it promised the destruction of all Protestants in the campaign to make the Pope ruler of the world. Billy Wright is one of those Protestants who actually believe that is what Sinn Féin/IRA are about. A sometime lay preacher, he sees loyalist terrorism as a Holy War against the murderous forces of Roman Catholicism. I formed a strong impression of a man who revels in his reputation. He certainly enjoys looking the part: six feet tall, lean and super-fit, he has cultivated an unnerving piercing stare and a style of conversation than combines extreme rationality with a carefully controlled underlay of menace. He of course does not even admit to membership of the UVF; he merely explains what he calls those who

---

* Conor Cruise O'Brien summed it up: 'Most people in both communities do not support violence, but are frightened and repelled by it. But *within* each community, there is a rather small but fanatically motivated section which resorts to murder for the furtherance of its political creed. And – again within each community – there are much larger groups who have a tendency to extenuate the crimes perpetrated by members of their own community, as having been provoked by the crimes perpetrated by members of the other community.'

are prepared to defend their people against the enemies of their religion and their state.

What surprised me about Wright was how intelligent he is. In fact he reduced me and my companion – another loquacious journalist – to silence in the end. We were trying to persuade him that if loyalists resorted to violence over the ban on parading down the Garvaghy Road they would be falling into an IRA trap. He was explaining courteously (he called me 'dear' throughout) that we were failing to grasp the central fact that government concessions to nationalists – beginning with the Anglo-Irish Agreement – had demonstrated conclusively that in Northern Ireland violence pays. Our counter-arguments sounded unconvincing even to us. Nor was there any point in arguing on moral grounds, for people fighting religious wars know they are serving God.

'The ceasefire is over,' he told us and I said desperately, 'You're not going to condone going back to murdering random Catholics, are you?' He shook his head pityingly and explained that loyalists didn't kill random Catholics; those murdered were republicans. I think he believed it, because, of course, to people like Wright, Catholics are by definition republicans.

At one stage in our conversation Wright pointed to the hundreds of Orangemen assembling for the parade and said: 'Look at them. I'll guarantee not one of them has a criminal conviction. They are the most loyal and law-abiding citizens in the United Kingdom and they're being denied their right to walk their traditional route because their government has given in to the people who're trying to destroy the state.' It was the only time he showed emotion. Arrogant, ruthless, cruel and a control-freak he may be, but he truly believes himself to be the saviour of his tribe. Like all such people, he is very very dangerous.

What was also becoming clear was that Wright, who had been on the fringes at Drumcree One, was determined to move centre-stage for Drumcree Two.

For light relief after the Wright encounter, Hugh Jordan introduced me to Belfast Annie, who goes to all the protests she can. She had brought her sleeping bag so that she could stay to the bitter end and opened her coat to show us her DRUMCREE 1995 NO SURRENDER T-shirt. There was then a crackling on the Tannoy and Harold Gracey appeared above us on a balcony to announce that the parade was about to start. 'We will not give in to Sinn Féin/IRA,' he shouted. 'Hugh Annesley said last night on the television that this was Custer's Last Stand. Well, friends, let me tell you that it was an Ulsterman, at the Alamo – Davy Crockett – and we will be like Davy Crockett at the Alamo.' I think Gracey was making the distinction between a siege (Alamo) and an attack (Little Bighorn); I don't think he realized that Davy Crockett and the rest of the Alamo defenders were wiped out.

During his speech came one of those surreal moments in Northern Ireland when the past and the future collide. Just as Gracey was saying 'Alamo', Hugh Jordan's mobile phone rang. At the other end was Tom Tracey who, almost alone among Irish Americans interested in Ireland, has taken the trouble to get to know unionists. He was ringing from California to inquire how things were in Portadown. As Hugh and then I talked to him and to Nancy Gracey of Families Against Intimidation and Terror, a Belfast group that fights paramilitary intimidation, whom Tracey had linked into his conference system, I revelled in the incongruity: as I talked on this most modern of communication systems, above me was Gracey talking about Davy Crockett and in the streets were a large group of men demanding rights they thought had been granted in the seventeenth century.

As we watched the two thousand or so Orangemen do their tour of the town, the cheering, clapping crowds of women and children and old people demonstrated graphically that Protestant Portadown expected that they stand their ground: one child in a pushchair carried a sign saying: 'DADDY DON'T LET THEM TAKE MY CULTURE AWAY'. It was clear that had the Orangemen backed down they would have been given the white-feather treatment. It was the sons of Ulster marching to the Somme all over again. And indeed the Somme was much in the minds of Ulster Protestants at that time. The first of July had been the eightieth anniversary of the day when the men of the 36th (Ulster) Division were mown down opposite Thiepval Wood.

I observed the Orangemen's walk as they went past, looking for signs of a triumphalist gait. But there were no 'kick-the-pope' bands and therefore no discernible swaggering. I noticed that because his legs were longer than those of most of his brethren, David Trimble was shortening his stride to keep pace; the effect was more of a mince than a strut. Hugh and I walked beside the parade as it left the town, and there, courtesy of Billy Wright, was an enormous new mural. Headed 'THE PEOPLE UNITED IN DEFENCE OF THEIR FAITH AND CULTURE', it featured, inter alia, two arrows: that on the left, over the legend 'SMASH PAN-NATIONALISM', represented 'Dublin, SF/IRA SDLP OPPRESSION'; that on the right, over 'FORWARD BRETHREN', pointed to 'Civil & Religious LIBERTY'. Across the road were mounted two trophies of a raid the previous night on Crossmaglen, headquarters of what is known as the bandit country of South Armagh: a 'Sniper at Work' traffic sign, featuring a balaclavaed rifleman, with UVF now inserted neatly at the top and a large sign in Celtic script with the legend 'My brother is a Criminal', placed in the centre of ten white crosses. We had been told about these earlier that morning and I had mentioned them to Billy Wright, who had smiled gently and said, 'It's important that republicans know nowhere is off limits to us.'

Along the 4-mile route various rumours were passed to us of what was thought to lie in store. The army had been instructed to fire on protesters, we were told; the hospital had been requisitioned, as massive casualties were expected. Looking at the loyalist thugs hanging around the route and at Drumcree itself, I could see them licking their lips over the prospect of violence.

During the first hour or so, there was an extraordinary combination of religion and politics. The Tannoy was broadcasting a religious service consisting of hymns, prayers and the rector talking about faith and righteousness; knots of journalists were trading gossip and predictions, and down the hill were the RUC in riot gear backed up by Land Rovers along with the British army – both now ranged against natural allies determined to resist the law.

There was plenty going on and no phone boxes. Another mobile phone provided me with an abiding image of the day. I had borrowed the phone of Toby Harnden, the *Daily Telegraph*'s Northern Ireland correspondent, to have a word with my friend Dean Godson, one of his London colleagues. When we finished, Dean asked me if he could talk to David Trimble. I took the phone to Trimble who was now sitting on a table which had been propped up outside the gates of the church hall for speakers to stand on. Like many other families, Trimble's had arrived to bring him supplies and show support. Standing on the table beside him was his youngest child, four-year-old Sarah, who was having trouble adjusting the knot in the sleeves of the sweater she had draped round her waist. As Trimble answered Dean's questions and then got involved in some abstruse aspect of the law relating to public processions,* I was

---

* I did not know our end of the phone-call had been taped until two years later, on a radio programme in which we were both participating, Tim Pat Coogan said: 'There is a celebrated tape-recording – I have a copy of it myself and it could always be produced if you want to play it here – of Ruth and David Trimble on the phone to the editor [sic] of the *Daily Telegraph* for a long conversation during which Ruth was retailing to the editor

knotting, unknotting and generally acting as lady's maid to Sarah. Toby Harnden stood by looking stricken as the life drained out of the battery of his phone. There were naturally no facilities for recharging in the press room – a hut normally used for children's playgroups. Throughout the days of Drumcree, press conferences were held in a room festooned with educational toys, tricycles and mini-tractors.

For the best part of twelve hours at Drumcree I watched and listened. I heard septuagenarian ex-servicemen explain that they were prepared to sit there for a year; I saw convoys of supportive spouses making tea and sandwiches for thousands; I saw pillars of the local community from other lodges – shop-keepers, farmers and ministers – marching up to join their beleaguered brethren; I heard the screams at the RUC of 'Spring's traitors' and 'Bruton's playthings', and was horrified to learn that Dublin parliamentarians were on the other side of the line, giving Paisley ammunition in his winding up of the crowd by talk of 'skunks from Dublin'; I heard Martin Smyth, the Grand Master, and others con-tinually make the distinction between 'decent Catholics' and 'rebels'; and I saw Wright, who made no such distinction, spending more and more time with Harold Gracey. As one Orange friend put it to me bitterly, 'Billy Wright has filled the vacuum that is Harold's head.' I saw the committed way in which 99 per cent of Orangemen stayed peaceful and tried to maintain discipline: 'There's trouble down at the line. Will twelve sensible Orangemen go down there immediately,' was a typical announcement. And I saw Trimble, continually condemning violence and calling for restraint and like an army officer defusing trouble as it was about to erupt, calming people down, trying to assuage the anger of his constituents without losing his influence for good and returning crestfallen from a civilized but unsuccessful meeting with the Deputy Chief Con-stable.

I hung around throughout the day listening to speeches from people

---

of the *Daily Telegraph* the information that not only was McKenna but a number of the other committee-people all had form, all were discreditable people with IRA background. And that was the impression being conveyed.' Putting Trimble's innocuous remarks into the public sphere is one thing, but I am surprised that an ex-newspaper-editor considers it ethical to repeat a private conversation between journalists. I would also like to know how he got hold of a copy of a tape made, I am told, by an IRA phone-bugging team located in the Garvaghy Road.

Coogan has, alas, broken his promise to send me a copy of the tape, so I can't comment on what I said to Dean Godson except to say that – allowing for what I referred to on the programme as Coogan's 'relaxed attitude to scholarship' – it sounds as if I was pretty accurate.

like Gracey and Smyth and Denis Watson and to Ian Paisley, who came
in briefly to stir everybody up and then left. I sat among different groups,
just listening. I heard a couple of octogenarians quite seriously discussing
whether it was likely that they'd be home in time for Christmas; there
was much talk about the length of the siege of Londonderry. Orangemen
queued patiently for food which the ladies had provided: you could get
a ham sandwich and a cup of tea for £1. They sat on benches in the
church hall and caught up with gossip and chatted about agriculture. It
was my first serious exposure to that capacity for sheer endurance that
marks out the rural Ulster Protestant. Providing the food kept coming, I
couldn't see that anything would shift them.

I brought my insight to Graham: 'I've discovered your community's
secret weapon – an infinite capacity to put up with boredom. In fact
they're rather like cows.'

'Of course,' said Graham. 'We're trained for it. What's a lodge meeting, but being bored in a hall? And what is the Twelfth of July but being
bored in a field?'

Graham was my consultant. It was to him that I went after a conversation with an Orangeman who explained that Gerry Adams was anti-
Christ and would live as long as Satan. 'I met a real live bigot,' I reported
excitedly. Graham listened and shook his head judiciously: 'There's a
difference between a bigot and a nut.' From time to time Billy Wright
would appear, often accompanied by other sinister-looking specimens
with earrings and shaven heads, and Trimble told me with extreme distaste
that Wright had spoken to him and that he was terrified about what he
might be planning. It was the early rumblings of the fear that grew all
week that Wright's gang was intent on massacring Catholics in the Garvaghy Road.

There were outbreaks of low-level violence as yobs screamed at the
police and threw stones, and throughout the day there was a barrage of
abuse directed at the security forces. Some Orangemen were involved
but most were passive. There was heavy marshalling going on and appeals
for discipline and order over the public address system. But, of course,
as at all parades where there is violence, the television cameras focused
on the trouble-makers and ignored the silent majority.

In the late afternoon Graham announced that this was clearly going to
be a long haul and one not to be lived through in a three-piece suit, so
he was going home to change; if I wanted to look at another parade in
Portadown I should come with him. So we drove to see the unprecedented

sight of Lurgan Orangemen, who are traditional rivals of their Portadown brethren, as a gesture of solidarity arriving to take the place of Portadown District at what should have been their evening service at Seagoe Church. Among them were Lurgan Orangewomen turned out in Sunday best. We drove on to Graham's house where his mother seized the opportunity to give us a large meal, and on the way back through Portadown spotted a woman walking down a street carrying a pile of big hats; for this we had no rational explanation.

We had to park the car a long way away from Drumcree Church, for by now Drumcree Road was packed with cars and thousands of Orangemen were arriving from all over Northern Ireland. When we got there, there was laughter when two women walked through the crowds carrying a large poster saying, 'IT MUST BE WAR – KATE ADIE'S HERE'. Adie-spotting became the popular sport: a nonagenarian, spotting that I looked and sounded foreign, asked me quite seriously, 'Are you her?'

The hat mystery was solved at about nine o'clock just as the light was going. Up the hill with their arms swinging came the Lurgan Orangewomen. They were bare-headed, having decided that hats are an encumbrance on a four-mile walk. It was the sight of these totally respectable women – the wives of shop-keepers and farmers, hard-working housewives and sandwich-makers and tray-bakers and the backbone of the Ulster Protestant community – joining their fathers and husbands and brothers and sons in defiance of the British government, that confirmed for me they would get down that road or there would be civil war.

Although I'd found the day fascinating, not being bred or trained to boredom, it was a relief to me that I couldn't stay at Drumcree indefinitely, though I felt treacherous as I left all these people cheerfully contemplating days of discomfort, frustration and danger. At midnight I arrived at the house of my host, another historian and teacher, and asked why after his local church parade he hadn't gone to Drumcree. 'It was awkward,' he said. 'A Roman Catholic neighbour dropped in for a chat and I thought it would be tactless to tell him I couldn't because I had to go to Drumcree. But I'll be there tomorrow night.' At which stage my long and extraordinarily healthy day (fresh air, endless walking, plain food and water) was mercifully finished off with 'a wee nightcap' (which with Presbyterians always seems to mean a treble Black Bush).

*   *   *

That Sunday night Michael McGoldrick, a thirty-one-year-old Catholic taxi driver, husband and father, who had just graduated in English from Queen's University Belfast, was shot dead outside Lurgan. Taxi drivers are a favourite target for loyalists looking to murder random Catholics, for it is simple to ring a Catholic taxi-firm and have a car sent to a convenient spot; there are loyalists depraved enough to call this the 'Dial-a-Taig' service. There was and is little doubt that Michael McGoldrick's killers were members of the dissident LVF, operating under the instructions of Billy Wright.

As Wright had intended, this murder petrified Catholics living in isolated areas. 'I would hate to be a local Catholic,' said my host, who insisted on driving me to the airport on Monday morning rather than letting me take my chances with public transport. I was relieved that I was not driving: it was not the best of days to have a southern Irish accent. Road blocks were no problem: one glimpse of Richard's collarette, displayed on his dashboard, and we were waved through. A week later I wrote:

> I went back to London, terrified for the decent people caught up on both sides of the stand-off, particularly for the residents of the Garvaghy Road and desperate that Annesley reverse a decision I believed would lead to civil war: a breaking of the loyalist ceasefire would have enabled the IRA to go fully back to work in the guise of defenders of their community. Against the background of mass protest and increasing loyalist intimidation, Orange friends rang to tell me of suggested deals and counter-deals; of desperate efforts of County and Grand Lodge officers as well as Trimble to get Gracey to see sense; of Wright's increasing influence over Gracey and Willie McCrea, DUP MP (recently described by Seamus Mallon as 'the village idiot' of the Northern Ireland Assembly); of the power-struggle between UVF HQ in Belfast and the local rogue elements; and of much else.
>
> It was on Wednesday, having failed to persuade London to countermand the Chief Constable's order, that Trimble asked for a meeting with the four church leaders. By then there was panic at Drumcree at the arrival of the huge mechanical digger, which by Wednesday lunch-time was armour-plated and capable of smashing through a brick house – let alone police and army lines. 'Don't they understand in London what's going to happen?' screamed one Orange friend at me down the phone. 'There are brainless hoods standing round this thing calling it "Baby, baby".' And he hadn't even heard what Trimble heard from security sources later that evening – that two more diggers and a slurry tank full of petrol were thought to be on their way to Drumcree, the idea being to put all these objects through the police lines

and enable terrorists to get at the Garvaghy Road residents. 'If no solution has been found before Thursday midnight [the beginning of the Twelfth],' said a despairing Orangeman reporting from the front, 'we face meltdown'.

With the church leaders as intermediaries, senior Orangemen and Trimble tried to find a compromise acceptable to Gracey/Wright: the deal agreed at 3.00 a.m. on Thursday morning was wrecked within minutes of his arrival by Ian Paisley. The church leaders, caught between two intransigent groups, could not deliver an agreement; to avoid carnage, Annesley had no option but to let the marchers through.'

Here are what the political magazine, *Fortnight* later selected as the highlights of Drumcree week:

MONDAY, 8 JULY. NI was at a standstill as rioting and disruption in support of the Drumcree Orangemen continued. Plastic bullets were fired at Drumcree, Sandy Row, Ballymena and north Belfast. The UUP, DUP and UK Unionists pulled out of the multi-party talks at Stormont. Unionist politicians condemned the RUC chief constable, Sir Hugh Annesley, for the trouble. The family of Mr McGoldrick blamed unionist 'fire and brimstone' speeches for his death.

TUESDAY, 9 JULY. 1,000 British troops were sent to NI as the RUC were stretched to their limits by escalating violence. In Belfast, Catholic families were moved out of the Torrens area, gunshots were reported in north Belfast, hundreds of roads were blocked by Orangemen and loyalists, including the motorway to Dublin and the Craigavon Bridge in Derry. Alliance party leader John Alderdice accused unionist leaders of 'holding us all to ransom'. Unionist leaders met the Prime Minister John Major in Downing Street, with Dr Paisley describing the Drumcree situation as 'a powder keg'.

WEDNESDAY, 10 JULY. As violence continued, SDLP deputy leader Seamus Mallon described the situation as 'the most tense in 25 years'. Mr Mallon's village, Markethill, was cut off, as were many other towns including Coleraine, Cookstown and Derry's Waterside. The UVF called for rioting 'to desist', while the Belfast Fire Service reported its busiest period in 25 years. The RUC stated that, since Sunday 7th, 156 arrests, over 100 incidents of intimidation, 90 civilians and 50 RUC injuries, 758 attacks on police, and 662 plastic baton rounds were reported.

THURSDAY, 11 JULY. 1,200 Portadown Orangemen silently marched down the Garvaghy Road after Sir Hugh Annesley reversed his decision to block them. Police forced protesting residents off the road, and riots soon followed in the Catholic estate. Rioting started in west and north Belfast, Derry, Armagh and other nationalist areas. The Catholic cardinal, Cathal Daly, called it a 'black day' and a 'disastrous decision' by the RUC. Condemnation also followed from all the southern Irish parties, as well as Alliance, the SDLP and SF. Over 1,000 police and army sealed off the lower Ormeau area after a judicial review brought by residents to stop the 12th parade failed. In the House of Commons, Sir Patrick Mayhew 'rejected the notion of surrender' to Orangemen.

FRIDAY, 12 JULY. Ballynafeigh Orangemen marched down the lower Ormeau. Gerry Adams said 'the peace process lies in absolute ruins'. John Major said that was 'absurd'. Speaking on the BBC's Nine O'Clock News, John Bruton [Irish taoiseach] blamed the British government for the violence: 'A state cannot afford to yield to force; a state cannot afford to be inconsistent; a state – a democratic state – cannot afford to be partial in the way it applies the law and I'm afraid we have seen all three basic canons of democracy breached in this instance'. Rioting continued in nationalist areas, with over 1,000 petrol bombs thrown and 1,000 plastic bullets fired in Derry alone. 22 were seriously injured, and a Catholic rioter, Dermot McShane (35), died after being hit by an armoured car on the Strand Road.

SATURDAY, 13 JULY. More riots. A bomb exploded outside the Killyhelvin Hotel in Enniskillen, Co Fermanagh, causing much damage but no injuries. The IRA denied it was responsible. The SDLP announced it would withdraw from the NI Forum.

SUNDAY, 14 JULY. Thousands of nationalists marched and rallied in Derry, Belfast and Lurgan. Loyalist leaders warned that the Combined Loyalist Military Command ceasefire was 'at breaking point'.

Orangemen had now risen to the first division of international pariah-dom. The international television and newspaper images of blood-stained protesters being hauled off the Garvaghy Road to make way for Porta-down District to go where they were not wanted were devastating in their power. A typical reaction came from a Dutch member of the European Parliament who announced that the 'misuse of the colour orange has been a matter of distress to us in Holland where orange is the colour of tolerance'. Other than brethren who sent messages of support from abroad, particularly Canada, Ghana and Togo, virtually no one outside the United Kingdom wanted to hear the Orange point of view. Nor did most people on the mainland have any sympathy whatsoever for their case – indeed, many swallowed wholesale the propaganda about Orangemen as Ku Klux Klan, National Front or neo-Nazis. Among the political and journalistic classes, in particular, the Orangemen at Drumcree elicited a fastidious shudder and a mindless repetition of words like 'triumphalism'. The

London *Independent* described Ulster's Catholics as 'white niggers' who had been 'stunned by the Orange victory'. Even *The Economist*, which prides itself on its intellectual rigour, showed alarming ignorance by blaming Drumcree wholly on 'the political bankruptcy of unionism'.

In the Republic of Ireland, there was a visceral outburst of rage. The public perception was that the British government had betrayed nationalists by giving in to loyalist violence. Not since the hunger strikes of 1981 had the island of Ireland been gripped by such tribalism. The truth was revealed, announced John Waters in the respected *Irish Times*, when 'the British government was seen as duplicitous, unionists as bigots and nationalists as a community under siege'. No nationalists wanted to hear about the origin and republican agenda of the residents' groups; people who had never met an Ulster Protestant, let alone an Orangeman, denounced them with the certainly born of complete ignorance. An atypical nationalist – Dick Keane of Glenageary, County Dublin – described the phenomenon in a letter to the London *Independent* on 18 July:

> For an instant our civilized veneer cracked. From every politician and church leader, from every TV, radio and newspaper commentator, from every phone-in and chat show, from every workplace and pub conversation, poured all the old tribal cliches. All the defeats, wounds, hurts and humiliations suffered by our tribe were rehashed with relish. All our myths, misapprehensions, fears, bitterness and hatred of the Unionist/British tribe were superbly articulated.
>
> The voices could have been Serb or Hutu, Croat or Zulu. There was enough rhetoric in the past week to sustain and justify our tribal warriors (IRA/INLA) in waging war on our tribal enemies for at least another 25 years.

Eoghan Harris, one of the few dissenting Irish commentators, castigated his fellow-citizens: 'How could the RUC protect residents of the Garvaghy Road if 100,000 Orangemen came over the hill on the 12th? Shoot them and start a civil war? No, the RUC made the right decision and the sole bright spot is that its action gave Trimble an asbestos suit which will allow him to talk to the taoiseach without Paisley lighting a bonfire under his backside.'

In Northern Ireland, things were even worse. The RUC, which through hard work had been gradually improving its reputation in the nationalist community, had hit new depths of unpopularity with both communities. And just to be an Orangeman was to share corporate responsibility for all the violence of Drumcree. A gentle, elderly Orangeman and Ulster

Unionist councillor told me in great distress how at his first council meeting after Drumcree he was screamed at by members of the SDLP with whom he had hitherto worked constructively and happily. 'I just sat there and took it, Ruth. But I was very upset that they would speak to me that way. I never in my life talked to anyone like that.'* But then the SDLP was under ferocious pressure to shout as loudly as Sinn Féin. As Harris put it in the Irish edition of the *Sunday Times* on 14 July:

> [Seamus] Mallon is a man strapped into the blazing car of the peace process. Hume is hunched over the wheel – but he is merely going through the motions because the Provos have the car under remote control. Whenever the car crashes – as it did after the Docklands bomb – Hume is comfortably cushioned by the air bag of public adulation while the SDLP is hurled through the windscreen. This makes Mallon mad. Since he cannot take it out on Hume, he takes it out on Trimble.†

Trimble was once again a particular hate-figure. His visits to the Irish Republic and his openness to dialogue were all forgotten. The revelation in a BBC television programme that he had had a meeting with Wright on Wednesday 10 July was widely seen as proof that they were in collusion, although its purpose had been to find out what Wright was up to and get

---

* In nationalist–unionist debate, nationalists are generally by far the ruder and more strident: Ian Paisley and his ilk on the wilder shores of Protestantism are atypical. There are, for instance, no mainstream unionist journalists who would ever write of John Hume or his SDLP colleagues in the abusive terms which many of their nationalist equivalents routinely apply to David Trimble and the rest of the Ulster Unionist Party. 'If one appoints a horse a consul, I suppose one can't be surprised if the animal craps all over the hall,' was Tim Pat Coogan's comment on David Trimble's thoughtful address in Oslo when in December 1998 he shared the Nobel Peace Prize with John Hume. As for Orangemen, consider the description by Brenda Power, a senior columnist with the Dublin *Sunday Tribune*, who described them as a 'gang of bigots with chamber pots on their heads and curtain pelmets around their necks'.

This is a manifestation of the licence granted to those who perceive themselves as the oppressed party and is reminiscent of the way in which, for instance, men are nowadays publicly routinely disparaged and traduced by women in terms which would never be tolerated the other way about.

† On several occasions Tim Pat Coogan has gone so far as to say and write that Trimble won the leadership of the Ulster Unionist Party on the back of Billy Wright. Trimble became UUP leader in 1995, after the first Drumcree stand-off, in which Wright had little involvement. He had met Wright once before 1996, when he had come to his constituency office, 'bold as brass', as Trimble put it to me, to complain of being harassed by the Ulster Defence Regiment.

him to use his influence to keep things calm at Drumcree. Although in 1996 Trimble had again not walked down Garvaghy Road and had stayed well away from any post-parade euphoric gatherings, the 1995 hand-in-hand-with-Paisley image was played and replayed and – particularly outside Northern Ireland – he was seen as the leader of Orange resistance and an accomplice of Billy Wright.

> Except for the ostentatious show of a mobile phone sticking out of his bulging pockets [reported John Cooney in the *Sunday Tribune*], Trimble, when dressed in the full regalia of the Orange Order,* is a sight to make any would-be Jacobite truly tremble. He is instantly distinguishable as a timeless Boyne bigot rather than the leader of a supposedly modern democratic political party . . .
>
> The television image will long remain in the public mind of a broad-bummed Trimble strutting around the Garvaghy road with the combined dizziness of a Charlie Chaplin and the verbal velocity of Glasgow Rangers' 'Gazza'.

Asked for his views by the Dublin *Sunday Tribune*, Trimble said bitterly: 'We know what the Irish government wanted. They wanted to see violence. They wanted to see soldiers shooting Orangemen. They wanted blood. They wanted the blood of unionists.'

In a Northern Irish newspaper I dissented:

> Trimble doesn't understand the Irish government any better than they understand him, largely because of the temperamental gap between the Ulster Protestant and the southern Catholic mind and the sheer ignorance of both sides that comes from a lack of contact.
>
> The Irish government is peopled by pleasant, well-meaning people, who – like the electors they represent – wanted at Drumcree what they always want: a bloodless victory. There would have been a secret tribal pleasure in seeing the Prods faced down, as well as relief that this would get whingeing northern nationalists off their back for a few minutes. But blood, no. Most southerners don't like it. They must not be confused with the IRA supporters who would have been thrilled to see the Paras shooting down Protestants.
>
> That the Taoiseach, John Bruton, who is a realist, and one with more

---

* Since Trimble neither wore a bowler nor carried an umbrella and had an ordinary collarette, this description is rather baffling.

understanding of unionists than any other member of his government, lost his temper so dramatically over Drumcree is indicative of how deep-rooted in the southern Irish psyche is the virus of wishful thinking – particularly where Northern Ireland is concerned.

Since I came back from Drumcree, I have tried to explain to many southern Irish nationalist friends, acquaintances and foes why I believed Annesley's first decision showed a profound ignorance about the Protestant state of mind and why – had he not changed his mind – there would have been many dead Catholics as well as Protestants. With only a couple of exceptions, they look at me as if I were speaking Urdu.

When I told them that everyone at Drumcree believed Dublin had insisted the march be rerouted, and that Orangemen screamed at the RUC that they were 'Bruton's playboys' and 'Spring's traitors' they shrugged. 'Nonsense', they responded. All that was required was firmness; then all those funny people in bowler hats would simply have backed down.

The simple truth is that the Irish people and their government have only a very limited understanding of northern nationalists and almost none of northern unionists. This is largely a product of laziness. Rather than embarking on a serious attempt to get to know and understand the population of Northern Ireland before deciding whether the Irish government had any business meddling, it has been easier to do what nationalist spokesmen tell them. More than a decade ago a senior adviser to Garret FitzGerald said privately to me: 'I've been telling Garret for years that it is wrong that our policy towards Northern Ireland should be dictated by John Hume.' Since then it's got worse. For most purposes, it is dictated by Hume and Gerry Adams, the first the fading high-king of his tribe; the second his challenger.

A particular conversation which I had all too often with people in the Republic around that time ran something like this. 'Of course, I blame Trimble.' 'Why?' 'Because he's the leader.' 'No, he isn't. He has no authority in the Orange Order. The person who calls the shots in Portadown is Harold Gracey, the District Master.' 'Don't be ridiculous. Trimble's the MP and leader of the Ulster Unionists. He should have just told them all to go home.' My efforts to explain how Trimble hadn't even been taken into the confidence of those Orangemen who had planned the blockades never got me anywhere. The Irish Catholic autocratic tradition has little in common with the divisive, dissenting, individualistic and ludicrously democratic cast of mind of Ulster Protestantism.

Early in August I wrote:

Drumcree was a double-whammy for the IRA. That the Chief Constable rerouted the Orange parade for fear of republican violence enraged the entire Protestant population, showed the ugliest face of loyalism to the TV cameras and as a bonus damaged David Trimble. The U-turn made to avoid mass slaughter enraged the Catholics, portrayed the British as cravenly sacrificing the rule of law to triumphalist bully-boys and caused a serious rift in Anglo-Irish relations.

To the annoyance of the IRA, Alistair Simpson, the Governor of the Apprentice Boys, accepted the invitation of John Hume, the local MP, to meet the residents' spokesman under his chairmanship. Hume, who has worked with Protestant and Catholic alike to bring foreign investment and tourists to Derry was desperate for a compromise.

When Simpson had made concessions to meet all local objections, MacNiallis demanded that the Apprentice Boys state publicly that they would give nationalists throughout the province the right to veto any parade in their area and when that was refused, the talks collapsed. In his own backyard, Hume has now learned the bitter lesson that republicans are sectarian and want peace agreements only on their terms.

Throughout the past few weeks inflammatory leaflets pushed through letterboxes in nationalist estates in Belfast have been just a small part of a campaign to whip up fears of loyalist pogroms. Simultaneously, in border towns with nationalist majorities where the two communities get on well, Protestants are being driven from their homes. Reinforcements – some from across the border – help local republicans break windows late at night, shout threats and intimidate Catholics into boycotting the shops of Protestants alleged to have participated in the Drumcree protests. Orangemen in little towns like Newtownbutler and Rosslea are being told that they may not parade from their hall down their main street.

Having tasted and cherished peace, the worsening polarization of the communities is agonizing for the majority of Northern Irish people. 'Throughout all the years of war,' said a moderate unionist in a border town last night, 'we never had anything like the bitterness that exists between the two communities this week. I have never been so afraid.'

Northern Ireland breathed again when the Apprentice Boys' parade (see Chapter 1) went off peacefully. But despite that setback, this was a wonderful time for Sinn Féin. The Manchester bomb of 15 June and the 200 injuries that it had caused had been excised by Drumcree from the nationalist memory. The orchestrated riots and boycotts of Protestant businesses were represented as a spontaneous expression of nationalist outrage, and anti-Orange propaganda reached new heights of viciousness.

In the weeks following Drumcree, I became ever more horrified at how decent, ordinary Orangemen were being subjected to a campaign of grotesque misrepresentation. And accustomed though I was to Sinn Féin's creativity and chutzpah, even I was taken aback by the scale and viciousness of the lies and distortions they were now proudly peddling in public.

Elaborate political murals are a dominating feature of Northern Irish ghettos: the godfathers like to ensure that the inhabitants of the areas they control are permanently reminded of their tribal grievances as well as their triumphs. Residents' groups had seen to it that the image of the faceless bowler-hatted figure in suit and collarette with a heavy line through it and the legend 'NO CONSENT NO PARADE' was to be seen in every contentious area. The month after Drumcree, there appeared a huge new mural in the Falls Road. Bearing the heading 'NOT ALL TRADITIONS DESERVE RESPECT', it featured a hooded and robed Ku Klux Klan horseman with an orange sash riding across a green landscape littered with skulls as well as with rocks daubed with the names of the places where Sinn Féin–IRA had with mixed success been trying to drive the loyal orders wild: Derry, Garvaghy, Ormeau, Dunloy, Castlederg, Enniskillen, Rosslea, Keady and Bellaghy. Plenty of room had been left for up-dates, for throughout the marching season there were confrontations and re-routings that kept the pot boiling.

Orangemen were not, of course, simply a target: they were a weapon with which to damage the British government and the police and further to demonize David Trimble. The day after the Apprentice Boys' August parade, I had an instructive afternoon in Belfast at the Sinn Féin republican rally against internment (abolished twenty-one years previously). At the end of the march I stood beside the platform outside City Hall where in addition to hearing the usual hail-to-the-freedom-fighters speeches from spokesmen from representatives of foreign organizations like ETA/Harri Battisuna* and NORAID, as well as home-grown luminaries like Gerry Adams, there was a dramatic performance by a street-theatre group starring and directed by the hard-line IRA veteran and convicted terrorist, Martin Meehan. In the forefront stood two men in Orange collarettes, one wearing a Klan hood, the other a John Major mask. A figure rep-

---

∗   Every time I see an ETA spokesman on a Sinn Féin platform, it amuses me that while IRA/Sinn Féin want a United Ireland, ETA/Hari Battisuna want to detach the Basque country from Spain. All they have in common is a belief that they are entitled to get their own way through violence.

resenting David Trimble spoke in the background on a mobile phone to one representing Billy Wright.

In the hearing of hundreds of police officers, who were on duty primarily to defend republicans against possible loyalist violence, seven artistes in RUC uniform came onstage singing: 'We are, we are, we are the rebel boys. We are, we are, we are the Trimble boys.'*

Introduced by a chief constable in an Orange collarette, they included Constable Baton, Constable Shoot To Kill and Constable Collusion†, all of whom were presented with a collarette and bowler. Since Sinn Féin hates the efforts the RUC make to get close to nationalist communities and to visit Catholic schools, the maximum venom was reserved for Constable Ever So Nice, who throughout the masque kept his hand over the mouth of a small squirming boy over whose head he tried to thrust an Orange collarette. The tiny patriot then struck him and, to the cheers of the crowd, broke away to freedom. It was an image with huge resonance in the Catholic community: Patrick Pearse, the leader of the 1916 Easter Rising, was the nationalist writer who most successfully incorporated into nationalist iconography the image of the defiant young boy who will face any trial, even death, for the sake of Ireland.

Over the next few months the anti-Orange propaganda fed off the rising sectarian tensions. Loyalists followed the republican lead in instigating boycotts in villages they controlled. Apart from those who welcomed the boycotts, there were many people in both communities intimidated against their will into participating, and many more who were ethically torn. For the customer who joined a boycott for fear of the local loyalist or republican thugs who hung around the shop in question, the issue was simply one of physical courage; in small communities, few people were

---

* A parody of the viciously sectarian Glasgow Orange song: 'We are the Billy Boys.'

† It is an article of faith with the republican movement that the RUC colludes with what it terms 'loyalist death-squads'. While some members of the security forces have certainly helped loyalists to target members of the IRA, the vast majority are as opposed to loyalist as to republican terrorism. However, the supremacist strain in the republican psyche believes that unionists are the stooges of the British government and loyalist paramilitaries but the instruments of the security forces. That is why, for instance, *The Committee*, a preposterous book by Sean MacPhilemy (which for libel reasons could not be published in Ireland or the United Kingdom), which alleges – on the evidence of one man who has since recanted – that loyalist godfathers including Billy Wright were controlled by a sixty-strong committee which included members of the security forces, Orangemen and unionists, is accepted as revealed truth by republican conspiracy-theorists and dismissed as a pack of lies by everyone else.

prepared to risk being assaulted or burned out. 'I understand that many of my Roman Catholic customers are afraid to come into my shop,' said one Orangeman to me. 'And I'm pleased to say some of them have phoned me to tell me that. Though of course some of them blame me for Drumcree.' But there were ethical problems too. What would you do, for instance, if your butcher was Catholic, but a local Protestant butcher faced ruin because of a nationalist boycott? It was a question I raised with several Orangemen. The Reverend William Bingham and his wife Janet spoke for many of them when they agreed they would stick with the Catholic butcher, fill up their freezer in the Protestant shop and eat more meat.

In addition to arson attacks on churches and Orange Halls, there was the near-destruction of Brownlow House, the headquarters of the peace-able Royal Black Institution. (The statement issued by its Imperial Grand Registrar at the end of August, prior to the Black's big day, the 'Last Saturday', was typical of its style: 'It is my earnest wish that our pro-cessions should go off in the fashion in which they have always done, namely in a peaceful manner. This is notwithstanding the fact that we have had a very provocative attack on our headquarters. It is my earnest desire that this institution does not do anything that would bring it into discredit.')

Another ugly sectarian manifestation came with the appearance of loyalist pickets outside Catholic churches in County Antrim on Saturday evenings* designed to intimidate mass-goers in mainly Protestant villages in revenge for the blocking of parades in nearby Catholic villages. Spear-headed by members of Ian Paisley's DUP, it had nothing to do with the Orange Order officially. The County Grand Master issued a statement saying that the County Antrim Grand Orange Lodge was committed to the principle of civil and religious liberty for everyone, 'utterly condemns the demonstrations outside Roman Catholic chapels and calls for mutual tolerance in our divided society'. But a few collarettes (Orange and Independent Orange) were seen here and there and the loyal institutions became guilty by association.

Like many others who were already worrying about Drumcree 1997, I was greatly troubled in the autumn of 1996 by the air of drift that characterized most of the Orange leadership. I was sitting one night in the house of Brian Kennaway listening to him, Denis Watson (the County

---

*   The Sabbatarianism of fundamentalist Protestants ruled out Sunday pickets.

Armagh Grand Master) and three others talking internal Orange politics. It was a couple of months after Drumcree. The politics were interesting but I started to get impatient when my companions began to disagree with each other on what seemed to me to be seriously unimportant issues compared to those of the forthcoming Grand Lodge elections and future strategy on parades.

Probably as a result of having heard over the preceding year or two so many sermons full of vivid biblical imagery I suddenly was inspired with a parable arising from an argument I'd had with a friend with whom I had stayed in the Welsh countryside the previous year. 'I love sheep,' I had said idly to Stephen. 'They're so soothing and undemanding.' Stephen looked at me aghast. 'I hate them. Their intense stupidity gets deeply on my nerves.' 'But surely that's half their charm,' said I. 'Not when it is taken to their level,' said Stephen. He waved out the window. 'Over there beside the beach there's a field with sheep in it. Sometimes a sheep gets through the fence and stands on the beach gazing vacantly into the middle distance. Time passes and the tide begins to roll in. The sheep doesn't move. Even when the water reaches its feet, the creature continues to gaze vacantly into the middle distance. The water slowly rises up his legs. Then, very quickly after it reaches his stomach, the sheep becomes waterlogged and is borne out to sea. At this stage he wakes up and you can hear him disappearing into the distance wailing: "maaa, maaa, maaa". I hate them.'

That, I said, is what the Orange Order reminds me of these days.

I'm not claiming this story had any dramatic effect, since the people in the room were of the intelligent, modernizing, communicating tendency and well in tune with reality and they just laughed. But it's not an unfair depiction of an awful lot of nice, decent Orangemen who think that you can win a war simply by standing your ground and ignoring the enemy sneaking up behind you.

17

The Road to Drumcree Three: William Bingham's Story

Among the Orangemen who had been horrified at seeing their community descend into lawlessness were Denis Watson and the Reverend William Bingham, from late 1996 Grand Master and Grand Chaplain respectively of County Armagh. William Bingham talked to me after Drumcree Three.

I was on holiday in '95 over the Twelfth in France and I had no idea what was happening at Drumcree. I'd listened to Radio 4 and heard Martin Smyth being interviewed about this stand-off situation and heard about thousands of Protestants arriving at Drumcree to be addressed by politicians on the platform. And then we'd heard how they'd come through the road and they'd got through fairly peacefully and apart from large crowds attending to protest, there didn't seem to be anything that would really make you feel that the situation was getting out of control or afraid, even, for the next year. But my involvement was very little after that.

Portadown District had really carried '95 themselves: I think probably the county had been mildly criticized for not helping them out, but I was a district officer, not a county officer. And '96 then came and of course that was the big one. The parade was banned by the RUC and I shared a great feeling of an injustice done towards our community – specifically to the Orangemen at Portadown – and felt that one needed to identify with them in their struggle to maintain their civil rights.

It was a much bigger issue than just Drumcree; it was really significant symbolically for the whole of Northern Ireland. We'd been continually having things forced upon us as a community: the Anglo-Irish Agreement, the Downing Street Declaration, the Framework Document – and all, we felt, were eroding our constitutional position within Northern Ireland. And we've always said if our constitutional position is eroded, then our rights would begin to be tampered with as well, and here we were in that situation – exactly as people had said. It was another step down the line to the erosion of people's civil liberties and to the destruction of the Orange culture in Northern Ireland.

So we felt it was a government attempt – a political decision – to smash Orangeism and take on the Orange Order, the biggest mass movement of Protestants in Ulster. And for that reason, to the total mystification and surprise of the police and the government, the Portadown Orangemen got overwhelming support.

For most of the time at Portadown things were very peaceful. Other things were happening elsewhere, but actually at Drumcree and at Porta-down, where I spent most of the week, people were coming in their thousands parading in lodges and demonstrating, walking up to the lines, and there was a kind of family atmosphere most of the evenings. It was a bit of a carnival there and there were mothers and fathers there with their children – five, six, seven, eight years of age. It was very peaceful: that's all I can say.

There were times then when tempers did get up and things got quite nasty during the day. I can remember standing down at the police lines trying to keep a little bit of order. And the torrent of abuse that was coming against the RUC I found offensive myself. I felt that the folk whose rights I'm seeking to defend are undermining their position; they're actually doing us a lot of harm by their attitude towards the legal forces of the country. I can remember one young policeman who was recognized by the crowd as being originally from Portadown. He was in the front line and I asked the guys to refrain from the language that they were using, but just got a real torrent of abuse. I asked if the young fellow could be removed from the lines, but the police refused to do that. So for an hour I made myself as big as I could and stood in front of the young man so that he was hidden from view, until after an hour or so he was taken off.

And then there were other insults hurled at the police. One person that recognized me as someone that buried members of the RUC said: 'You didn't bury half enough,' which I found grossly offensive. Then he turned on them and said that they were a disgrace for not identifying with the Orange Order and should go home.

There were a number of these people wearing collarettes – no doubt about that – but most of them were outsiders. But at the same time, if you call people on to the streets and call people to protest you cannot abdicate responsibility. So I think there were mixed emotions. There was the feeling of great frustration and of anger that here a walk home from a church service that had taken place for almost two hundred years was being denied. That a group of people who we believed were (at least manipulated by) Sinn Féin were able to stand and to block a legal parade. And that these folk who were just purely anti-Orange had had grievances that they had brought to our attention – things like flute bands and music being played up and down their street, Paisley and Trimble doing their dance, medals being struck; all those things we felt we'd dealt with. There was no music being played, no flute bands taking part and not even the sound of the drum. People would just walk down the road; in fifteen minutes it would be all over. No matter what we had done, whatever compromises we had made, there seemed to be this adamancy that there was no toleration of Protestant culture here in Portadown.

We were being told to be the tolerant people. Now to me, tolerance is accepting things that you don't like. We all tolerate or accept things that we do like. But tolerance is actually showing acceptance of things that you don't like. So in actual fact the ones who were being intolerant were the nationalist group on the Garvaghy Road, because no matter what we'd have done they were not willing to accept us.

So that was one side of the feeling. The other side of it was a deep sense of wonder and bewilderment and fear for our own community in the way that many were responding to the police and the attitude to the security forces that day. I'd always been brought up to respect law and order and to believe as a Christian in Romans 12, which clearly states that the government has a God-given responsibility to bring laws and we have the God-given responsibility to respect those who are in authority over us; at the end of the day no matter what one thinks of the RUC, there's no alternative to them. They're what stands between this community and anarchy; and though we may want changes, though we may not be happy with the way they're going at times, we have no credible alternative. Therefore you just cannot willy-nilly say: 'Smash the RUC.' That's just not on.

So there was this real upset in my mind that folk were actually playing into the hands of the Provisional IRA by attacking the police force. Here were unionists taking on the crown which we were seeking to defend, taking on the government of our country. I began to think that the Provos were probably the only ones that were very happy at this particular time. And I think as we did walk down the Garvaghy Road – although I didn't walk down the Garvaghy Road – there was a hollowness in the victory. There was the violence throughout the whole of the country – well, we've had violence for years, there's nothing new in that – but there was something, something in the back of many Orangemen's minds that felt we had walked into a trap, that we had actually given the Provisionals a propaganda victory.

So after that I felt that, if I was involved in the institution, a number of things had to be looked at. First was how Orangemen respond to crises. In my view, it's a Christian organization and there are certain Christian parameters outside which we cannot step and within which the organization has to operate. That was the fundamental one.

The second one was that for too long we had danced to the tune of the Provos and perhaps had blindly walked into their traps; we needed to be much more aware of their strategy and have a counter-strategy to that. And I suppose the third thing was the stability of the whole country. It wasn't in our interests to have the country up in turmoil. We wanted to prove to people in the world that Northern Ireland works, whereas the Provos wanted to prove it didn't, which was how it looked when in '96 the country was brought to its knees. And together with that was also the sense of injustice towards our people – our people, who are pushed and shoved and battered about and alienated, and when alienated, they will react. So there was a mixture of emotions.

So after '96, I suppose County Armagh officers felt the most important thing was to work alongside Portadown District. Portadown District were the crucial folk. It was a problem that had been created by nationalists, but it was a problem that was going to be addressed by Portadown District and though Portadown District itself could work out how to proceed in the future, our view was that the bottom line was that the parade had to go ahead in '97. There was no question about that: it was a civil right and that right was unnegotiable.

However, we did feel that in the exercising of our rights we had certain responsibilities to face up to and that your rights are not *carte blanche*: you have to exercise those rights in the way that is seen to be responsible. I'm not saying that was a departure or a new way of thinking but I'm just saying that we brought a greater emphasis to that way from the end of '96 onwards.

There also began then a process which we felt was necessary: one of educating people as to what the institution was about. We felt there was no end to who had to be educated. Here was an organization which in '96 had been portrayed as being bigoted, as being militant, as an organization that was bringing Northern Ireland to its knees. So we felt, well, we've been maligned, we've been the target of much criticism, but we haven't really addressed the criticism.

So we targeted Britain specifically: the media there, as well as people in government and others with influence, needed to hear our side of the story. We targeted the United States of America as best we could and we targeted the Republic of Ireland as well. We felt the Republic had been our traditional enemies – and we still feel that they are our enemies in actual fact – but we felt that they had acted so irresponsibly that they needed to be told what we were about. That way, if they ever did the same again, we could always say, 'Well, we told you what we're about and the difficulties we faced and that if you poured fuel on the fire again this time it wouldn't be from a position of ignorance but from one which you hold responsibility for.' We had a lot of help from some sympathetic outsiders who helped clarify our position, especially as far as the Residents' Coalition was concerned.

There was no doubt that the big push after Drumcree '96 was to get the two sides together and get an agreement so everything would go well in '97. There had been an abortive attempt to do something like that in the Carpetmills factory during the crisis of '96, when some Orangemen had agreed to proximity talks with the church leaders and a group from Garvaghy Road which would not include Brendan McKenna [Breandán MacCionnaith]. Now Brendan McKenna remained throughout the whole time as a stumbling-block in this process of seeking consensus or agreement. Basically, he insisted from day one that he would be involved in everything to do with the Garvaghy Road, and the Orangemen in Portadown justifiably felt they didn't want to sit down beside someone who had a terrorist conviction and had been involved in an attempt to blow up part of the town in which they lived. Why should such a person, who had shown hatred towards the people and the town of Portadown, have more influence in the town? Surely he should have less. So at no stage and at no time did we ever meet with him or did we ever seek to meet with him. Portadown District, and I share their feeling, felt that he was not a person that we could do business with.

At the time we were criticized for that, because it was the perception of many people that the Orange institution had dealt with Billy Wright; certainly his name was not a name that many folk thought was divorced from terrorism. Our point all along was that at no time did the Orange Order have dealings with Billy Wright. Certainly at no time have I or Denis Watson ever met Billy Wright; nor did I ever feel that he had something to say to this community. At Drumcree in '96 I was not aware that David Trimble had been involved in talks with him. He was not involved directly or as far as I know indirectly with the Orange Order's position at Drumcree, so therefore I felt very clear of conscience not meeting Brendan McKenna on the same basis that I wouldn't meet with Billy Wright.

We did feel that this group was Sinn Féin-orientated and that McKenna had Sinn Féin connections, although he had denied it – said he'd walked away from that. But the longer that talks about talks were drawn out and we didn't see any willingness on their part to meet with us, we felt that the Residents' Coalition agenda – at least McKenna's agenda – was political. It was my view that at all costs McKenna wanted the Orange parade forced down the Garvaghy Road; he wanted the world to have pictures of the police battering the nationalist community off the road to let Orangemen through. His second choice would have been to have the parade banned but have the Orange Order face down the security forces and maybe even burst their way through on to Garvaghy Road.

We decided that since it was a civil right, the right to walk was not negotiable, but that we had a responsibility to at least listen to those of different opinions and take on board maybe things that they felt were genuine grievances that we hadn't seen from the other side of the fence. Although we did try to talk to members of the coalition, agreement was never forthcoming because of McKenna: 'You meet no one if I'm not there,' was his position.

So we had to by-pass the coalition. We talked to some of the Roman Catholic clergy on the route and we talked to some folk who lived there; they said that their main problems had been the fact that their community seemed to be under siege by the security forces. Our reaction was that would not be the case if you agreed to peaceful and legal protest and we have a legal and peaceful procession and then a limited amount of police would do. I said we looked forward to the day when a traffic warden could lead the parade down the town; it wasn't us who wanted thousands of police. I said as well that for their part, they had to face up to their responsibilities for bringing this situation about as we were willing to face up to ours. I think they hadn't thought about that before. I think they had felt this heavy police presence was something we had demanded and wanted.

Other things were the dance that Ian Paisley and David Trimble had taken part in after '95. They felt that was rubbing salt into the wound. And I didn't excuse that, but I said that, trying to understand that, one has to realize that whenever people are under a tremendous amount of pressure, when that pressure is lifted euphoria is a natural reaction. I quoted examples in Pomeroy where I live: the nationalist residents' group had blocked the road for an Orange parade and for a while we weren't sure what we were going to do. When finally we turned and walked away there was great euphoria, clapping and cheering and cat-calling at us. Or in more recent times, in England, there was criticism that when the news came through in the Louise Woodward trial case that the judge had let her off, the whole display in the village pub was cheering and clapping and that this was brilliant. And then people misunderstood their euphoria, and said: 'Well, you shouldn't be like that because a baby's dead.'

Well, in the cool light of day, yes, maybe that was wrong. But if your emotions are so entwined on a little girl of nineteen you feel is entirely innocent and suddenly she's been released from prison, your tendency is to put your hands up in euphoria. So I think that played a big thing in Paisley and Trimble doing that. I don't think that should be harped on. It should be set in the context of the sense of relief that this was all over: that was the context people have got to understand. It wouldn't have been the way I'd have planned it, but it happened and I understand why. But I also understand the perception taken by the Catholic community that it was an offence to them. But it definitely wasn't done in that spirit. And definitely anyone who was there would tell you that.

Another thing they thought had been an offence to them was the striking of the medals – the misspelt medals. Yet that was purely a fund-raising thing, not even organized by Portadown Orangemen but just by a few. The other thing was the feeling that they couldn't get to their own place of worship, their chapel, for mass. I could identify with them: I just would not want my congregation being prevented from going to worship on a Sunday morning. That was something that needed to be looked at.

And the other thing – and I think this was a very big one for them – which wasn't anything that we as an institution could do anything about was long-term grievances within Portadown, in terms of fair employment, in terms of people working and maybe finding it difficult coming up to the top because they worked in a Protestant factory and there were union flags being draped over their looms and things. And feeling that their young people couldn't go into the village or the town centre without fear. And also the fact that the St Patrick's Day parade to a chapel had been blocked. They were saying: 'We're not treated with equity here.' And the fact that there were so many loyalist parades and Orange parades in Portadown.

So when we sat down to analyse that, the point we made was that they'd grossly over-stated the number of parades in Portadown. Yes, there were quite a number of parades, but in actual fact as Orange Order parades go, you could count with the fingers of one hand the number of parades in a year. There were many band parades and other parades – British Legion parades that you have in England, Boys' Brigade parades that you have in England, youth organization parades as you have in England – but those are on a Sunday afternoon, most of them, and go to places of worship. There shouldn't really have been a problem with commerce or traffic because of that.

There was also the issue then of employment and unemployment and the point that we were making was that throughout Northern Ireland unemployment has affected all communities and every community has suffered from unemployment. And we felt that if they had cases of unfair partiality towards Protestants, there were proper courses to take and bodies set up to deal with that, and that was the way they should go, not blaming the Orange Order at Drumcree because of that.

And then there's the whole area of the use of the town, and having their own parades and the young people going into the town. And yes, above all else, I want to see a Northern Ireland where people have learned to accept and live with their differences. I want a culture that's diverse, which everybody has the right to express in a proper way – an ordered and dignified way. And within Portadown, there's a lot of work to be done at that level in building up trust within the community. The Orange Order can play a part in that, but it's only a small part in a bigger picture; it cannot be blamed for all that is wrong in Portadown, just as I don't blame all nationalists for all that was wrong in Portadown and Northern Ireland. These are issues that they'll have to address long-term, but are not solved over Drumcree.

So that was how we addressed them. We admitted faults in the past: we admitted that there were times things had gone wrong. But we also said to them that they had to ask the question why twenty years ago there were many, many Protestants living in the Garvaghy Road but now there are very few. They had to address questions like why a UDR man, for example, who had taken children to school regularly in his car, was told one night not to bother in the morning and they would arrange their own transport. And when he went into the car the next morning he was blown to pieces. There were serious questions that they had to address. They had to address the movement of Protestants out that area because of fear and intimidation and why that happened. And why in actual fact they talked of mutual respect and toleration and parity of esteem, when in fact a lot of the signals to Protestants were completely the opposite. That's a big question for anyone to address.

These were people who I would call reasonable-minded people and I think they were prepared to address these things. But I think they are issues that their wider community needs to address.

Denis and I had little or no contact with the Garvaghy Road Residents' Group apart from a meal to which we'd been invited to meet Father Eamon Stack and Sister Laura Boyle.* I had been asked there to talk about my faith, about how I became a Christian and why I was involved in the Orange Order, so that they might have a better understanding of it. There were some within our own side who saw that as us going to make a deal with Eamon Stack over Drumcree, when in actual fact neither he nor I was willing to do so. In fact it was very clearly stipulated by them that they weren't going to discuss making deals over the Garvaghy Road; obviously they felt that they had no freedom to do that.

I just think that from their backgrounds they had obviously no under-standing of the Ulster Protestant. To me these people were a hindrance to the whole situation; by the time I left them I thought they didn't want an Orangeman on the face of the world. I think their perception is that the Orange is a bunch of bigoted men that want to walk over Catholics and keep them down. It never was that, but as we go on into the new millennium, it's even less credible to say that. To think that any group in society can do that, even if they wanted to, it's just totally ridiculous.

They were annoyed when the dinner party was made public.† And I had difficulties about that. But the problem was that McKenna kept saying: 'The Orangemen will not talk to any of us.' We were sick to death listening to that man, so we were, knowing that he was just being economical with the truth.

And then we had to deal with folk who would say to even talk or educate is negotiation. I think you once, Ruth, said that the Ulster Prot-estant feels that because he's right he doesn't have to explain it to anyone

---

* Among the reasons Father Stack gave in the *Irish Times* on 27 May 1997 why 'No one on the Garvaghy Road wants this parade' (he had forgotten the Protestants at the bottom of the road), was that, 'It expresses a permanent socio-economic imbalance in the town, where nationalists are four times more likely to be unemployed.' That baffling observation turned out to be related to clothes. As Sister Laura Boyle explained to one Orangeman, poor residents were offended by the Orangemen's suits. Apart from the fact that most Orangemen wear cheap suits, as Orangeman Richard Whitten pointed out in the *Belfast Telegraph* on 8 July, this criticism 'displays a gross ignorance of the mind-set of the Ulster Protestant, who demonstrates his respect for God in the form of his dress'.

† Denis Watson referred to the dinner in a radio interview.

and I think that could be true. But I think there's a dawning realization among Orangemen and among any unionist people that perhaps we've sat back for too long on that basis and now it's time to explain to the world what we are. And if you believe in Orangeism, if you're committed to the principles of Orangeism, if you're an evangelical Christian, part of your evangelical faith is that you take it out and share it with people: you're not evangelical unless you're doing that.

I would have to say that the majority of our own people did not want a re-run of 1996. If hardy came to hardy, I would say they would be prepared to be there again. But a lot of folk were saying, 'Look, we just can't have this every year. We can't have our country destabilized. We need to come to some situation where our rights are maintained. Yes, the parade must go ahead, but make sure every effort is made to show that if it doesn't happen, it's not because the Orange Order haven't tried.' And many people out there prayed and prayed for months that it would never happen again. Ulster Protestants are law-keepers, not law-breakers. They're loyal to the crown forces; they don't want to be opposed to them. They want to remain part of all that is British and retain that British identity and not be seen as anarchists within society. So that was the solid base that we had to work upon.

The institution, like any mass organization, is diverse. Within it there are people from different denominations, different political parties, different social and economic backgrounds. That can be its strength as well as its weakness. But that's the reality of it. There were those who I felt were not listening carefully enough to what was being said by us and for months would continually talk about secret deals being made behind closed doors and secret meetings. And when July came, it was proved to all that there were no secret deals being made or had been made.

As we had said right from the beginning, as far as we were concerned it was Portadown District's ultimate decision. Whatever course of action they would take or whatever route they wanted to take or whatever strategy they wanted to develop, at no time would Denis Watson or William Bingham attempt to force anything on them. But we did ask them to look harder at their strategy and look harder at how they were going to face '97 and at the education process. And out of that came the letter to the residents and all those kind of initiatives.

While we might have been the prime movers within that it certainly was not done at any time without the consent of Portadown District behind us. But we had folk who were outside of the area saying, 'We demand this, that or the other. What's going on?'

What right had they to know? It was a Portadown District matter. It's County Armagh. And that was important. We were keeping within the parameters of Grand Lodge policy as well as County Armagh and Portadown District.

It was also my view that there were those extremists on both sides, who, when they looked over the precipice in '96, liked what they saw and were quite prepared to bring our country to another '96 in '97, if not worse. And we were continually aware – and I talk about extremes without the Orange Order on this – that it was in the interests of both the Provisional side and the maverick loyalist side to further great sectarian division within Northern Ireland. My view was that the mainstream people of Northern Ireland – folk who when they saw over the precipice didn't like it – had to take a stand against this at whatever cost: we should not allow ourselves to be shaped and moulded by extremists and play into their hands. And my fear was that there would be some who, maybe unintentionally, could have done just that.

With regard to the Orange Order as an institution, I can only say that we had massive support throughout the province for all that we tried to do. Massive support from without the Orange Order as well. And, yes, sure we made mistakes along the road, but if I were doing it all over again – which I hope I never have to do – there would be very little that I would change.

That's the background.

Now, there were certain groups that we felt we had to have lines of communication opened up with: the RUC, the government, the Secretary of State, the wider government at Westminster and obviously our own people – those who were the main players in this whole thing. Church leaders also were important. Let's deal with them first.

After '96, Cardinal Daly had retired and was replaced by Archbishop Brady. The feeling that we got was that the Roman Catholic Church felt they'd got their fingers burnt in '96. Daly certainly seemed to be bitter the way things had worked out. And they seemed to be very reluctant, very reluctant, to get involved in the thing and certainly at no time met with us or wanted to meet with us to discuss the problem. Archbishop Brady had been written to by the Orange Order over another matter and they're still awaiting his reply. We had pushed through Archbishop Eames [of the Church of Ireland] to try and set a meeting up but we didn't push the issue too hard. If Archbishop Brady felt like that, he felt like that.

Archbishop Eames has been maligned by our community over his ecumenism and for his failure at times to stand up for the Ulster Protestant. All I could say is that any time I met with Lord Eames, although he too had had his fingers burnt in '96, he was most courteous towards us, most accommodating and willing to listen, met with County and with Portadown District officers and offered all the help he could. But he had been so maligned by the Residents' Coalition, who seemed to think he'd acted with the Northern Ireland Office to get the parade through, that he felt that even if we had agreed to have a go-between, it was likely he wouldn't have been regarded by them as an impartial chairperson or somebody who was uninvolved.

The Presbyterian Moderator was a Portadown man, Harold Allen, and he was most helpful; we felt that anything he could do he would be willing to do. He had meetings with some Portadown Orangemen, expressed his concerns, his views and his ideas and the way forward and certainly he also took with him wherever he went the sense of why Drumcree happened – the feeling of the Ulster Protestant and the Orangeman on how they had felt that they had been pushed and pushed and shoved and that this had happened too often and that governments had to listen to what they were saying.

So we felt that although not an Orangeman, he at least understood our position, had a degree of sympathy towards us and also as a Christian man wanted to see what way '97 could go in a peaceful way: I give him great praise. We didn't really meet the Methodist president: the Moderator and the Archbishop were the main players from the Protestants' point of view; and we were aware they would be keeping him updated. But though from November on we saw a lot of them, it became increasingly obvious that church leaders were not going to be as significant in '97 as in '96.

Then we had the government side in all this and along the line, in May, we had a new government. The civil servants stayed the same, and Sir Patrick Mayhew was replaced by Mo Mowlam. We had two meetings with Sir Patrick Mayhew: the first in the January and the second in March. The message from Sir Patrick was: 'Sit down and talk with the residents.' But I think he realized the difficulties that were there with McKenna.

We did find him slightly distant in his approach to us, which is maybe understandable after the summer he had in '96. He hadn't too many nights' sleep in the first week of July. He was the kind of guy that rarely if ever would have opened his heart and you wondered what he really was thinking. There was a feeling towards March (dare I say it?) that the Tories were on their way out, he was going anyway and wouldn't have July '97 to worry about to the extent that he did in '96. I think he was resigned to knowing that someone else was going to have to deal with it and therefore he was needed much more in England canvassing in the Tory cause.

And then Mo Mowlam came on scene and was totally different in her approach to people. She had immense interpersonal skills and I think when the Residents' Coalition blamed her for going against them or going back on promises, I think it was because they probably had misread her approachableness for being on their side. Because I remember the first time we met her in Hillsborough Castle, she was just totally different to Sir Patrick Mayhew. She sat down in the chair. She'd been receiving chemotherapy and the wig was itching and she took it off, sat it down beside her and sat down to crackers and cheese and talked away. There was a refreshing difference about her, but at the same time, we never for a moment believed necessarily that she was on our side. We felt that she was the kind of person that could sit down with anybody and make them feel at home, make them feel at ease, make them feel that she was with them whether she was or not.

As I said to Denis afterwards, she's probably as happy with us with the cup of coffee as she is across the road with a pint in her hand with somebody else. Which is fair enough. And it's been to her advantage at times, but long-term it might not be to her advantage. Because a person who is like that, when it comes to asserting authority, sometimes it's not easy to do it because of that.

She basically said from day one that she was going to throw her whole self – those were her words: 'I will throw my whole self into this process and I will do what I can to bring about a resolution to this problem in Drumcree.' And she certainly did and in no time at all she was meeting people left, right and centre all over the place. She was being very closely guided by her Northern Ireland officials both in Belfast and in London and I think the most frustrating thing for us was that they were always concerned with balance: everything had to be balanced. Whether something was right or wrong, she had to get somewhere in the middle all the time.

For example, we were called to meet her in Hillsborough one night – asked at five o'clock to be with her at half seven. Now we didn't realize that her agenda for the next day was to go around all the residents' groups, on the day of the council elections or the day before. And we were sitting with her in Hillsborough and she said: 'Actually, I'm meeting the residents' groups tomorrow.' And then the significance dawned on us: that was why we were sitting there. And well, we thought, we've been used here. And sure enough in the morning, it said on the news that she'd met with representatives of County Armagh Orange in Hillsborough and now she was off to meet the residents' groups. Throughout there was that kind of balancing thing, even right down to the wire in July when the decision was made. In her statement she went against them and she went against us. But she'd actually said to us that we had made a genuine effort this year – but that was lost in the balancing act.

That happened throughout the whole political process: everything had to be worded to accommodate both sides. Principles seemed to be less important than balance. At least that was my view. I wouldn't want to be too hard on her either, because she was very open. If we wanted a meeting, we could have had a meeting within twenty-four to forty-eight hours. She was very, very good that way.

I can remember on one occasion very close to Drumcree – a propos the proximity talks that hadn't worked, never could have worked – we discussed what would be the wider implications for the community if the government seriously addressed some of our issues as Orangemen; then maybe it might be possible to look at Drumcree in a new light.

On the phone I told her that I had met with Portadown District last night and that we had four proposals to bring to her: 'You can come in two-and-a-half hours,' she said. On the way to Hillsborough Castle we stopped – we were a wee bit early – and I said we should buy her an ice-cream. We saw one called 'Orange Crunch' so we thought we'd better have three tubs of that.

We went into Hillsborough through the security gates, pulled up at the front door and rang the door bell. It was a lovely warm summer's day, and there was no reply. We went to the side door: no reply. We went back to the front door, turned the handle, walked into the entrance hall and let a few shouts out of us to see if anybody was about. There was nobody and I had landed Denis with ice-cream which was now beginning to melt and spill over the floor.

So we went through the corridor into where the Queen's Dining Room is, and again, we could find nobody and the ice-cream was melting all over the place and Denis was getting quite frustrated, as you can imagine only Denis can get. And so we went out of the castle again and looked around us, saw a security man, called him and said, 'You're going to have take us to where the Secretary of State is.' So eventually we made our way up to her suite of apartments and found her and shared our ice-cream and we put forward our proposals. First was that the Public Order Order would be repealed; that the principle of traditionality would be enshrined with regard to traditional church parades; and that the Parades Commission would actually be disbanded, since it had been set up at the behest of nationalists reacting to '96, was very anti-Orange and really went back to the 1850s and 1860s legislation.

Second, we said that there were other aspects of cultural identity that people found difficult. We especially mentioned the GAA – not that there was anything wrong with people playing Gaelic sport and not in any sense would we want restrictions put upon people playing sport – but the GAA are not seen by Protestants as a purely sporting organization: there are politics behind it. That was seen very clearly at the time of the hunger-strikes when the GAA was heavily involved in organizing and orchestrating protests and in its law that said that members of the security forces could not participate. And you can see it in the cavalcades of cars that precede Gaelic matches, with tricolours waving through villages that are Protestant as well as Catholic, sounding their horns and playing rebel music through loud-speakers. We were saying that these were processions just as much as Orange processions.

The third thing was our request that freedom of assembly would be enshrined in the Bill of Rights which the Labour Party had committed themselves to in their manifesto.

The last one was obviously a very big one: that the Anglo-Irish Agreement, which many people had felt had been the big step in the erosion of our rights, be put to the people of Northern Ireland to decide what to do with it, in the same way that Scotland and Wales were being given the right in a future referendum to decide their constitutional position.

And I think if Portadown District had got all those, which we felt were not really even negotiating positions, but were ours by right anyway, I think Protestants would have felt that no longer was Drumcree the last stand.

So she promised. Well, let's say she said that one, two and three were possible, but four absolutely wasn't possible. We left it at that in order to address these issues, that she should in actual fact come and address the Portadown District officers, which, again was a big decision for her to make. She had addressed on numerous occasions the Garvaghy Road

Residents' Coalition, but she hadn't addressed Portadown District.

So having put those points to her, a meeting was set up on Friday 27th June, nine days before Drumcree. We had several meetings that day, the big press conference at tea-time and then the meeting with Portadown District where we informed them they should have their entire district at Brownlow House in Lurgan at, I think, 10.30 that night. For security reasons, we wouldn't tell them who else to expect.

Then a meeting of officers took place with myself and Denis and we told them Jim Molyneaux would be coming and so would Mo and that she would speak and then take questions. 'She is a representative of Her Majesty's government, who should be treated with respect and courtesy,' I said. Not that I had any fear that they wouldn't do that.

When she arrived she received a standing ovation. Then they sat down and she addressed the gathered brethren with regard to the issues that they had brought via us to her and about her commitment to civil rights and liberties for people. And she also said she thought it was an IRA strategy to destabilize Northern Ireland, and that we shouldn't be walking into the traps. Then there were a series of questions from the floor and she answered them very well. She was very professional. In fact I think she did superbly well coming into that situation.

The big issue in everybody's mind including my own was: 'It's OK to have promises. Let's see the reality.' And like many Protestants in the past, Portadown District felt that nothing was ever guaranteed by politicians: they were expedient, they were pragmatic and just concerned to get the crisis over. That was very much the feeling of the meeting. Yet she listened to what Portadown men had to say. They were courteous but passionate and said: 'Promises are promises. We want reality.'

At the end she left to a standing ovation, but also to a realization among Orangemen that not now, not ever, would their rights be enshrined into law. And therefore they couldn't enter into an arrangement with the government. They couldn't trust the government.

She had promised, for example, that the right of procession would be enshrined in law – but with the qualification that that did not mean that every year they would go down the Garvaghy Road. That was not really much of a help, so it wasn't. She promised that the Parades Commission would be looked at, and that she couldn't give any promises on the Anglo-Irish Agreement. And the Public Order Order thing on tra-ditionality she promised would be enshrined. My recollection is that she gave no specific commitment on the GAA.

So that was the history of our links with the Secretary of State, who did try very hard. And although she was coming in afresh, she was going in as a stranger into a strange land and in many ways – though she never fully grasped the whole picture as we would see it – she did try very hard. And I think whenever she was accused by the Coalition of going back on her word, of not going down to tell them her decision, I think they've got to understand that that was the decision she had to make because of security reasons. Her promise to them had been sheer naivety, but it was typical of her openness at that stage: 'I will do anything and everything.'

I've heard people say that Harold said that he would walk down the road alone even if everyone else agreed to be re-routed. Certainly when Harold spoke at that meeting he very clearly demonstrated the commitment of Portadown Orangemen to walk down Garvaghy Road from church. Harold would have been at the most significant meetings with Mo, not at the peripheral ones. Denis and I probably attended around ten.

Now, the proximity talks in Hillsbrough in mid-June: a last-ditch attempt by the government to get representatives of the Coalition and representatives of Portadown District and County Armagh together, though not to meet face-to-face. The Secretary of State would be there with her advisers, along with the Chief Constable and the chairperson of the Parades Commission.

We agreed and attended and put forward the ten concessions we were offering. Once again a very simple message came from the Garvaghy Road: no parade down this road; no parade; no parade. There was just no ground on which we could reach consensus no matter what we did.

I think that the proximity talks exposed them, showed that eventually they had nothing to offer. The compromise that they were asking for was no compromise. It was asking for the Orange Order to give them all that they wanted. So the talks broke up in the afternoon. Again – and it'll show you the difference between the two groups – we just did not want publicity. Not that we were unwilling in principle to go on the media, but we believed that talking in public put on extra pressure that only acted to harden rather than soften positions; people hanged themselves on hooks they couldn't get off. Therefore we tended to talk to the media much less than they did.

So before the Hillsborough talks, for example, we said that we were not willing to run the media gauntlet. We went in the back way, believing that McKenna was to do the same. But he refused: 'I'm not going in the back door. I'm going in the front door.' And then of course he addressed the media. At one stage we thought that this man was just media-crazy, but in actual fact his whole strategy was a propaganda thing.

The closer it got to Drumcree and the more pressure we exerted on him, the more his true colours came out. At one stage he was just talking pure republican language – comparing Orangemen to child-abusers – and yet the Garvaghy Road Coalition was supposed to be cross-community. I think we did put him under pressure. Certainly the letter that we sent out to all the Garvaghy Road residents explaining our position put him on the back foot. I think then more people began to realize that McKenna – who if you like had used '96 so well and had so cleverly demonized the Orange Order – was actually not just the innocent man who wanted to secure the rights of Catholics in the Garvaghy Road but someone with a much bigger agenda.

That is certainly the pragmatic argument for talking to people like him. But there are principles and there is pragmatism. Not that the two are opposites, but the principle of not talking to unrepentant terrorists is a principle that we have in Portadown District and one which I think the Orange Order should stick to: it boils down to the fact that you're negotiating your rights with somebody who has an antipathy towards your rights.

The American constituency was one that we didn't sufficiently address, but we certainly attempted to get our side across to their diplomats in the United Kingdom.

Another constituency we had to address was the wider British government and the British public. We thought it was important to meet with any Labour MPs who would take an interest in Northern Ireland. It became apparent to us how little knowledge had even the MPs who were supposed to be interested and just how many didn't want to be bothered with it. Though there have been two governments that have made Northern Ireland a top priority, a lot of MPs just didn't want to understand. But we had some good meetings, including the cross-party New Dialogue group, the Labour Backbench Committee on Northern Ireland, and with Lord Holme, the Liberal Democrat in the House of Lords.

We needed to explain our position to the British media, so folk would realize that the Orange Order was committed to the principles of civil and religious liberties and that we were an institution that held to the values of liberal democracy. So we had meetings including that one you helped with in the Reform Club in London with key journalists ranging from the sympathetic to the unsympathetic.* And those were probably the best meetings we had. We looked at how we were going to have to go on the media much more and how we should go about it, bearing in mind that as an institution we're not very public, we're not political, we're not good at public relations because basically we've never thought in those terms. But '96 had changed all that; this was something that wasn't going to go away. Like it or not we were going to have to develop links with the media and be prepared to put people on the box. And we identified some who we felt had at least some capabilities that way. They're not professional; they haven't done courses and media training. But they were honest, direct people who could go on to discuss our case and not get hot under the collar, but be calm and collected and reasonable about the whole thing and could cope with the pressure of that.

We had our day with Eoghan Harris† and that was useful. But there still has remained a reluctance in people to do this kind of thing. But there's going to have to be lots more Orangemen doing it. There was a recognition through articles and interviews that we were much more proactive, and our radio and television interviews had quite an impact back home. I can't quite gauge the impact in England, although I did breakfast television there and several other programmes there and Graham Montgomery did 'Newsnight'. But it's hard for us to gauge how it comes across in England. I think back home in Northern Ireland more and more people did begin to think that the Orange had something to say and actually something worth listening to.

Then there were the police. I still am someone who would give my whole heart in support of the security forces. I've buried too many of them and have had too many friends killed, not to back them up. But I think they've got to seriously address how they relate not just to the Protestant community but to the whole community.

I think in their efforts to address what they saw as an imbalance against the Catholic community, they alienated the community from which they traditionally received support. Issues like reverse discrimination, these

---

* Having previously taken William Bingham and Denis Watson to my London club, they thought it a good venue for a press conference. It amused some of the journalists that the entrance hall is dominated by a huge picture of Daniel O'Connell, of Catholic emancipation fame.

† Corkman and Dublin-based political commentator and media consultant, Harris has made tremendous efforts to appreciate and explain the unionist position. I put him in touch with some of my Orange friends and he generously offered to coach several of them in media techniques.

are serious things. And I think also the fact that they've actually handed over this law-and-order problem of parades and allowed it to become a political problem could be a very serious mistake. Whatever the police do now, they're going to be seen as being a political police force and they're going to be on very dangerous ground. And that's something that has to be properly addressed.

In '96, Sir Hugh Annesley, the Chief Constable, just seemed distant: he didn't want to know. The burden of the whole of Drumcree had been placed on Ronnie Flanagan, who then became Chief Constable. And I'll say first of all that Ronnie Flanagan is the most able Chief Constable that perhaps Northern Ireland has ever had. He is articulate, he is highly qualified. I can remember the first time I went into his office that he had a certificate on his wall referring to some course he'd done with the FBI in America. And he had international respect as well.

Many people have said: 'Ronnie Flanagan's not to be trusted.' But my experience of '97 is that either you trust nobody, or you trust everybody. In fact, at times you trust nobody, and at times you trust everybody. I had to accept Ronnie Flanagan as someone who was going to be making crucial decisions in '97. I had to accept his word unless I could prove and know differently.

We had discussed with him what the situation would be. One of the strong points of the Orange Order was that this was our traditional route. And as we were coming to the end of our first meeting on the 30th January '97, I said to him: 'What if originally the first parade and the first few parades did not go along the Garvaghy Road? If we could historically prove that they took a different route. Do you think the government would identify and open up the route?'

Now this could do one of two things. This could either get us all lucky and we could all end up happy ever after and we could go back to the traditional route, or alternatively, it would strengthen the Orange case even more if it was proved that it did go down the Garvaghy Road. So we spent some time in the Public Record Office in Belfast trying to get this sorted out. There were maps that went back to 1795 done by a French cyclist in Ireland, then the first Ordnance Survey of Northern Ireland was done in about 1847. What we came up with was a map that went back to 1820. Lo and behold, the Garvaghy Road existed at the time of our first Orange parade. So we went back to the minute book and the first reference to the walk was in 1827: it turned out that almost certainly the Drumcree Church parade actually went up and came back down the

Garvaghy Road. So really, we should be asking now for the right to be going up and down the Garvaghy Road.

And that – certainly for Denis and myself – was that. We had been assured that should it cost twenty million, that the money was there if it was anyway practical. But in actual fact it strengthened Portadown's position. So be it.

The police line from day one was: 'We couldn't get you down the Garvaghy Road.' There was all kind of pressure to get together and talk it out. And off and on we had meetings with the Chief Constable and every time we went to him we said: 'As far as our reading of the situation is, the bottom line is this has to go down the Garvaghy Road.' As the situation got closer and we were getting more and more tense, quite a lot of other factors began to come in. There was a real genuine feeling of both paramilitaries going on the offensive: the IRA ceasefire was broken at this stage. The loyalists who had murdered Mr McGoldrick in '96, they were upping the ante in kidnapping and murder. All this we were aware of, that the LVF of Portadown were ready for action. And the Chief Constable obviously felt the whole province could go up in flames: with the Ormeau Road, Armagh, Londonderry, Newry and other areas, he felt his men were going to be stretched to the limit.

After Drumcree [when, at the last minute, the parade was permitted down the road], everybody in Northern Ireland seemed to be holding their breath, and as they say here, you could cut the atmosphere with a knife. There was a desperate fear the Provos were going to go berserk. They were talking of thousands of people being brought on to the streets, of IRA movements, of snipers taking up positions in certain areas. The Orangemen were faced with the decision: either you believe what you're hearing from the security forces or you don't. And if you plough on and don't believe, you end up with women and children being massacred in bands, because our bands have women and children in them – four-year-old children playing triangles and tambourines in bands. Now are you going to put those children at risk? I wouldn't want that. I would say again that that no road is worth a life. And I think it would have been grossly irresponsible to take the risk. Thus the decision came on the 10th of July for the sake of peace in the country to postpone and re-route and basically to pull the country back from the brink of what many people feared would be civil war.

People said it was a tactical move by the Orange Order that wrong-footed the Provos. That was a bonus out of a bad situation. The reality was that at the end of the day we love our country, we love our people. Looking at it from a County Armagh position, the district officers met to discuss it and spoke with one mind.

The difference with the Garvaghy Road was that right up to forty-eight hours prior to the parade it looked as if it was going to be banned. And up to five days before that, there was a ring of steel put around Portadown and movements of people were noted and therefore there was less chance of that. The thing that probably enabled the parade to go down the Garvaghy Road was the element of surprise. The Orangemen were surprised to get down it: we were getting blamed by some militants on the Saturday night, that once again it was shown that the government are against us and we were wasting our time. And the element of surprise was there. And this area is so small that if IRA terrorists get into it, they'll not get out of it.

I think they've a right to go down the road next year. I think unless the political climate in Northern Ireland changes, and unless people who are the moderates in society and are supposed to be the tolerant folk that represent nationalists and the Roman Catholic Church are prepared to get involved in this and to not allow the hard-liners to dictate what happens in Portadown, we'll be into another similar situation as '96 or '97. Whether it gets down or not, God only knows.

As for Dublin, our traditional enemies. In '96 it came out with some such ridiculous statements about the Orange institution and triumphalism as to be unbelievable. We told those in Dublin that after John Bruton had made a speech in the Dáil in which he said that the prime minister had gone back on his word, back on his agreement, that Dublin had helped thereby to put more Orangemen on to the streets.

But behind this lay the real problem again that Dublin speaks from a position of not understanding the psyche of the Ulster Protestant – just does not realize the serious impact for disorder that some statements that it makes can bring about. Our position is: (a) they don't understand what Orangeism is about, they don't understand the Ulster pysche, they probably don't really want to understand us, but we've got to give them no excuse for not understanding us. And (b) would be to say to them that having been forewarned is forearmed and come '97, if similar things happen, if you are not more cautious with your language and more, if you like, understanding of our position, you'll only have yourselves to blame and you'll have a moral responsibility to face up to it.

So our position was that we were quite prepared to put them in the position where they were going to have to face up to moral responsibility as to how they made any statements on the situation. And whether they paid any heed to that it would remain to be seen, but if they did come out of line again, then we would be the first to point the finger and say: 'We warned you.' From an Orange position, what happened at Drumcree and in Portadown is none of Dublin's business and they should keep their nose out of it.

There were two key players in the south at that time. There was taoiseach, John Bruton and there was Bertie Ahern, who was leader of the opposition. We knew at some stage there was going to be a general election in the south. At the time it seemed to be heading towards the autumn, after Drumcree. But the closer it got to Drumcree, the more it seemed as if it would be close to our own general election. So we decided to meet John Bruton first. Out of office, at least, he had been one of the conciliatory voices towards unionists and had made some attempt to understand our position. But since going into office he seemed to have kind of upped his greener card more. But that would be political expediency again. So we met with him. We had talked to Roy McGee at some stage, really to see if he'd got any soundings from the paramilitaries that they might break a ceasefire over Drumcree in '97, what was actually going on in their minds. Because the last thing we wanted – even worse than the IRA responding to the violence – was that the loyalists would respond to violence. And although we weren't willing to talk and negotiate with them, we certainly wanted them to know from our position that to take up a gun in the name of Orangeism was not what the Orange Order was wanting.

So we just said to Roy about Dublin, look, this is an area that we're cautious, we want probably a one-off thing and certainly not to develop links.

So a meeting was set up with John Bruton in his office in Dublin and I think Bruton was apprehensive to begin with. He had a prepared statement beside him and far from us being the ones who were under pressure, he seemed to be much more than we were. But after about fifteen minutes he put his papers away and was totally relaxed and a meeting that was supposed to go on for twenty minutes went on for an hour and three-quarters. Unlike a lot of politicians, Bruton listened a lot. And it was very good. And we left, not having any plans to meet again, but satisfied that we had made our position clear.

And on going out, the officials were wanting to become more involved in the thing. Their line was: 'If there's anything we can do to help you, we'll do it.' And our line was: 'Yes, there is. Stay out of it.' They were wanting to get in more and more but we said: 'None of your business. It's not part of your jurisdiction. Remember we are British.'

And the other key player was Bertie Ahern, whom we were under no illusions about: in my view he was as green as Gerry Adams. And he comes from the traditional republican party. But then you can be very green in opposition and less green in power which is the opposite to the other guy. But we did again play it straight down the line with him. But they were certainly not going to be committed to keeping out of it. Not be committed to not making statements from the nationalist viewpoint of the Garvaghy Road area.

Bertie did listen, to be fair to him. And so did his adviser, Martin Mansergh, who is from a liberal Protestestant tradition. But we felt that really, in opposition at least, there was no difference between him and Gerry Adams. And when he made that statement just prior to Drumcree saying that we should not get down the road, it certainly proved to Denis and me what we believed all along. That they won't listen to you.

I hope what we did wasn't wasted, but there's always a feeling that whatever politician you're dealing with, they will do what is expedient for them at that particular time. And therefore you really don't know where you are with them except that they're going to be expedient.

DRUMCREE HOLIDAYS '97
* SPECIAL 4/5 DAY SUMMER BREAKS *

New Thrills - Ride on the Big Orange Digger

Inflatable Dolls : Paisley £7 ; Trimble £5
(The Paisley Doll is Bigger and holds more Hot Air)

RUBBER BULLET SOUVENIRS
(Available ONLY after the 4th day!)

Hear Rev. McCrea Sing ; "The Men Behind the Wire"

VINTAGE CAR RALLY
* ALL NEWLY BURNT OUT CARS *

The Sky at Night
See Portadown skyline lit up with spontaneous Bonfires

Siege Medals Still Available
Please state Year : ('95, '96, '97)

Let your friends abroad see you on TV !
Camera crews from Canada, Australia & the USA will be in attendance

* <u>Special this Year</u> *

* Spirit of Drumcree *
in standard and litre size bottles
(Bottles Non-Returnable)

Ireland's largest Outdoor Holiday Camp

Flyer circulating in Orange circles, 1997.

18

Drumcree Three: The Rest of the Story

A crowd o'the lads wuz whoopin it up in a Sandy Row Saloon,
To the sound of an aul piano, that was badly out of tune.
The night was July 11 and they made the rafters roar
With a most harmonious rendering of 'The Sash my Father Wore'.

Outside, the blazin' bonfires made night as bright as day
And everyone was dancin' in a wobbly sort of a way.
They were singin', they were shoutin', and all the din they made
Nearly drowned the clangin' of the Belfast Fire Brigade.

There was educated men there, cultured men, you know –
Men like Billy Bothwell from the village of Drumbo.
A painter by profession, but an artist to his friends,
He had painted many's the masterpiece on Protestant gable ends.

And poor wee Tommy Ferguson, a Prod from Donegal,
Especially invited and beloved by one and all –
A ballad singer was Tommy – he's singing still I hope –
He was well-known throughout Ulster for his songs about the Pope.

There were shipyard men and dockers, all wi' glasses in their hand
And transport men an' fitters – ay, the toughest in the land.
And standing there among them and drinkin' aff her fill,
Was a well-known local lady by the name of Orange Lil.

But over in the corner, a stranger stud his loan
And nobody paid no heed to him as the gaiety went on.
A very weary traveller, he'd tramped for many a mile,
He'd just come in to sit there and rest hisself a while.

But Orange Lil soon noticed him, as her sort often does,
So she went over and sat beside him, and asked him who he wuz.
'Ach, I'm a very weary traveller, but a civil one you'll find
I just came in to hear the craic. I hope the boys won't mind.'

Now Orange Lil, for all her faults, had a heart as pure as gold,
So she turns and says to the fellas: 'Luk, sure someday we'll all be old.
So get this man a drink or two and make him feel at home.'
And so they did and soon the whiskey and the beer began to come.

Then somebody says to the stranger: 'Come on and sing a song.'
But the stranger says: 'I'm sorry, but my singin' days is gone,

Though I used to play the piano and so if that's all right,
I'd like to play some music in honour of this night.'

His coat was all in ribbons and you should have seen his hat
And his tattered sleeves were flappin' at the keyboard as he sat.
Everybody pitied him. He was a sad and a terrible sight,
But I somehow can't help mindin' that his eyes were kinda bright.

And as he started playin' and the notes riz in the air,
A mighty hush descended on the whole assembly there.
The transport men and fitters, they never made a sound,
The shipyard men and dockers stood rooted til the ground.

And as the sweet notes tinkled on, the place grew deathly still –
I even saw a tear roul down the face of Orange Lil.
As long as I am on this earth, I'll not forget that night
I mind it just like yistry – a sad and moving sight.

But the saddest part I've yet to tell – a tear I know you'll shed.
Before the night was over, that poor old man was dead.
He lies now in his earthly grave, away from worldly strife
And up above his head, a tombstone tells the story of his life.

It says 'Here lies a brave brave man, who'll be remembered long,
Because one night in Sandy Row, he played "A Soldier's Song'.*

A S I WAS FINISHING this chapter, I saw myself described in an article by my most enthusiastic public adversary, Tim Pat Coogan, as the successor to 'Orange Nell, whom we used to see appear on TV screens swathed in Union Jacks, dancing to the beat of the Orange drum on the twalfth'.† He meant 'Orange Lil', so I thought I'd include the above loyalist parody of Robert Service's 'Dangerous Dan McGrew' just for the fun of it. Such attacks are nothing new. It is impossible for someone from either tribe in Ireland to write sympathetically of the other without incurring a backlash. Build a bridge across the divide and you will become alienated from most of your own; indeed, there will be those who will try to blow up the bridge behind you.

As I became closer to the loyal institutions and made more friends

---

* The Irish national anthem.

† Southerners often attempt to mimic a Belfast accent by calling the Twelfth the Twalfth.

within them, I was constantly angered by the sheer unfairness of the way in which they were perceived outside their own community. I thought, and have thought constantly, of two people who would have appeared on the television cameras at Drumcree 1996 looking mad and bad. One was a man who is one of the thousands of brethren whose border community has suffered thirty years of terror at the hands of the IRA and its sympathizers but who I've never heard utter an uncharitable word about even his per-secuters. At Drumcree, to the consternation of friends, he briefly succumbed to frustration and rage and was seen screaming at the RUC. The other – a pillar of his local community – completely lost control when he saw the razor-wire, for it conjured up an image of the trenches at the Somme. He was seen by a horrified fellow-Orangeman tearing at the wire with his bare hands, unconscious that they were streaming with blood.

I became gradually drawn into Orange politics in the autumn of 1996, mainly because I started to tell influential Orangemen what a hash I thought they were making of things. One of the endearing characteristics of many Ulster Protestants is that they take criticism well, perhaps because they associate it with straightforwardness. When I first met Denis Watson, County Grand Master of Armagh, at a friend's house prior to the 1996 'Black Last Saturday', I was in an irritable mood, partly because I'd got up at 5 a.m. to fly to Belfast. I'd been 'lifted' at the airport by Brian Kennaway and we had engaged in our usual handwringing about the aftermath of Drumcree. Over an enormous post-breakfast spread of sand-wiches and sausage-rolls and buns and cake, I became snappish when Denis said Trimble had been useless during the Drumcree crisis and added that Trimble had not, anyway, been taken into the confidence of the Orange leadership. 'So you think you had a great success, do you?' I asked by way of openers. Instead of taking umbrage at an outsider's effrontery, Denis listened courteously to my harangue about the culpable stupidity of the internecine strife within unionism, left with reluctance when his official duties called and sent me messages later saying he'd like to meet again.

In the ensuing months, I became involved in trying to help Orange moderates by introducing them to people who might give them useful advice or help them to make their case to the outside world. One of those was Robert Saulters, a sixty-one-year-old accountant and the Grand Master of Belfast, who had become the Orange Order's Grand Master in December 1996 almost by accident. At least two senior Orangemen who had contemplated taking over from Martin Smyth, who was stepping down after a quarter of a century, had backed off because their wives were terrified that they might become IRA targets. Saulters did not want the job, but he is an obliging man who allowed himself to be persuaded. He would be the first to admit that he was politically out of his depth. But then, who would not have been?

Saulters's election produced further bad publicity, for newspapers reported that months previously he had said that Tony Blair, then leader of the opposition, had 'sold his Protestant birthright by marrying a Romanist'. Inevitably I tried and failed to explain to horrified English and Irish people that such a remark did not mean that Saulters was a mad bigot, but instead that he took his religion seriously in a way which was incomprehensible to a secular world. 'My remarks were taken completely out of context,' he said wearily a few months later. 'I don't care who Tony Blair or anyone else marries. We all have our own problems.'

Bobby Saulters is as nice and as non-sectarian as they come in Northern Ireland. He grew up in a Catholic area and his friends were and are from both communities. 'People have become more aggressive and less tolerant,' he told a journalist. 'Over the past six years I have seen decorum going down within the institution among members, what with groups such as the Spirit of Drumcree forming.' A modernizer by instinct, he wants to separate the institution from the Ulster Unionist Party: 'I see the Orange Order as being to uphold law and order and civil and religious liberty. I think it would be much better to get back to the old type of Orange.'

One of Saulters's first public actions was to travel to Harryville in January 1997 with a group of senior Orangemen, including Brian Kennaway. Carrying a banner saying, 'ORANGEMEN SUPPORT CIVIL AND RELIGIOUS LIBERTY FOR ALL', they stood outside the Catholic church as a mark of solidarity with the mass-goers who by now had endured months of intimidation, abuse and sometimes violence by loyalist riff-raff enraged at the blocking of parades in nearby Dunloy.* Their gesture was applauded by decent people; it was ignored or savagely condemned by the indecent. Some Orangemen who participated in the 100-strong picket the following Saturday showed their defiance by wearing their collarettes. Saulters was now marked out as a traitor by, among others, Joel Patton and the Spirit of Drumcree.

---

* The group set off late and had to drive fast to get to Harryville on time, causing one of their number, Graham Montgomery, to remark that it had to be the first time that a car-load of Orangemen were in a panic lest they miss mass.

In February, I arranged a meeting between Saulters, three of his colleagues and Sean O'Callaghan.* We spent the best part of a day in an anonymous hotel near Heathrow, where Sean spelled out republican strategy, laid bare the trap into which the Orange Order were falling in contentious areas and particularly in Portadown, and gave strategic and tactical advice. Over the next few months, as William Bingham and Denis Watson struggled to find a way of avoiding another confrontation at Drumcree, Sean and I helped to arrange meetings in London between Orangemen and journalists, peace activists and politicians from all parties. Typically, Bingham in his interview says little about the sacrifices he and Watson made, but I was closely enough in touch with them to know their lives had been turned upside down with innumerable and interminable Orange and non-Orange meetings virtually every day of the week. Watson, a self-employed mortgage-adviser, was only just managing to keep his business going and had suffered badly financially; his wife was very worried by the threats made by fringe loyalists who opposed all attempts to make a deal.

The Orange Order, predictably, was in turmoil. In a County Armagh Grand Lodge meeting in February 1997, Watson had to defend himself against Orange enemies, mostly from the Spirit of Drumcree.

> I am concerned, like the greater number of Orangemen and right-thinking people throughout this land, that the actions of some in the name of Orangeism brought and continue to bring much discredit on the colour we proudly wear and the institution we dearly love. Let us not forget why we process to and from Drumcree. Is it to worship God or to kick the pope? Sadly, I have come to the conclusion that there are those within our ranks who do not wish to see the parades issue in the province resolved.†

---

* From County Kerry in the Republic of Ireland, Sean O'Callaghan joined the IRA at fifteen to fight against the British presence in Northern Ireland and left four years later having realized he was involved in a squalid sectarian war. He rejoined the IRA in 1979 to work as an unpaid informer for the Irish police, rose to a very senior level in the IRA and became a Sinn Féin councillor. In 1988 he gave himself up for his teenage crimes and served eight years of a life sentence. He is now a distinguished political analyst and peace activist.

With very few exceptions, Ulster Protestants have no inhibitions about meeting that rare creature, a repentant ex-IRA terrorist. I have been amazed, however, at how warm and welcoming towards Sean have been people from localities where he murdered and bombed for the IRA in the early 1970s.

† Before anyone attacks Denis Watson for revealing lodge secrets, let me say that he did not tell me what he had said.

He was absolutely right. As William Bingham puts it, 'there were those extremists, who, when they looked over the precipice in '96, liked what they saw'. Residents and Orangemen who wanted a quiet life faced intimidation from their own extremists. And, as usual, the extremists were each other's best allies. The Spirit of Drumcree were overjoyed early in March 1997 when an RTE programme quoted Gerry Adams's remarks to a Sinn Féin meeting about the hard work party activists had put into creating the confrontations at Derry, Drumcree, the Lower Ormeau Road and elsewhere.

The little Tyrone village of Dromore, which is about 90 per cent Catholic, was one of the battlegrounds between peaceable and aggressive Orangemen that spring. An Orangeman and member of the band described the background. 'It would have been in 1981, I think, that a group decided to create a flute band. I would have to call them Ian-men. They had Big Ian [Paisley senior] down to help the fund-raising for the band . . . We had no part of it. Our band were invited and we wouldn't go out. I've been in the band now since I was twelve and never once going out the door was it my intention ever to cause anyone offence. I went out because it was a holiday for me. Or we went out as a family. We're proud of our wee band. Never did anything to tarnish the reputation.'

This was the time of the hunger-strikes, a period of high sectarian tension. According to my source, a local hard-line Orangeman said as every band formed up: 'Give it to the bastards, boys, when you turn up Church Street. It's a Fenian hole.' And as each of the fifteen bands turned up Church Street, they struck up 'Derry's Walls', 'The Green Grassy Slopes', 'The Sash' and any other provocative tune they could think of. 'There were two well-known republicans at the top of that street and the organizers had those two republican houses identified. And they kicked their doors and they shouted abuse.

'Instead of the bands going up to the top of the street as in the normal parade and coming back down again, the first band stopped, the second band stopped and they used it as a staging post. And they beat and they thumped – you know their blood-and-thunder drums – and they drummed and they beat and they shouted abuse. The next morning the tricolour was flying from one of the lampposts. And really and truly, those were the boys who sowed the seeds.

'And if you went round a lot of these contentious areas – Newtownbutler, Bellaghy, Dunloy or whatnot – you would find that in recent history a bunch of hangmen like that might well have been there. We disowned ourselves completely from them and let everybody in Dromore know that we thought it was a disgrace.'

Paisley came back for the actual dedication of the band a year later, 'and there were about 500 police in Dromore because the people of Church Street said: "You're not getting up it this time." And it was quite understandable. So they were kept out of Church Street.' There was no further trouble until 1996 after Drumcree. As the local lodge came out over the hill, the bars near the corner of Church Street disgorged perhaps sixty people, who closed the street off. 'Now we had the right to go up that street,' said Charlie Kenwell, secretary of the local lodge. 'It was an illegal blockade and we were very annoyed and it caused a lot of friction but we went on, we ignored it, we left that street out, we walked to the bottom and came back and ignored it again. Everyone in the parade behaved impeccably. And what was potentially an ugly scene was avoided.

'There were an awful lot of rough words spoken between Orangemen and bandsmen and everybody throughout the Twelfth, but it probably was a good thing that we did not get the police to get us up that street, because people probably would have been hit with truncheons or people would have been trampled to the ground, band uniforms would have been torn and instruments broken – a real ugly scene. And it might have taken years for it to blow over.

'We didn't like it, but in hindsight, and the way everything turned out this year, it probably was the best course of action. Because those people were seen to have acted illegally and nobody could find fault with our behaviour. So they couldn't justify what they'd done. In fact they felt so bad at not having had a confrontation that they actually fought with each other as the day progressed in the bars in the town.'

With the help of a false rumour that the Orangemen intended to parade again, the day finished off with riots which brought the little village into the headlines. 'As the year progressed,' said Kenwell, 'everybody then started to realize that the main Twelfth demonstration in all the towns in West Tyrone and Strabane, Omagh, Newtownstewart, Castlederry, Fintona and all was to be held in Dromore. And quite a few of the nationalist people in Dromore – shopkeepers and other people with an interest in good community relations – were worried about the Twelfth and what might happen with 10,000 people.'

Historically, Dromore village had had good inter-community relations. The master of the lodge for forty years had been Charlie's father Alfie, a popular local businessman who was very proud of having turned out for the Gaelic football team as a teenager when they were short of a man. 'The people running Dromore GAA I grew up with,' he recalled. 'The GAA here isn't run as a sectarian organization, but for the benefit of the GAA and the sports-loving people of Dromore. I haven't a bad word to say of it.' Alfie's son Charlie, an ex-master and now secretary of the lodge, was chairman of Dromore 2000, a cross-community group, dedicated to improving the village. 'The foundations of trust laid in the group between myself and a few others helped.' Yet there were ominous signs of polarization. Not only were young nationalists responding to republican propaganda, but the Spirit of Drumcree was making its presence felt among the Orangemen. Like many other lodges, Mullinagoagh LOL 669 had acquired some hard-line recruits after Drumcree Two.

In a sadly untypical partnership,* the parish priest, Father Breen, and the Church of Ireland rector, Reverend Gamble, took control of the situation before Sinn Féin could set up a residents' group and invited to a meeting a cross-section of the community, chosen from the electoral roll according to location rather than politics. Charlie Kenwell told the meeting of his plans for the parades: 'I said that hope for the future was the sentiment with which the clergymen initiated the meeting. I also said that it was time for Dromore to drift out of the headlines, but that before it did, I would like to mention the quiet people of Dromore who had stood behind this understanding [between the lodge and the residents] as, unfortunately, our tragic opera had played its way over the airwaves. I told people that I was born in Dromore, loved Dromore and wanted Dromore to be the place where my children would be proud to grow up.'

Though the few Sinn Féiners present objected to any parade, the vast majority of nationalists present were quite happy with Kenwell's suggestions, though afraid that with so many people there might be some vandalism in Church Street. 'So I had to assure them that that wouldn't happen and it was agreed that just a small number would parade up. Nobody wanted a Drumcree to end up, where 100 people swole to 1,400 people.

---

* Another unusual but effective partnership exists in Crumlin, North Antrim, between the Presbyterian minister, the Reverend Brian Kennaway and Father David Delargy. Their joint leadership has helped to hold the two communities together despite trouble-making bands, Sinn Féin provocation, the burning of the Catholic church and the sectarian murder of a Catholic student. Brian Kennaway threw the incipient residents' group into confusion by telling them he wanted to join. After two years, he had still had no answer to his application, but the group has never been properly set up.

Everyone was happy enough with the normal parade going on in a normal way. I gave guarantees that would happen. Of course an element would say: "Why should you have to give guarantees at all?" But these were neighbourly guarantees.'

To Charlie Kenwell, this outcome was ideal. Until the next meeting of the lodge he did not realize that Joel Patton was in cahoots with Gerald Marshall, the deputy master of the lodge, who tabled a motion of no confidence in those who had attended the meeting. 'It isn't what was in the agreement. It is the fact that there was an agreement at all,' was Marshall's position. After four-and-a-half hours, with forty-three voting, the censure motion was defeated by just one. One anti-SOD Orangeman said of Kenwell's opposition: 'People like that should be smart enough to know they're used in a bigger issue when the person who uses them would have to find a map to get to the town that he's so interested in. It was obvious from the word go where all the manipulation was coming from.'

Kenwell and his supporters set out to win over more of their brethren: 'As we educated the people they saw this was no betrayal, it was sensible.' And though Patton kept up a barrage of criticism of any discussions with outsiders, his angry and vociferous supporters won no converts at the County Grand Lodge meeting where there were sixty-eight votes for Kenwell, nine against and three abstentions.

Kenwell had help from Catholic neighbours who made sure their side of the bargain would be kept. 'Whenever the whole situation hit the media, two men in particular rallied round to support what had been done: a former chairman of Omagh District Council and a local schoolteacher. The schoolteacher has since stood as a local councillor and been elected. It showed that the nationalist people of Dromore agreed with what they were doing.' Kenwell had been under attack for having been at a meeting with Sinn Féin, but 'in all my discussions and in all interviews I gave, I said that it would have been pointless to have any meeting without the Sinn Féin views being expressed, because then they could have legitimately stood at the bottom of the street saying, "We weren't represented. We will defeat this." But their view got its say and the majority of people didn't agree with it. They were carried along on the tide.'

There were seven resignations in the little lodge. 'We get a good couple of new members every year. Unfortunately with Drumcree, an unsavoury element has been applying to join. Four of the most vociferous had joined in 1996, but they resigned. But anyone joining has to be of good character and attend church.

'The brethren are good, decent law-abiding people. They can't see why people generally don't understand the good motives and they don't feel they have to go and explain themselves. They think that anybody with any brain would understand that they were right and they shouldn't have to say they were right. And that's perfectly true. I could say, "Well, the people round here know me and know my father." And so they do. But sometimes you do have to get up and speak and I would say this year if we hadn't, it would have been a disaster for Dromore. But nine times out of ten nobody wants to speak.'

What had made Charlie Kenwell's job much more difficult was that at every stage of the proceedings the media kept rushing to Joel Patton, even after the county meeting had shown how small was his support. 'I suppose it's no fun going to somebody who says, "Well, we've got to try to live together, so let's all try to work together." That's not a statement anybody wants. Joel Patton's really good at giving soundbites; they're a distortion of the facts, but look good on TV.'

That spring, Patton and his cohorts had kept up relentless pressure on Bobby Saulters and the other senior Orangemen who were trying to resolve problems through mediation. One of the worst episodes of intimidation occurred in Carnlea Orange Hall, near Ballymena, at the end of March. Patten and 500 or so hard-line Orangemen from across the province packed into the hall alongside the 200 county Grand Lodge representatives invited to discuss a possible resolution to the impasse over Dunloy. With the backing of Bobby Saulters, the County Antrim Grand Master Robert McElroy, who had given such firm leadership in his condemnation of the Harryville pickets, had with other brethren been involved in discussions with the Northern Ireland Mediation Network; it was widely reported that residents might accept two parades the following month. The Pattonites refused to give McElroy a hearing and after he and other members of Grand Lodge had walked out into the path of picketing SODs, Patten took over the platform, denounced 'surrender to republicans on parades' and passed a vote of censure on McElroy. 'The county Grand Master, Robert McElroy, was bullied and threatened at that meeting,' said Bobby Saulters. 'It was ironic that this thuggery should take place on the eve of Good Friday, when our Lord was betrayed by Judas Iscariot. Strange that the leader of this so-called group's name begins with a "J" as well. He [Joel Patton] calls himself a born-again Christian.

But some advertise that they are born-again Christians, but never seem to learn the true message of Easter.'

Two weeks later, sixty uninvited protestors pushed their way into the reconvened meeting and after a stormy meeting, along with County Antrim hard-liners, they voted down McElroy's proposals. The placard declaring 'STOP TALKING, START WALKING' summed up the mood of the rejoicing SODs. Sean Farren, a local SDLP representative who had worked ceaselessly to try find a peaceful solution, said: 'The goodwill of the Dunloy residents having been rejected, the prospects for the marching season are now full of foreboding.' The leader of the protesters pronounced it a great day for the Orange brethren of County Antrim: 'The County Grand officers actually faced a fairly humiliating defeat when they were forced to send a resolution to the Grand Lodge of Ireland not to talk to Mediation Network or any residents' groups as well, and we hope that all the other counties in the province will follow suit.' Asked if the passing of the resolution was worthwhile even if it brought about another Drumcree, he said: 'Even if it means another Drumcree.'

It meant death for Constable Gregory Taylor, one of the RUC officers who had to hold back jeering loyalists who tried to force through a banned Orange march in Dunloy in May. As one journalist described it: 'One by one the officers' names, their wives' workplaces and the schools their children attended were recited. In the language of Ulster it was a menacing reminder that, no matter how meticulous the RUC's security precautions, they were no longer safe.' Two weeks later, as Constable Taylor left a pub in Ballymoney, his home town, he was attacked by a crowd of loyalists and beaten to death.

By June, the best efforts of people like Bingham, Watson and Saulters were foundering on the rock of hard-line intransigence. In June, with two Conservative unionists, Viscount Cranborne, then Shadow Leader of the House of Lords, and Andrew Hunter MP, Sean O'Callaghan went to Portadown to plead with Harold Gracey and his brethren to seize the high moral ground. The advice was that, if allowed to walk down Garvaghy Road, Portadown District should voluntarily re-route themselves as a gesture of goodwill; if banned, they should emulate Alistair Simpson, Governor of the Apprentice Boys, accept the prohibition in the interests of peace in Northern Ireland and say they would walk the disputed territory in the future at a time of their own choosing.

'If you walk down Garvaghy Road this year,' Sean warned, 'you will probably never be permitted to do so again.' Gracey and other Portadown officers listened politely, smiled benignly and explained they would be walking down the road. In Portadown District they do not talk of the art of the possible.

It was clear that no one could move Gracey from his belief that this issue was simply a matter of right and wrong. He believed, as the Book of Common Prayer puts it, that he that 'doeth the thing which is right, and speaketh the truth from his heart . . . shall never fall'. Gracey knew that right would prevail against the forces of darkness. And there was nothing that the Grand Master, County Armagh Grand Lodge, David Trimble or anyone else could do about it.*

At a Grand Lodge meeting a few days later, fearful that they would lose a test of strength, members backed down from their threats of suspending Patton and just gave a vague warning that Orangemen bringing the Grand Lodge or the Order into disrepute would be liable to disciplinary action. Gracey told the gathering there would be no talks with anyone. 'We will not be talking to anyone ever, and I mean anyone. I will be going into Drumcree Church with Portadown District and I will be coming out of church and going down the Garvaghy Road and that's it.'† Although Grand Lodge ruled that there could be talks, it reiterated that they could not include alleged representatives of Sinn Féin or convicted terrorists.

Five days later, the IRA shot dead two RUC constables. They find it hard to operate in Portadown, so they had done the next-best thing and committed their murders in neighbouring Lurgan. William Bingham, Harold Gracey and Denis Watson sent a letter to Tony Blair, who by now had been in office for six weeks:

Dear Prime Minister,
On behalf of County Armagh Grand Orange Lodge we would like to congratulate you on becoming prime minister. We assure you of our support and cooperation as you try to bring peace to Northern Ireland. It is the deepest desire of our hearts to avoid a repetition of the terrible

---

* For the record, and because he sought to deny it later, Joel Patton orginally agreed to meet the trio, but later ducked out of meeting O'Callaghan because he was afraid that it would weaken his line on refusing to talk to ex-IRA terrorists.

† Memories are unclear as to whether it was at that or another meeting that Gracey made his celebrated statement that even if every other Portadown Orangeman agreed to be re-routed, he would walk the Garvaghy Road alone.

scenes of violence and intolerance that occurred as a result of the ban on the parade at Drumcree last summer. It is only in the interests of Sinn Féin/IRA and loyalist extremists to have another summer of bloody conflict.

For the last year we have worked night and day to try to bring about a peaceful solution to the dispute over our annual traditional walk from morning prayer at Drumcree church down the Garvaghy Road. Orangemen feel strongly that the right to walk in a peaceful and dignified manner from church should not be denied anyone – whether it be our Roman Catholic neighbours in Harryville or our brethren in Portadown, but they accept also that such freedoms bring responsibilities.

For many months now we have been engaged in discussions with local residents, with senior politicians in the United Kingdom and the Irish Republic, with clergy, police, officials, diplomats and the business community. We have also had a lengthy process of consultation within the Orange Order itself. Drumcree is a very emotional issue for us, especially since we have given up nine of our ten annual Portadown parades.

Having secured agreement from our brethren we wrote to all the residents of the area offering what we believe to be a fair and sensible basis for agreement, which could promote harmony and mutual respect within the community.

Our proposals were:

1. The Walk from morning prayer will be by people from the local community only. No one outside of Portadown District will be permitted to participate.

2. No bands which could be perceived by our nationalist neighbours to be antagonistic will take part. Accordion bands will play hymn tunes only which are common to both traditions.

3. The Orangemen will walk four deep so that the parade will pass any one given point in less than five minutes.

4. The Order will marshal and discipline its own members to ensure there will be no confrontation on our part. If this can be reciprocated then there would be need only for a minimal police presence.

Further to this, as an Order we gave assurances that there would be no triumphalism, and that in keeping with our belief in civil and religious liberty, we acknowledge that the cultural and religious heritage of both traditions in Portadown should be afforded equal respect.

We are sad that the response from the spokesmen of the Garvaghy Road Residents' Coalition was negative.

We have no ground left to give. If the parade is banned, the moderate Orange national and local leadership will be discredited and our influence destroyed.

It is the sincere hope of the Orange Order that the vast majority of the people in Portadown will work together for real peace in a new spirit of tolerance. We certainly will do our best to build up confidence and respect within the community as a whole, so that we can look forward not only to a peaceful summer but to a more peaceful and tolerant future.

May we assure you that the Secretary of State will have our full cooperation and prayers over the next few weeks in her praiseworthy efforts to defuse the terrible sectarian tension, which has been made so much worse by the murder of two of our local community policemen.

Mo Mowlam went on rushing around energetically, and still ended up between a rock and a hard place. By late June, newspapers were predicting Armageddon. Joel Patton explained to one journalist that parades 'are all we have left. In the past ten years, Protestants have vanished from large areas of the west and the borders. Nationalists control two-thirds of the geographic areas and both the major cities. Protestants are corralled in the south and north-east. We are being ethnically cleansed and no one wants to know.'

His analysis was pretty accurate, but his conclusions were open to question: those senior Orangemen seeking accommodation 'are living in another century, tugging their forelocks, and trying to stay in with the British, but the British don't want to know'. The Union was finished, and Protestants should be asking themselves, 'How do we preserve a distinct race of people who have the right to self-determination and survival?'

Lots of ideas were tried and failed: John Hume and David Trimble were among those whose peace efforts were tossed aside. I arrived in Northern Ireland the weekend before Drumcree, mainly to attend a press conference organized by County Armagh Grand Lodge in the modern surroundings of the civic centre in Craigavon, near Portadown. By Orange standards this was a remarkable occasion, having as it did the sole purpose of explaining to the press the efforts that had been made to reach accommodation with the residents. An information pack included copies of the letters Bingham and Watson had sent to the prime minister and to all the residents of Garvaghy Road, a substantial amount of information on the background to the dispute and a reasoned analysis of Orange objections to the report of the North Committee, set up under the previous government to examine the parades issue. There were tables laden with food, for the press conference was being held at tea-time, and the Orangemen could not bear to think of the journalists going hungry.

After the opening explanations had been given, an English journalist said to Harold Gracey: 'Could I ask you what may sound like a simplistic question. If you chose not to march down the Garvaghy Road and just went back into Portadown by the route that you'd taken to the church there would be no trouble and you would gain the admiration of the world. What would you lose?'

'And likewise,' said Harold Gracey, 'we have to say to the residents' coalition that if they were to have a legitimate protest along the side of the road. I mean I would have to query what happened between 1994 and 1995 as someone who has along with all these gentlemen been in that parade for a number of years; 1994 was one of the quietest parades in existence for the Orange institution of Portadown.'

'Forgive me for interrupting,' said the journalist, 'but we all know the climate that we're in at the moment. Given the awful foreboding about this weekend, what can you lose by making concessions that would gain you the admiration of the world? You would be seen to be the wiser side of this conflict, wouldn't you?'

'That's something for Portadown to consider,' said the weary Denis Watson.

'Do you think that they should consider that?' asked the questioner.

'I think they have already considered it and made their decision quite clear on that matter.'

'You think they should consider it further?'

'I have said Portadown District has made their position clear on the matter.'

'So that's the bottom line?'

'Yes.'

That was when everyone gave up hope. When I went over to Gracey after the press conference, he smiled benignly and asked if I would be writing something supportive. 'If there's something to be supportive about,' I said. 'Like you re-routing yourselves.'

'England will rise in our defence if we're not let down the road,' said his companion.

'It will not,' I said.

He smiled and shrugged. 'Then we'll be on our own like we were in 1914.'

I looked at these two pleasant, ordinary, stubborn old men, despaired and went off with a couple of more sophisticated brethren to drive down the Garvaghy Road, look at the Women's Justice Camp and the latest murals and to talk to journalists, who reported that Breandán MacCionnaith was giving nightly pep-talks to residents about how to comport themselves in front of the television cameras.

Later that night Bingham and Watson made their last throw by bringing Mo Mowlam to address Portadown District. Afterwards, there was nothing much anyone who wanted a peaceful outcome could do except hope that she and Ronnie Flanagan, the Chief Constable, would make better decisions than had their predecessors in 1996.

By the following weekend, after days of veiled and direct threats from paramilitaries and a tribal intervention from the Irish taoiseach, Bertie Ahern, that raised the temperature further, the speculation was intense and the general view was that the parade would be banned. On Saturday I sped from Rossnowlagh (see Chapter 1) to the 'mini-Twelfth' at Lurgan to find out what was going on. There was a slightly bizarre twist to the proceedings here, as far as I was concerned. Some time previously a newspaper had outed the involvement of Sean O'Callaghan and me in the parades issue, so the team who were making a television programme about Drumcree, and particularly about William Bingham and Denis Watson, wanted my comments on what was going on. I had to walk backwards for the benefit of the cameras, explaining why I thought Denis Watson, parading in full regalia and speaking into his mobile phone, was talking to Ronnie Flanagan.

At the end of that parade, William Bingham led the prayers. And after a rousing rendition of 'God Save the Queen', the colour party marched off and the sisters and brethren were dismissed. Some of us went for tea in Brownlow House where we speculated fruitlessly on what would happen the next day. At around 1 a.m., Graham Montgomery and I drove up Drumcree Road to see what was going on. By now the army had moved in around Drumcree Church and, like everyone else, we assumed the march would be banned. In a state of gloom we left to get some sleep and woke the next morning to the news that, during the night, troops and police had taken over the Garvaghy Road. After three hours of violence and bloodshed they had succeeded in moving the protesters, whom

MacCionnaith had summoned on to the road with a siren, and had lined the road with around seventy-five armoured Land Rovers.

At 12.45 p.m. on Sunday, around a thousand members of Portadown District walked silently down the road, six-abreast, looking straight ahead. Walking backwards ahead of them in a scrum of hundreds of cameramen and journalists was one of the most depressing fifteen minutes of my life. From behind the barricades, residents blew whistles, crashed dustbin lids on the ground, banged saucepan lids with sticks, threw bottles and stones and cans and shouted at their Protestant neighbours, 'Youse bastards', and 'Scum, fucking scum'. When the parade reached the Protestant areas, a joyous crowd screamed a welcome and one woman shouted, 'Victory'.

What had happened was a disaster, not because the parade was let down the road, but because of the reasons given by Mo Mowlam and Ronnie Flanagan. Mowlam could have said that, unlike the previous administration, she did not yield to force, but that Orangemen were being rewarded for having done much more than the GRRC to reach accommodation. Such a statement would have strengthened moderate leadership in both communities. Instead, catastrophically, she said it was purely a matter of public order and backed up the Chief Constable's remark that he had taken the decision on the basis of 'how much life was liable to be lost'. His conclusion that Billy Wright's Loyalist Volunteer Force (LVF) posed a greater threat than the IRA was not lost on the paramilitaries, the hoods and the thugs of Northern Ireland who set to work that day with stones and petrol bombs and the rest of their paraphernalia of violence. 'The very criteria employed by the police,' pointed out Malachi O'Doherty, 'were an invitation to both sides to compete to provide the greater threat. It hardly seems creditable that a modern government would give insurgents such a message, but the implications of the decision taken at Garvaghy Road in 1997 were as simple and obvious as that.' And as the *Daily Telegraph* put it, Mo Mowlam had admitted 'what (as they say in Northern Ireland) "every dog on the street knows" – that it is the gangster-terrorists, be they republican or loyalist, who are making the running in everything that the "peace process" touches. A parades commission to oversee marches, on which so many people are now pinning their hopes, cannot even begin to address this problem.'

As usual, most of the press knew whom to blame. 'MARCHERS TRAMPLE PEACE HOPES', screamed the London *Independent* headline, and the Irish nationalist press were mostly hysterical. The Belfast nationalist *Irish News*, which had for weeks cooperated responsibly with the *Belfast Newsletter*, its opposite number, in trying to find a solution, ran for a whole week a photograph of Father Eamon Stack gazing with consternation at a bloodstained Sister Laura Boyle. Events followed the predictable pattern of violence and destruction and the good people of Northern Ireland looked towards the Twelfth with dread.

Then on 10 July a fax emerged from the House of Orange announcing that 'after several days of discussions involving Grand Lodge officers, the appropriate authorities, and the four relevant constituent bodies within the Instititution', for the sake of the community, four contentious parades would be re-routed or cancelled. Newry District L O L No. 9's statement included an appeal 'to the genuinely concerned citizens of Newry, of all religious denominations, to cast out this cancer of sectarian hatred from our midst. Let us get back to when we lived together as a mixed community, respecting each other's traditions and culture and tolerating their expression and existence.' Most of the province sighed with relief, though the rough fringes of loyalism branded the Orange Order the 'Yellow Order' and republican frustration was evident in sporadic outbreaks of violence. 'For once Orangemen have used their heads instead of their feet,' said a moderate. 'What these people have done will strengthen the Union. You only have to listen to the Shinners today, they're gutted.'

I saw some stark evidence of that on the afternoon of the Twelfth. I had spent most of the day in Brookeborough, at a parade of the kind that responsible Orangemen wish all parades could be: a family affair. Brookeborough is mainly Protestant; there had been no protests. All day there had been an air of relief so intense as to be almost palpable and Orangemen and their families and local residents got on with enjoying the Twelfth in traditional style with bands and ham sandwiches and flasks of tea, meeting and chatting – or as they would put it, bantering – with friends and brethren and neighbours. I and my motley group of companions from London and Dublin walked behind bands, watched from the sidelines, were fed as honoured guests in an Orange Hall and occasionally went to a pub to escape the relentless County Fermanagh rain. Towards the end of the parade, as the Orangemen gathered for their service, someone said, 'There'll be trouble in Pomeroy this afternoon.' So half-a-dozen of us decided to go and have a look.

Pomeroy is a small village in County Tyrone, which by 1997 was 97 per cent Catholic. As demographic changes came, there had been tensions

about parades. Since Drumcree Two, as in several predominantly nationalist border villages, there was a boycott in operation: in this case, two
of the three remaining Protestant businesses in the village had been
destroyed.

Pomeroy's main street is on a hill, at the bottom of which is the
Protestant enclave. Paddy O'Gorman and I were on our way into Pomeroy
when we got a call from a nervous English friend who had got there
ahead of us. 'Don't go through to the top of the village,' he said. 'It's
full of Provo thugs.'

Provo thugs didn't bother us since we both come from southern Irish
stock and are both journalists – the most safe of all combinations in the
very public-relations-oriented republican world. But we still drove very
carefully through their massed ranks and joined up with our friends at a
car park at the other end of the village just beyond the Protestant enclave.

The few remaining Protestants are now grouped round the Presbyterian
manse and church. William Bingham, who has been the minister there
since 1986, has buried in his little churchyard five Protestants murdered
by the IRA on the excuse that they were part-time members of the
security forces. Bingham had been much in the news in previous weeks
because of his attempts to resolve the problem at Drumcree; he was
well-known for his contribution to creating a climate which had enabled
Orangemen to pull back from the brink. There was no reciprocal generosity in Pomeroy.

At the top of the hill were assembled about a hundred or so young
men and a handful of young women. The local youths came from the
Catholic housing estate at the back of the village but according to the
RUC assessment, which was corroborated by neighbours who knew who
were locals and who weren't, about two-thirds of the protesters had been
brought in from the local republican towns of Cappagh and Carrickmac-
ross. The police thought that three IRA active service units were in
Pomeroy that afternoon. Although there was no sign of weapons, every
so often a door would open in a darkened shop or pub and five or six
people would emerge. You didn't have to be an experienced riot-watcher
to know that there were caches of petrol bombs ready to hand.

The protesters' spokesmen were delighted to talk to press and
cameramen. They had prepared statements, they had soundbites and they
were friendly. Down at the bottom of the hill where Protestant men and
women stood in small groups, the reaction to the press was equally
typical. 'What's the use in talking to you? The media never write about

things like this.' And then, after some wooing, came the remark from a middle-aged woman: 'The IRA won't rest until they've killed all of us or driven us away. But I'll not be going. Now, why don't you write about that?'*

In the distance, to the south, some activity started around the heavily fortified police station, Land Rovers emerged and up towards the village came khaki-clad soldiers of the British army, who took cover in alleyways, and police in riot gear who took up their stand halfway up the hill. Half of them faced the threatening mass of young men and the others faced south ready to deal with Orangemen.

The disputed area was less than one hundred yards, for while in the past parades used to go round the village, latterly they had confined themselves to the short stretch from the bottom of the hill up to the Church of Ireland church at the top, which they would circle, before going down the hill again. This was unacceptable, said the residents' group leader, because this was now a predominantly Catholic area. The disputed territory in fact was just over 50 per cent Catholic: none of the Catholics was in the residents' group and none was visible that afternoon. They were people who got on well with their Protestant neighbours and were keeping out of sight.

Everyone was tense – both those who wanted a riot and those who didn't. Then William Bingham arrived, fresh from speaking at a parade in County Armagh. He emerged from his manse carrying a document which he hoped would defuse the situation and went up the hill to greet the coaches that were just delivering local Orangemen back to their village. There were were about fifty of them, young, middle-aged and old; the flute band included many young men who would have liked nothing better than to have a show-down with their tormenters.

For half-an-hour, William Bingham talked to the master of the local lodge and his senior colleagues and then to almost everyone in the parade and he sold them a solution. As I passed through the Protestant enclave again, its inmates' attitude was a mixture of resentment, fear, bitterness and no surrender, all infused with a longing that none of their own people would be hurt or their little village laid waste. The RUC – piggy-in-the-middle once again – waited in trepidation to see who would be their enemies today. No one standing there in the village itself knew at that moment whether thirty minutes hence there would be peace or war.

---

* I did, but the newspaper to which I sent it didn't publish it because there had been no violence.

The band had been playing beside the coaches for about twenty-five minutes by now, thus causing much bafflement in republican ranks, where it was not realized that Bingham was buying time. As he negotiated with his brethren, he was also giving the band time to work off some of their anger. Eventually, led by Bingham and the senior members of the lodge, the parade moved off and walked steadily into the village, past the couple of dozen or so Protestants and up to the RUC lines, where the Worshipful Master asked for permission to pass. Having been formally told the parade was now banned and having formally protested that a legal parade had been blocked because of an illegal protest, William Bingham read out his prepared statement.

POMEROY DISTRICT LOYAL ORANGE LODGE NO. 5
PRESS RELEASE, 12TH JULY 1997
The Officers and members of Pomeroy District Loyal Orange Lodge deeply deplore the denial of their civil rights by nationalist protestors in Pomeroy to parade their own town in a peaceful and dignified manner.

For the past 30 years the Protestant people and the Orange Order has borne the brunt of a vicious and sectarian campaign by Republicans to drive them from this village and countryside. Many of our members have been murdered and intimidated from their homes, others continue to suffer from a highly organized boycott of their businesses and in recent days we have even been denied access to the Parish Church for morning worship.

The goodwill to the Nationalist Community shown by the Order throughout the Province has been met here in Pomeroy today with derision and open sectarian hatred by the Republican-orchestrated Residents' Group.

Pomeroy District Orange will not enter into negotiations with such people nor make deals over what are our inalienable rights. The Orangemen at Pomeroy call on the government to move on towards a political settlement for Northern Ireland without Sinn Féin who have demonstrated today that though they are part of the problem they can never be part of the solution.

SIGNED
R. H. Sinnamon, District Master
W. T. Bingham, Deputy Grand Chaplain of Ireland.

Then Bingham and Sinnamon wheeled around and walked back down the hill and round to the back of the manse, followed by the band and lodge members. As an operation it had been perfect, until one member of the band, overcome with rage and (inevitably) in full view of the television cameras, waved a fist towards the line of police and shouted: 'I hope you fry tonight.'

The republican protesters melted away, the police went thankfully home to their families, the media reports showed the residents' association's leader uttering apparently reasonable soundbites about dialogue and consensus and triumphalism and when I told William Bingham about the undisciplined bandsman, he ground his teeth because, once again, an Ulster Protestant who was loyal to the state and to the Queen had taken out his frustration thuggishly and publicly with the forces of the crown.

Still, the summer passed unexpectedly peacefully, though the struggle between Orange heads and feet did not diminish. William Bingham made the intellectual and spiritual case for Orangeism at a fringe meeting of the Labour Party Conference in Brighton at the end of September, which ended with:

> History is not a road that rolls behind us. It isn't over just because it is done, nor does it have to dictate the direction we travel into the future.
>
> We all bring our past with us. The Order in Ireland is like any individual. There are parts of its past that it arguably could have done better without. We have a duty to acknowledge that, come to terms with that and resolve never to go that way again.
>
> There is also much in our past that is good and of which I am proud and which has been positive and constructive. We have a duty to the future to bring that with us.
>
> We are in a key position to build real understanding across our community divisions, to help forge a future of mutual respect and tolerance in a land free from the pain and tragedy of the past.
>
> Orangeism has much to offer in the building of such a future. The road ahead is fraught with many difficulties and challenges, but we must give no quarter to sectarian bigotry in our quest to promote the principles of Christianity, democracy and justice.
>
> I finish as a Christian minister with the words of the Christian author, E. M. Bounds – words which I often remind myself of.
>
> 'The world is looking for new ideologies, new methods, new causes to advance society. God is looking for new men and new women, men and women that the Holy Ghost can use, men and women of prayer, mighty in prayer, men and women who are godly. These can mould a generation for God.'
>
> The time has come for Orangemen to have done with mere militancy and answer the call of Orangeism and the gospel.

It was an appeal which was being reiterated by other Orange ministers like Brian Kennaway and Warren Porter as well as by laymen like Bobby Saulters and Denis Watson, but Joel Patton and the SODs were having none of it. Character-assassination and intimidation of moderates were increasing. Early in December, 200 SODs forced Watson out of a building where he was presiding over a disciplinary meeting. A few days later came the occupation of the House of Orange in an unsuccessful attempt to block Saulters's re-election. Some weeks later, the SODs invaded the building and held hostage members of the Education Committee to protest against a few of their number having talked to the Parades Commission. It was an indication of the weakening of the moderate Orange leadership that it continued to waver over how to deal with the increasingly militant SODs. There were few Orangemen who didn't agree that 1998 would almost certainly be a bad, bad year for the institution.

Drumcree Four, 5 July 1998–?

T HE CONTINUING BATTLE BETWEEN Orange moderates and extremists proceeded against the background of talks on a constitutional
settlement. An IRA ceasefire in July 1997 had led to the inclusion of
Sinn Féin, despite promises by successive governments that decom-
missioning of terrorist weapons was a prerequisite. This had led Ian
Paisley's DUP and Robert McCartney's UK Unionist Party to quit the
talks and had greatly weakened David Trimble's UUP. As unionists
turned on each other, nationalists united. For reasons of emotion as well
as electoral considerations, there was little to choose now between the
SDLP and Sinn Féin on the parades issue. Loyalist and republican
paramilitaries represented in the talks continued to mutilate and occasionally murder people in their ghettos and sectarian violence increased. And
the Real IRA, a group of dissident Provisionals, began to let off bombs
in Protestant villages which caused massive destruction but received little
media or government attention because no one died.

Throughout the talks, Drumcree cast a dark, dark shadow over several
of the participants. 'It's like the Sword of Damocles hanging over David,'
said Daphne Trimble to me in May 1998. By that time Trimble – up to
then, because of Drumcrees One, Two and Three, seen outside unionist
circles as a villain – was getting a good press, because despite huge
pressure he had stayed in the talks and had finally cut a deal with nationalism. During the period of the Good Friday Agreement referendum campaign, it was recognized that with his own party seriously split on the
agreement and with the two other main unionist parties strongly against
it, he was risking his career – even his life – on a gamble for peace. He
had first to get through the hurdle of the referendum and the assembly
elections and then Northern Ireland would be facing Drumcree Four.

Throughout this period views had hardened on both sides in Portadown.
Whenever Breandán MacCionnaith was quoted in the media, he was
making ominous noises about asking republicans throughout the province
to come to the aid of the residents. The kicking to death in Portadown
of the Catholic Robert Hamill by loyalist thugs, and the murder of Adrian
Lamph, a Garvaghy Road resident, almost certainly by the LVF, had
increased fear, loathing and defiance in the Garvaghy Road itself and
helped MacCionnaith win a council seat. Protestant opinion had hardened
as well, as a result of the murder by the INLA in the Maze prison the
previous December of Billy Wright, the LVF's vicious but charismatic
leader. Among those attending Wright's funeral were Harold Gracey and
Joel Patton.

The Parades Commission was becoming a perfect case history of how the well-meaning English belief in balance and compromise can make everything worse in Northern Ireland. From the British and the southern Irish perspective, it seemed perfectly reasonable to bring a group of non-politicians to weigh up the rights and wrongs of various sides and come to impartial conclusions; I had myself once, briefly, thought it an idea worth running with. But as the legislation went through parliament with little evidence that more than a handful of M P s and peers understood the issues and sensitivities, it became clear to those of us preoccupied with the issue that the Parades Commission was a disaster waiting to happen.

Had the British government paid more attention to the loyal institutions and less to pressure from Dublin, the Commission might not have been doomed from the start. But once it became clear that, for instance, noisy cavalcades of supporters going through Protestant areas on their way to and from G A A matches were being excluded from the legislation, the loyal institutions rightly felt they were being targeted unfairly as a part of the British and Irish governments' policy of appeasing republicanism. And so, predictably and stupidly, Grand Lodge took a decision not to speak to the Parades Commission, thus putting itself firmly in the wrong from the very beginning.

It was in the appointment of members to the Parades Commission that its inadequacy became swiftly clear. It would have been difficult to find anyone with the imagination, authority and wisdom to handle a job like that. The decent Yorkshire trade unionist Alistair Graham was simply not up to the job to which Mo Mowlam appointed him. With sincerity and the best of motives, he came to the Parades Commission completely ignorant of Northern Ireland and imbued with the conviction that compromise was all: find against Orangemen here, but for them there, and everyone will be happy. Such thinking takes no account of the enormous importance of local issues and the local sense of territory.

Nor was Graham helped by the choice of ordinary members to his Commission. It would be fair to say that of the many approached to serve, most of those who understood the problem refused or soon resigned. There were notorious instances of Graham's inability to understand the sheer tribalism with which he was dealing. In February 1998, for instance, he had insisted against disinterested advice in calling a public meeting in Portadown. What the Cassandras had predicted was what happened: the Garvaghy Road Residents' Coalition refused to attend on the grounds that they would not be safe, and, knowing the thugs that would turn up, most decent Portadown Orangemen stayed away too.

The Good Friday Agreement hardened attitudes among the Portadown Orangemen even further. Denis Watson, who had been tireless in his search for accommodation the previous year, was so appalled at what he regarded as the immorality of letting prisoners out early for pragmatic reasons, and so fearful that unionists might be expected to sit in an executive with Sinn Féin while the IRA still kept their weapons, that he had determined not only to oppose it but to stand against David Trimble in the assembly election.* He was one of those pressing the Orange Order to line up against the Agreement, thus pushing it once more into the forefront of politics at a time when its best chance of survival was to move away from politics and towards religion. One of the ironies of that period was that many of the very people who believed that it would be in the interests of both the UUP and the Orange Order to sever their formal relationship were egging the Order on to play a powerful political role.

The leadership was split. While Grand Lodge deliberately did not say no to the Agreement, on the grounds that it was a matter of conscience, its statement that it could not recommend it because it was 'fatally ambiguous, morally objectionable, and constitutionally flawed' gave everyone the impression that the Orange Order was saying an unequivocal 'No'.

In County Armagh, the problem could be seen starkly. Most Portadown Orangemen were bitterly anti-Agreement, but many others in the county were in favour and many more were in the category of 'soft no' – those people who desperately wanted the Agreement to work but found it virtually impossible to swallow the pragmatic concessions to terrorists. Watson was a 'hard No', his old ally William Bingham 'soft', but together they followed the spirit of the Grand Lodge statement and, instead of launching a County Armagh Orange campaign against the Agreement, they set up a series of information meetings within Orange lodges in which the case was put for and against. One soft no was converted to a

---

* With Lord Cranborne, who was in Northern Ireland to support David Trimble and the 'yes' campaign, I had breakfast in Belfast with a group of senior Orangemen of differing opinions on the Agreement. As the huge divisions within Orangeism and unionism became ever more apparent, Cranborne observed: 'I used to believe in the truth of Dr Johnson's dictum that "when a man knows he is to be hanged in a fortnight, it concentrates his mind wonderfully." Now I realize it just makes him sillier.' All those present laughed merrily.

soft yes when in answer to the statement from the yes proponent that
'40 per cent of people are nationalists and we have to deal with them',
a cry of 'Annihilate them' came from some LVF supporters.

With a split in unionism in the referendum which was close to 50/50
and with fears heightened by the overwhelming nationalist vote in favour
both north and south of the border, tensions within the Orange Order
were exacerbated. The internal struggle went on between those who
wanted to keep the Order neutral and those who wanted to throw its
weight behind the 'No' candidates. To a media hyped-up on the pro-
Agreement side, the fact that the majority of well-known Orangemen –
Saulters, the Grand Master, John McCrea, the Grand Secretary, George
Patten, the Executive Secretary, Denis Watson and Joel Patton – had
been publicly so fervently anti-Agreement served to copperfasten the
impression that the Orange Order was wholly negative. In the Assembly
election in June, the UUP won only just enough seats to enable David
Trimble to become First Minister Designate.

As Drumcree loomed, there were once more many forces desperately
seeking a solution. The British, Irish and US governments now all realized that the split in unionism was potentially disastrous for the future
of the Agreement and that it was vital that self-confident nationalism
should make a conciliatory gesture. Their emissaries tried and failed to
persuade MacCionnaith to allow a small parade down the road. David
Trimble who, for the third year running, was trying to secure agreement
behind the scenes did no better in the search for a formula that would
save everyone's face.

The hopes of many were centred on John Hume who, it was felt, was
the only individual in Northern Ireland with the moral authority to call
on nationalism for a gesture of generosity. Pressure was brought to bear
on him from American, British and Irish diplomats and politicians behind
the scenes. Inexplicably – apart from calling on Orangemen to talk to
residents – he refused to get involved. The benign explanation was that
he was so exhausted after the months of talks that he couldn't face a
challenge like this. A less charitable explanation was that, unlike Trimble,
Hume was not prepared to take the risk of losing face.

It was widely understood that the Parades Commission had decided to
ban the parade down Garvaghy Road unless an agreement was arrived
at between residents and Orangemen. And as the days went on and
MacCionnaith became ever more intransigent, Harold Gracey refused to
give way on the principle and Hume stayed out of sight, Dublin, London,

Washington and most parts of Northern Ireland looked on aghast as the province's stability was once more put at risk by a handful of people fixated on a small patch of territory.

What confused matters further was that it was beginning to emerge that the republican leadership was unable to control its own creation. It was believed by diplomats that Gerry Adams had discreetly suggested to MacCionnaith that he give a little ground, for this time around the Sinn Féin agenda would not be helped by mayhem at Drumcree. But by now MacCionnaith was in his third year as a focus of international attention. Like Gerard Rice, he had been to America that spring to parade his community's wrongs in front of Irish American die-hards. Journalists who had known MacCionnaith for three years confirmed to me that he seemed megalomaniacal. There were rumours that he had aligned himself with the 32-County Sovereignty Committee (the political wing of the Real IRA). Unable to control him, Sinn Féin had to be seen to be with him, so Martin McGuinness was sighted publicly walking with him down the Garvaghy Road to give succour to the beleaguered residents.

The Parades Commission duly confirmed almost everyone's worst fears by banning the Garvaghy Road parade and trying to give the appearance of balance by approving one which would go through the Ormeau Road eight days later. It was clear to anyone who knew anything about Tony Blair that although the British government would put huge efforts into finding a last-minute compromise acceptable to both sides, it would not and could not back down on its commitment to implement the Commission's decisions. So the week before Drumcree, the army and the RUC arrived at Drumcree to build a massive barricade, dig a huge trench, flood it and line it with razor-wire. A last-ditch attempt by David Trimble and Seamus Mallon, Deputy First Minister Designate, to persuade Portadown Orange and the GRRC respectively to give ground failed miserably. Mallon was barracked in the Garvaghy Road and the security forces indicated to Trimble that in Portadown, the biggest town in his own constituency, his safety could not be guaranteed. In isolated rural areas with minority Catholic populations, not far from strong loyalist towns, ten Catholic churches were destroyed by fire. Blair flew in and, like many other people, made fruitless appeals to both sets of intransigents.

So, for the third year in succession, Dublin, London, Washington and the whole of Northern Ireland held their collective breath on the morning of the first Sunday in July. This time there would be no Trimble to take the lead and try to control loyalist excesses, for he could not now participate in an illegal procession. Indeed, it was made clear to him that he might well be killed if he went near Drumcree. So on that Sunday morning, he had become an irrelevance.

With my friend Mark, I had gone to Garvaghy Road the night before to view the small group who had assembled on a hillock to protest against the perceived fear of a British government sell-out; MacCionnaith announced there would be an all-night vigil on the road itself. Rumour abounded in both camps. Neither seemed to understand that this was Tony Blair's Falklands. He might have privately wished that the Parades Commission had made a different decision, but he had no choice but to stick by his word.

We arrived in the centre of Portadown on Sunday morning and, as we walked around the corner to Carleton Street Orange Lodge, I looked at the Orangemen assembling outside and the sadness of previous years swept over me. Here were people I liked – decent, honourable men like George Patten and Denis Watson – once again looking over the precipice into an abyss which held no attractions for them. This year, they and their brethren were even more unpopular than before, for those who had voted against the Agreement for the best of reasons – because they were unable to stomach what they saw as the appeasement of terrorism – were being lumped with bigots and branded as fascists by many nationalists, including John Hume.

Watson was now an Assembly man, elected principally on the votes of County Armagh Orangemen. He wanted no confrontation, he was fearful yet again of bloodshed, but he had no choice but to set off again following Gracey on a path to nowhere. 'I'm respectable,' announced Gracey to the assembled Orangemen. 'I'm law-abiding and I'm going to the church. Every step of the way. And I'm staying until I come home by Garvaghy Road. As long as it takes.'

So, for the third year running, along with other journalists, I walked beside the Orangemen of Drumcree wondering who this year would die for a small stretch of road. On the way we passed the Catholic church, in front of which MacCionnaith, for the benefit of the cameras, had gathered a large group of GRRC members whom he was instructing to behave properly and not be provoked.

The most farcical moment for me on this occasion took place outside Drumcree Church itself. For the second year running I had been asked to talk over a mobile phone to 'The Sunday Show', a midday radio programme in Dublin. So as the hymns came over the Tannoy relaying the service to the crowds outside the church, I was trying to explain the point of view of the Portadown Orangemen and describe some of the attempts that had gone on behind the scenes to reach agreement. Even Adams and McGuinness would have gone along with a small parade, I said, but 'in the end, Brendan McKenna',* one man, has actually managed to flout the will of virtually everybody. The Orangemen have refused to speak to McKenna because he is an unrepentant ex-terrorist who assisted in blowing up their local Royal British Legion Hall . . . McKenna is now out of control. The residents' groups were set up by Sinn Féin, but some of them have now gone out of control and McKenna is a classic – he's now moving towards the 32-Counties lot . . .'

At this stage, it was announced that MacCionnaith, who would have been only a few hundred yards away from me physically, had telephoned the show. I reproduce part of the transcript here because it tells a lot about how republicans take advantage of the state of fear in which the media live in the Republic because of its draconian libel laws.

'First of all,' he said, 'I would ask Ruth Dudley Edwards to make a complete public retraction of the remarks and allegations that she made on air a few moments ago and I would ask that RTE completely dis-associates itself from those remarks.'

'Which remarks now?' asked the chairman, Andy O'Mahony.

'I think that's the remarks in relation to the bombing of the British Legion. I think it's the remarks in relation to myself being supposedly out of complete control and being unrepresentative. I think that people should bear in mind that I am an elected representative for the Portadown area. Ruth Dudley Edwards will be aware that a public meeting was held in the local parochial hall on Friday night† attended by well over 1,000 local residents at which the media were present and can state that, far from being out of control or unrepresentative, I am actually the authentic voice of the community in Portadown. That can be authenticated by the Irish government, by the British government, by the SDLP and anyone else who wishes to deal with this problem seriously and not merely to go and utter propaganda and defamy on air.'

Asked to reply, I said: 'I fear that the tragedy – and it may very well be that Brendan McKenna feels he is doing the best thing for his com-

---

* I apologize to Breandán MacCionnaith for not using the Gaelic version of his name in this broadcast, but it was not until later that I discovered that he is genuinely an Irish-language enthusiast.

† The one where Seamus Mallon had been barracked.

munity – is that what he and people on the other side who are intransigent have done is once again stir up tribalism. People who in the last couple of weeks were actually looking to a new future are now drawing back into their own tribe and becoming unreasonable again.'

'Is it true, Breandán, can I ask you – ?' began O'Mahony, but MacCionnaith interrupted.

'First of all, I have asked Ruth Dudley Edwards to give a total retraction of the remarks and allegations made. She has failed to do so. I would now like RTE to completely disassociate themselves from that remark because I have standing beside me my legal adviser listening to everything which is actually being said and if RTE and Ruth Dudley Edwards do not make a retraction then we will have no alternative but to lodge papers against her and RTE.'

'What specific retraction do you want, Breandán?' asked O'Mahony.

'Well, I think everyone knows the comments and the allegations that were made.'

'Andy, perhaps I could say something now,' I said. 'This idea seems to have come to Brendan McKenna because the other day he was thrown off Ulster television for claiming that the Orange Order had burned down the churches. I am retracting nothing – '

MacCionnaith interrupted. 'Ruth Dudley Edwards, I'm glad you've heard that, because Rosemary Nelson [his solicitor, murdered the following March by loyalists] is now standing beside me. Now she can contact you and RTE.'

A few minutes later, after MacCionnaith had denied meeting Gerry Adams, had made his case and was about to ring off, O'Mahony said: 'Before you go, Breandán, we should let you know that RTE does not stand by those allegations of Ruth Dudley Edwards, who was merely expressing her opinion. Thank you very much for taking part.'

'Before he goes . . .' I said.

'Are you still there, Breandán? I think he's gone.'

'Oh, well, I hope he's still listening . . . I find this quite funny really. You know, in olden days they threatened to kill you. Then they got to a stage when they just sent one filthy letters. Now they threaten you with the law because they've become so respectable. And I'm not alarmed by it because he doesn't actually have a case.'

And nor did he have a case, and he knew it, which was why neither he nor his solicitor wrote to me, but they did to RTE, presumably in the hope that, like many Irish newspapers, it would dish out a few thousand pounds to shut him up and warn its presenters to be careful with him.

I was not on that programme to defend Portadown Orangemen, merely to explain why they felt as deeply as they did. But by any standards of rationality and political pragmatism, they were behaving foolishly. Had they the previous year taken the advice of their sympathetic advisers and the wisest of their brethren and voluntarily forgone their route, they would have captured the moral high ground. Instead, they had made it inevitable the cards would be stacked against them in 1998. All they had going for them was a mood in the decent nationalist community that recognized the divisions and fears within unionism and felt this was a time for nationalism to make a gesture of generosity.

In so far as Portadown District had a strategy, it was, once again, to win their walk through numbers: 6,000 Orangemen had turned up to attend a service in a church which could hold 700–800, thus undercutting the argument that this was an ordinary group of local Orangemen seeking merely to follow their forefathers' route. Yet, on that first day, the proceedings were dignified and disciplined. In close formation and in step with the hymn music, Harold Gracey and the district officers proceeded to the barricade at the head of the parade to make their protest. Humiliatingly, there was no one there to receive them; the RUC had made a decision to have no one manning the barricade. Men in bowlers and collarettes milled around aimlessly for a while. There was a brief disagreement as to whether the band should be allowed to play 'The Sash', but Sabbatarianism won out. There was nothing to do except turn, form up again and walk defiantly back up the hill.

That Sunday there was a determination to keep control of events. The place was heavily marshalled and there was no trouble. Ladies arrived and the tea-and-sandwich-making began as before. Enterprising local vendors of burgers and soft drinks began to make arrangements to set up shop at Drumcree.

With much less enthusiasm than previous years, Orangemen from around the province set off to demonstrate their solidarity with their Portadown brethren. Many others, who were there in 1996, stayed at home, for, as one of them put it to me: 'We are fed up with being held to ransom every year by Portadown District.' Some leading lights in County Fermanagh, for instance, concentrated their energies on persuading their hot-heads that Drumcree was a matter for Portadown and for Portadown alone.

But already, on Sunday night, the first sinister elements began to emerge. First was the high visibility of Joel Patton and his cronies, wandering about, as someone put it, 'as if they owned Drumcree', although most of them came from a different county. He told one loyal Orangeman, whose crime was to favour dialogue, that he was as welcome as Gerry Adams. Patton and his henchmen were practising low-level intimidation – insults and jostling – but it was intimidation for all that and it frightened a lot of people. Particularly in rural areas, individuals feel vulnerable and few put their heads above the parapet for fear of being denounced as traitors or Lundys or of being physically assaulted. Ian Paisley turned up for a while to tell Orangemen that this was a battle that had to be won. Then loyalist thugs – L V F and freelancers – began to trickle in late on Sunday night. With the two-week holiday period stretching ahead, respectable people looked nervously at this violent, drunken minority screaming abuse at the police and the soldiers across the ditch. The following night, serious violence erupted.

Although Orangemen continued to turn up in large numbers, there were few loyalist road blocks – just enough to encourage one to stay at home rather than go out unnecessarily. In the middle of that week in Belfast, I ran into one that consisted of a few large women, some children and at the side just one or two burly chaps. It is curiously humiliating to be blocked by children from continuing one's journey, but I've always made it a rule in Northern Ireland never to tangle with any group that includes shaven-headed, tattooed loyalists who can recognize a southern accent as a lion recognizes the sound of a hyena. And besides, I had the highly recognizable Sean O'Callaghan in the car and that would make anyone nervous.

As the incidence of violence grew and Portadown District seemed to cede control, non-confrontational Orangemen became increasingly unhappy. Mid-week, Denis Watson and William Bingham went with a delegation to London to meet Tony Blair, thus leaving Portadown District without the moderating leadership of County Armagh. It was that evening that two of the two least belligerent counties – Down and Tyrone – arrived to demonstrate their solidarity.

Harold Gracey called upon Joel Patton to speak and as he harangued those present for having failed to do enough to support Portadown, he alienated yet another substantial group of brethren. The polarization was splendidly symbolized by the moment when Willie Thompson, most uncompromising of the U U P's anti-Agreement M P s, arrived in the field to be denounced as 'Sinn-Féin Willie', for the previous year he had refused to condemn the Dromore agreement on parades. 'Decent people want no part of this,' was what a senior Tyrone Orangeman said to me afterwards. 'Joel Patton is a disgrace to his collarette.'

It was mystifying how self-deluding the Portadown Orangemen were. People I knew to be sensible were utterly convinced that the question was not would they get down the road, but when. 'Blair can't give way,' I said to one senior marshal. 'We'll go down on Tuesday night,' he replied with absolute certainty. Coming up to the weekend I met Harold Gracey sitting on a wall outside the church hall. Only about 100 yards away were that day's consignment of thugs screaming abuse at the security forces, but Gracey didn't seem to notice them. We exchanged pleasantries about a 'BORN TO WALK THE GARVAGHY ROAD' bib I had bought as an improbable gift for an English baby of my acquaintance and he suggested it might set a trend. His major concern seemed to be that because he had a sore foot he might have to drive down the road rather than walk.

'Even if King Billy himself told the Portadown Orangemen they wouldn't get down the Garvaghy Road,' observed a senior Orangeman gloomily towards the end of the week, 'they wouldn't believe him.'

'And they'd shoot his horse,' added his Orange companion.

We were sitting in a Chinese restaurant, racking our brains to think of any way out.

'You're going to get an awful press again,' said Sean O'Callaghan, the fourth of our party. 'The home counties already think you're blockheaded bigots.'

'We are blockheaded bigots,' said the first Orangeman, and the other one nodded.

Day after day, the scum of the Protestant tribe continued to flaunt itself in front of the press along the moat that the army had created to keep protesters and security forces apart. My most memorable encounter during my Drumcree peregrinations was the fat woman in red who was screaming across the barrier at the two soldiers within earshot, 'I hope you die like dogs.' Observing my facial response to this attempt to seduce the British army into mutinying in defence of the loyal people of Northern Ireland, she placed her hands on her extensive hips and inquired, 'What's wrong, missus? Isn't it better I'm telling them what I think to their faces instead of behind their backs?'

During this period, two academics, Professors Paul Bew and Liam Kennedy, Sean and I, and a few other like-minded people, got together to draft a speech for the prime minister which we thought might help (see Appendix). Sean and I had had some contact with a Downing Street official over the preceding months whom we had put in touch with thoughtful and articulate Orangemen. Neither of us would have disclosed this, but we were seen going into Downing Street one day and a tabloid produced a mad headline about a 'TOP TERROR BOSS NOW BLAIR AIDE'. There would have been no need to mention this draft either, had not two newspapers run front-page stories about us having written a pro-Orange speech. It was in fact an attempt to get a British politician to show he had some understanding of and respect for ordinary Northern Irish people. And though subsequent events made the speech irrelevant, echoes of it have subsequently appeared in prime ministerial utterances and in a letter from his chief-of-staff to the Orange Order.

At this time, too, I wrote an article for the cross-community *Portadown Times* which included two sets of questions that remain pertinent today.

FIRST, TO THE RESIDENTS:
When you think back to the days before the foundation of the Garvaghy Road Residents' Coalition, was life worse or better around the first Sunday in July? If you think it was worse then, why is that? Because it was less exciting? Because you enjoy having the international media focused on you every year? Or because you truly could not bear the ten-minute Orange parade and regard all the violence and destruction of the last few years as worthwhile? If that is the case, how many lives are you prepared to sacrifice to keep even a token parade off the road?

If you think life was better in 1995, why do you continue to support the people that have brought this fear and tension to the Garvaghy Road? Most of you voted for the Good Friday Agreement, yet Breandán MacCionnaith's refusal to give an inch may result in terrible bloodshed and the collapse of the Assembly. You believe you are non-sectarian. What efforts have you made to make common cause with your frightened Protestant neighbours at the end of your road? Has anyone sympathized with those who in the last few weeks have had petrol bombs through their windows?

TO THE PORTADOWN ORANGEMEN:
You definitely think life has got worse. Do you think it is entirely the fault of the Residents' Coalition? Has your refusal publicly to meet Breandán MacCionnaith worked to his advantage or yours? You know he was chosen by those republicans who set up the GRRC because they knew you wouldn't talk to him. Do you ever wonder if it is sensible to behave as republicans want you to behave? In Derry, Alistair Simpson gritted his teeth, talked to Donncha MacNeilis and won the

argument. Does that make him unprincipled? Or intelligent? You are a Christian organization. Do you feel that when Robert Hamill was kicked to death, you did enough to demonstrate your abhorrence of his murderers? Do you ever think that many Catholics genuinely are afraid to go into parts of Portadown? And that if you had tried to address their fears, they might be less anxious to see you defeated?

You pride yourselves on being law-abiding, yet you know very well that your intransigence fuels paramilitary fires. Is that not as hypocritical as it is dangerous? How many lives are you prepared to sacrifice to get down Garvaghy Road?

On Thursday, the night before that article appeared, soldiers and police were fired on and attacked with blast bombs, and when a police line was breached, a mob of loyalists and Orangemen stormed through. Around the province, attacks on Catholic people and their property were increasing. Trimble and Mallon met church, business and trade union leaders but, despite intense activity, there seemed no hope. It was the end for Trimble, said many newspapers. Drumcree was shaping up to be his Waterloo. The Twelfth was on Monday, and it was feared that tens of thousands of Orangemen might come to Drumcree after their demonstrations.

And then, on Sunday morning, came the news of the murder of Jason, Mark and Richard Quinn, three little boys with a Catholic mother, living in a Protestant area, burned to death when a petrol bomb was thrown into their Ballymoney home. There had been many other such attacks that week, so the protestations by people like Ian Paisley Junior and the officers of Portadown District that it had nothing to do with Drumcree went down badly. In a sermon in Pomeroy, William Bingham, close to tears, called for the protest campaign to be called off. 'I believe wholeheartedly in the principles of Orangeism,' he said. 'I believe in civil and religious liberties for everyone. I believe in the right of Orangemen to walk. But I have to say this: that after last night's atrocious act, a fifteen minute walk down the Garvaghy Road by the Orange Order would be a very hollow victory, because it would be in the shadow of three coffins of three small boys who wouldn't even know what the Orange Order was about . . . No road is worth a life.'

Bingham's plea was broadcast on radio and television. I heard it in a BBC studio, waiting with Chris McGimpsey to appear on the 'Seven Days' programme. 'Do you think this is a defining moment?' I was then asked. And in words that were to have an unexpected effect the following day, I said, 'I see this as the defining struggle between democrats and extremists . . . It's a defining moment when nationalists decide do they want to listen to Seamus Mallon or Brendan McKenna or Orangemen decide to they want to be led by William Bingham or Joel Patton.' Rather incoherently, for I was very upset, I added that 'people are in this position because of the leadership they have followed. That's anyone who is following, as I said before, Gerard Rice or Brendan McKenna or on the other side, Joel Patton, or are allowing themselves to have their emotions stirred up by Ian Paisley, anyone who is following sectarian leadership, call it what you will – they'll call it political on the nationalist side, but it is sectarian. That's the problem.'

Trimble and Mallon were among the many who publicly echoed Bingham's plea that day. Saulters tried privately and others cited the example of the Orangemen who that morning had abandoned their 'Freedom Camp' outside Mo Mowlam's official residence, leaving behind them three bunches of flowers. But though Portadown District agreed with Saulters that protests would be massively scaled down the following day, they would not abandon Drumcree. They stood on the hill snatching at the straws of self-justification offered them by loyalist agitators: the Quinns had been murdered for family reasons; the murders were drug-related; they had nothing to do with Drumcree protests; the boys were Protestant anyway – all the time ignoring the fact that, using Drumcree as an excuse, loyalists had been fire-bombing Catholic houses throughout the week. They did not have the imagination to realize that this decision was to lose them the sympathy of the vast majority of their now sickened and horrified brethren. (Gerard Rice and the Lower Ormeau Road were much cleverer. They cancelled their plans to block the march the next day and instead, as the parade went past, released black balloons and held placards saying 'Shame'.)

For me, there was strange drama the following day in Pomeroy, which was hosting the South Tyrone Twelfth. Like most Orangemen, I approached the day in a gloomy spirit. Hanging over what should have been a festive day were the three dead brothers, the continuing impasse at Drumcree and dreadful weather. (David Trimble, who had intended to walk with his lodge to the assembly point and then go home, got his times muddled up and didn't appear at all.)

In the midst of all that tragedy, farce broke in again, for, en route to Pomeroy and in the assembly field, my mobile phone kept going off: Fleet Street was hunting my twenty-nine-year-old niece, Sara, who after seven years in a Dominican convent had left to marry a fifty-two-year-old friar who was the head of the Blackfriars Theological College in Oxford.

Having been acquainted with that news the previous night by the *Daily Telegraph*, I had uttered some supportive words and thus unwittingly laid myself open to the chase, for Sara and Paul were not speaking to the media. So there was I, in a corner of the world where the madder elements are convinced that the Church of Rome abounds with wicked priests forcing themselves on imprisoned nuns, fending off questions from a pack of hacks who seemed to be in a corporate state of passionate prurience. If only Joel Patton had known that when he caught sight of me in the assembly field, things might have been even more interesting than they were.

I had located Killyman District and Joel Patton at the request of the journalist John Lloyd. When he approached Patton and introduced himself, Patton said, 'I'll talk to you', and then glared over his shoulder and added, 'but I'll never speak to Ruth Dudley Edwards again.' Upon which – along with a few companions – he promptly did. He was going to sue me for libel because, he claimed, I had said on radio that he was inciting people to riot. (I thought of pointing out this would be slander, not libel, but I let it go, pleased as I was to have this threatened law suit to balance that of Breandán MacCionnaith.) Patton and his brethren made it clear that I had no right to be in the field and should leave it forthwith.

I pointed out that it wasn't their field, but since they were continuing to be noisy and nasty, I decided to leave them. Unfortunately, the direction I chose led me to Sean O'Callaghan. Incautiously, as he later admitted, Sean had come with John Lloyd to Pomeroy in his journalistic capacity. Dark glasses notwithstanding, he was instantly recognized by the Patton contingent, who conveniently forgot what they knew – that he had been an enemy of the IRA for twenty years – and began to shout, 'Sean O'Callaghan IRA'. Sean made no excuses but left hurriedly, suddenly realizing that his presence would almost certainly be used against William Bingham, who was to give the address from the platform, for it was already clear that Patton and the SODs were fuming over what they saw as Bingham's treachery.

The next hour or two were awful. It was pouring with rain for a large part of the time, I had neither coat nor umbrella and there was nowhere to shelter. John Lloyd and I wandered up the Pomeroy main street wistfully, vainly seeking an open pub, wiggled round the side of the police Land Rovers blocking the road and stood in front of the Church of Ireland. There were a few people there from the residents' groups – perhaps five or six in all. John engaged Dessie Grimes, the group's leader, in conversation. I stayed on the side-lines, for the previous Monday I had been on a Dublin political television programme popular with northern nationalists and I reckoned I had enough enemies to be going on with. I chatted instead to a couple of bored soldiers and then we wandered down the hill again to stand watching the tail-end of the parade going into the assembly field. When it began to hail, John chivalrously shared his jacket with me. It was, I think, the nadir of my experiences at parades: it was very cold, the hail was very heavy, the participants were finding it hard to look cheerful and everyone was aware that the Orange Order was in more disarray than ever before in their lifetime.

We squelched into the field and it became clear that there would be a longish wait for the service and the speeches: the dignitaries were being fed. After hanging about for a while having a cup of tea and a bun, we separated – John to go and talk to the Patton contingent, me to climb on the platform to talk to the solitary person there, a pleasant and decent man whom I knew to be an officer in the Pomeroy lodge and a member of William Bingham's congregation.

We talked about the events of the previous week which had caused him immense distress: he was deeply shaken at the Quinn murders. As we talked, one of Patton's acolytes – a thin, hatchet-faced man whose bowler did not suit him – sped up to the platform and began to deliver to my companion a number of home truths about me: I had vilely libelled Joel Patton and I had brought Sean to Pomeroy. My companion, politely, got up to listen and I, prudently, left the stage and went to sit under the tarpaulin along with a couple of children, hoping to shield myself from the rain and the possibility of an embarrassing scene.

A few minutes later the dignitaries began to assemble and move towards the stage. I stood in front of the stage for a moment or two, and then Hatchet-face began shouting again and John Lloyd arrived and said, 'They'll use you to get at William. For his sake you'd better get out.' It was excellent advice, so, much though I hate to leave the scene of potentially interesting events, I departed, retrieved my car and drove out of Pomeroy to the sound of hymn-singing. I missed the drama. To the delight of one of my friends, who switched on the BBC's-24-hour news programme late that night, Joel Patton was to be seen screaming at William Bingham: 'Ruth Dudley Edwards, Sean O'Callaghan. Provos, Provos.' (He was later to allege that we had been working for the Irish government and/or MI6 to split the Orange Order.)

Bingham retired to a chair and entered into private prayer. Patton and a henchman or two shouted on for a while longer, denouncing Bingham for having 'stabbed the men of Portadown in the back when they were at their most need' and accusing him of having invited Sean O'Callaghan to the field. Later on, as they began to parade again, one of Patton's supporters grabbed Bingham by the throat and tried to throw him into the ditch.

As own-goals go, it was the stuff of which legends are made. Joel Patton, so adept in interviews at seeming deceptively reasonable and calm, had lost all control in public in his rage against Bingham, the man who was felt by the vast majority of Orangemen to have saved their institution's honour. Over the next few weeks, Bingham was to receive many hundreds of phone-calls and letters in support. And from my point of view, it was a pleasure that Patton's fury at me for having said he stirred people up had been quickly followed by him being televised stirring people up to assault and violence. It would take a few months, but Patton and my assailant, Walter Miller, were eventually expelled from the Orange Order for interrupting a service.

While responsible leaders called for calm reflection and Grand Lodge officers dithered about what to do next, a substantial group of Orange chaplains expressed their 'utter revulsion' at the murders and

> to the Roman Catholic community in Northern Ireland our deep sorrow that so many of them have been intimidated out of their homes, and that several of their churches have been burned. Our bitter shame at all this, allegedly carried out in the name of Protestantism, is not in any way lessened by the fact that many of our own people are the victims of terrorism.
>
> The spectacle of people attempting to injure or murder policemen and soldiers in Portadown, and the intimidation of police families, has brought shame on the Protestant community, and all the more since it has been done under the guise of supporting the Portadown District's protest against the determination of the Parades Commission.

All eyes were on the next likely focus for confrontation: the Apprentice Boys' parade in August. But the Apprentice Boys were boxing clever and had hammered out a deal with the Parades Commission which was so reasonable that the residents' group had no grounds for objection and the event passed off with little trouble (see Chapter 1).

Proximity talks failed, the RUC seized weapons from Drumcree and only a handful of protesters remained. Harold Gracey brought up a caravan and settled in, and from time to time there was an occasional rally of a few hundred people, but essentially the Orange Order across the province was fed up and sick at heart. At the last parade of the season – the Black Last Saturday in August – there was a coda to the Pomeroy event.

This time the venue was Dungannon; once again William Bingham was speaking. It was a sunny day and I had with me a Dubliner from the Peace Train organization (set up years ago to protest against the tendency of the Provisional IRA to bomb the railway line from Belfast to Dublin in the interests of pursuing a United Ireland). Rhondda was a frequent visitor to Belfast but her only visit elsewhere in Northern Ireland had been to Pomeroy in 1996 with two Dublin colleagues to buy a substantial amount of meat in solidarity with a boycotted Protestant butcher.

Rhondda had never been to a rural parade therefore and it was a pleasure to see a happy family occasion once more through the eyes of a newcomer. Being a Black parade, there was a huge variety of bands: silver, accordion, pipe, flute and only the merest sprinkling of blood-and-thunder. We met up in the field with my friends Mark, Margot, Paul and his Chinese friend, Shelly, who had adapted to rural Northern Ireland with apparently no difficulty, loved the parade and happily consumed ham sandwiches and tea in the Presbyterian tea-tent. (Mark could have only buns; he is a vegetarian, an unknown concept in rural Ulster.)

We emerged from the tea-tent for the service and listened to William Bingham speak about the gospel. A few minutes after he sat down, a shaven-headed young drunk came thundering down the hill. His friend, more prudent, stood behind him and said: 'We're too late.' Undaunted, the yob stood screaming, 'He brought an IRA man to Pomeroy', and made a lurch towards the platform.

It had been clear from conversations with Blackmen from Pomeroy that they were on this occasion determined and ready to protect Bingham; indeed, he had been flanked by two of the fittest of them as he walked on parade. So upon the shouting yob fell perhaps a dozen men, mostly middle-aged and a couple elderly, determined to keep the youth under control yet anxious not to hurt him. It was the most curious fight I ever witnessed. He was young, fit, violent and so drunk he could feel no pain. They, hampered not only by their scruples but by their suits, bowlers, aprons, white gloves and embroidered cuffs, were trying to restrain him, and outside the scrum, a friend of mine, a part-time policeman, had handed me his hat and gloves and was trying to get through to administer the scientific blow on the side of the head that would stun the would-be assailant without causing him any harm. He was ultimately removed from the field without anyone getting hurt, and the speakers got back to passing their resolutions.

Rhondda and I had been to Omagh that morning to see the bombed buildings and the hundreds and hundreds of bouquets, many of them from ordinary families and groups of shop-workers throughout the Republic of Ireland. Omagh, where twenty-nine people were murdered on 15 August, and where Lorraine, Erin and Thomas Reid just escaped death, had been the second cataclysmic event in the history of Northern Ireland that summer. Gruesomely, like the deaths of the Quinn children, it had actually helped the peace process. Had the bombs earlier planted by the Real IRA in the Protestant towns of Moira and Portadown and Markethill and Newtownhamilton caused deaths rather than simply destruction, the consequences would have been entirely negative. As it was, because the casualties were Catholics and Protestants, nationalists and unionists, loyalists and republicans, decent people from the two communities of Northern Ireland were moved to pull together against the terrorists.

Omagh offered Portadown District their third opportunity to walk away with their heads held high. Their first chance had been when blast-bombs were thrown at the security forces at Drumcree, the second on the Sunday the Quinn children died. In October they were to have a fourth, when a policeman hit by a blast-bomb early in September died of his injuries.* But doggedly they kept their token presence there, being cynically used by some anti-Agreement politicians as a focus for anti-Trimble agitation. Paisley was an assiduous supporter. 'There can be no weakening and there can be no giving up,' he told them on a typical visit. 'We must not fall by the wayside, we have to keep going.'

The effect on Portadown was appalling. In an October stocktake, Martin Fletcher of *The Times* wrote of how the town was being poisoned by the unresolved confrontation:

∗ Frank O'Reilly, a Catholic married to a Protestant, was a friend of William Bingham's. The remark by the Portadown District spokesman, David Jones, that 'Unfortunately, when you are standing up for liberties, sometimes the cost of those liberties can be very high,' caused a great deal of offence. An angry Orangeman rang me to report. 'When Portadown District have laid *their* lives on the line,' he said, 'then I'll support them. For years they sacrificed everyone else. That's why they blame William.'

Even as the rest of Northern Ireland inches towards peace, Portadown is being
sucked back towards the dark days . . . Ignatius Fox, a nationalist SDLP councillor,
said community relations were now 'non-existent . . . I've seen it bad, but never this
bad.' Mark Neale, a Unionist councillor, agreed: 'Community relations are gone.'

In the past month, three Catholic shops have been burnt; six police officers have
been injured in street clashes with loyalists . . . school buses have been stoned; the
police are being taunted and abused. Last week, David Trimble, the town's Unionist
MP and Northern Ireland's First Minister, had to be bundled into his car by
bodyguards after being accosted by a baying loyalist mob outside an Orange hall.

With Catholics increasingly afraid to go into Portadown, the Garvaghy
Road had become 'a town within a town'; shops had opened to service
the residents. Thousands of Protestants now avoided the town on Saturdays, when there was frequent violence, sales had halved and shops were
laying off staff. As Fletcher noted ruefully: 'The irony is that the Parades
Commission banned this year's Orange Order march from entering the
Garvaghy Road on the ground that it would have "a serious adverse
impact" on community relationships. In past years the police forced the
march through and after a few days of rioting, normality returned.'

The release of terrorist prisoners and the refusal of paramilitaries to
decommission any weapons helped to exacerbate the problem and led to
an increase in loyalist violence coming up to Christmas. More solutions
were floated. An Orange delegation to Downing Street which included
Harold Gracey and Denis Watson resulted in a reconvening of proximity
talks which duly failed. (A balancing visit by the GRRC in January also
produced nothing.) The award of the Nobel Peace Prize to John Hume
and David Trimble only added to Trimble's unpopularity in Portadown.

Fletcher took stock again just before Christmas:

In icy rain Harold Gracey, a silver-haired grandfather who is district master of
Portadown Orange Lodge, performed the same ritual on Sunday as he had on the
previous 22.

He attended the family service in Drumcree's parish church, then donned his
regalia and led 300 Orangemen in a dignified procession down the lane that leads
to Portadown via the nationalist Garvaghy Road. At a bridge across a stream three
slate-grey armoured police Land Rovers blocked their way.

Mr Gracey formally complained to the officer in charge about this denial of the
Orangemen's civil and religious rights. A colleague read a passage from Psalms
through a loudspeaker and invoked God's help 'as we take a stand here for God and

Ulster'. Most of the Orangemen then went home for Sunday lunch, but not Mr Gracey. He returned to the battered caravan behind the church where he has spent every one of the 163 nights since . . . July 5.

Summer has turned to winter, and the grass around his caravan has turned to mud, but the 63-year-old 'Man on the Hill' has not once gone home to his wife. 'If somebody had told me in July that I'd still be here at Christmas, I would not have believed them,' Mr Gracey said. But he will not budge until the Orangemen complete their parade, and if he dies first, 'somebody else will take my place'.

Protests increased in size around Christmas, as did the intensity of loyalist violence, which was 'totally and unreservedly' condemned by Grand Lodge: 'There is a simple message for those who would sully the name of Orangeism and use the pretext of a peaceful protest for their own ends. Stay away, we don't want you.' But Grand Lodge was not prepared to disassociate itself entirely from the protest. Saulters had stayed on as Grand Master, but he was weary and in the December elections, hard-liners had scored over moderates. Many people who had been Orangemen all their adult lives were sickened. On Garvaghy Road, every night, republicans and loyalists fought over inches of territory, scoring the occasional success with a tricolour on a lamppost here, an extra kerbstone of red-white-and-blue and the occasional prize of a family of the other tribe forced out of their home.

Harold Gracey left his caravan when his mother died, but soon returned. And as winter turned into spring, there he sat, enduring, indomitable, principled, stubborn and inflexible, a graphic symbol of those Ulster Protestant qualities that kept them going through the Siege of Derry and a three-century siege of their whole community, and yet have made them so often play into the hands of their enemies.

Draft Speech for the Prime Minister

T HE UNITED KINGDOM OF Great Britain and Northern Ireland is not just a legal and constitutional entity. It is much more than this. It is underpinned by ties of emotion and a shared history, not least the sacrifices endured in two world wars.

This week, Northern Ireland is in the news again – sadly, in a negative way. Once more, there are scenes of violence – of intimidation, of destruction. The anger and the conflict have been focused, once again, on the issue of the opposition by residents to a walk by Orangemen down the Garvaghy Road in Portadown.

People in Northern Ireland must understand that, to most people outside the Province, such confrontation is incomprehensible. Yet people from outside owe it to those in Northern Ireland to understand that the negative images they see in the media fail to show the extraordinarily positive side of the province.

Over the past fourteen months, since I became Prime Minister, I have had a great deal of contact with our people of Northern Ireland. And I have been humbled. Humbled by those I have come into contact with who have emerged without bitterness from terrible experiences. They have had their loved ones murdered and maimed because of political conflict. They have suffered in a way we have not experienced in the rest of the United Kingdom for fifty years. And the vast majority of them have come through with courage and without bitterness. I honour them.

All the people of Northern Ireland have been dealt a difficult hand of cards by history. They have inherited a conflict between two communities of the kind which has led to wholesale slaughter in Bosnia. That they have kept a civil society in place has much to do with a shared sense of Christian values. After every atrocity, there have been bereaved people who rose up and called for forgiveness and for dialogue with those who have suffered in the other community. I could never praise too much the ordinary Catholic and Protestant people who in their daily lives have shown friendship to those with different political loyalties. That is the true spirit of Northern Ireland. The overwhelming majority of its people have opted for tolerance rather than revenge.

In the last year we have seen remarkable progress in Northern Ireland. An Agreement has been reached and has been strongly supported by a referendum in which a record number of people voted. David Trimble has been elected as First Minister with Seamus Mallon as his Deputy. I am sure that the vast majority of the people want to give them a chance to break the destructive patterns of the past. The tragedy we are facing is that – because the beginning of the Assembly has coincided with tensions of the marching season – all that has been gained could be lost.

What is happening at Drumcree and elsewhere is not a battle between those who were for and against the Good Friday Agreement. There were people on both sides of the referendum debate who cared passionately about peace. It is a polarization of political tensions between people of two traditions who feel their neighbours are failing to give them enough respect. I believe that – such is the will towards peace in the province – these problems could be resolved locally. My fear is that high emotions could allow decent people in Northern Ireland to allow malign elements to wreck their precious but precarious peace.

I am talking to you with respect and still in hope, but I must make it clear that the government will uphold the decisions by the Parades Commission. I understand that members of the Orange Order, denied the right to walk, feel a sense of injustice as acute as those residents whose objections have been overridden. But the government set up the Parades Commission. And we will abide by its decisions. There will be no buckling under to violence – threatened or actual.

The anti-parade case is better understood outside Northern Ireland than is the case of the loyal institutions: the Orange Order, the Apprentice Boys and the Royal Black Institution. We know that members of these organizations feel their culture is under attack. But let me assure them that, as far as my government is concerned, this is not the case. In fact, as a result of valued efforts made by the loyal institutions to reach out to the other community, we are looking at ways of helping to show to a wider world the positive contribution to British culture that the Orange Order and other loyal institutions have made, both locally and internationally. They are international organizations, many of whose principles are deserving of admiration.

How many of those who dismiss the Orange Order and its sister institutions as sectarian, because they are exclusively Protestant, recognize that their shared guiding principle is a commitment to upholding civil and religious liberties. In England, we tend to ignore the Glorious Revolution of three centuries ago which ended monarchical tyranny and replaced it by a commitment to democratic rights and liberties. And while the loyal institutions have often during their history been involved in secretarian conflict, they have also been a force for stability and community cohesiveness. And no one could doubt their commitment to their country.

I appeal now for an act of patriotism by the Orange Order. Part of this act of patriotism is recognizing the danger of a larger, mutually destructive conflict in Northern Ireland which is entirely disproportionate to the issues at stake at Drumcree. But I appeal also to those the Orange Order believes threaten their way of life to give them reassurances. The vast majority of Orangemen fear that democracy is giving way to republican terrorism, just as the vast majority of residents in contentious areas are terrified of loyalist terrorism.

In these emotion-charged times, there is an onus on all of the paramilitary organizations to say and show that the war is over. Nothing would ease our problems more. Such declarations would lock Northern Ireland into peace very quickly.

I said, as Leader of the Opposition, and again as your Prime Minister, Labour would not be a persuader for Irish unity. Rather, I said, the new Labour government would be the facilitator of the will of the people of Northern Ireland. My predecessor, John Smith, said: 'These are my people, and I will never desert them.' I repeat that assurance to the people of Northern Ireland, Catholic and Protestant, Nationalist and Unionist. As Prime Minister of all of the UK, I cherish both nationalist and unionist culture as equal expressions of important traditions which have helped shape us all.

In my May speech of 1997 I outlined my vision of the future. I have stuck to the principles and policies outlined then. I said the principle of consent guided our policy, that I wanted to see a Northern Ireland assembly alongside that of Scotland and Wales. I wanted to see sensible cross-border cooperation. The legitimacy and security of Northern Ireland's place within the UK has never been more secure.

We are trying to manage the problems of this year. The government is set on its course of action. But this is not the long-term answer. The government does not believe in apartheid, cultural, religious or physical. We want to see the development of mutual respect and tolerance – an inclusive society. We have to get through the next few weeks. We must determine that before the marching season of 1999, locally and nationally, the people of Northern Ireland will have solved their territorial problems themselves. I hope and believe that next year, there will be no need for government to act as arbitrator.

The people of Northern Ireland have courage in abundance. This is the time for them to show vision. The shared values of the community must triumph.

Select Bibliography

I HAD ACCESS TO MANY booklets, brochures, programmes, rule-books, newsletters, newspapers, newsheets, song-books and so on, produced here and abroad by the loyal institutions and by the Ulster Society. I owe a huge debt to Jonathan Bardon. Any quotations without an obvious source have probably come from his magisterial *A History of Ulster* (Belfast, 1992).

Of the numerous books, pamphlets and articles I have consulted, I found the following small selection particularly useful:

Barrington, Donal, *Uniting Ireland* (Dublin, 1959)
Beattie, Geoffrey, *We Are the People* (London, 1992)
Bell, J. Bowyer, *The Protestants and a United Ireland* (Dublin, 1996)
Bew, Paul, *Ideology and the Irish Question: Ulster Unionism and Irish Nationalism 1912–1916* (Oxford, 1994)
Bew, Paul and Gillespie, Gordon, *The Northern Ireland Peace Process 1993–1996* (London, 1996)
Bowman, John, *De Valera and the Ulster Question 1917–1973* (Oxford, 1982)
Bruce, Steve, *God Save Ulster! The Religion and Politics of Paisleyism* (Oxford and New York, 1986)
———— *No Pope of Rome: Anti-Catholicism in Modern Scotland* (Edinburgh, 1989)
Bryan, Dominic, Fraser, T. G. and Dunn, Seamus, 'Loyalist Parades in Portadown' (Centre for the Study of Conflict, University of Ulster, 1995)
Buckland, Patrick, *James Craig, Lord Craigavon* (Dublin, 1980)
Cielou, Robert, *Spare My Tortured People: Ulster and the Green Border* (Lisnaskea, 1983)
Darby, John, *Conflict in Northern Ireland: The Development of a Polarised Community* (Dublin and New York, 1976)

———— *Northern Ireland: The Background to the Conflict* (Belfast and New York, 1983)

Dewar, Rev. M. W., Brown, Rev. John and Long, Rev. S. E., *Orangeism: a new historical appreciation* (Belfast, 1967)

Dunlop, John, *A Precarious Belonging: Presbyterians and the Conflict in Ireland* (Belfast, 1995)

Ferguson, Tom, *The Independent Orange Order* (Ulster Society, Lurgan, 1997)

Flackes, W. D. and Elliott, Sydney, *Northern Ireland: A Political Directory, 1968–1993* (Belfast, 1994)

Gray, Tony, *The Orange Order* (London, 1972).

Harbinson, Robert, *No Surrender: An Ulster Childhood* (Belfast, 1960)

Hill, Jacqueline, *From Patriots to Unionists: Dublin Civic Politics and Irish Protestant Patriotism, 1660–1840* (Oxford, 1997)

Jones, David R., Kane, James S., Wallace, Robert, Sloan, Douglas, and Courtney, Brian, *The Orange Citadel: a History of Orangeism in Portadown District* (Portadown Cultural Heritage Committee, 1996)

Kennedy, Billy (ed.), *A Celebration: 1690–1990 – The Orange Institution* (Grand Orange Lodge of Ireland, 1990)

Kilpatrick, C. S., Murdie, William and Cargo, David, *History of the Royal Arch Purple Order* (Belfast, 1994)

Kilpatrick, Cecil, *The Formation of the Orange Order 1795–1798: The edited papers of Colonel William Blacker and Colonel Robert H. Wallace* (Grand Lodge of Ireland, Belfast, 1994)

———— *William of Orange: A Dedicated Life* (Grand Lodge of Ireland, Belfast, 1998)

Laffan, Michael, *The Partition of Ireland 1911–1925* (Dundalk, 1983)

Long, S. E., *Orangeism in Northern Ireland* (Belfast, n.d. circa 1970)

Lee, Joseph, *Ireland 1912–1985: Politics and Society* (Cambridge, 1989)

Lucy, Gordon, *Stand-Off! Drumcree: July 1995 and 1996* (Ulster Society, Lurgan, 1996)

Lucy, Gordon and McClure Elaine, *The Twelfth: what it means to me* (Lurgan, 1997)

McCartney, Clem and Bryson Lucy, *Clashing Symbols? A report on the use of flags, anthems and other national symbols in Northern Ireland* (Belfast, 1994)

McClelland, Aiken, *William Johnston of Ballykilbeg* (Ulster Society, Lurgan, 1990)

———— 'The Battle of Garvagh' in *Ulster Folklife*, vol. 19 (Ulster Folk and Transport Museum, 1973)

McDowell, R. B., *Crisis and Decline: the Fate of the Southern Unionists* (Dublin, 1997)

Marshall, William S., *The Billy Boys* (Edinburgh, 1996)

Miller, David, *Queen's Rebels: Ulster Loyalism in Historical Perspective* (Dublin, 1978)

Meredith, Ian and Kennaway, Brian, 'The Orange Order: An Evangelical Perspective' (Grand Lodge of Ireland, Belfast, 1993)

Miller, Derek, *Still Under Siege* (Ulster Society, Lurgan, 1989)

Montgomery, Graham and Whitten, Richard, *The Order On Parade* (Grand Lodge of Ireland, Belfast, 1995)

Neal, Frank, *Sectarian Violence: The Liverpool Experience, 1819– 1914* (Manchester, 1988)

O Connor, Fionnuala, *In Search of a State: Catholics in Northern Ireland* (Belfast, 1993)

O'Doherty, Malachai, *The Trouble with Guns: Republican Strategy and the Provisional IRA* (Belfast, 1998)

O'Malley, Padraig, *The Uncivil Wars: Ireland Today* (Belfast, 1983)

Orr, Philip, *The Road to the Somme: Men of the Ulster Division Tell Their Story* (Belfast, 1987)

Parkinson, Alan F., *Ulster Loyalism and the British Media* (Dublin and Portland, USA, 1998)

Senior, Hereward, *Orangeism in Ireland and Britain 1795–1836* (London, 1966)

Stewart, A. T. Q., *The Narrow Ground: Aspects of Ulster, 1609–1969* (London, 1977)

———— *Edward Carson* (Dublin, 1981)

Walker, Brian, *Dancing to History's Tune* (Belfast, 1996)

Walker, Graham and English, Richard, *Unionism in Modern Ireland* especially Peter Hart, 'The Protestant Experience of Revolution in Southern Ireland', Jane Leonard, 'The Twinge of Memory: Armistice Day and Remembrance Sunday in Dublin since 1919,' Thomas Hennessy, 'Ulster Unionism and Loyalty to the Crown of the United Kingdom, 1912–74' (Belfast, 1997)

Williams, Thomas Desmond, *Secret Societies in Ireland* (Dublin and New York, 1973)

Whyte, John H, *Interpreting Northern Ireland* (Oxford, 1990)
Wright, Frank, *Northern Ireland: A Comparative Analysis* (Dublin, 1987)

index

This book may be retained for three
per week or portion of a week plu
charged.
The latest date entered below is th
be returned.

BM	

C/820